CANADIAN TAX PAPER NO. 102

Financing the Canadian Federation, 1867 to 1995: Setting the Stage for Change

DAVID B. PERRY

Canadian Tax Foundation
L'Association canadienne
d'études fiscales

A forum for tax analysis and research
Une tribune pour l'analyse et la recherche fiscales

Canadian Cataloguing in Publication Data

Perry, David B.
  Financing the Canadian Federation, 1867-1995 : setting the stage for change

(Canadian tax papers ; no. 102)
Includes bibliographical references and index.
ISBN 0-88808-125-1

1. Federal-provincial fiscal relations — Canada.* 2. Federal-provincial tax
relations — Canada.* 3. Grants-in-aid — Canada — History. I. Canadian
Tax Foundation. II. Title.

HJ793.P47 1997   336.71   C97-932594-3

© 1997 Canadian Tax Foundation

Contents

Tables

Foreword

The Canadian federal system is unique in many respects, not least in its capacity to reinvent itself. Again and again in the 130 years since Confederation, the relationship between the federal government and the provinces has changed in fundamental ways. Canada is not the only federation that has carried out significant structural change within the framework of an essentially stable constitution, but few other federal systems have changed so frequently and to such an extent. This adaptability augurs well for the future, as we once again contemplate redesigning the relationship between Ottawa and the provincial capitals.

The purpose of this book is to review the changes in the financial framework that sustains and in large part defines Canada's federal system. It traces separately the evolution of our present system of tax sharing and cooperative tax collection, the development of extensive conditional grant programs involving huge sums of money, and the growth of an equalization system that has made it possible to convert cash payments under conditional grant programs into transfers of tax room under block-funding arrangements. An appendix provides a summary of federal payments to the provinces over the past 50 years.

Federalism is a constantly changing concept. Its financial arrangements are regularly adjusted to reflect current priorities and concerns. The weakness of any book like this one is that it must draw a line at some point even as change continues. To help the reader keep apprised of the latest developments, the Foundation's annual publication, *Finances of the Nation*, provides regular up-dates of current developments.

David B. Perry is the senior research associate of the Canadian Tax Foundation. He is the author of the Fiscal Figures feature in the *Canadian Tax Journal* and co-author of the journal's provincial budget roundup articles. He also co-authored the foundation's annual publication, *The National Finances*, and its biennial publication, *Provincial and Municipal Finances*, and is currently co-author of the foundation's new annual publication *Finances of the Nation*.

Alex Scala edited the manuscript, and Michael Gaughan verified the references. Paula Pike of WordsWorth Communications prepared the index.

Robin J. MacKnight
Director
December 1997

Preface

Books about the evolution of Canada's federal system are not in short supply. What has been lacking in recent years, however, are books that deal broadly with the fiscal aspect of that evolution. The present book attempts to fill the gap.

The constitutional debate that has absorbed Canadian academics, government officials, politicians, and stout-hearted citizens over the past few years is only the most recent phase of a discussion that has been in progress since before Confederation. From the beginning, the essential question has been that of Canada's appropriate place on the continuum between a strong federation and a weak federation. Should the federal government dominate the provinces or defer to the provinces? Or is Ottawa's proper role located somewhere between these extremes?

In 1867, the answer seemed obvious. Britain's colonies in North America found themselves alone on the continent with a United States that had just finished asserting, through the medium of a civil war, the primacy of the federal government over the states. The American war had provided interested onlookers in what would become Canada with a striking example of what can befall a federation that fails to establish a clear division of powers and responsibilities between the central government and the regional governments. After the war, the reconstituted United States, large, strong, and potentially aggressive, provided the same onlookers with a sufficient reason for undertaking an experiment in federalism of their own. The new federation, it was agreed, would have to be strong; otherwise it might not survive at all. Thus the British North America Act of 1867—Canada's founding document—took care to reserve the lion's share of power and responsibility for the central government.

Any state is, among other things, a matter of money—of revenue and expenditure. The fathers of Confederation took care to assign the most important areas of expenditure, and consequently the most important sources of revenue as well, to the center. "Important," of course, is a relative term. The prevailing assumption, in 1867, was that government should be unobtrusive and cheap. Its job was to prepare an environment in which private enterprise could thrive, and then stand to one side. So, although the federal government was to be stronger than the provinces, it was not to be very strong, or very expensive, in its own right.

The founders could not foresee that time would change everything. The very idea of what government was *for* would change, and the result would be an enormous enlargement in the size, the range, and the cost of public-sector

activity. Moreover, these changes would reverse the values of the constitutional formula: what had been the less important areas of government
responsibility would become the more important areas of responsibility. The
art came in adjusting revenue sources to reflect this change.

The shift in emphasis from one set of responsibilities to another took a
long time to mature, but it was complete, more or less, by the end of the
Second World War. This shift created problems for every level of government, but most of all for the federal government. If the federal government
had any purpose at all, that purpose was to address the interests of the nation
as a whole, however those interests might change over time. At the beginning
of the post-war era, in fact, it seemed plain that during the Great Depression
of the 1930s the federal government had failed to identify the national
interest properly, and that its adherence to the old formulas of fiscal
conservatism and small government had produced fiscal chaos and massive
distress. Yet if the federal government was to address the interests of the
nation as a whole, as it was reasonable to define those interests in 1945, it
would have to exert itself in areas of responsibility that the constitution
reserved to the provinces.

The federal government could not, for the most part, act in these areas
directly, but its control of the most important sources of public revenue
would give it the power to act indirectly to no small effect. By dispersing a
large share of its revenues judiciously among the provinces, it should be able
to reduce disparities in levels of public services among the provinces,
promote the growth of services for which there was a large public demand,
enforce universal access to those services, and ensure that a given minimum
level of services was available to all Canadians. Taken together, these goals
constituted a "national" agenda for social welfare, broadly defined.

There was a difficulty. In order to exert federal influence in areas of
provincial responsibility through the use of transfers to the provinces, Ottawa
would have to maintain its dominance of the most lucrative fields of direct
taxation—in particular, personal and corporate taxes. Under the constitution,
however, the provinces' claim to these fields was as good as Ottawa's claim.

The consequence of this somewhat awkward state of affairs was a unique
federalism in which the leadership of the central government was the result
of negotiation and voluntary subordination rather than the automatic product of a constitutional supremacy. The federal government could not, in the
last analysis, compel the provinces; it could only persuade them that their
own interests coincided with the federal definition of an overarching national
interest. In practice, this meant provincial acceptance of federal control
over the major tax fields, over the disbursement among the provinces of
much of the revenue harvested from those fields, and even over the use to
which the provinces put some of that revenue.

Until fairly recently, the provinces generally went along with Ottawa's
"national" view and accepted federal leadership in fiscal matters. Over the

past 20 years or so, however, the provinces have become less tolerant of federal leadership and have taken increasing advantage of the substantial freedom of action that the designers of the constitution made available to them—unintentionally—by giving them access to direct taxation and exclusive authority in the area of social welfare.

This book traces the course of Canadian federalism in its fiscal dimension from 1867 to the present, with an emphasis on events since the end of the Second World War. The first part of the book reviews developments from 1867 to the end of the war, and the balance of the book, apart from a final, summary chapter, examines developments since the war in each of three main areas: tax sharing, equalization, and conditional grants. A brief overview precedes each part.

The book does not discuss in detail the intricate and often subtle bargaining that has been the essence of provincial-federal fiscal relations over the years, but it does show how the arrangements in place at any given time were the result of trade-offs between the competing priorities of the federal government and the provinces. In order to allow the narrative to flow, statistics have been kept to a minimum and are largely confined to tables rather than allowed to proliferate through the text. Most of the figures given are estimates made during the relevant fiscal year. As a rule, the post-war tax-sharing and transfer arrangements have provided that the final calculation of the amounts due to the provinces will be made only after all of the relevant data have been determined—an undertaking that generally requires several years to complete. Although the final figures are of interest, they are not relevant to an understanding of contemporary perceptions. For the provinces, the current cash flow has been at least as important as the final reckoning.

The staff of the Foundation showed remarkable forbearance as the book inched its way along. Doug Sherbaniuk was especially supportive. Mary Gurney was of tremendous assistance in many ways, not least in preparing the appendix. Alex Scala was an editor who transformed disparate grains of sand into a string of pearls.

This book is built on the first two editions of *Financing Canadian Federation*, published by the Foundation in 1953 and 1966. To their authors, Milton Moore, J. Harvey Perry, and Don Beach, this book is dedicated. To J. Harvey Perry, who had the courage to revisit the topic and wrestle a first draft into a coherent manuscript, goes also my heartfelt appreciation.

David B. Perry

PART I

THE HISTORICAL BACKGROUND

Introduction

The arrangements that constitute the financial dimension of Canadian federalism have been a source of friction between the federal government and the provinces since Canada was new. These arrangements have been changed again and again, but the changes have usually failed to satisfy either level of government. They have also failed, as a rule, to keep pace with the changing requirements of Canadian society. These two failures are closely related.

From the start, the problem has been twofold: first, to find an appropriate balance between the tax powers and the spending responsibilities of the federal government and those of the provinces; second, to find a formula that will minimize the fiscal disparities among the provinces.

The British North America (BNA) Act of 1867 gave the larger share of both powers and responsibilities to the federal government. Yet limited as provincial responsibilities were, it was soon apparent that for many provinces the cost of meeting these responsibilities exceeded the revenue resources at their command. For the first few decades after Confederation, the two levels of government were generally able to bridge the gap between provincial resources and provincial responsibilities by negotiating ad hoc federal subsidies for the provinces. However, the lack of systematic arrangements to balance the responsibilities of the two levels precluded any lasting peace between them.

The twentieth century imposed new demands on both the provinces and the federal government and aggravated the friction between them. Two world wars and a major depression pushed them into new tax fields and new realms of expenditure. The BNA Act had made direct taxes such as income taxes available to both the federal government and the provinces. In 1867, however, no one had expected income taxes to become an important source of revenue, and during the first half-century of Confederation they were levied, in a limited way, only by the provinces and some municipalities. When Ottawa introduced the first federal income tax in 1917, it acknowledged that it was violating the spirit—though not the letter—of the BNA Act, a violation made necessary by the extraordinary fiscal demands of the First World War.

After the war, the problems inherent in the original division of powers and responsibilities were exacerbated by the very process that the original arrangements had been intended to promote—the development of Canadian society. The public services now most needed and demanded by Canadians—schools, highways, social services—fell within areas of responsibility that the BNA Act

1

had assigned to the provinces. Moreover, these services required levels of expenditure that the fathers of Confederation had never contemplated.

The pressures on the financial arrangements of the federation were relentless, and these arrangements threatened to unravel altogether during the depression of the 1930s, when Ottawa and the provinces competed for the same severely contracted tax bases. The Second World War resolved the issue in favor of the federal government, to which the provinces surrendered their primary tax powers for the duration of the war.

In planning for the peace to come, the federal government was mindful of two considerations: first, that the creation of a stable post-war economy would require government intervention; second, that the provinces were too weak financially to sustain a significant role in the reconstruction process. Ottawa was determined, in fact, to retain the dominant role that it had recovered during the war—the role envisaged for it by the fathers of Confederation.

This part of the book reviews the history of the financial arrangements between the federal government and the provinces from 1867 to 1947—that is, from Confederation through the termination of the Wartime Tax Agreement system after the Second World War. Chapter 1 carries the story from the 1867 to the threshold of the depression of the 1930s. Chapter 2 considers how the financial structure in place at the end of the 1920s fared in the context of depression and war.

1

The Financial Basis of Confederation: 1867 to 1930

The design for Canadian federalism reflected the concerns and hopes of the founding fathers at Confederation. The development of our federal system since Confederation has reflected changes in political and economic conditions. A number of major studies have discussed the evolution of the system of government put in place in 1867, and I shall not describe that evolution in detail here.[1] The financial basis of Canadian federalism, like its political basis, has evolved sometimes slowly, sometimes rapidly, and has presented a wide variation over time in the division of powers and responsibilities between the federal government and the provinces.

The Basic Design

The stated intention of most of the colonial leaders involved in the debate that led to Confederation was to create a strong central government. Given the example of the United States, where the relative weakness of the central government had led ultimately to civil war, and given the serious problems of development and finance that faced the new nation, it was inevitable that the constitution should allocate the major revenue resources and expenditure responsibilities to the federal government.

The designers of the constitution assumed, however, that the occasions for expenditure—and hence the need for revenue—would be limited. The British North America (BNA) Act of 1867[2] reflected the prevailing laissez-faire approach to economic and social issues. It was framed to suit the needs of a central federal government that would concern itself mainly with transportation and communication (that is, the provision of facilities such as railways, canals, and harbours), the development of the frontier economy, and defence.

---

[1] Canada, *Report of the Royal Commission on Dominion-Provincial Relations* (Ottawa: King's Printer, 1940) (herein referred to as "the Rowell-Sirois commission") and the studies prepared for it, all published in 1939, provide a wealth of detail for the period up to the Second World War. In addition, the reader is referred to such classic works as A.R.M. Lower, *Colony to Nation* (Toronto: Longmans, Green, 1946); Donald Creighton, *The Road to Confederation: The Emergence of Canada* (Toronto: Macmillan, 1964); J.A. Corry, *Democratic Government and Politics*, 2d ed. (Toronto: University of Toronto Press, 1951); J.A. Maxwell, *Federal Subsidies to the Provincial Governments in Canada* (Cambridge, Mass.: Harvard University Press, 1937); and R.M. Dawson, *The Government of Canada* (Toronto: University of Toronto Press, 1947 and subsequent editions).

[2] British North America Act, 1867, 30-31 Vict., c. 3 (UK); since renamed the Constitution Act, 1867.

Government involvement in education, health, and social welfare was rudimentary: school was not compulsory, and the provision of welfare services was left largely to private charity. Nor was this state of affairs expected to change.

The capital expense of building extensive facilities for transportation had left the finances of the colonies in a precarious state. The provinces were willing, therefore, to turn over to the new federal government the responsibility for major transportation projects, such as the transcontinental railway and the improvement of the St. Lawrence River canal system.

Sections 91 to 95 of the BNA Act set out the main features of the division of responsibilities and taxing powers between the federal government and the provinces. Section 92 gave the provinces exclusive authority over prisons, hospitals, asylums, and charitable institutions, public lands, and the administration of justice. Two general subsections of section 92 were intended to provide a limited degree of latitude in determining provincial responsibilities: the provinces were given jurisdiction over property and civil rights and over all matters of a merely local or private nature. Section 93 assigned education to the provinces, subject to guarantees of the rights of certain religious minorities.

Section 91 gave the federal, or dominion, government the power to make laws for the peace, order, and good government of Canada in relation to all matters not assigned exclusively to the provinces. The section listed 29 functions to illustrate but not restrict this general principle, including defence, the postal system, and the regulation of trade, commerce, and banking.

Accordingly, section 92 left the provinces in control of local works and undertakings but gave the federal government authority over international and interprovincial transport, an authority that included the power to assume responsibility for a local work by declaring it to be for the general advantage of the nation or of two or more provinces.

To make it possible for the federal government to carry out the costly functions that the provinces had relinquished, the latter surrendered to it (in section 91) the power to use indirect taxes such as customs duties and excise taxes, the main sources of colonial revenue. The assignment of indirect taxes to the central government also ensured that no province could use such taxes to control interprovincial trade in the new nation. The BNA Act gave both levels of government the power of direct taxation, the taxation of incomes, wealth, or property. It was expected, however, that unless extraordinary circumstances forced the federal government to resort to direct taxation in other forms—all of which were highly unpopular at that time—the main direct taxes would be property taxes, which the provinces would assign to their local governments. The provinces did not expect to use the power of direct taxation themselves. They anticipated both an expansion in revenue, from the sale of public lands and from various licences and fees, and a substantial reduction in expenditure, thanks to the federal government's assumption of the heavy debts they had incurred, primarily for transportation facilities, when they were colonies.

These expectations proved to be excessively optimistic even before Confederation was an accomplished fact, and in its final form the BNA Act provided for a system of federal grants to the provinces. These subsidies, although prompted in large part by projected deficits at the provincial level, were also justified as compensation for the transfer of the main taxing power to the federal government. The Act specified four types of subsidies:

1) *Debt allowance subsidies*: The federal government assumed the large colonial debt related to capital assets used for development, but the level of debt was not the same for all colonies. Provinces with actual debt below the national average per capita received an annual grant equivalent to 5 percent of the difference, and provinces with debt above the national average (Ontario and Quebec) were to pay a comparable amount.[3]

2) *Per capita subsidies*: The debt allowance formula did not alleviate disparities in provincial finances that reflected existing disparities in the development of local government and local revenue; projected per capita deficits ranged from 38 cents in the Province of Canada (Ontario and Quebec) to $1.70 in Nova Scotia.[4] A compromise was reached when Nova Scotia revised its deficit down to 80 cents per capita, an amount that was set as a federal per capita subsidy to all provinces.

3) *Government support subsidies*: Each of the provinces received an additional subsidy for the support of its legislature and administration.

4) *Special subsidies*: New Brunswick received grants in view of its particular hardships, as did Nova Scotia after 1869.[5]

The subsidies were to be in full settlement of all future demands on the central government. To limit the importance of the per capita subsidies, the federal government stipulated that they were to be payable only on the first 400,000 of population. The annual subsidies granted to each of the first seven provinces in the year in which it joined Confederation were as follows:

	Per capita subsidy	Grants in support of government	Special grants	Total
	thousands of dollars			
Nova Scotia	264	60		325
New Brunswick	202	50	63	315
Quebec	890	70		960
Ontario	1,116	80		1,196
Manitoba (1870)	14	30		44
British Columbia (1871)	48	35	100	183
Prince Edward Island (1873)	75	30	45	150

---

[3] As is shown later in the chapter, the formula was adjusted so that neither province made such payments.

[4] Estimated by Galt in 1864. See Alexander Galt, "Speech on the Proposed Union of the British North American Provinces," delivered at Sherbrooke on November 23, 1864 and quoted in the Rowell-Sirois report, supra footnote 1, book I, at 45.

[5] See below.

The Evolution of Federal Transfers: 1869-1913

The grant provided to New Brunswick of $63,000 per year for 10 years established a precedent for relief of special hardship. In 1869, Nova Scotia also found itself faced with reduced budget projections and successfully petitioned Ottawa for a grant of approximately $80,000 per year for 10 years, plus $60,000 annually with no time limit.

With the entry of Manitoba in 1870, British Columbia in 1871, and Prince Edward Island in 1873, the original terms of the subsidy scheme were altered further. Manitoba's basic subsidy, as determined by the formula, was to be $67,000, but with no revenue from land sales and little from other sources the province was forced to press for increased assistance. Its annual subsidy was increased four times in the province's first 15 years. The debt allowance for all provinces was gradually raised, so that by 1872 even Ontario and Quebec (the provinces with the highest pre-Confederation debt) received transfers in respect of the debt allowance.

During the first seven years of Confederation, the federal government enjoyed buoyant revenues. It was able to improve the financial terms of union for the original provinces and to make the conditions for new provinces more generous than would have been possible before 1867. At this time, Ottawa was the dominant force in government. It changed the provincial subsidies without full provincial concurrence and often without reference to Westminster. Several provinces had come to rely on federal subsidies for most of their revenue: in 1874, New Brunswick got 92 percent of its revenue from this source, and even Quebec and Ontario received 40 to 50 percent of their revenue from the central government. Ontario and Quebec were, however, the only provinces with no continuing deficits.

This prosperous interval was ended by the worldwide depression that began in 1873, although its full effects were not felt in Canada until 1875. The recovery did not begin until 1895.[6] The federal government's commitment to transportation expenditures, the drying-up of the investment market, and a reduction in imports (and hence in customs duties) imposed severe strains on Ottawa's financial position. The depression also created financial problems for the provinces, which, except in a few notable instances, found no federal subsidies forthcoming to fill the gaps. When the 10-year special grants provided to Nova Scotia and New Brunswick ended, a deficit-plagued federal government would not agree to extend them. On the other hand, Ottawa made a number of special arrangements for Manitoba—which did not get natural resource rights and ownership of Crown lands as the earlier entrants had—because of its role as the focus for development in the West. The subsidies to Manitoba increased almost tenfold between 1870 and 1905, and over three-quarters of the net increase in subsidies between 1873 and

---

[6] See Stewart Bates, *Fiscal History of Canadian Governments*, a study prepared for the Royal Commission on Dominion-Provincial Relations (Ottawa: King's Printer, 1939), 36.

1905 went to Manitoba. This period also saw another adjustment in the debt allowances. In 1884, the federal government yielded to the argument that the 1873 increase in the allowances, which made Quebec and Ontario eligible for subsidy, should have been made retroactive to 1867. It granted a further increase to all provinces, adding $360,000 to the total annual subsidy.

In 1887, the Quebec premier called a conference of all provincial leaders to discuss their financial problems and federal subsidy structure. Prime Minister Sir John A. Macdonald, who considered the conference an affront to the federal government, refused to attend, as did the premiers of Prince Edward Island and British Columbia. The remaining five premiers passed resolutions that called for substantially increased grants. One resolution called for an increase in the arbitrary grants in support of the provincial governments and legislatures and their distribution on the basis of population. Another called for a removal of the population limit on the per capita grant. These resolutions went unheeded: even if the conference had been politically acceptable to the federal government, the federal treasury did not have the money to meet the provinces' requests.

In 1902, another premier of Quebec hosted a similar conference, but this one had the support of all the provinces. The premiers reiterated the demands made 15 years earlier, then took the resolutions back to their legislatures and had them ratified. The federal government again rejected the provincial initiatives.

A study prepared for the Rowell-Sirois Commission characterized intergovernmental fiscal relations from 1873 to the end of the century as "a constant wrangle between mendicant provinces and a stingy federal government, each haggling at times over a few thousand dollars in grants."[7] As the depression ended, however, federal government revenues increased, making it possible for Ottawa to consider increasing its assistance to the provinces. The first indication of the change in the federal position was Ottawa's relatively generous treatment of Saskatchewan and Alberta when they entered Confederation in 1905. Both provinces had large populations on entry and both were at the centre of frontier development. Each province received the following subsidies:[8]

	$000
Grant for government	50
Population	200
Debt allowance	405
Subsidy in lieu of land	375
Building allowance (for five years only)	94
	1,124

---

[7] Wilfrid Eggleston and C.T. Kraft, *Dominion-Provincial Subsidies and Grants*, a study prepared for the Royal Commission on Dominion-Provincial Relations (Ottawa: King's Printer, 1939), 30.

[8] Ibid, at 28.

In 1905, Prime Minister Sir Wilfred Laurier agreed to meet with provincial leaders to discuss the grant system, but no date was set. In September 1906, nearly a year after a joint request from the provinces for a meeting to discuss grant terms, Prime Minister Sir Wilfrid Laurier convened the first federal-provincial conference on fiscal arrangements. The Provincial Conference, as it was called, endorsed the recommendations of the 1887 and 1902 conferences. The federal government then took the recommendations to Westminster for incorporation in the British North America Act. British Columbia unsuccessfully sought a special study of further aid that it required because of special circumstances. The other provinces and the federal government offered the Pacific province $100,000 per year for 10 years, a subsidy that was incorporated in the amendments to the BNA Act passed at Westminster. In the view of British Columbia's government, however, the amount was insufficient.

The effect of the revisions is shown by a comparison of the grants to the provinces in the fiscal year 1906-07, under the old system, with the new grants paid in 1907-08. The two newest provinces, Saskatchewan and Alberta, received an increase of less than 8 percent, but the other provinces received increases that ranged from 33 percent for Prince Edward Island to 70 percent for British Columbia. The old and new subsidies were as follows.[9]

	1906-07	1907-08
	thousands of dollars	
Nova Scotia	433	610
New Brunswick	491	621
Prince Edward Island	212	282
Quebec	1,087	1,687
Ontario	1,339	2,129
Manitoba	621	751
Saskatchewan	1,130	1,218
Alberta	1,124	1,212
British Columbia	307	522
	6,745	9,033

The schedule for the grants for government and the legislature was set on a sliding scale based on population:

Population	Dollars
Under 150,000	100,000
150,000 or more but less than 200,000	150,000
200,000 or more but less than 400,000	180,000
400,000 or more but less than 800,000	190,000
800,000 or more but less than 1,500,000	220,000
1,500,000 or more	240,000

The population limit was removed from the per capita grants. The revised grants were 80 cents per person for population up to 2,500,000 and 60 cents

---

[9] Ibid, at 33.

per person on the excess. The population figures for Manitoba, Saskatchewan, and Alberta would be adjusted for grant purposes every five years; the grants for the other provinces would change in accordance with the decennial censuses.

Table 1.1 shows the amounts paid to the provinces in the fiscal year 1908-09, by which time the new grant structure had stabilized.

Although the revised subsidies introduced in 1907 were intended to be "as final and unalterable" as the original subsidy structure devised in 1867, the provinces continued to press for additional allowances. British Columbia was unsuccessful, but in 1912 Manitoba received increases in both the subsidy in lieu of land and the debt allowance and Prince Edward Island received an additional special grant. In 1913, a provincial conference heard pleas by the provinces for an increase in the subsidies equivalent to 10 percent of the federal collections of customs duties and excise taxes. This early proposal for federal-provincial tax sharing was looked on favourably by the federal government and might have been implemented had not war broken out in 1914, before concrete action could be taken. Minor adjustments to the statutory subsidies have been made since, but the subsidies are no longer an important source of revenue for the provinces.

The Development of Strong Provincial Governments

During the first 40 years of Confederation, the provinces were unable to solve their financial problems with increased transfers or subsidies from the federal government. These problems arose in the first place because, in all of the provinces except Ontario, municipal development failed to meet expectations. The provinces were called on to provide municipal services but did not

Table 1.1 Statutory Subsidies to the Provinces, Fiscal Year July 1, 1908 to June 30, 1909

	Allowance for government and legislature	Per capita grants	Special grants	Debt allowance	Total
		thousands of dollars			
Prince Edward Island	100	87	56	39	282
Nova Scotia	190	368	—	53	610
New Brunswick	180	265	150	26	621
Quebec	240	1,319	—	127	1,687
Ontario	240	1,746	—	142	2,129
Manitoba	180	293	100	179	751
Saskatchewan	180	206	469	405	1,260
Alberta	180	200	469	405	1,254
British Columbia	150	143	200	29	522

Note: Totals have been rounded.

Source: Wilfrid Eggleston and C.T. Kraft, *Dominion-Provincial Subsidies and Grants*, a study prepared for the Royal Commission on Dominion-Provincial Relations (Ottawa: King's Printer, 1939), statistical appendix.

develop the complementary levies on real estate. They were forced, therefore, to examine options for new taxation, and, as table 1.2 shows, a number of new provincial taxes were introduced between 1874 and 1896.

British Columbia began to exploit its power to impose direct taxation when its request for additional federal assistance was turned down. It introduced a provincial income tax and land taxes in 1873. Prince Edward Island imposed a land tax from 1877 to 1882. Quebec also reacted to the federal government's refusal to increase grants, and to the pressing problems of financing railway lines, by imposing new taxes. The province levied a charge on insurance companies in the late 1870s, but the Privy Council declared the tax ultra vires. Capitalizing on this experience, Quebec successfully introduced a series of charges on places of business, paid-up capital, and related bases beginning in 1882. The other provinces gradually adopted the same system of special taxes on business. In 1892, Ontario established the precedent of a succession duty that was constitutionally valid, and over the next four years the Ontario tax was copied by the other provinces. In 1894, Prince Edward Island reintroduced its land tax and began levying a personal income tax.

The exploitation of a range of direct taxes by provincial governments had not been a part of the design of the fathers of Confederation, who had given the provinces the power to levy such taxes mainly so that municipalities could impose taxes on real property. Yet given the federal government's failure to respond to provincial requests for increased assistance, it was almost inevitable that the provinces, in order to maintain financial stability, would enter the direct tax fields.

**Table 1.2   Provincial and Federal Revenues on
Current Account, 1874 and 1896**

	Provincial		Dominion	
	1874	1896	1874	1896
	thousands of dollars			
Federal subsidies	3,842	4,301	—	—
Taxes				
Customs	1	—	14,443	19,479
Excise	—	—	5,617	9,170
Corporation taxes	—	156	—	—
Succession duties	—	428	—	—
Real and personal property	42	288	—	—
Other	—	82	213	—
Subtotal	43	954	20,273	28,649
Licences, permits, etc.	651	1,756	14	266
Public domain	1,413	2,801	351	299
Other	716	160	963	744
Grand total	6,665	9,972	21,601	29,958

Source: same as table 1.1, at 64.

The direct taxes introduced in this period were more important as precedents than as sources of revenue. In 1896, they provided only about 10 percent of all provincial revenues. In the maritime provinces and Manitoba, federal subsidies continued to be the principal revenue source. Nevertheless, these small direct taxes firmly established provincial occupancy in fields that were later to be very important to both the provinces and the federal government. For the time being, however, the federal government relied exclusively on indirect taxes (customs and excise duties) and made no moves to exercise its power to levy direct taxes.

The early decades of Confederation were marked by a number of important decisions by the Privy Council at Westminster that not only supported provincial tax measures but also, by giving a broad interpretation of the provincial power to legislate in matters relating to "property and civil rights," established provincial priority over the federal power to legislate for the "peace, order and good government of Canada." Thus the provinces were given responsibility for areas of expenditure, such as relief and social welfare, that would create demands on provincial revenue resources far greater than those contemplated at the time of Confederation.

By the turn of the century, the "Great Depression" had yielded to an era of general prosperity, stimulated by both an influx of settlers to the western plains and an influx of foreign capital for building new cities on the prairies, new transcontinental railways, and a substantial industrial base in central Canada. The provinces and municipalities began a period of expansion that would continue through the 1920s, interrupted only by the First World War and the short depressions that preceded and followed it. Industrial development led to increasing urbanization and, with it, a need for high capital expenditures on roads, schools, public buildings, and basic infrastructure. In addition, the widespread adoption of the motor car necessitated extensive spending for better roads and highways. These developments caused new strains on intergovernmental finance, strains that were largely eased during the prosperity of the 1920s by the further exploitation of provincial taxing powers.

Wartime Tax Measures: 1914-1918

The pressure of financing Canada's participation in the First World War forced the federal government to introduce direct taxation. This action contradicted the implied principle that the provinces had exclusive use of the direct tax field—a principle so well established that the provincial premiers regarded the federal move as an invasion of provincial taxing powers. Notwithstanding this assumption, the federal government imposed income taxes on individuals and corporations in 1917; it later added increased and new excise taxes and a general sales tax. These new taxes decreased the relative importance to the federal treasury of the traditional customs and excise duties, which fell from 78 percent of revenue in 1913 to less than one-third in 1921.

The provinces increased their own taxes significantly during the war, particularly by imposing a temporary provincial property tax that was collected by their municipalities. In 1912, the land boom on the Prairies collapsed; only the stimulus provided by the war effort prevented economic difficulties. The depression of 1912-1915 and the war seriously limited provincial and local capital expenditures until the end of the war. In 1912, the federal government acceded to Manitoba's request for improved terms in its grants in lieu of land sales and gave a small additional subsidy to Prince Edward Island. The war prevented any further changes in federal-provincial fiscal relations, forestalling, for example, a promised royal commission to investigate British Columbia's grievances.

The Post-War Period

The federal role in the development of a pioneer economy seemed to come to an end after the war. The burden of war debts and war pensions and the costs of running the continental railway system, which Ottawa had taken over during the war, forced the federal government to adopt an extremely conservative financial policy. The only concession that it made to the provinces during the 1920s was to assume one-half of the cost of the old age pension system that it introduced in cooperation with the provinces in 1927.[10] The federal revenue structure reverted to its pre-war pattern: by 1930, the personal and corporation income taxes had been substantially reduced, the sales tax rate had fallen from 6 to 1 percent, and customs and excise revenues had rebounded to two-thirds of all tax revenue.

The provinces assumed the responsibilities of nation-building, since the major demands for public services arose in fields under their jurisdiction. Highway and hydroelectric projects forced provincial debt for capital expenditures sharply upward during the 1920s. Several provinces drew upon loans from the federal government to finance public telephone systems and government housing projects. Public buildings and other capital expenditures associated with rapid urbanization further added to provincial and local debt, which was financed largely by 12- to 15-year debentures that matured during the depression of the 1930s. Current provincial expenditures remained at about the per capita levels reached in 1914, but the emphasis shifted from services related to justice and legislation, the public domain, agriculture, and transportation to education, mother's allowances, child welfare, mental hospitals, and other welfare expenditures—including direct relief for the unemployed in the depression of 1921-22.

To finance these expenditures, the provinces and municipalities moved aggressively into new revenue fields. During the early 1920s, after the repeal of wartime prohibition, most provinces undertook to channel the distribution

---

[10] This development is examined in more detail in chapter 12.

of alcohol through provincially run organizations. The result was that the control and sale of alcoholic beverages became an important source of revenue. As the automobile gained general acceptance, licence fees and gasoline taxes also became major sources of provincial revenue. The established provincial taxes, succession duties, and corporation taxes continued to produce significant revenues, and municipal tax receipts were buoyed up by expanding residential and business construction.

The provincial financial structure that developed in the 1920s contained an unappreciated vulnerability to cyclical fluctuations that was to exacerbate the problems faced by the provinces in the depression of the 1930s. High capital expenditure led to increasingly rigid outlays for interest on debt, and other forms of expenditure involved high fixed costs. Moreover, most of the new revenue sources were sensitive to general economic conditions. The only stable element, statutory subsidies, had become a relatively unimportant source of revenue for most provinces.

The first conditional grant programs were introduced during the decade after the First World War. The initial programs involved federal grants to fund programs undertaken by the provinces under strict conditions set down by the federal government. For most provinces, however, they were not a significant source of revenue. They were most useful to those provinces that had sufficient resources to finance their share of the relevant expenditures.

Royal Commissions on Federal-Provincial Fiscal Relations

The Royal Commission on Maritime Claims, the Duncan commission, which reported in September 1926, was the first of a series of federally appointed royal commissions with mandates to examine aspects of the financial relationship between Ottawa and the provinces.[11] The "claims" arose from the fact that the post-war depression lasted longer in the three maritime provinces than in the rest of the country, widening the regional disparities in wealth that had been a feature of Canada since Confederation. The international market for the basic products of the maritime provinces—lumber, fish, agricultural products, coal, and steel—was characterized by intense competition and low prices, the populations of Prince Edward Island and Nova Scotia had declined between 1920 and 1926, and the budgets of Nova Scotia and New Brunswick had been in deficit positions almost continually since the war. The maritime provinces argued that the debt allowance discriminated against them, that they lacked the vast virgin territory—and thus the potential wealth—of other provinces, and that national policies such as the tariff had reduced the capacity of their citizens to bear taxation.

---

[11] Canada, *Report of the Royal Commission on Maritime Claims* (Ottawa: King's Printer, 1926). As was noted above, a royal commission on federal-provincial financial relationships in general was proposed earlier but did not meet because of the First World War.

The Duncan commission agreed that the maritime provinces had a "genuine claim to a readjustment of the financial arrangements between the Dominion and themselves, and that in any readjustment their territorial limitations entitle them to still further consideration."[12] It recommended immediate lump-sum increases in annual subsidies of $875,000 for Nova Scotia, $600,000 for New Brunswick, and $125,000 for Prince Edward Island, amounts that nearly doubled the annual statutory payments to the three provinces. The commission also recommended a complete revision of the financial arrangements between the federal and maritime governments, but it made no attempt to determine what the "readjustment" should be. The federal government acceded to the proposal for interim additional grants reluctantly and then only after a federal-provincial (then called dominion-provincial) conference early in 1927 showed that all of the other provinces approved of the increase. The grants were introduced for the 1927-28 fiscal year and continued until a further revision was made in 1935.

Not surprisingly, all of the other provinces except Quebec and Ontario immediately requested increases in their own subsidies, arguing that their fiscal resources also were inadequate. Provincial proposals ranged from a demand that the federal government take over expensive new services to suggestions that Ottawa withdraw from certain tax fields—in particular the income tax field. The federal government was unmoved; it argued that it had a responsibility to reduce its debt and maintain the nation's good credit standing in order to encourage investment by foreigners.

The spirit of cooperation evident at the 1927 conference encouraged the federal government to reopen negotiations with the prairie and western provinces on a more liberal basis than had been possible earlier. In 1927, the federal and Manitoba governments agreed on the appointment of a royal commission to determine what financial readjustments were necessary to place Manitoba on an equal basis with the other provinces in the administration and control of its natural resources. The Turgeon commission,[13] reporting in May 1929, recommended a compensatory grant to Manitoba of $4,584,000 and continuation of the subsidy in lieu of lands at the existing level. The federal government implemented the recommendations in 1930, when it also gave over control of resources to the province.

Saskatchewan, Alberta, and British Columbia, meanwhile, pressed their concerns about the ownership of natural resources and the level of federal grants. The federal government accepted the principle that the three provinces be given jurisdiction over natural resources, and in the late 1920s royal commisisons were set up to determine appropriate compensation for each province for the previous federal jurisdiction over public lands and natural resources.

---

[12] Ibid., at 19, and quoted in Eggleston and Kraft, supra footnote 7, at 54.

[13] Canada, *Report of the Royal Commission on the Transfer of the Natural Resources on Manitoba* (Ottawa: King's Printer, 1929).

The Saskatchewan and Alberta commissions recommended flat one-time grants of $5 million to each province,[14] but Saskatchewan objected on the basis of the minority opinion of one commissioner, who had recommended $58 million. Alberta refrained from agreement until Saskatchewan had settled. Both cases remained unresolved until shortly after the Second World War. The royal commission investigating the British Columbia claim did not recommend a similar flat one-time grant, since in this case the federal jurisdiction had been limited;[15] the province did not accept the alternative of a three-year extension of the related subsidy, and again the matter was not settled until after the war.

The three royal commissions were also expected to determine new levels of basic subsidies comparable to the higher grants awarded to the Atlantic provinces. The basic structure of statutory subsidies to Saskatchewan and Alberta did not change. Additional annual grants were provided to British Columbia.[16]

Conclusion

By the end of the 1920s, the financial arrangements embodied in the original British North America Act had long since proved to be unrealistic. Regional disparities were more intractable than the fathers of Confederation had expected them to be. In the course of the 60 years since Confederation, the Privy Council in Westminster had interpreted the Act in a way that had caused a significant shift in powers and responsibilities from the federal government to the provinces. Technological developments and the changing character of the national and regional economies had reinforced this trend.

The federal subsidies to the provinces, despite a long series of increases, were no longer of major significance outside of the Maritimes: in total, they amounted to less than 9 percent of provincial revenues in 1929. Federal conditional grants had been introduced, but they had brought problems that prevented them from becoming a significant source of provincial revenues.[17] Thus the provinces had been forced to develop their own tax systems. The provinces with buoyant economies were beginning to exploit direct taxes, but only British Columbia relied on such taxes for a major part of its revenues.

As the 1930s dawned, the provinces and municipalities were spending, in total, almost half as much again as the federal government. Although the

---

[14] See Canada, *Report of the Royal Commission on the Natural Resources of Saskatchewan* (Ottawa: King's Printer, 1935); and Canada, *Report of the Royal Commission on Natural Resources of Alberta* (Ottawa: King's Printer, 1935).

[15] Justice W.M. Martin reported the recommendations of his one-person royal commission in 1928. See Canada, *Report of the Royal Commission on the Reconveyance of Land to British Columbia* (Ottawa: King's Printer, 1928).

[16] The changes are discussed in chapter 2.

[17] See chapters 12 and 13.

provinces were very far from exhausting their powers of taxation, the provincial revenue structure was built on a base that was highly vulnerable to changes in economic conditions. Provincial and local responsibilities too had become more directly related to economic conditions. The system of government in Canada had been able to cope with the First World War and minor depressions, but it would not be strong enough to cope with the depression of the 1930s.

2

The Financial Arrangements in Depression and War: 1930 to 1947

The evolution of Canadian federalism during its first sixty years into a system of strong provinces and a relatively weak central government contradicted both the intentions and the expectations of the designers of Confederation. This result came about in part because of the way in which the division of revenues and expenditures between the provinces and the federal government operated under the pressures of nation-building and industrialization. The structure that evolved was not capable of withstanding the major shocks of the depression of the 1930s and the Second World War. The highly centralized federal system in place by 1947 represented Canada's response to these two challenges.

The Depression of 1930-1939

During the late 1920s, international trade became unstable as each country strove to protect its own basic producers. A surplus of agricultural goods and base metals accumulated. International borrowing and lending failed to rationalize protectionist policies. After the collapse of the stock markets in the United States in 1929, international lending eased, raw materials prices fell, the gold standard was abandoned, and the international economic system fell into chaos. Canada was severely affected, since its main exports—wheat, newsprint, and metals—were among those hit hardest by falling prices. As the depression deepened and many countries devalued their currencies to assist their exporters and, particularly the United States, increased tariff barriers to protect their domestic producers, international competition in the sale of these commodities became even more severe. Canada did not devalue, but over the period 1930-1932 it did increase its tariffs, a step that seriously damaged foreign trade and exacerbated regional disparities within Canada. The problem posed by regional disparities led to the shift of power from the provinces to the federal government, since only a national government could alleviate regional distress by redistributing resources from one region to another.

The depression put a tremendous strain on the public finance system in Canada. Unemployment relief was a provincial responsibility, but up to this time the function had been delegated to the municipalities. At various times during the 1920s, the provinces and the federal government had provided ad hoc grants to help underwrite local "relief" payments, but no system had been

17

developed. During the depression, neither local nor provincial governments could afford the rising costs of relief, and a new series of federal grants (also ad hoc) was instituted to assist the provinces and, through them, the municipalities. During the period 1930-1937, these grants covered approximately 40 percent of all relief expenditures. This assistance was not sufficient, however, and the provinces and local governments were forced to borrow to meet the cost of relief (see table 2.1). Some of these loans were obtained from the central government. The prairie provinces had exhausted their borrowing capabilities by 1932 and relied entirely on federal loans for the remainder of the depression. Only Quebec and Ontario were able to weather the depression without additional ad hoc assistance from the federal government.

The process by which higher levels of government funded aid for relief expenditures developed from a sequence of crises. When municipalities could no longer finance their relief expenditures, even by borrowing at prohibitive interest rates, they appealed to the provinces, most of which soon found themselves in the same position. The provinces appealed in turn to the federal government, which provided grants and large loans or advances to provinces that could not borrow further on their own.

Federal relief grants differed from earlier subsidies: they were hastily devised to meet an emergency that was expected to pass quickly, and they were continued on this basis from year to year. The first grants were given to cover public works to create employment and for direct relief. They were later expanded to cover agricultural relief (including assistance for farm operation, seeding, and so forth) and rehabilitation, the care of transients, the placing of unemployed persons on farms, agricultural settlement, training camps, and other projects. At first, some conditions were attached to the aid,

**Table 2.1 Statutory Subsidies to the Provinces,
Fiscal Year 1936-37**

	Allowance for government and legislature	Per capita grants	Special grants	Debt allowance	Total
	thousands of dollars				
Prince Edward Island	100	87	431	39	657
Nova Scotia	190	410	1,300	53	1,953
New Brunswick	190	327	1,050	26	1,593
Quebec	2,225	240		127	2,592
Ontario	2,559	240		142	2,941
Manitoba	190	569	562	382	1,703
Saskatchewan	220	745	750	405	2,120
Alberta	190	618	563	405	1,776
British Columbia	190	555	850	29	1,625

Note: totals have been rounded.

Source: Wilfrid Eggleston and C.T. Kraft, *Dominion-Provincial Subsidies and Grants*, a study prepared for the Royal Commission on Dominion-Provincial Relations (Ottawa: King's Printer, 1939).

but in later years the grants were simply merged in the general receipts of the provinces.

In drought-stricken areas, the federal government initially covered 50 percent of the costs of relief, but later it took on the whole burden. In other areas, the costs were at first usually shared equally among the three levels of government; later, the federal government made monthly payments to the provinces, which then made their own arrangements with their municipalities.

Meanwhile a search was undertaken for long-term solutions to the problems of the provinces. The White commission, a royal commission that reported in September 1935,[1] followed up the work of the Duncan commission[2] by examining the financial relations between the federal government and the maritime provinces. The commission recommended replacing the interim subsidies described in chapter 1 with permanent annual grants of $1.3 million to Nova Scotia, $0.9 million to New Brunswick, and $275,000 to Prince Edward Island. These subsidies were first paid in 1935-36. Table 2.1 summarizes subsidies and grants to the provinces during the fiscal year 1936-37.

British Columbia pressed its claims for additional assistance, arguing that the amounts recommended by the Martin commission[3] were insufficient and that it was receiving substantially less, in relative terms, than the maritime and prairie provinces. The federal government recognized that more aid was needed and beginning in 1934-35 provided an interim special grant of $750,000 per year.

The prairie provinces, where a long series of crop failures had reduced revenues and increased expenditures, were already in poor shape when the depression began. With the added problems brought on by the depression, these provinces had difficulty in meeting their obligations. After 1930, they relied extensively on federal loans, which by February 1937 had reached $127 million. The situation was worst in Saskatchewan, which had to provide not only unemployment relief but also assistance for farm operations. The province's resources were depressed, and it soon exhausted its borrowing powers by borrowing to meet relief expenditures. For several years, federal aid covered the entire cost of rural relief and agricultural aid in the drought area. Alberta, the newest province in terms of development, had a high debt load to carry in the depression. It was primarily the problem of debt load, not the pressure of relief payments, that caused the worst provincial crisis of the period. That crisis arose when the statutory authority for federal advances to Alberta expired and the province was unable to honour a debt issue that matured on April 1, 1936.

---

[1] Canada, *Report of the Royal Commission on Financial Arrangements Between the Dominion and the Maritime Provinces* (Ottawa: King's Printer, 1935).

[2] Canada, *Report of the Royal Commission on Maritime Claims* (Ottawa: King's Printer, 1926).

[3] Canada, *Report of the Royal Commission on the Reconveyance of Land to British Columbia* (Ottawa: King's Printer, 1928).

Saskatchewan and Manitoba were not in default, but their positions were precarious. In early 1937, the governments of Canada, Manitoba, and Saskatchewan requested the newly formed Bank of Canada to examine the problems of the two provinces. The bank reported quickly, recommending a commission of inquiry into the financial powers and responsibilities of all three levels of government. The bank also recommended temporary financial aid for the two provinces until such a commission could investigate and report. Manitoba, accordingly, received $750,000 per year in 1937 and 1938, and Saskatchewan received $1.5 million in each of the same years. In 1937, Saskatchewan suffered its worst drought and was given an additional $2 million. The bank also reviewed Alberta's position, at the province's request, but recommended against extra assistance.

It is clear from this brief review that there was no coordinated or carefully planned relief policy in Canada during the depression. In these unprece- dented circumstances, government followed a policy of expediency that failed either to promote maximum welfare or to safeguard the financial position of the various governments. The Rowell-Sirois report (discussed in detail below) made the following point:

> Although the Dominion provided nearly one-half of the total funds, and over 70 per cent in the case of the western provinces, it did not have adequate control over the money which was spent and administered by nine different provinces and by hundreds of municipalities.[4]

The report went on to discuss in more detail the problems caused by the de- pression. A lack of uniformity in the rules used by local authorities to grant relief had seriously impaired labour mobility; moreover, the level of assistance provided to those in need varied greatly from locality to locality. The provision of federal funds had done nothing to alleviate the financial problems of local governments, and the result was a number of municipal bankruptcies. Municipalities and the provinces alike suffered from very high levels of debt. In 1937, debt charges ranged from 16 to 27 percent of current provincial revenues, and the average over the nine provinces was 19 percent.[5]

As tables 2.2, 2.3, and 2.4 show, all three levels of government were in a precarious financial position, the consequence not only of extraordinary expenditures but also of an almost desperate revenue picture. As the depres- sion took hold, the tax revenues of all governments fell drastically, and municipal revenues fell farthest of all. At the beginning of the depression, the provinces' opportunities for raising additional revenues were limited, since the BNA Act prohibited the provinces from imposing indirect taxes and the federal government was already occupying the personal income tax field. As the depression deepened, all three levels of government scrambled for addi- tional tax revenues.

---

[4] Canada, *Report of the Royal Commission on Dominion-Provincial Relations*, book I (Ottawa: King's Printer, 1940), 173.

[5] Ibid., at 174.

Table 2.2   The Cost of Relief and Municipal-Provincial Finances, 1930-1937

	1930	1931	1932	1933	1934	1935	1936	1937
					millions of dollars			
Total municipal-provincial current revenues	492.38	479.26	479.53	479.34	484.47	508.49	529.65	558.36
Total municipal-provincial current expenditures[a] excluding relief	490.65	491.69	490.28	478.91	481.96	485.27	482.56	514.02
Total relief from municipal-provincial agencies	16.93	91.82	92.14	90.16	141.11	134.04	133.82	152.38
Deficiency of revenue	-15.20	-104.25	-102.89	-89.73	-138.60	-110.82	-86.73	-108.04
Less share of relief assumed by federal government	3.22	33.48	33.75	28.12	43.22	40.69	51.52	54.68
Municipal-provincial deficit	-11.98	-70.77	-69.14	-61.61	-95.38	-70.13	-35.21	-53.36
Federal loans for relief and general purposes[b]	—	17.00	11.00	8.30	25.80	29.60	15.80	17.30

[a] Including municipal sinking fund contributions and debt retirement. [b] $18,505,000 of these advances was written off by the federal government in 1937.

Source: Canada, *Report of the Royal Commission on Dominion-Provincial Relations*, book I (Ottawa: King's Printer, 1940), 164-72.

Table 2.3   Government Expenditures on Current Account, 1930 and 1937—All Governments

	Municipal		Provincial		Federal		Total[a]	
	1930	1937	1930	1937	1930	1937	1930	1937
					thousands of dollars			
Net debt charges	55,740	54,813	29,476	50,911	149,098	167,043	232,522	271,339
Defence	—	—	—	—	23,256	33,614	23,256	33,614
Pensions and aftercare	—	—	—	—	55,341	54,437	55,341	54,437
Public welfare	31,510	53,223	34,678	87,806	17,698	109,998	83,882	251,010
Education	84,705	76,506	33,775	32,121	702	272	119,191	108,899
Agriculture and public domain	—	—	21,241	20,636	23,298	17,909	44,484	38,545
Transportation	42,159	30,559	28,328	25,191	29,083	18,000	99,570	73,750
Subsidies to provinces	—	—	—	—	19,036	21,210	—	—
General expenditures—justice, legislation, general government, and miscellaneous	71,614	66,936	35,902	41,835	70,332[b]	55,685	177,849[b]	164,456
Total	285,728	282,037	183,400	258,500	387,844	478,168	836,095	996,050

[a] Less duplications. [b] Includes post office deficit—$6,081,000.

Source: Same as table 2.1, at 177, table 73.

Table 2.4 Government Revenues on Current Account, 1930 and 1937—All Governments

	Municipal		Provincial		Federal		Total	
	1930	1937	1930	1937	1930	1937	1930	1937
			thousands of dollars					
Federal subsidies	—	—	14,276	21,184	—	—	—	—ᵃ
Taxes								
Customs import duties	—	—	—	—	131,209	112,077	131,209	112,077
Excise duties	—	—	—	—	57,747	52,037	57,747	52,037
Manufacturers' taxes	—	—	—	—	10,474	17,185	10,474	17,185
Sales taxes	—	4,412	—	1,893	20,147	138,055	20,147	144,360
Corporation taxes	—	—	18,520	34,002	45,961	71,742	64,481	105,744
Succession duties	—	—	20,780	35,757	—	—	20,780	35,757
Income taxes on persons	2,381	1,870	2,122	11,884	26,624	50,597	31,127	64,351
Gasoline taxes	—	—	23,487	38,906	—	—	23,487	38,906
Real property taxes	257,118	244,936	6,708	5,875	—	—	263,826	250,811
Amusement taxes	—	—	4,525	2,838	—	—	4,525	2,838
Other taxes	23,275	20,337	1,534	3,005	4,531	7,391	29,340	30,733
Subtotal	282,774ᵇ	271,555ᵇ	77,676	134,160	296,693	449,084	657,143	854,799
Motor vehicles, automobile licences, etc.	—	—	19,907	25,937	—	—	19,907	25,937
All other licences, permits, fees, and fines and penalties	11,294	10,454	10,024	8,905	3,703	2,539	25,021	21,898
Public domain	—	—	17,037	21,135	2,297	2,484	19,334	23,619
Liquor control	—	—	30,985	29,798	—	—	30,985	29,798
Sale of commodities and services	3,171	6,175	1,159	965	2,745	6,269ᶜ	7,075	13,409ᶜ
Other	19,916	20,881	2,759	2,390	8,605	3,948	29,457	25,753
Total	317,155	309,065	173,823	244,474	314,043	464,324	788,922	995,213

ᵃ Excludes transfers from the federal government. ᵇ Particulars not available; included with "all other licences, permits, fees, and fines and penalties."
ᶜ Includes Post Office surplus—$3,250,000.

Source: Same as table 2.1, at 178, table 74.

In 1930, only the federal government, Prince Edward Island, and British Columbia taxed corporation profits, but 10 years later all of the provinces had entered the field. In the same period, the number of provinces occupying the personal income tax field increased from three to seven, and federal rates doubled. The federal sales tax rose by stages from 1 to 8 percent, and many new excises were introduced. Provincial gasoline taxes increased by an average of 50 percent during the depression. Saskatchewan, Alberta (for one year), and the city of Montreal introduced retail sales taxes. The provinces increased succession duties and stiffened enforcement. Some provinces increased or introduced flat rate taxes on corporations. Manitoba imposed a tax on wages.

The depression-inspired tax system, which had squeezed an increase in revenues of 30 percent from the prostrate economy, placed an unprecedented burden on the taxpayer. Even more disturbing, however, was the complexity and inefficiency of this improvised system. The burden of compliance implied by a tax system in which some fields were occupied by all three levels of government was a source of serious concern. This concern created a favourable environment for the introduction of a coordinated tax system in which the central government would play the dominant role. In the long run, the perceived shortcomings of the depression-era tax system made it easier for the provinces to accept federal dominance of the tax system in the post-war period.

The extraordinary revenue measures undertaken during the depression failed to establish a sound fiscal position for any of the three levels of government. Because the special federal grants to the provinces were on an ad hoc basis, they provided no stable basis for recovery. The federal grants also failed to solve the basic problems of regional disparity and the uneven incidence of the depression. Indeed, by the middle of the 1930s the prairie provinces had almost become wards of the federal government.

The Rowell-Sirois Commission

By 1937, it was clear that a major realignment of the federal system was needed if the tax and expenditure problems of the federal and provincial governments were to be solved. To this end, the federal government set up the Royal Commission on Dominion-Provincial Relations, the Rowell-Sirois commission, in August 1937. The commission's task was to investigate the distribution of functions and revenues between the federal government and the provinces; it was instructed to express what, in its opinion,

> subject to the retention of the distribution of legislative powers essential to a proper carrying out of the federal system in harmony with national needs and the promotion of national unity, will best effect a balanced relationship between the financial powers and the obligations and functions of each governing body, and conduce to a more efficient,

independent and economical discharge of governmental responsibilities in Canada.[6]

Over the next three years, the commission held hearings across the country and produced 18 studies of aspects of the Canadian economy and Canada's system of government. It also developed the first consistent set of public finance statistics for the federal and provincial governments. The commission's work was still pertinent long after the initial crisis, the depression, had passed and continues to stand as a landmark in the study of government and public finance in Canada.

The commission addressed itself to two basic tasks. The first and immediate task was to recommend changes in the fiscal relationship between the federal and provincial governments that would enable the federal government to coordinate the activities of all levels in the alleviation of the hardships of the depression. The second task was of long-term significance: to suggest a new division of government responsibilities and revenues that would be efficient, meet the increased needs of the provinces and local governments, and reflect current national objectives—objectives never envisaged at Confederation.

The commission held that the federal government was mistaken in regarding relief for the unemployed as a provincial-local function. Although it shunned the responsibility for relief, the federal government in practice directed large expenditures to provincial relief programs over which it had no control. As a result, it was unable to prevent marked regional differences in standards, the barriers to labour mobility created by these differences, and imprudent loans. Further, the costs of relief forced the junior levels of government to restrain other expenditures, and thereby exacerbate the depression, and put most governments deeply into debt.

The commission recommended that relief of unemployed employables should become a federal responsibility. This advice received the agreement of the federal and provincial governments, and in 1941 Ottawa introduced compulsory unemployment insurance. This step did not, however, completely relieve the junior levels of government of responsibility for unemployment relief. It was not until 1955 and 1957 that the federal government extended aid to provincial programs of unemployment assistance for those not qualified for benefits under the federal program.[7]

The commission made no other recommendations for changes in the distribution of social welfare responsibilities. It felt that responsibility for all other forms of social welfare (except a contributory old age pension system, should this be adopted) should remain at the provincial level and be financed by the provinces. It opposed joint jurisdiction over social welfare and

---

[6] Ibid., at 10.

[7] This development is described in chapter 12.

criticized the shared-cost system of financing social welfare programs. It recommended that the federal government be responsible for providing relief to primary industries, such as agriculture, that found themselves in severe distress. It made no other recommendations for transfers of functions.

The commission recommended that the federal government assume all outstanding provincial debt. Under the commission's plan, provincial revenues related to existing self-supporting debt would be turned over to the federal government (the commission proposed special adjustments for Quebec, which had undertaken significant borrowings on behalf of hospitals and charitable organizations). New borrowings, in the commission's view, would be necessary only for development projects (that is, self-supporting debt), and for these issues the provinces could borrow through a proposed finance commission.

These transfers of relief expenditure and debt to the federal level would increase federal spending. In compensation the federal government would, under the commission's plan, receive exclusive jurisdiction over personal and corporation income taxes and succession duties. This step would also improve the design, administration, and equality of the tax system, and thus effectively end the tax problems that the commission had identified. To compensate the provinces for the costs of developing their mineral and petroleum wealth and for its depletion, the federal government would turn over to the provinces 10 percent of corporate income tax derived from this sector. The provinces would surrender the subsidies described in chapter 1.

The transfers of functions and tax revenue, although they would have greatly improved the financial position of the poorer provinces, would still have fallen short of establishing the desired degree of provincial equality. The commission therefore also proposed a system of national adjustment grants, unconditional transfers designed to equalize the basic elements of provincial finances. This proposal represented a complete break with the traditional subsidy system, the principles underlying it, and the political bargaining that was its essence. The national adjustment grants would be calculated to make up the shortfall, if any, between the cost to a province of average standards (as established in a pre-depression period) for certain specified services and the yield of its new taxes at national average rates. This general system would have to be adjusted to reflect differences in provincial circumstances. In Quebec, for example, many social and health services were carried out by church and charitable organizations. In the prairie provinces, natural resource revenue was not as well developed as it was elsewhere in the country. The national adjustment grants would be designed to ensure the provision of minimum standards of public service, but the provinces would be free to levy additional taxes in order to finance programs at levels appropriate to their own needs or wishes.

The adjustment grants would be irreducible but subject to review every five years and, if necessary, would be supplemented by emergency grants (this stipulation was designed to give immediate aid to Saskatchewan). The review would be carried out by the finance commission, a national body assisted by a technical staff equipped to determine grants objectively and scientifically and to administer the proposed debt system described above.

The national adjustment grants proposal proved to be unacceptable to the provinces, as noted below. Given its similarity to the equalization system introduced more than 20 years later, however, the proposal represents an important stage in the evolution of federal-provincial fiscal relations. The proposed system recognized provincial autonomy, which the Rowell-Sirois commission considered vital given the wide differences in the social philosophies and the economic and social conditions of the provinces. The grants would not influence directly the level or nature of services provided by the provinces, nor would they take account of specific provincial tax measures. The grants would be determined objectively, by a body insulated from direct political influence or bargaining, and they would be subject to reasonably frequent review. The proposal also recognized that, although some form of federal assistance for social programs was necessary, many social services required the detailed and personal administration available only at the local or provincial level. Only when programs did not require detailed administration or when differences in local conditions were irrelevant, as in the case of contributory old age pensions, did the commission recommend federal administration. The commission also stressed the importance of regular federal-provincial conferences, which became a feature of the post-war period.

The commission's proposals would have increased federal expenditures by $115 million—$65 million for interest on the assumed provincial debt, and approximately $50 million for relief. The elimination of unconditional subsidies would have decreased expenditures by $6 million. Federal revenues would have increased by $65 million. Table 2.5 compares the actual subsidies in the 1937-38 fiscal year with the proposed national adjustment grants.

The Federal-Provincial Conference of 1941

The Rowell-Sirois commission presented its report to the federal government in May 1940, after the Second World War had become the major preoccupation for Canada. The war may have precluded any consideration of long-term revision, but it also necessitated high federal income taxes and federal use of tax fields previously occupied exclusively by the provinces. Some minimum agreement with the provinces was required to permit the maximum federal exploitation of tax resources and to avoid adverse effects on provincial finances. The federal government called a federal-provincial conference for January 1941 to accomplish these objectives, if possible, by securing adoption of the recommendations of the Rowell-Sirois commission.

Adoption proved to be impossible. The transfer of taxing powers to the federal government was a matter of serious concern to all provinces, but especially to Ontario and British Columbia. The three provinces that stood to lose federal money under the national adjustment grants system, Ontario, Alberta, and British Columbia, refused to accept the proposals. The premiers

Table 2.5 Federal Unconditional Subsidies to the Provinces in 1937-38 and Grants Proposed by the Rowell-Sirois Commission

	Total of existing subsidies in 1937-38	Proposed national adjustment grant
	thousands of dollars	
Prince Edward Island	657	750
Nova Scotia	1,953	800
New Brunswick	1,567	1,500
Quebec	2,592	8,000
Ontario	2,941	—
Manitoba	2,453	2,100
Saskatchewan	5,620	1,750[a]
Alberta	1,776	—
British Columbia	1,625	—
	21,184	14,900

[a] In addition, Saskatchewan was to have received an emergency grant of $4 million in 1937-38.

Source: A. Milton Moore, J. Harvey Perry, and Donald I. Beach, *The Financing of Canadian Federation: The First Hundred Years*, Canadian Tax Paper no. 43 (Toronto: Canadian Tax Foundation, 1966), 14.

of some of the other provinces expressed only modified acceptance. As a result, the commission's recommendations were abandoned—at least until the end of the war—and in that sense the conference was a failure.

The Second World War

The federal-provincial conference of 1941 did produce an agreement by all of the provincial premiers to cooperate fully with the federal government in the prosecution of the war effort, although no specific proposals were agreed to. The federal finance minister, J.L. Ilsley, made it clear at the conference that the new federal tax levies would fall very heavily on the citizens of some provinces if the problems inherent in existing provincial taxation were not remedied. He stressed that in the absence of an agreement on taxation the federal government would not be able to compensate the provinces for any revenue decline that resulted from war measures such as gasoline rationing, which would reduce provincial gasoline tax revenue.

In his budget address of April 1941, Ilsley announced drastic increases in all existing federal taxes and introduced an inheritance tax. He offered to compensate the provinces if they would abstain temporarily from taxing personal and corporation incomes, thus enabling the federal government to increase such taxes to "the maximum levels which would be reasonable at this time, if the provinces were not in those fields."[8] Since the nation was engaged in a serious and expensive war, the provinces had little choice but to agree. When the federal government passed its Wartime Tax Agreement

---

[8] Canada, Department of Finance, Budget Papers, Budget Speech, April 29, 1941, 11.

Act,[9] all nine provinces enacted legislation that authorized their governments to enter into agreements with Ottawa. These agreements provided the
federal government with sufficient freedom to expand and develop its financial system in order to meet the increasing demands of the war. The agreements also put an immediate end to the chaotic tax system developed during
the depression. Individual and corporation income taxation was solely under
federal jurisdiction for the calendar years 1941 to 1946 inclusive, and
corporations were free of other provincial corporation taxes from September
1, 1941 to September 1, 1947.

In return for surrendering these tax fields, the provinces received payments and guarantees. The payments, detailed in table 2.6, were made in
addition to the existing statutory subsidies and based on two options. The
first option provided an amount equal to the interest paid on provincial debt
(less interest received) less inheritance taxes collected by the province in its
fiscal year ending nearest to December 31, 1940. Saskatchewan and the
maritime provinces, whose receipts from income taxes in 1940 were lower
than their debt service charges, accepted this option. The second option
provided an amount equal to provincial and local revenues from the re-
nounced taxes in the provincial fiscal year ending nearest to December 31,
1940. This option was to the benefit of Quebec, Ontario, Manitoba, and
British Columbia. Alberta initially chose the second option, but the debt-
charge option was later recalculated to that province's advantage.

The federal government also guaranteed the existing level of provincial
revenues from gasoline and, later, liquor, both of which were rationed during
the war. The federal government also taxed gasoline for the first time.
Federal payments were made to maintain provincial gasoline tax revenues at
their level in the fiscal year ending nearest to December 31, 1940. Liquor
revenues were guaranteed at their level in the year ending June 30, 1942, but
in the event no federal payments were necessary. Table 2.7 summarizes all
federal payments under the agreements.

The federal government proposed to drop the special grants discussed in
chapter 1 while the wartime grant arrangements were in effect. These special
grants were the subsidies to the maritime provinces proposed by the Duncan
and White commissions and the depression-initiated grants to the prairie
provinces and British Columbia. This proposal was modified by the addition
of "fiscal need" and "loss of revenue" grants, which continued a substantial
part of the pre-war transfers to the maritime provinces, Manitoba, and
Saskatchewan. British Columbia received no funds under these additional
grant schemes. The Maritime Subsidies Act, 1942,[10] provided that the special subsidies to Prince Edward Island, Nova Scotia, and New Brunswick
would be restored in full as permanent statutory payments when the Wartime
Tax Agreement Act expired. The payments began anew in 1947.

---

[9] Dominion-Provincial Taxation Agreement Act, 1942, SC 1942-43, c. 13.

[10] Maritime Provinces Additional Subsidies Act, 1942, SC 1942-43, c. 14.

Table 2.6 The Wartime Tax Agreements: Calculation of Basic Payment Under Two Options Based on Fiscal Years Ending Nearest to December 31, 1940

	PEI	NS	NB	Que.	Ont.	Man.	Sask.	Alberta Original terms	Alberta 1945 recalculation	BC	All provinces (original terms)
							thousands of dollars				
Option "A": (tax option):											
Revenues from suspended taxes:											
Provincial revenues	242	1,488	1,066	18,189	28,964	5,055	2,093	4,081	4,081	12,048	73,226
Municipal revenues	10	123	1,384	2,397	—	—	—	—	—	—	3,914
Total	252	1,611	2,450	20,586	28,964	5,055	2,093	4,081	4,081	12,048	77,140
Option "B" (debt option):											
Interest on gross debts excluding debentures, discount, amortization, discount, amortization, and sinking fund or debt retirement	388	4,284	4,718	12,107	29,846	5,807	6,953	4,736[a]	7,835	8,220	77,059
Less: interest receipts	80	1,209	891	2,803	8,955	2,030	2,308	1,590	1,590	1,703	21,569
	308	3,075	3,827	9,304	20,891	3,777	4,645	3,146	6,245	6,517	55,490
Less: succession duty receipts	43	490	548	7,602	11,463	603	315	417	417	1,014	22,495
Net total	265	2,585	3,279	1,702	9,428	3,174	4,330	2,729	5,828	5,503	32,995
More favourable option[b]	Debt	Debt	Debt	Tax	Tax	Tax	Debt	Tax	Debt	Tax	
	265	2,585	3,279	20,586	28,964	5,055	4,330	4,081	5,828	12,048	81,193

[a] Excludes unpaid interest on funded debt. In 1945, the calculation of the debt option offered to Alberta was revised to include the unpaid interest on its funded debt, and the federal government made retroactive payments on this basis. Alberta was also paid an additional subsidy of $600,000 for the years 1938-1941. These two adjustments formed part of the refinancing of the Alberta debt. [b] In addition, the federal government made up the short-fall in provincial gasoline taxes below receipts in the fiscal year ended nearest December 31, 1940.

Source: Compiled mainly from the provincial acts authorizing the tax agreements.

Table 2.7 The Wartime Tax Agreements: Composition of Payments to the Provinces

thousands of dollars

	PEI	NS	NB	Que.	Ont.	Man.	Sask.	Alberta Original terms	Alberta 1945 recalculation	BC	All provinces (original terms)
1. Rental payment under more favourable option (from table 2.5)	265	2,585	3,279	20,586	28,964	5,055	4,330	4,081	5,828	12,048	81,193
Fiscal need subsidies:											
2. Annual subsidy temporarily discontinued	275	1,300	900	—	—	—	—	—	—	—	2,475
3. Minus excess of debt option over tax option	13	974	829	—	—	—	—	—	—	—	1,816
4. Net fiscal need subsidy	262	326	71	—	—	—	—	—	—	—	659
5. Additional subsidies	175	—	300	—	—	600	1,500	—	—	—	2,575
6. Annual payments under the agreements (items 1, 4, and 5)	702	2,911	3,650	20,586	28,964	5,655	5,830	4,081	5,828	12,048	84,427
Deduct:											
7. Revenues from suspended taxes	252	1,611	2,450	20,586	28,964	5,055	2,093	4,081	4,081	12,048	77,140
8. Special grants discontinued	275	1,300	900	—	—	750	1,500	—	—	750	5,475
9. Subtotal	527	2,911	3,350	20,586	28,964	5,805	3,593	4,081	4,081	12,798	82,613
10. Gain or loss (−) of revenue under the agreements, excluding Dominion guarantee of gasoline tax revenues (item 6 minus item 9)	175	—	300	—	—	−150	2,237	—	1,747	−750	

Source: Compiled mainly from the provincial acts authorizing the tax agreements.

Annual payments under the Wartime Tax Agreement system were approximately $100 million, consisting of $83 million for tax reimbursement, $3.2 million for fiscal need and loss-of-revenue subsidies, and $14.4 million for statutory subsidies. The gasoline tax guarantee cost the federal government $34 million.

The federal government had proposed the wartime tax arrangement as a temporary measure,[11] and in its agreement with each province it undertook to reduce, in the year after termination, "its rates of taxes by such an amount as will enable the Province[s] again to use the income tax and corporation tax fields, and in particular the Dominion undertakes to reduce its rates of tax on corporation incomes by at least ten per cent of such incomes."[12] Throughout the war, however, two major problems dominated planning for the return of peace. The first was the fear of a major depression, since the demobilized armed forces would enter the labour market just as domestic industry was gearing down from the war effort. The second was the unresolved issue, examined by the Rowell-Sirois commission, of the unbalanced distribution of taxing and spending powers among the three levels of government. The temporary assumption by the federal government of exclusive occupation of the personal and corporation income tax fields presaged the approach taken under the reconstruction program.

---

[11] The Minister of Finance stated "I should like to emphasize that this is not an attempt to get the provinces out of these tax fields permanently." Supra footnote 8, at 12.

[12] Dominion-Provincial Tax Suspension Agreement, section 20, concluded under the Dominion-Provincial Taxation Agreement Act, 1942, supra footnote 9, and found in Canada, *Dominion Subsidies to Provinces, Including Other Transfers*, reference book for Dominion-Provincial Conference on Reconstruction (Ottawa: Secretariat of the Cabinet Committee on Dominion-Provincial Relations, 1945), 66.

PART II

SHARING TAX FIELDS

Introduction

As Part I has shown, Canada's fiscal structure before the Second World War fell well short of providing a model of tax harmony in a federation. The war changed this state of affairs. What is more remarkable, the change survived the peace and persists to this day. The wartime and post-war tax rental agreements and the subsequent development of true joint occupancy of tax fields resulted in a tax structure—at any rate, an income tax structure—that is notable for the extent to which it harmonizes the tax systems of the federal government and the provinces. This is so even though Canada is in many other respects far more decentralized than, say, the United States, where conflicting and competing tax systems are accepted as a matter of course.

The key to Canada's success in the income tax field has been acceptance by all of the provinces of common rules for the allocation of income. These rules provide that, for a given tax year, an individual is to be treated as a resident of the province in which he or she resided as of December 31. A corporation that operates in more than one province must allocate its income according to certain formulas. The most important formula uses sales and wages and salaries to determine the allocation of taxable profits. Other formulas apply to special operations such as transportation and banking. Even the provinces that are not party to the collection agreements use these formulas and in general keep their systems close to the federal system.

The price of this harmony has been periodic discord between the federal government and the provinces when the tax agreements come up for renegotiation. The post-war period began with the entire income tax field under the effective control of the federal government. Thus the provinces' concern in the early post-war decades was to recover a share—and a growing share—of that field in order to finance, on their own terms, their rapidly growing expenditure for education, health care, social services, and transportation. The federal government, for its part, was anxious to retain a share of the field large enough to allow it to use income taxation to further national economic objectives and to finance the growing equalization and conditional grants programs. In other words, the federal government wanted to use income taxes to establish national standards of public services, whereas the provinces wanted to use them in order to tailor public expenditure to suit their own priorities.

During the first few decades of the post-war period, it proved to be possible to reconcile these separate agendas. The economy grew fast enough, and the income tax base with it, to allow the two levels of government to share and share alike—not without conflict and mutual resentment, but peacefully enough on the whole. In the late 1970s and 1980s, when government revenues began to fall seriously short of expenditures, the balance between Ottawa and the provinces implicit in the tax collection agreements began to shift in favour of the provinces. More and more tax room went to the provinces, which also sought a larger freedom under the agreements to introduce income tax provisions that suited their particular purposes. Ottawa accepted this erosion of its original dominance gracefully enough. The essential harmony of federal-provincial relations in the area of income taxation was not seriously disturbed, even when some provinces chose not to participate in the collection agreements.

Harmony has not characterized federal-provincial relations in other tax fields. The last chapter in this section describes the struggle between Ottawa and the provinces—in particular, Alberta and the other oil-producing provinces—for the lion's share of natural resource taxation. More recently, the sharing of the retail sales tax field has become an issue. It remains to be seen which precedent—income tax harmony or resource tax discord—will prevail in this area.

Chapter 3 discusses the first post-war tax rental agreements. Chapter 4 describes the transition, during the 1950s, from tax rental to tax sharing. Chapter 5's subject is the refinement of the concept of tax sharing in the tax collection agreements introduced in 1962. Chapter 6 carries the history of the collection agreements through the era of federal tax reforms in the 1970s. Chapter 7 carries the story of the collection agreements through to the late 1990s. Finally, chapter 8 discusses the special problems associated with natural resource taxation, particularly during the oil-price crisis of the late 1970s and early 1980s.

3

Bridging the Gap to Peacetime: The 1947-1952 Tax Rental Agreements

In its white paper on employment and income, tabled in April 1945,[1] the federal government assumed responsibility for the maintenance of a high and stable level of income and employment. The white paper set the basis for a series of acts, passed in 1945, that, among other things, provided for price supports for agricultural and fishery production, universal family allowances, and the transition, in many areas, to a peacetime economy. In addition, federal and provincial officials had been working together to design a system of provincial health insurance that would be funded in part by federal grants.

The Conference on Reconstruction

The negotiations that the 1941 federal-provincial conference should have carried to a conclusion were resumed at the federal-provincial Conference on Reconstruction, which met in August 1945. The wartime experience of co-operation had moved the participants far beyond the recommendations of the Rowell-Sirois commission;[2] instead of these recommendations, they had before them an extensive and explicit set of "green books," federal reference studies designed to reflect the change in the social and economic outlook that had taken place during the war. The green books were not merely financial analyses, for they also covered social security and public investment policy. They reflected the three main aims of the federal government: to divide public revenues among the three levels of government in the most efficient manner possible, to initiate social insurance plans for old age and health care, and to coordinate the economic influence of all Canadian governments in order to reduce the possibility of further depressions.

Under the green book proposals, the federal government was to retain exclusive occupancy of the personal and corporation income tax fields and assume exclusive occupancy of the inheritance tax field. Its "rent" for these fields would be an unconditional per capita grant to the provinces based on 1941 population. The minimum per capita subsidy would be $12, but this

---

[1] Canada, Department of Reconstruction, *Employment and Income, with Special Reference to the Initial Period of Reconstruction* (Ottawa: the department, April 1945).

[2] See Canada, *Report of the Royal Commission on Dominion-Provincial Relations* (Ottawa: King's Printer, 1940).

amount would be increased in proportion to the increase in the national per capita gross national product (GNP) since 1941. The term of the initial agreements would be three years.

The proposed payments, which were considerably more generous than the payments under the Wartime Tax Agreements, were to replace all existing statutory and special subsidies and unconditional grants. The guaranteed minimum, based on 1941 figures, would have given about $138 million to the provinces, and the adjusted payment for 1944 was calculated at nearly $207 million, compared with a total of $125 million under the wartime agreements and from provincial succession duties.

The green book proposals included a universal old age pension for those aged 70 or over, for which the federal government would provide full funding, and a health insurance plan, for which the federal government would provide 60 percent of the funding (see chapter 13). In addition, the federal government was to assume responsibility for full employment; it would extend unemployment insurance to all employees, provide assistance equal to 85 percent of insurance benefits to unemployed employables not eligible for insurance benefits, and meet up to 20 percent of the costs of provincial and municipal public investment projects designed to create jobs in times of high unemployment.

These proposals differed substantially from those of the Rowell-Sirois commission, whose plan had included a system of equalizing provincial revenue sources. The green book proposals for conditional grants and for joint federal-provincial responsibility in the areas of health insurance and assistance to the aged contrasted with the commission's recommendations for a clearly defined separation of functions and a minimum of conditional grants. The tax proposals, based on a series of three-year periods, were at odds with the commission's recommendations for permanent transfers.

In the green book proposals, the federal government presented an integrated program for social security and economic stability unprecedented in Canadian history. It is an open question, however, whether the federal government had a pressing mandate from the people to implement so far-reaching a project. The proposals amounted to fishing in what many considered to be exclusively provincial waters, and each of them—unconditional grants, unemployment assistance, old age pensions, and health insurance— would have substantially increased the burden carried by the federal government.

The main conference produced no general agreement, but the coordinating committee, which met in November 1945 and January and April 1946, fostered continuing efforts to resolve the differences between the federal government and the provinces. Few provinces were fully satisfied with the federal proposals, but several seemed ready to enter agreements. Ontario was the only province to present a complete set of counterproposals:

• The two levels of government would share personal and corporation income taxes, which the federal government would collect. Inheritance taxes would fall to the provinces alone.

• Ten percent of provincial revenues from income and inheritance taxes would go into a "National Adjustment Fund," which would be redistributed among the provinces on the basis of fiscal need.

• The statutory subsidies would continue, but other federal payments would be applied to the provinces' debt to the federal government.

• The provinces would have exclusive jurisdiction over the taxation of gasoline, amusements, pari-mutuel betting, stock transfers, and electricity.

• The federal government would meet 75 percent of the cost of assistance to unemployables.

• The universal pension would apply to everyone over 65.

• The level of assistance under the proposed system of support for capital projects would be determined by the coordinating committee, not by the federal government alone.

Ontario's proposals were acceptable to neither the federal government nor several of the provinces. During the five months of negotiations, a number of provinces expressed reservations of their own about specific aspects of the federal scheme. Just before the April 1946 session, Prime Minister Mackenzie King offered to increase the minimum basic annual rental to $15 per capita, using either 1941 or 1942 population. The payments would increase annually in proportion to both provincial population growth and the average growth over the three preceding years in national GNP per capita. Two provinces were offered flat payments somewhat larger than the payments they would be entitled to under the per capita rental formula: British Columbia would receive 150 percent of the payment it received under the wartime tax agreements, and Prince Edward Island would receive a guaranteed payment of $2 million. These payments would not increase with population and GNP. The revised federal proposals would have increased guaranteed payments to the provinces from the $138 million offered under the original proposals to $181 million. The revised proposals also provided that the statutory subsidies would be continued, but that they would be deducted from the payments described above.

The federal government also offered further concessions in the tax fields. If an agreeing province chose to continue to levy its own succession duties, a credit for succession duties equal to 1946 provincial rates would apply to the taxpayer's federal tax, but the equivalent amount would be deducted from federal payments to the province. The federal government proposed to refrain from taxing real property or automobiles in users' hands, and to hold constant its rates of tax on gasoline, amusements, and pari-mutuel betting. It would continue its 8 percent tax on household gas and electricity but would refund to the provinces 50 percent of the federal corporation tax on electrical or steam-producing utilities, less any similar provincial tax. The federal government offered to seek an amendment to the British North America Act that would allow it to delegate to the provinces the power to levy indirect retail sales taxes. It also offered to withdraw from gasoline taxes, in exchange for dropping its offer to share the cost of pensions to those aged 65 to 69, and from amusement taxes, in exchange for dropping the proposed public health grants.

The full Conference on Reconstruction reconvened on April 29, 1946 to discuss these proposals and a new set of counterproposals by Ontario. Bitter debate produced little agreement, for both Ontario and Quebec were still opposed to the federal plans. Ontario's new counterproposals involved (1) a slight departure from the federal formula for compensation; (2) federal withdrawal from succession duties and from taxes on gasoline, amusements, pari-mutuel bets, stock transfers, and electricity and gas consumption; and (3) federal assumption of the full cost of pensions and relief for the employable unemployed. The federal government felt that the costs of the Ontario scheme were too high. The full conference broke up on May 3 unable to agree even on a future meeting date. No further meetings of the full conference were held.

Negotiations Outside the Framework of Federal-Provincial Conferences

Finance Minister James Ilsley's budget speech of June 29, 1946 abandoned the attempt to get the general agreement of all of the provinces; instead, the federal government would seek to secure tax agreements with any provinces that were willing to negotiate. The terms of the budget offer were, however, designed to avoid putting undue pressure on provinces that elected to continue their own taxation.

The federal government proposed to pay to any province that entered into a tax agreement the per capita payment (as modified before the last session of the conference) of $15 per capita of 1941 or 1942 population, adjusted for growth in population and GNP per capita, and not less than 150 percent of the Wartime Tax Agreement payment or $2 million. The province, in turn, would refrain from levying its own personal income tax and impose no taxes on corporations other than a 5 percent tax on corporate income within the province, which would be collected by the federal government. The province could choose to continue to levy succession duties. The proceeds of the provincial corporation income tax and succession duties would, however, be treated as part of the annual tax rental and thus be deducted from the nominal amount of the rental.

The proposals for non-agreeing provinces were as follows. In compliance with the Wartime Tax Agreements, the federal government would reduce the standard personal and corporation income taxes as of January 1, 1947. A maximum credit of 5 percent of federal personal income tax would be allowed for any provincial personal income tax, and the provinces would also be free to impose the 5 percent corporation income tax. The federal succession duties would be doubled, but a credit of up to 50 percent would be provided for provincial duties. Thus the non-agreeing provinces could impose taxes up to a given level without detriment to their taxpayers relative to taxpayers in agreeing provinces.

The federal government also agreed to permit a deduction from corporate taxable income for taxes imposed by the provinces on mining and logging activities. This proposal recognized the fact that some provinces used such special income taxes in place of royalties on the exploitation of natural resources. The earlier welfare and public investment proposals would be withdrawn until all of the provinces had completed their tax negotiations with Ottawa.

The idea of bilateral negotiations did not sit well with some provinces, particularly Quebec. These provinces called for a new conference, but others were in favour of the revised federal proposals. Most of the latter provinces were dismayed that the non-tax proposals had been delayed. Prince Edward Island, New Brunswick, Manitoba, and Saskatchewan had agreed in principle within a month of the June offer, and in October Alberta indicated that it too was ready to sign. The four remaining provinces would not accept the federal budget proposals. British Columbia pressed for the scaling-down and refunding of provincial treasury bills of nearly $175 million that the western provinces had issued to the federal government during the depression of the 1930s to finance relief. The premier of Nova Scotia called for immediate federal withdrawal from certain tax fields, in particular gasoline and amusements.

In December 1946, Premier John Hart of British Columbia announced federal concessions in the matter of the treasury bills. What was more significant, the federal government would enrich its proposal to pay the province 150 percent of its allowance under the Wartime Tax Agreements by making the payment subject to the general formula for adjustment upward to reflect increases in provincial population and gross national product per capita. These changes drew complaints from other provinces that the federal government had changed the terms of its offer. In the face of this opposition, the federal government presented yet another set of new proposals in January 1947.

The final offer combined the principle of per capita payments with compensation for tax sources and the existing statutory subsidies (which were thrown in to retain the advantage of the historic bargaining process that some provinces had found wanting in the 1946 federal budget proposal). The per capita payments would increase with per capita GNP and provincial population, as proposed earlier.

The federal government offered the provinces three options for guaranteed minimum payments. The first consisted of $12.75 per capita of 1942 provincial population, 50 percent of the provincial revenue from personal income and corporation taxation in 1940, as determined under the Wartime Tax Agreements, and the statutory subsidies payable in 1947. This was the most favourable option for all of the provinces except Prince Edward Island, Nova Scotia, and Saskatchewan. The second option consisted of $15 per capita of 1942 provincial population and the 1947 statutory subsidies. This was the most favourable option for Nova Scotia and Saskatchewan. Under either option, the current year's payment would be adjusted to reflect any increase in the province's population and any increase in the three-year moving average of national GNP per capita over the per capita GNP in 1942. The third option was for Prince Edward Island and consisted of a flat annual payment of $2.1 million.

As table 3.1 shows, these options guaranteed to the provinces minimum payments of $25.1 million more than they had been guaranteed under the offer of six months earlier and $68.5 million more than the green book proposals. Table 3.2 shows the estimated payment for each province under each of the three options and the options chosen to produce the figures in table 3.1.

In return for their grants under these formulas, the provinces would agree to impose no taxes on personal incomes. They would restrict corporation taxes to a 5 percent tax on net income, which would be imposed by uniform legislation and collected by the federal government in conjunction with its own tax. The provinces would be free to levy taxes on income from mining and logging operations as substitutes for royalties. Such taxes would be deductible from net income in computing taxable income for federal corporation income tax.

Table 3.1 Comparison of Federal Proposals for
Guaranteed Minimum Payments

	August 1945 offer	April 1946 offer	January 1947 final offer
	$ millions		
Prince Edward Island	1.1	2.0	2.1
Nova Scotia	6.9	8.9	10.9
New Brunswick	5.5	7.0	8.8
Quebec	40.0	50.9	56.4
Ontario	45.5	58.3	67.2
Manitoba	8.8	10.9	13.5
Saskatchewan	10.8	13.4	15.3
Alberta	9.6	11.9	14.2
British Columbia	9.8	18.1	18.1
Total	138.0	181.4	206.5

Source: Canada, *Dominion and Provincial Submissions and Plenary Conference Discussions*, Dominion-Provincial Conference on Reconstruction, 1945-46 (Ottawa: King's Printer, 1946), 384; Canada, Department of Finance, Budget Papers, Budget Speech, June 27, 1946, 14; and Canada, House of Commons, *Debates*, July 9, 1947, 5417.

Table 3.2 1947 Tax Agreements—Calculation of Guaranteed Minimum Annual Payments Under the Three Options

	PEI	NS	NB	Que.	Ont.	Man.	Sask.	Alta.	BC	Total
						$ thousands				
First option										
$12.75 per capita on 1942 population[a]	1,147	7,535	5,916	43,222	49,521	9,297	11,262	10,169	11,093	149,164
50% of provincial income and corp. tax revenue for year ending nearest Dec. 31, 1940 (Wartime Tax Agreements)	126	805	1,225	10,293	14,482	2,527	1,046	2,040	6,024	38,569
Statutory subsidies payable in 1947	657	2,005	1,632	2,867	3,155	1,716	2,042	2,018	1,003	17,095
Total	1,930	10,345	8,773	56,382	67,158	13,540	14,350	14,228	18,120	204,828
Second option										
$15.00 per capita on 1942 population[a]	1,350	8,865	6,960	50,850	58,260	10,938	13,250	11,964	13,050	175,487
Statutory subsidies payable in 1947	657	2,005	1,632	2,867	3,155	1,715	2,041	2,018	1,003	17,094
Total	2,007	10,870	8,592	53,717	61,415	12,653	15,291	13,982	14,053	192,581
Third option (PEI only)	2,100									
Most favourable option	Third	Second	First	First	First	First	Second	First	First	
Amount under most favourable option	2,100	10,870	8,773	56,382	67,158	13,540	15,291	14,228	18,120	206,463

Note: For Manitoba, Saskatchewan, and Alberta, 1942 population determined by straight line between 1941 and 1946 census figures; for all other provinces, 1942 population as estimated by Dominion Statistician.

Source: Canada, House of Commons, *Debates*, July 9, 1947, 5417.

The federal government would refund to all provinces one-half of its collections of corporation taxes on producers and distributors of electricity, gas, and steam. Certain provincial taxes imposed on such corporations would be deducted from the federal payments. In return for providing these payments, the federal government would keep its 8 percent sales tax on the household use of gas and electricity.

To provinces that imposed inheritance taxes, the federal government would provide credit for up to one-half of its own inheritance taxes. The equivalent of the credits would be deducted from the rental payments. In the event, none of the agreeing provinces chose to impose inheritance taxes.

Seven provinces accepted the federal proposals and signed tax rental agreements for the five-year period 1947 to 1952. Newfoundland, on joining Confederation, accepted the same conditions for the three years 1949 to 1952. Ontario and Quebec did not enter into the agreements.

The federal tax rental proposals of 1946 and early 1947 did not contain anything equivalent to the national adjustment grants recommended by the Rowell-Sirois commission or to equalization as such. They did, however, agree with the general objectives of the federal government in this era, a circumstance reflected in Mr. Ilsley's June 1946 budget speech:

> It has been said that the proposed payments by the Dominion to the provinces are not based on the principle of fiscal need. That criticism fails to grasp the true facts of the situation. What is essentially valid in the position taken by the financially weaker provinces is their claim that the great bulk of the wealth and income of the country is concentrated in the two or three large provinces, that most of the head offices of the corporations doing business all over Canada are situated in Ontario and Quebec, and that the larger provinces, therefore, get an unfair share of the tax revenues which are based on the corporate profits and the personal incomes and estates resulting from the business done throughout the country. Now, what the Dominion's proposal does is to provide a method whereby the three maritime provinces and the three prairie provinces will be enabled to derive from these sources the same per capita revenue as Ontario and Quebec. By selling certain rights to the Dominion for the term of the agreement, they are put in a position of sharing with the two central provinces equally on a per capita basis the productivity of the three great fields of direct progressive taxation—corporation taxes, taxes on personal income and succession duties. Surely this is going very far to meet the test of fiscal need. If, in spite of such assistance, any one province should still find itself under normal conditions faced with a fiscal problem, that could only be due to a higher relative level of expenditure or a failure to tap other sources of tax revenue to the same extent as other provinces. In such a case, a further fiscal need subsidy would be impossible to justify, although this does not of course mean that occasionally a province or region may not be affected by a calamity which might justify special temporary assistance.[3]

---

[3] Canada, Department of Finance, Budget Papers, Budget Speech, June 27, 1946, 15.

The tax rental agreements fell well short of ensuring that each province would be able to provide a level of services equivalent to the national average without resorting to a level of taxation above the average. They came closer to realizing that concept, however, than any previous financial arrangement between the federal government and the provinces. Another significant advantage for the provinces was the assurance that revenues from the agreement could not fall below a given minimum, and in fact they rose quickly with increasing economic activity and a rapidly increasing population. Had the guaranteed minimum been in effect for the five years of the agreement, the total payments would have been $413 million; the actual payments were $558.8 million, thanks to the unexpected increases in population and GNP.

Developments During the Period of the Agreements

When the provincial obligations under the Wartime Tax Agreements expired in 1947, Ontario and Quebec imposed taxes of 7 percent on corporate income and reintroduced special corporation taxes equivalent to about 1.5 percent of corporate income on specific bases (capital and place of business). Thus the two provinces imposed taxes on corporations at an effective rate of about 8.5 percent, compared with a rate of 5 percent in the agreeing provinces. At this stage, Ontario and Quebec used their own systems for the allocation by province of the income of interprovincial corporations.

Neither Ontario nor Quebec imposed an individual income tax, although a credit of up to 5 percent of the federal tax was available to residents of non-agreeing provinces. In 1950, Ontario passed legislation to impose a tax equal to 5 percent of the federal levy, but the act was never proclaimed; the province tried unsuccessfully to have the federal government collect the tax on its behalf.

In 1947, the federal government doubled its rates for succession duties. The non-agreeing provinces continued to levy their own inheritance taxes, which were creditable against up to 50 percent of the new federal taxes. This credit was generally equal to the levies in Quebec and Ontario, and so there was at least rough uniformity in death taxes between these provinces and the agreeing provinces, where no provincial inheritance taxes were imposed. Quebec and Ontario subsequently agreed on measures to end the double taxation of inheritances, a step that largely eliminated one of the most serious inequities of the depression years.

During the early post-war period, the federal government withdrew from a number of fields that it had pre-empted during the war. In April 1947, Ottawa withdrew the federal gasoline tax of 3 cents per gallon; its place was immediately taken by a two-cent-per-gallon tax levied by all of the provinces except Manitoba, Saskatchewan, and Alberta. In November 1947, the federal government repealed its 8 percent sales tax on the residential use of electricity and gas. In May 1948, it withdrew its taxes on amusements, cabarets, and pari-mutuel betting. During the same period, British Columbia, New Brunswick, Quebec (and its municipalities), and Newfoundland (on its entry into Confederation in 1949) imposed retail sales taxes and Alberta and Prince Edward Island dropped their provincial property taxes.

By 1948, the provinces had become concerned about the difference between the revenues they obtained from Crown-owned provincial utilities, whose total net income flowed directly into the provincial treasuries, and the minor revenues they obtained from investor-owned utilities, whose net revenue flowed to the shareholders and the federal corporation tax collectors. To lessen the differential, the federal government agreed to transfer to the provinces 50 percent of the federal income tax paid by investor-owned public utilities on income that was attributable to the generation or distribution to the public of electrical energy, gas, or steam. The transfers were unconditional; some provinces retained the money, others arranged for rebates to the customers of the utilities. The federal tax rental legislation provided the statutory authority for the transfers to the provinces.

Table 3.3 shows the federal payments to the provinces in the fiscal years 1946-47 to 1951-52.

Table 3.3 Federal Subsidies, Grants, Tax Agreements, and Conditional Subsidy Payments to the Provinces, Fiscal Years 1946-47 to 1951-52

Fiscal year ending March 31	Statutory subsidies	Transitional grant to Newfoundland	Wartime tax agreements	1947 tax agreements	5% provincial corporate income tax	Provincial share of utilities tax	Conditional subsidies	Total payments
				millions of dollars				
1947	14.4	—	88.4	6.0	—	3.1	60.7	172.6
1948	17.1	—	63.0	59.5	—	2.9	70.4	212.9
1949	17.1	—	—	84.4	28.8	3.7	88.8	222.8
1950	19.2	6.5	—	78.3	20.2	1.4	115.5	241.1
1951	18.7	6.5	—	98.7	17.4	4.6	149.1	295.0
1952	20.1	6.5	—	96.9	25.1	3.7	128.4	280.7

Source: A. Milton Moore, J. Harvey Perry, and Donald I. Beach, *The Financing of Canadian Federation: The First Hundred Years*, Canadian Tax Paper no. 43 (Toronto: Canadian Tax Foundation, 1966), 33, table 8.

4

Transition to a More Permanent System: The 1952-1957 Tax Rental Agreements and the 1957-1962 Tax Sharing Agreements

In December 1949, Prime Minister Louis St. Laurent proposed that a federal-provincial conference be held in the fall of 1950. Although there was general agreement that a conference was appropriate, there was no consensus on the agenda. The Korean war had begun when the conference met on December 4 to 7, 1950, and the federal government, once more under pressure to finance a war effort, restricted the agenda to three items—renewal of the 1947 tax rental agreements, a provincial proposal for a constitutional amendment to permit the provinces to levy indirect sales taxes, and old age pensions.

In opening the conference, Prime Minister St. Laurent reviewed the existing tax agreements. They were

> designed to provide an assured and stable source of revenue to the provinces and to remove, as far as possible, competition between the federal and the provincial governments in the direct tax field. On the whole, I think it will be generally acknowledged that they have fulfilled both purposes to a degree which few could have anticipated four or five years ago.[1]

The federal position was that

> the federal government is not renting the tax fields themselves but merely the exclusive use of those fields .... What ... we are making agreements about is the allocation of the revenues from certain of these direct taxes between the federal and provincial governments.[2]

In discussing the terms of renewal of the agreements, the prime minister had this to say:

> Faced with the world situation to which I have referred, it is obvious that the federal authorities will have no option but to impose direct taxes to a degree commensurate with the gravity of the situation. In view of

---

[1] Canada, *Proceedings of the Constitutional Conference of Federal and Provincial Governments*, held at Ottawa, December 4-7, 1950 (Ottawa: King's Printer, 1951), 6.

[2] Ibid., at 7.

that circumstance and with the prospect of further expenditures for
social security that I shall mention later, it will not be possible for the
federal government to make changes in the tax agreements which would
add materially to their immediate over-all cost.[3]

The prime minister took pains, however, to stress that the new tax agreements offer would

not be specifically related to any other aspect of federal-provincial
relations. Universal acceptance will not be a condition of action, or a
commitment to action, in any other field.[4]

The minister of finance presented proposals for the new tax rental
agreements, which the provinces agreed to consider, and the federal government undertook to draft an amendment to the constitution that would enable
the provinces to levy indirect retail sales taxes. These points are discussed
below. The conference was deemed a success by all participants, in marked
contrast to the early post-war meetings. The federal government moderated
its approach, and the provinces, especially Ontario, adopted a more concilia-
tory attitude.

The Proposed Amendment for Indirect Retail
Sales Taxes

Newfoundland, New Brunswick, Quebec, Saskatchewan, and British Columbia were levying retail sales taxes in 1950. The taxing statutes satisfied the
definition of direct taxation in the BNA Act, since they imposed a direct levy
on the purchaser at the time of the retail sale and did not tax the sales
transaction itself, the goods sold, or the vendor.

In 1935, the House of Commons had passed a proposal to permit the provinces to levy indirect sales tax, but the bill had been defeated in the Senate. In
the 1945 and 1946 conferences, the federal government had offered to try
again, but in the absence of universal agreement it had taken no action. The
premiers of several provinces revived the idea at the 1950 conference. They
argued that indirect retail sales taxes were both less unattractive than direct
taxes and easier to collect. The federal government prepared a draft amendment, which it circulated early in 1951, that would have permitted indirect
taxation within a province on the sale of goods (except goods sold for
shipment outside the province) for consumption rather than resale. The rate
of the tax could not exceed 3 percent of the sale price, and the tax could not
discriminate between sales of goods produced within the province and sales
of goods produced outside the province.[5]

---

[3] Ibid. Social security proposals are discussed in chapter 11.

[4] Ibid.

[5] Canada, House of Commons, *Debates*, February 1, 1951, appendix, at 43-44.

The proposal met with some active public opposition, but it was eventually approved by all of the provinces except Quebec. Premier Maurice Duplessis of Quebec expressed misgivings about the amendment in April 1951, but he did not refuse approval until later, in a press interview. Prime Minister St. Laurent did not favour the admission of the provinces to this tax field, but he was willing to concede the point in the interests of intergovernmental cooperation, if all of the provinces accepted the federal proposal. In the absence of Quebec's approval, the proposed amendment was dropped.

The 1952-1957 Tax Rental Agreements

The negotiations at the 1950 conference were opened by federal Finance Minister Douglas Abbott, who proposed a five-year agreement for the tax years 1952 through 1956. The new agreements would be substantially the same as the 1947-1952 agreements, but there would be important changes in the provisions governing the federal payments.

In the first place, the new agreements would increase the minimum payments under the existing agreements by the ratio of the changes in provincial population and gross national product per capita between 1942 and 1948. This formula would have increased the floor payments by about 50 percent, but it would not have increased actual payments, since they had already been raised above this level by the regular adjustments for population and economic growth.

Mr. Abbott outlined the proposed formula for determining the guaranteed payment as follows:

> Since the payments under the agreement are primarily for the rental of tax fields, it can be argued that a more up-to-date evaluation of the rental value of these tax fields than the one which is included in the first option provided under the present agreements should be developed. You will recall that this was based on actual tax receipts by the provinces from income and corporation taxes in the year 1940. This argument seemed to us to be a valid one and we are therefore providing that any province may ... take as its guaranteed minimum annual payment the sum of the following amounts:
>
> 1. The yield of a personal income tax at 5 percent of 1948 federal rates applied to 1948 incomes in the province.
>
> 2. The yield of a tax of 8.5 percent on corporation profits earned in the province in 1948. (The rate of 8.5 percent, I might explain, is taken as a fair measure of the corporation tax potential and takes account of the separate or specific taxes traditionally levied by provinces as well as taxes on corporate profits.)
>
> 3. The average revenue received by the province from succession duties. (For the agreeing provinces we have taken the average of the revenues received during the last two years before their succession duties were suspended, and for Ontario and Quebec, the average of the three fiscal years 1946-47, 1947-48, and 1948-49).

4. Statutory subsidies payable to the province for 1948 .... Except in the case of one province, the amount produced by this new option is lower than that produced by adjusting the present guaranteed minimum payments up to the 1948 base. The exception is the province of Ontario, where the new option gives an amount higher by a little over $2 million.[6]

The federal minister also proposed two changes in the adjustment formula. Under the 1947 agreements, the adjusted payments had been calculated on the basis of changes over the three years preceding the year of payment. This term would be reduced to two years, to make the payments more sensitive to current conditions. GNP at factor cost would replace GNP at market prices—a technical change designed to eliminate the effects of indirect taxes, which were considered to be irrelevant to an accurate measure of economic growth.

The provincial premiers took these proposals home for consideration and subsequently made some suggestions for further change. In January 1952, Finance Minister Abbott responded in a letter to each province:

> The representations I have received have mainly been directed towards obtaining the guarantee of a higher level of minimum payments than that originally offered, with a consequent increase, of course, in the adjusted payments. In considering these representations we have been forced to balance the increasing needs of provincial governments, the nature of which is fully appreciated, with the continuing heavy burden on the federal treasury for defence and other outlays. We have been forced to conclude that it would be unwise for the federal government, in the extreme uncertainty of the years immediately ahead and the very heavy burdens it is now carrying, to assume any heavier fixed commitments than those involved by the guaranteed minimum payments under the original proposals.

Although the minister rejected the possibility of any major revisions to the federal proposals, he did make one significant concession to provincial demands:

> At the same time, I have been impressed with the argument advanced by some that due to the effect of the averaging of the adjustment factors over a period of years, the present adjusted payments may not be sufficiently sensitive to rapid growth in provincial population or rapid acceleration of economic activity such as the last five years have seen, both of which factors bring sharply increased demands on provincial budgets. In the offer made at the conference this argument was recognized in the proposal that the averaging period of three years provided for in the present agreements be reduced to two years. After further consideration, I am now prepared, on behalf of the federal government, to allow any province the further option of having the adjustments of the guaranteed minimum payments necessary to calculate the adjusted payment for any given year determined either on the basis of the two-year

---

[6] Supra footnote 1, at 142.

average or on the basis of data relating solely to the year preceding the
year of payment. Under this arrangement, of course, a province would
have to elect between one method or the other for the whole period of
the agreement.[7]

The minister's statement also contained a table showing the increases in
payments that would result from using the preceding-year option. In table
4.1, the figures in the original table have been adjusted to incorporate revised
data; the original table did, however, show clearly the effect on the calculations of moving from a three-year average to the previous year alone.

All of the provinces accepted the change to the previous-year data base.
There were also a few less important changes: the quarterly payment schedule was advanced to begin in June instead of September, the calculation of
population was altered slightly, and several minor changes were made that
affected individual provinces only. On the whole, however, the final federal
proposal was little different from the one advanced at the 1950 federal-
provincial conference. The financial implications of the program are detailed
in table 4.2, which shows the guaranteed minimum payments available under
the 1947 and 1952 proposals and the adjusted payment for 1952-53.

Under the terms of the 1947 agreements, each province levied a 5 percent
tax on the share of corporation income allocated to its jurisdiction, an
allocation based on a set of rules acceptable to all of the agreeing provinces.
Although intended to be temporary (to be repealed at the request of the
federal government), the tax stayed in place for the full term of the agreement; that is, the calendar years 1947 through 1951. The tax was administered by Ottawa and kept in conformity with the federal legislation.

In his letter to the provinces of January 1952, Finance Minister Abbott
announced that the provincial tax would be repealed. Later, in his April
budget, he outlined an arrangement, applicable to agreeing provinces only,
under which most of the 5 percent would be incorporated in a higher federal
rate. For non-agreeing provinces, the minister originally proposed a tax credit
system that would allow a deduction from federal tax payable of provincial
corporation income taxes up to a limit of 5 percent of the taxable corporation
income allocated to that province. The legislation, however, provided that a
credit of 5 percent of corporate income earned in a non-agreeing province
could be deducted from federal tax, whether or not provincial tax was in fact
payable. Since by this time Ontario had agreed to participate in the 1952-
1957 arrangements, only Quebec corporations could claim this credit.

No full-scale federal-provincial conferences had followed the 1950
meeting, so negotiations with the provinces proceeded on a bilateral basis.
By the summer of 1952, seven of the former agreeing provinces had passed
legislation to enter into the new arrangements and Nova Scotia had indicated

---

[7] Letter from Finance Minister Abbott to the provinces, reproduced in Canada, Department
of Finance, *Release*, January 15, 1952.

Table 4.1 Tax Rental Payments for 1952-53[a]

	Estimated payment for 1952[a]	Payment for 1952 if 1947 agreement extended without change
	$ millions	
Newfoundland	12.2	10.7
Prince Edward Island	3.9	3.4
Nova Scotia	20.1	17.7
New Brunswick	16.6	14.6
Quebec	114.4	99.9
Ontario	137.4	118.3
Manitoba	24.6	21.6
Saskatchewan	24.6	21.9
Alberta	28.7	24.8
British Columbia	41.2	35.6
Total	423.8	368.5

[a] First year (1952-53) if adjusted payment is based on previous year only.

Source: Canada, Department of Finance, *Release*, January 15, 1952. The payments include statutory subsidies.

Table 4.2 Guaranteed Minimum Annual Payments Under 1947 and 1952 Agreements and Annual Adjusted Payments for 1952-53

	Guaranteed minimum payments		Annual adjusted payments for 1952-53
	1947 agreements	1952 agreements	
	$ millions		
Newfoundland (1949)	6.2	9.2	12.3
Prince Edward Island	2.1	3.0	3.9
Nova Scotia	10.9	15.3	20.2
New Brunswick	8.8	12.6	16.6
Quebec[a]	56.4	85.1	115.0
Ontario[a]	67.2	101.8	137.2
Manitoba	13.5	18.6	24.7
Saskatchewan	15.3	20.0	25.6
Alberta	14.2	21.0	29.4
British Columbia	18.1	29.6	41.4
Total	212.7	316.2	426.3

[a] The amounts shown for Ontario and Quebec are the amounts that would have been payable if these provinces had entered the 1947 or 1952 agreements; the total of tax credits allowed to taxayers on account of succession duties paid to the Ontario government were deducted from the rental payments to Ontario under the 1952 agreement, since Ontario continued to collect its own succession duties.

Source: Canada, House of Commons, *Debates*, June 23, 1952, 3550-51.

its intention to follow suit. Parliament passed the necessary federal legislation in June 1952.[8] Ontario had remained publicly unenthusiastic during the 18 months since the December 1950 conference. Premier Leslie Frost had indicated at the conference that he had no settled intention of entering into the new agreements. After he received the federal letter of January 1952, he is reported to have said "I don't think this offer means a great deal to Ontario. We don't want to accept something which is artificial and far removed from the realities of Ontario's tremendous growth in recent years."[9]

In April 1952, Ontario claimed that the federal government was obliged to pay Ontario the amount of personal income tax that the province could have collected had it taken advantage, in 1951, of the federal credit of 5 percent. The federal government publicly rejected this claim; meanwhile, however, negotiations between Ottawa and Toronto had apparently begun in earnest. In August, Premier Frost announced that he and Finance Minister Abbott had agreed on an arrangement substantially the same as the federal offer of December 1950. The only change was that the province retained the right to levy succession duties, at the expense of a reduction in its payments equal to the credits allowed by the federal government for duties paid to Ontario on deaths that occurred during the new agreement. Ontario dropped its corporation income tax.

Quebec did not change its position and remained outside the 1952-1957 tax rental agreements. The province levied corporation income tax at a rate of 7 percent (in addition to the special taxes noted in chapter 3) and succession duties but no personal income tax. In 1953, the federal government rectified the situation to some extent by increasing its credit for provincial corporation income taxes from 5 to 7 percent of taxable profits, to match the 7 percent rate imposed by Quebec.

The basis of the post-war negotiations had been an understanding that no province should feel forced to accept the rental arrangements. The federal government had committed itself, accordingly, to avoid penalizing taxpayers in non-agreeing provinces. Yet in spite of the increase in the credit for provincial corporation taxes, Premier Duplessis could with justification complain that Quebec was receiving far less in abatements than it would have received under an agreement. The problem was exacerbated when, in early 1954, Quebec imposed personal income taxes equal to about 15 percent of the federal rates. The federal government responded to this move by increasing its personal income tax credit to 10 percent. The value of the abatement did not bring the compensation up to the level of the rental payments, however, and so did not eliminate so-called double taxation—a phenomenon long decried by the federal government.

---

[8] Tax Rental Agreements Act, 1952, SC 1952, c. 49.
[9] *The Globe and Mail*, January 16, 1952.

From Tax Rental to Tax Sharing:
The Background

In April 1955, federal and provincial representatives met to plan the agenda for a full-scale federal-provincial conference in October. The conference was to concentrate on new fiscal arrangements to replace the tax rental agreements, which would expire on March 31, 1957.

The 1947-1952 and 1952-1957 rental agreements contained a significant element of equalization for the poorer provinces. At the same time, the provision of tax room, which left the provinces with a measure of choice, meant that the agreements were free of any major element of coercion, or of interference with provincial autonomy. Quebec's imposition of a personal income tax, however, had made it clear to the federal government that, even given the tax room built into the agreements, the province had no intention of entering into the rental arrangements in their existing form. Any future arrangements with Quebec would have to be based on the granting of a greater degree of tax room.

Originally, the granting of tax room—that is, the allotment to each agreeing province of 5 percent of the corporation taxable income, 5 percent of the federal personal income tax, and 50 percent of the estate taxes generated within its borders ("5-5-50")—had been in fact simply a move to make tolerable the position of the one or two wealthier provinces that were not expected to participate in the agreements. Had the federal government intended to provide tax room equivalent to rental payments for all of the provinces, it would have had to provide credits for some of the poorer provinces of from 50 to 100 percent. Credits of this magnitude, or indeed any abatements greater than those provided by the 5-5-50 formula, were not acceptable to the federal government, which wanted to maintain a tax system that was capable of rapid change in the event of war or national emergency. Had Quebec pressed only for additional money in 1954, it would probably have met with success, but tax concessions that would have impeded federal tax policy and manoeuvrability would not have been acceptable to Ottawa. The federal government was also concerned that if it increased Quebec's abatement Ontario and the other provinces would press for an increased share of personal income taxes, which Ottawa could not grant without once more putting Quebec at a relative disadvantage if it remained outside the rental arrangements and the additional federal payments implicit therein.

It was recognized that the methods used for calculating tax rental payments were in need of revision. No unifying principle underlay the options available to the provinces, since they had been designed simply to yield the amount of money necessary to induce each province to enter into an agreement. Two of the formulas were based on provincial tax yields, but the bases were defined in different ways. One formula reflected tax effort; that is, it was based on actual provincial tax revenues in the pre-war period. The other reflected tax potential; that is, it was based on the yield of a set of standard rates applied in the province. The third option was essentially a per capita payment to provide relief for low-income provinces. All three options included the statutory subsidies described in chapter 2, and they too aided the low-income provinces.

The need for a detailed review and overhaul of the existing fiscal arrangements was obvious by 1955. In sum, the federal government had to develop a proposal that would

• satisfy Quebec;

• give some recognition to the financial demands of other provinces;

• meet the apparent aspirations of certain of the high "tax potential" provinces for more room for their own taxes;

• recognize the historical imperative of granting assistance to the low-income provinces;

• be neutral to the choices of individual provinces—that is, the proposal would have to ensure that any province's position would be the same whether it chose to sign an agreement or not;

• embody a new formula, preferably of universal application, that was calculated on the basis of some up-to-date criteria; and

• not worsen any province's position in comparison with its position under the existing tax rental agreements—at a minimum, the proposal would have to improve the position of all of the provinces moderately.

The participants in the April 1955 meeting agreed that the agenda for an October conference should include federal-provincial fiscal relations, the desirability of establishing a federal-provincial continuing committee (a technical committee of federal and provincial officials that would meet between regular conferences to carry out the necessary studies and other preparatory work), and the timing and scope of such other special conferences as might be desired.

The October 1955 Conference

In earlier conferences, the problems of financing the Second World War, rebuilding a peacetime economy, and financing the Korean War had given the federal government a strong bargaining position. By 1955, however, the nation was more concerned with social security, health care, education, highway construction, and other expenditure programs that fell within provincial jurisdiction. Thus the position of the provinces was significantly stronger at the October 1955 conference than it had been at the earlier ones.

The federal government brought up a number of proposals for preliminary discussion at a conference of officials held in September. When Prime Minister St. Laurent opened the full-scale conference on October 3, he outlined publicly his government's proposals for a new system of fiscal arrangements for the period April 1, 1957 to March 31, 1962. The four main proposals were as follows:

1) The provinces would no longer be required to participate in tax rental agreements in order to receive the federal assistance implicit in those provisions of the tax rental agreements that did not necessarily restrict federal payments to a province to the level of federal collections in the province.

2) The federal government would provide new unconditional grants designed to bring each province's yield from its share of the standard taxes up to the level of the two wealthiest provinces.

3) Provinces not participating in the tax rental agreements would continue to be free to impose and administer their own taxes. Participating provinces would receive an agreed share of the proceeds from the standard taxes collected by the federal government from their residents.

4) A stabilization clause would ensure that each province received as much under the new arrangements as it would have received under a continuation of the existing arrangements, even if economic conditions and tax yields declined.

The federal offer contained two fundamental departures. First, the federal government was willing, for the first time, to provide a form of equalization independent of the tax arrangements; that is, with no conditions attached. This innovation was important because it soon became a basic element of federal-provincial relations—to the point, finally, of being enshrined in the Constitution Act of 1982. The second remarkable feature of the federal offer was the linking of rental payments to tax yields, a step that identified a provincial right to a share of the major direct tax fields. The federal proposals set the tone for all future federal-provincial fiscal arrangements by establishing the clear separation of tax and equalization measures and the principle of unconditional equalization, and by recognizing the provinces' rights in major tax fields.

The replies by the provincial premiers had one common theme: postwar economic development and population growth had put a severe strain on provincial and local government resources. The wealthier provinces—Quebec, Ontario, Alberta, and British Columbia—pointed out that although their rapid economic growth had resulted in higher costs, the existing tax system returned little of this increased wealth to the provincial treasuries. The less wealthy provinces pointed out that their lower tax capacities did not allow them to provide the level of public services enjoyed in the "have" provinces.

Premier Duplessis' opening remarks set out Quebec's view of its place in the federal system: he made it clear that the province was determined to continue to impose and collect its own taxes. Premier Frost of Ontario stressed his province's need for a greater share of personal and corporation income taxes, but he did not preclude Ontario's participation in some form of rental arrangements. Premier W.A.C. Bennett of British Columbia took a neutral position: he indicated a willingness to accept either a continuation of the tax rental system or joint occupancy of the major tax fields. New Brunswick proposed a system of grants designed to bring the per capita revenue of the poorer provinces up to the national average yield from 85 percent of the per capita national average personal income.[10] The other provinces were generally in favour of a continuation of the rental agreements and some system of equalization.

The October conference adjourned with no conclusions on fiscal arrangements for the 1957-1962 period, but all parties took the proposals home for study. The participants did agree to the establishment of a Continuing Committee of federal and provincial officials who would meet from time to time to exchange information and examine technical problems associated with federal-provincial fiscal and economic relations.

The Federal Offer of January 1956

A letter of January 6, 1956 from Prime Minister St. Laurent to the provincial premiers outlined revised federal proposals for the taxation years 1957 to 1961 inclusive. The new proposals were intended to ensure that the decision by a province to impose its own taxes did not affect its financial position.

The federal government offered 10 percent of federal individual income tax collections in each province in the form of either payment or abatement, a choice that would provide all provinces with the same treatment as that afforded to Quebec. It offered 9 percent of corporate taxable profits (as defined in the federal Income Tax Act), again either as a payment or an abatement. This figure represented an increase over the 8.5 percentage points provided to Ontario under the 1952-1957 agreements.

The treatment of estate taxes and succession duties was also changed. For some time, only Quebec and Ontario had occupied this field, so no data were available on provincial yields in the other provinces. The federal government therefore offered the provinces 50 percent of federal estate tax rates, as payment or as abatement, instead of the average yield of provincial levies. This arrangement had the advantage that it put estate taxes on a basis consistent with the sharing of the two income taxes.

The provincial shares of these standard taxes at standard rates—10, 9, and 50 percent—would be based on federal rates in 1956, an arrangement that would insulate the provinces from any changes in federal rates during the life of the agreement.

Equalization under the January 1956 federal proposal was to bring the per capita yield from the standard taxes in any province up to the average of the per capita yields in the two provinces with the highest yields. An element of stabilization was introduced to ensure that the per capita yield would not be

---

[10] Further details on this proposal and the text of Premier Duplessis's statement are provided in the appendices of A. Milton Moore, J. Harvey Perry, and Donald I. Beach, *The Financing of Canadian Federation: The First Hundred Years*, Canadian Tax Paper no. 43 (Toronto: Canadian Tax Foundation, 1966).

less under the new arrangement than it had been during 1956-57, the last year of the old tax rental agreement, and that for any province the total yield under the new arrangement would not fall below 90 percent of the average of the province's total yields in the previous two years of the new arrangements.

The January 1956 federal proposal also outlined changes in the treatment of corporation taxes (as distinct from corporation income taxes), a category that included special taxes such as capital and place-of-business taxes. These special taxes would not be allowed as a deductible expense for corporation income tax purposes unless they exceeded 9 percent of taxable profits (or the applicable provincial corporation income tax). The excess would be allowed as a deduction, but the cost of that deduction would be offset against the federal payments to the province. Table 4.3 compares the financial effects of these proposals with the effects of a hypothetical extension of the 1952-1957 arrangements.

Subsequent Negotiations

In a statement issued a week after the October 1955 conference, Premier Frost announced that Ontario would re-enter the corporation income tax field. By mid-February 1956, however, the provincial government had still not set a rate for the tax or introduced the relevant legislation. The other provinces, meanwhile, had raised specific questions about the January proposals, but none had announced plans.

The federal finance minister, Walter Harris, addressed the specific questions in a memorandum to the provinces dated February 18, 1956. According to the memorandum,

• the federal government would cede to the provinces the taxation of insurance premiums (thus providing additional tax room of about $23 million for provincial treasurers);

• the federal government would collect provincially imposed income taxes (but not succession duties) if the provinces adopted standard legislation and did not set provincial rates in excess of the standard rates;

• the calculation of equalization payments would use data for the current fiscal year rather than data for the preceding year, a change that would increase the payments;

• the calculation of the tax-sharing payment or the tax abatement would include the tax on Canadian income of non-residents but exclude withholding tax and old age security tax collections; and

• the allocation rules contained in the regulations to the federal Income Tax Act would be used to allocate profits among the provinces.

Premier Duplessis announced shortly after receipt of the federal memorandum that Quebec would accept the equalization payment. Given the position taken by the premier, however, it could not enter the proposed tax sharing arrangements.

Table 4.3 A Financial Illustration of Federal Proposals Based on Assumed Economic Conditions[a] for Fiscal Year 1957-58

	Nfld.	PEI	NS	NB	Que.	Ont.	Man.	Sask.	Alta.	BC	Total
	all dollar figures in thousands except per capitas										
Estimated population in 1957 (000)	432	108	703	578	4,700	5,509	867	929	1,172	1,377	16,375
Yield of standard taxes	4,355	840	9,725	7,375	129,965	213,500	18,765	13,255	26,100	49,525	473,405
Per capita yield of standard taxes	10.08	7.78	13.83	12.76	27.65	38.75	21.64	14.27	22.27	35.97	—
Equalization per capita to top 2 ($38.20)	28.12	30.42	24.37	25.44	10.55	—	16.56	23.93	15.93	2.23	—
Equalization payment for 1957-58	12,150	3,285	17,130	14,705	49,585	—	14,360	22,230	18,670	3,070	155,185
Standard taxes plus equalization payment	16,505	4,125	26,855	22,080	179,550	213,500	33,125	35,485	44,770	52,595	628,590
Per capita	38.20	38.20	38.20	38.20	38.20	38.75	38.20	38.20	38.20	38.20	38.39
Stabilization payment for 1957-58[b]	—	145	—	—	—	—	—	—	—	735	880
Revenue available from 2% provincial insurance premium tax	235	70	780	565	6,325	10,170	1,110	660	1,580	2,100	23,595
Total revenue available 1957-58	16,740	4,340	27,635	22,645	185,875	223,670	34,235	36,145	46,350	55,430	653,065
Per capita	38.75	40.19	39.31	39.18	39.55	40.60	39.49	38.91	39.55	40.25	39.88
Tax rental payment available in 1956-57[c]	14,155	4,165	21,975	18,505	140,515	169,875	28,620	28,625	35,265	50,715	512,415
Per capita (1956 population)	33.54	38.56	31.71	32.58	30.48	31.78	33.36	31.49	31.51	37.82	32.08
Increase in proposed formula in 1957-58 over 1952 agreement formula in 1956-57	2,585	175	5,660	4,140	45,360	53,795	5,615	7,520	11,085	4,715	140,650
Percentage increase	18.3	4.2	25.8	22.4	32.3	31.7	19.6	26.3	31.4	9.3	27.4
Per capita increase	5.31	1.63	7.60	6.60	9.07	8.82	6.13	7.42	8.04	2.43	7.80
Tax rental available in 1957-58 if the 1952 agreement formula were continued[d]	14,890	4,270	22,865	19,320	146,620	179,290	29,620	30,010	37,990	53,330	538,205
Per capita	34.47	39.54	32.52	33.43	31.20	32.54	34.16	32.30	32.41	38.73	32.87
Increase in proposed formula in 1957-58 over the 1952 agreement formula in 1957-58	1,850	70	4,770	3,325	39,255	44,380	4,615	6,135	8,360	2,100	114,860
Percentage increase over 1952 formula	12.4	1.6	20.9	17.2	26.8	24.8	15.6	20.4	22.0	3.9	21.3
Per capita increase over 1952 formula	4.28	0.65	6.79	5.75	8.35	8.06	5.32	6.60	7.13	1.53	7.01

[a]The yield of standard taxes and the insurance premium tax have been increased by 6 percent per annum over the basic 1955 data. The distribution of taxable incomes, profits, and successions among provinces is based on the data available. The calculations use the 1956 federal rates for individual income tax and succession duty. [b]To bring up to tax rental payment available in 1957-58 if the 1952 agreements were to be extended. [c]Estimated on GNP at factor cost of $23.56 billion (corresponds to GNP of $26.77 billion at market prices). [d]Estimated on GNP at factor cost of $24.70 billion (corresponds to GNP of $28.00 billion at market prices).

Source: Canada, House of Commons, *Debates*, July 16, 1956, 5989.

Federal and provincial representatives met on March 9, 1956 to consider provincial requests for substantially larger payments or tax abatements. At the meeting, and in subsequent correspondence, the federal government rejected these requests. In a letter dated March 19, 1956, the prime minister told the provincial premiers that he was willing to raise the stabilization level from 90 to 95 percent of the average of the two previous years' payments and to ensure that the new payments would be at least equal to provincial entitlements under an extension of the 1952-1957 arrangements. The federal government's final word appeared in the budget of March 20, 1956: the federal offer, as outlined above, stood. As far as Ottawa was concerned, the negotiations were over.

The Legislation

Parliament passed the Federal-Provincial Tax Sharing Arrangements Act, 1957, on July 31, 1956. Under the Act, the provinces were to receive payments or abatements equal to 10 percent of federal individual income tax, excluding the old age security tax (this figure was raised to 13 percent for the taxation years 1958 to 1961), 9 percent of taxable corporation profits, and 50 percent of federal succession duties (later, estate tax). The standard taxes thus became "10-9-50" in the terminology used at the time. The legislation also provided for equalization payments, which would bring each province's per capita share of the standard taxes up to the weighted average per capita yield of the two provinces with the highest per capita yields. Chapter 9 describes this formula in detail. The federal government would, in addition, make stabilization payments, which would bring each province's yield from the standard taxes plus equalization up to the largest of the following amounts:

• the amount calculated by extending the 1952-1957 arrangements unchanged,

• the per capita yield in 1956-57, or

• 95 percent of the average payments in the previous two years of the 1957-1962 arrangement (for 1957-58, this proviso was not effective, and for 1958-59 it applied to 1957-58 only).

Provincial Positions

Only Quebec and Ontario turned down the federal proposals. The other eight provinces duly signed agreements under which they waived their rights to impose individual and corporation income tax for the taxation years 1957 to 1961 inclusive and to levy succession duties in respect of persons dying between April 1, 1957 and March 31, 1962. In return, each province received payments equal to the yield of the standard taxes in that province.

Ontario re-entered the corporation income tax field with a rate of 11 percent—a rate 2 percentage points higher than both the abatement and the rate in Quebec. The province justified this rate, in its February 1957 budget, by arguing that the fruits of its rapid economic expansion were being enjoyed mainly by the business sector and that many provincial expenditures were related to this expansion. Ontario also reimposed special capital and place-of-business taxes, effective January 1, 1957; these taxes were payable only to the extent that they exceeded the corporation income tax of 11 percent. The province changed its allocation rules for corporation income taxes to conform to the federal system. In April 1957, it signed an agreement to rent its individual income tax rights to the federal government. Ontario continued to levy and collect its own succession duties.

All of the provinces moved to impose a tax of 2 percent on insurance premiums, effective January 1, 1957; they thus picked up the tax room provided by the federal government, which had repealed its tax as of December 31, 1956. Quebec extended its corporation income tax to cover banks and insurance, railway, and mining companies, and it increased its general corporation income tax rate from 7 to 9 percent. However, because the province did not use the federal rules for allocating profits, the Quebec corporation income tax payable did not necessarily equal the federal abatement.

Subsequent Developments

The 1957-1962 agreements were far from satisfactory even to the provinces that had signed them—all the less satisfactory given that the provinces continued to struggle with deficits, whereas Ottawa was budgeting for a surplus. In 1957, however, the provinces saw an opportunity to improve their position. The federal election in June swept the Liberals out of office and installed the Conservatives under John Diefenbaker, who had promised to convene a fall federal-provincial conference with a mandate to review the existing tax arrangements. Prime Minister Diefenbaker and the provincial premiers assembled for a two-day conference on November 25, 1957.

All of the premiers made the point that economic growth and the demand for more government services had put intolerable strains on provincial resources. British Columbia's premier called for a 25-25-50 system of standard taxes. The premiers of Manitoba and Saskatchewan sought a minimum of 15-15-50. Ontario too pushed for greater tax room. The Atlantic provinces, on the other hand, emphasized the need for greater equalization (see chapter 9). In the end, the assembled provincial premiers agreed on both points: the provinces in general needed a larger share of the standard taxes (either as an increase in rental payments or as larger abatements), and the poorer provinces needed greater equalization if they were to provide a level of services equivalent to some minimum national standard.

The federal government responded in January 1958 by increasing the provincial share of the federal personal income tax from 10 to 13 percent for the taxation years 1958 to 1961 inclusive. Because the additional 3 percentage points were included in the equalization formula, the recipient provinces automatically received additional equalization.

In 1960, the abatement for corporation income tax was increased from 9 to 10 percent of taxable profits for provinces that chose not to receive federal per capita university grants. Quebec was the only province that refused the grants, and so Quebec alone received the increased abatement.[11]

[11] This is discussed further in chapter 11.

5

A New Approach to Tax Sharing: The 1962-1967 Tax Collection Agreements

Background

The 1957-1962 tax agreements had run less than half their course before the federal government and the provinces began to prepare seriously for the next round of negotiations. During the campaign for the 1958 federal election, which the Conservatives won handily, Prime Minister Diefenbaker promised to call still another full federal-provincial conference. The federal and provincial finance ministers and treasurers met in Ottawa in July and October 1959 to prepare for the conference and to consider problems that had arisen under the current arrangements. The provinces were also concerned about the condition of capital markets in Canada, since federal deficits and the re-financing of war bonds had made borrowing difficult for provincial and local governments.

The July meeting produced a long list of topics that were to be examined at length by the federal and provincial officials in the Continuing Committee. The subjects for detailed study included the following:

• Alternative federal-provincial fiscal arrangements.

• The Canadian revenue system and its jurisdictional distribution, including the allocation of revenue sources and the feasibility of introducing cooperative taxing or collection procedures.

• The expenditure responsibilities of the various levels of government, including the municipalities, and the appropriateness of the existing division of responsibilities in the light of current conditions.

• The principles and methods employed in measuring fiscal need (see chapter 9).

• Conditional grants and shared-cost programs—what their place should be in the scheme of intergovernmental financial relations and possible means of coordinating and simplifying them (see chapters 12 to 16).

• The taxation of natural resources and the economic and financial implications of the tax burden on primary industries.

• National development and long-range regional development problems—how the federal government and the provinces might cooperate in developing the country's resources.

In addition, the finance ministers themselves were to study the need for changes in the last two years of the existing arrangements, the policy aspects of shared-cost programs, and the problems of obtaining capital funds.

The Continuing Committee was also charged with several short-term studies that were to be completed in time for the October meeting. These studies were to address various questions about natural resource taxation, the calculation of preliminary federal payments to the provinces, sales tax exemptions for Crown agencies and foreign powers, conditional grants and shared-cost programs, and the distribution among the provinces of their share of the newly imposed federal estate tax, which had replaced federal succession duties on January 1, 1959.

Although the October meeting of finance ministers and treasurers produced little in the way of final agreement, the federal finance minister, Donald Fleming, used the occasion to announce that a full conference would take place in mid-1960. Prime Minister Diefenbaker issued the formal invitations on March 24, 1960 for a conference that would begin on July 25. On July 8, he circulated a draft agenda among the provincial premiers. According to this agenda, it would be the task of the conference to

• develop tax arrangements to replace the 1957-1962 agreements when they expired, including (1) arrangements for the treatment of personal income tax, corporation income tax, and succession duties, (2) formulas for equalization and fiscal need payments, and (3) a formula for stabilization payments;

• resolve the question—pressed by Ontario—whether or not to allow indirect provincial retail sales taxes;

• establish uniform rules for allocating corporation profits and the income of individuals to the provinces;

• examine the taxation of the natural resource industries;

• establish a basis for sharing with the provinces federal income tax collected from corporations whose main business was the distribution or the generation for distribution to the public of electrical energy, gas, or steam;

• consider the possibility of applying sales tax to Crown agencies; and

• discuss the role in provincial financing of conditional grants and shared-cost programs.

Thus, the main items of contention between the federal government and the provinces remained to be resolved by the full conference. The conference was all the more important because it would see the first appearance on the national stage of the new Liberal premier of Quebec, Jean Lesage, who had been in office for only four weeks.

In the event, three full federal-provincial conferences were held in 1960 and 1961—on July 25 to 27 and October 26 to 28, 1960, and February 23 and 24, 1961.

The July 1960 Conference

In his opening speech at the July 1960 conference, Prime Minister Diefenbaker asserted his government's continuing support for the current system of equalization, stabilization, and shared occupancy of the three major tax fields. He indicated that his government was willing to consider substantial changes but did not mention any specific measures contemplated by the federal authorities.

Premier Leslie Frost of Ontario made a direct request for either 50 percent of personal and corporation income taxes or a constitutional amendment that would enable the provinces to levy an indirect retail sales tax. Premier Lesage expressed his acceptance of the existing system under which Quebec received equalization payments and yet was free to levy its own taxes. He did request an increase in the provincial share to 25 percent of personal and corporation income taxes and 100 percent of death taxes, and a continuation of equalization based on the yield of personal and corporation income taxes in the province with the highest yield from these taxes.

Premier W.A.C. Bennett of British Columbia suggested that equalization be tied to provincial need rather than to tax capacity, an approach that took no account of the variation in the local costs of provincial programs. The other provincial leaders made many of the same points, calling for a larger share of standard taxes and larger equalization payments, and also pushed for reform of the taxation of natural resources, including deductibility for such taxes under the Income Tax Act.

Most provincial spokesmen criticized the recent proliferation of conditional grants and shared-cost programs as a serious threat to provincial autonomy. The administrative and budgetary rigidity imposed by the grants caused problems for many provinces. Premier Louis Robichaud of New Brunswick pointed out that it was often difficult for the poorer provinces to fund their shares of the joint programs but even more difficult for them to refuse to participate. He suggested that the grants be modified to take into account the varying fiscal capacities of the provinces.

Chapters 12, 13, and 14 discuss conditional grants in detail. It is important to note here, however, that it was at the July 1960 conference that Premier Lesage formally introduced the idea that the federal government should abandon conditional grants and provide in their stead additional tax room and equalization.

The July 1960 conference proved to be largely an opportunity for all parties to present their views. There were few concrete results. The federal government, which had incurred three consecutive deficits, was not in a position immediately to decrease its share of the standard taxes and increase its commitment for equalization. In summarizing the provincial position at the end of the conference, Finance Minister Donald Fleming noted that the current formula for the standard taxes of 13-9-50 gave the provinces about 37 percent of total revenues from these fields, and that if all of the provincial demands were met over 80 percent of these revenues would go into provincial coffers. He further noted that three provinces were receiving in federal payments more than 100 percent of the standard taxes, five were receiving more than 50 percent, and no province was receiving less than 26 percent. Nearly a year later, in his June 1961 budget, Finance Minister Fleming estimated that meeting the provincial demands put forward at the July conference would have cost over $2 billion per year—a figure that the provinces disputed.

The October 1960 Conference

Even before the round of conferences began, there had been some suggestion that the Diefenbaker government disliked carrying the entire responsibility for levying the standard taxes, particularly the personal income tax. This arrangement—federal taxation for provincial purposes—scarcely enhanced the federal government's popularity with the electorate. Meanwhile, the demands on provincial treasuries had grown so severe that a number of provincial governments intimated a willingness to forgo their "invisibility" in the major tax fields in return for the ability to impose their own taxes in these fields at rates sufficient to meet their requirements.

As Quebec's example made clear, there were in fact no constitutional impediments to unilateral provincial action, and, under the 1957-1962 arrangements, the equalization entitlement was not jeopardized by such action.

The federal government proposed a solution at the October 1960 conference. It was willing to reduce its share in each of the three standard taxes by the equivalent of the provincial share (13-9-50), giving the provinces tax room in which to impose their own taxes. For most of the provinces, however, especially the smaller ones, it would have been difficult or impractical to set up their own collection machinery. The provinces were further deterred by the political cost of such a move, which the public would probably interpret as double taxation. The federal government did not, however, offer at this point to put its collection machinery at the provinces' disposal. Consequently, the federal proposal did not generate a consensus, and the meeting adjourned with the provinces still looking for additional resources.

The February 1961 Conference

At the February 1961 conference, the federal government announced that it would not seek to renew the tax rental system. Instead, it would introduce legislation to reduce its tax on corporate income by 9 percentage points and its personal income tax by 16 percent initially and 20 percent eventually; these reductions would be phased in over the next five years, and the resulting tax room would be available to the provinces. Finally, the federal government would pay 50 percent of its estate tax collections to any province that did not levy a similar tax. Moreover, and more significantly for the future, the federal government was willing to collect provincial taxes at no cost to the provinces, provided that the provincial tax base was identical to the federal base.

The federal proposal recognized the provinces' demands for both more fiscal autonomy and greater fiscal resources. Each province would be free to set its own personal and corporation tax rates in accordance with its own particular needs, and to increase its share of personal income taxes, without having to set up its own collection machinery and impose additional administrative burdens on its taxpayers; the only limitations on provincial rates would be those imposed by public opinion.

The centralized system of tax rentals had been designed to maintain both uniform tax laws and uniform tax rates across the country. A centralized system had been seen as important to the economic development of Canada and an appropriate way of reducing the number of tax returns that had to be filed—a distinct advantage from the taxpayer's point of view. Although the federal proposal maintained the practice of centralized collection, it ended—in theory, at least—the imposition of uniform rates. In practice, the legacy of uniform rates left provincial politicians with a compelling reason not to impose rates of income tax higher than those in other provinces. Only Saskatchewan and Manitoba raised their income tax rates when they had the opportunity in 1962, but seven provinces imposed new or increased general sales or gasoline taxes in their 1961 budgets.

The federal proposals not only introduced significant changes in the form of tax sharing but substantially increased the tax resources available to the provincial governments. What is perhaps more significant, it indicated the philosophy to which the federal government would adhere for a number of years to come—that is, to increase provincial resources without regard to differences in provincial wealth. In an address to the House of Commons in July 1961, Finance Minister Fleming stated that the federal government had chosen the personal income tax as the vehicle for transferring fiscal resources to the provinces because it regularly exhibited steady and rapid growth, and because the provincial share of corporation income tax already amounted to nearly 23 percent of total collections. He pointed out that the corporation income tax was a less appropriate vehicle for the transfer of fiscal resources because "many corporations operate on a national scale and corporation profits are therefore generally regarded as more appropriate for taxation by the federal government."[1] The February offer also included some major and far-reaching changes in the equalization system; these changes are discussed in chapter 9.

Provincial Responses

The federal offer provided both less tax room and less equalization than the provinces had anticipated. The consequence was that a number of provinces were obliged to introduce major and highly unpopular increases in taxation in order to meet the heavy demands on their treasuries. Ontario introduced a retail sales tax, and Nova Scotia, New Brunswick, Manitoba, Saskatchewan,

[1] Canada, House of Commons, *Debates*, July 11, 1961, 7911.

Alberta, and British Columbia all increased their sales taxes, gasoline taxes, or both. As noted above, only Saskatchewan and Manitoba moved immediately to increase their personal or corporation income tax rates.

The 1962-1967 Arrangements

The new arrangements were embodied in the Federal-Provincial Fiscal Arrangements Act, which Parliament passed on September 29, 1961.[2] The arrangements covered the five fiscal years April 1, 1962 to March 31, 1967 and the taxation years 1962 to 1966, inclusive. Federal personal income tax was to be abated by 16 percent in 1962 and by 1 additional percentage point in each of the next four years until, in 1966, the abatement reached 20 percent. The agreeing provinces were free to impose whatever personal income tax rate they desired, provided that the rate was expressed as a percentage of basic federal tax (a term of art that has become an important part of tax sharing); the federal government would collect the provincial tax at no cost to the province or the taxpayer. Federal corporation income tax was abated by 9 percent of taxable income, and the provinces were free to impose their own rates provided that they were expressed as a percentage of taxable income as defined for federal tax purposes. The federal government was willing to collect this tax free of charge. The provinces had the option of accepting either 50 percent of federal estate tax collections, which would be allocated to them under federal rules, or an abatement of a similar amount, which would be applied against provincial succession duties.

Before January 1, 1962, only Quebec had levied its own personal income tax. On that date, the other nine provinces imposed their own rates under the terms of the collection agreements. As was noted earlier, only Manitoba and Saskatchewan took advantage of the opportunity to impose rates higher than the rates that had prevailed under the old agreements. Both provinces set their 1962 rates at 22 percent of basic federal tax. Ontario and Quebec were already imposing separate corporation income taxes; the other eight provinces moved to impose their own rates under the collection agreements. Again, Manitoba and Saskatchewan were the only provinces to set their corporate rates above the abatement—at 10 percent of federally defined taxable income. Only Quebec and Ontario had their own succession duties at the beginning of the period, and both chose the death tax abatement; the other provinces accepted the federal payments.

Quebec did not sign tax collection agreements and continued to levy its own personal income tax at rates ranging from 2.5 percent to 13.2 percent of taxable income, as defined in its legislation. Quebec's corporation income tax rate was 12 percent, but because the province continued to receive an additional 1 percent abatement in lieu of the federal grants to universities the rate was in effect 2 percentage points above the abatement.[3] Ontario levied

---

[2] Federal-Provincial Fiscal Arrangements Act, SC 1960-61, c. 58.

[3] See chapter 15 for further details.

and collected corporation income tax at a rate of 11 percent, also 2 percentage points above the abatement.

The tax collection agreements made the revenue of the agreeing provinces dependent on the structure of the three federal taxes. If an agreeing province wished to change its rate, the change could not become effective until the following year. If the federal taxes were reduced by 3 percent or more, however, the provinces could increase their rates retroactively to offset the effects of the federal reduction.

The new arrangements settled the long-standing problem of allocating income by province. Both the agreeing and the non-agreeing provinces accepted the convention that personal income (except income from partnerships or unincorporated business) would be allocated according to the taxpayer's province of residence as of December 31. Corporation income was to be allocated among the provinces according to a formula based on sales and wages paid (with special formulas for interprovincial transportation and other special cases). Quebec and Ontario agreed to these formulas as well.[4]

During debate on the legislation in the House of Commons, the federal government tabled its projections of payments under the Act and compared them with hypothetical payments under an extension of the old arrangements; these calculations appear in table 5.1. As the table shows, Ontario benefited from the extra personal income tax room, the Atlantic provinces benefited from the increased equalization, and Alberta and British Columbia suffered a net decline in revenue by entering the new arrangements. The revenue positions of Quebec, Manitoba, and Saskatchewan did not change.

Subsequent Developments

British Columbia felt that the federal estate tax legislation allowed tax avoidance at the expense of the province's treasury. In 1963, therefore, it moved to impose its own succession duties.

Following negotiations with the provinces, the federal government's 1962 budget introduced an income tax credit of two-thirds of any provincial logging tax of 10 percent or less. The federal government had not allowed provincial logging tax as a deduction for income tax purposes, thus creating an element of double taxation that had been a problem for Quebec, Ontario, and British Columbia. The provinces were expected to match the federal move by allowing the remaining one-third as a credit against provincial corporation income taxes. In 1963, Quebec and Ontario duly introduced such a credit, but British Columbia enacted a credit of only 18 percent, the equivalent of the provincial share of corporation income tax on nondeductible logging taxes.

---

[4] A more detailed discussion of the terms of the tax collection agreements appears in the appendix to this chapter.

Table 5.1 Hypothetical Illustration of Provincial Revenues for 1962-63 Under New and Old Formulas[a]

	Nfld.	PEI	NS	NB	Que.	Ont.	Man.	Sask.	Alta.	BC	Total
					thousands of dollars						
New formula (16-9-50): revenues projected to 1962-63 from first estimate for 1961-62											
Standard taxes at 1962-63 rate of federal withdrawal (16-9-50)	6,037	1,314	13,052	10,371	169,193	314,480	29,482	20,201	45,758	72,835	682,723
Equalization	14,397	3,399	19,459	15,394	72,307	—	12,814	22,327	12,617	977	173,691
Atlantic provinces adjustment grants	10,500	3,500	10,500	10,500	—	—	—	—	—	—	35,000
Additional grant to Newfoundland	8,000	—	—	—	—	—	—	—	—	—	8,000
Total	38,934	8,213	43,011	36,265	241,500	314,480	42,296	42,528	58,375	73,812	899,414
Formula (13-9-50): revenues projected to 1962-63 from first estimate for 1961-62 using same assumptions as with new formula. Total revenues from standard taxes at 13-9-50, equalization, stabilization, Atlantic provinces adjustment grants, and additional grant to Newfoundland	37,277	7,381	41,315	35,762	241,500	296,170	42,296	42,528	61,294	76,069	881,542
1957 formula (10-9-50): revenues projected to 1962-63 from first estimate for 1961-62 using same assumptions as with new formula. Total revenues from standard taxes at 10-9-50, equalization, and stabilization	19,556	4,881	30,430	25,426	217,284	266,865	38,056	38,268	55,144	76,026	771,936

[a] The calculations assume a rate of growth in tax yields of 5 percent per annum and no change in the 1961-62 percentage distribution by provinces of tax yields or population. [b] The projection of the new formula is based on standard taxes of 16-9-50; that is, on rates equal to the federal withdrawal.

Source: Canada, House of Commons, *Debates*, July 11, 1961, 7927.

The defeat of the Diefenbaker government in 1963 coincided with a shift in the emphasis in federal-provincial discussions from tax room to equalization and shared-cost programs, which are discussed in later chapters. During the campaign, the Liberal party put forward what would prove to be an important new idea—the idea of allowing provinces to opt out of conditional grant programs in return for increased federal tax abatements. As will be noted later in this study, opting-out was to become a major issue in federal-provincial relations.

In November 1963, a full federal-provincial conference convened in Ottawa, primarily to discuss equalization and conditional grants. Premier Lesage of Quebec used the occasion to renew his demands for 25 percent of personal and corporation income taxes and 100 percent of death taxes. Prime Minister Lester B. Pearson offered an additional 25 percent of death taxes (not equalized), effective April 1, 1964. The seven provinces that received payments equal to the original 50 percent share agreed to accept the additional 25 percent as a payment. Quebec and Ontario chose to accept the additional funds as a payment rather than tackle the technical complexities involved in revising their succession duties, pending the reports of various royal commissions on taxation.[5] British Columbia, on the other hand, revised its duties to incorporate the additional 25 percent abatement; it was thus the only province to opt for the extra abatement.

Following a further meeting early in the spring of 1964, the prime minister announced in April that the abatement of federal personal income tax was to be raised an additional 2 percentage points in each of the next two years, bringing the abatement to 22 percent in the 1965 tax year and 24 percent in 1966. He further announced that the provinces would be allowed to opt out of the Canada Student Loan program and the youth allowances.[6]

In the spring meeting, Ottawa and the provinces agreed to set up the Tax Structure Committee, a unique mixture of appointed and elected officials from both levels of government. The committee's terms of reference included a charge to study "the tax fields that should be used exclusively by the federal government and by the provinces and municipalities, and the fields in which joint occupancy is desirable; and the arrangements to be made in

---

[5] Canada, *Report of the Royal Commission on Taxation* (Ottawa: Queen's Printer, 1966) (the Carter commission); The Ontario Committee on Taxation, *Report* (Toronto: Queen's Printer, 1967) (the Smith committee); Quebec, *Report of the Royal Commission on Taxation* (Quebec: Government of Quebec, 1965) (the Belanger commission); Saskatchewan, *Report of the Royal Commission on Taxation* (Regina: Queen's Printer, 1965) (the McLeod commission); New Brunswick Royal Commission on Finance and Municipal Taxation, *Report* (Fredericton: Queen's Printer, 1963) (the Byrne commission); and Manitoba, *Report of the Manitoba Royal Commission on Local Government Organization and Finance* (Winnipeg: Queen's Printer, 1964) (the Michener commission).

[6] Chapter 13 discusses the details of the opting-out negotiations.

respect of jointly occupied tax fields."[7] It was hoped that the committee's report, expected early in the spring of 1966, would spell out the proper balance of revenues and expenditures for each level of government. In the interim, debate on tax matters was deferred. The committee's full report was never released; a summary was made public immediately after a federal-provincial conference held in October 1966. The summary provided projections of revenues and expenditures for each level of government, which proved useful in the debate on tax shares, but the committee stopped well short of proposing any resolution to the debate.

At a full federal-provincial conference held in July 1965, the federal government offered to increase the transfer to the provinces of federal income tax on privately owned power, gas, and steam utility corporations from 50 percent to 95 percent, effective January 1, 1966.[8] The federal government retained 5 percent to cover the cost of the dividend tax credit available to shareholders of private corporations operating in this area. The federal minister of finance, Walter Gordon, attached no conditions to this offer, but he expected that the provinces would pass the benefits along to the companies and that the companies would lower their rates accordingly.

Appendix: Further Details on the Tax Collection Agreements

The level of provincial participation under the tax collection agreements for personal and corporation income taxes was similar to what it had been under the tax sharing agreements: Quebec continued its own collection of both personal and corporation income taxes; Ontario participated in the personal income tax collection agreement but continued to collect its own corporation income tax; the other eight provinces signed agreements covering both taxes.

Nevertheless, the introduction of the tax collection agreements represented a major change in both the form and the substance of federal-provincial arrangements to share the three major tax fields. For the first time in the postwar period, the provincial part of income taxation was clearly identifiable by the taxpayer.

In the case of the personal income tax, the federal government introduced the concept of basic federal tax (BFT)—not defined in the federal Income Tax Act—which represented the tax calculated by applying the rate structure to taxable income, after application of the dividend tax credit and the foreign tax credit. Thus, any federal tax provision that applied after the calculation of BFT did not figure in the calculation of provincial income tax. The special

---

[7] Canada, *Federal-Provincial Tax Structure Committee*, proceedings of a meeting held in Ottawa, September 14-15, 1966 (Ottawa: Queen's Printer, 1966), 6.

[8] From 1957 to 1966, the transfer of federal income tax on public utilities was separated from other aspects of the tax sharing or collection machinery. The federal expenditure was authorized by an expenditure item to be voted annually in the main estimates.

federal tax for the old age security fund, for example, was not shared. The social development tax, levied later to help finance the introduction of the national medicare plan, was similarly kept out of the provincial tax base.

The federal legislation established a fundamental distinction between tax room or tax points for the purposes of the personal income tax and tax points for the purposes of the corporation income tax. A personal income tax point was 1 percentage point of BFT; a corporation income tax point was 1 percentage point of taxable corporation income, as defined in the federal Income Tax Act.

In 1962, the federal government abated the BFT by 16 percent to allow room for provincial taxation and provided a line on the tax form for the calculation of provincial income tax, expressed as a percentage of the BFT. Although the federal government subsequently made adjustments to the calculation of federal tax to provide tax reductions or surtaxes, it was careful to make most of these changes apply only after the calculation of the BFT. The provinces, by basing their taxes on the BFT, automatically adopted the federal levels of exemptions and allowable deductions (that is, the federal definition of taxable income) and the progressive rate structure set by the federal governments. No province was forced to adopt a rate of tax—that is, a percentage of the BFT—equal to the abatement, but any deviation would be readily apparent to the taxpayer. Thus the provinces were free to increase their tax rates, but the federal government would not get the blame when they did. The divorce between federal and provincial taxation was not complete, however, since the taxpayer still wrote only one cheque (to the federal government).

The federal corporation income tax was abated by 9 percent of taxable income—not tax—for nine provinces and by 10 percent for Quebec (in keeping with the special arrangement with that province for university grants). Each of the eight agreeing provinces was then free to impose any rate it chose on its taxable corporation income, as defined for federal purposes. The taxpayer corporation in an agreeing province still filed one return for both federal and provincial corporation income taxes and wrote only one cheque (to the federal government).

In order to terminate a collection agreement, the federal government had to give notice a full year before the beginning of the next taxation year. A province had to give notice three months in advance of the next taxation year. Because the agreeing provinces were obliged to express their personal income tax as a percentage of basic federal tax and their corporation income tax as a percentage of federally defined taxable income, the provincial legislation and regulations had to conform to their federal counterparts. Each province duly passed an income tax act of its own that was modelled on the federal Act and referred specifically to it. The provinces also accepted the federal system of allocating personal and corporation income among provinces. The rule that allocated non-business personal income according to the taxpayer's province of residence on December 31 of the tax year was an arbitrary one, but it and the other allocation rules were accepted by both the agreeing and the non-agreeing provinces.

The collection agreements required the provinces to strike a single rate for individual income tax for the entire taxation year, and changes in rates required notification by October 15 of the year before the rate change went into effect. Because the taxation years of corporations vary, they were required to pay the provincial corporation income tax rate (also held constant through the calendar year) applicable to the calendar year in which their fiscal year ended. A province could impose only one corporation income tax rate, and notification of rate changes was required by April 15.

The federal government made payments in respect of provincial tax collected on a regular basis, four times per month. The payments began on an estimated basis, and the estimates were revised on a regular basis. Final adjusting payments were made 15 months after the end of the taxation year on the basis of income tax assessments by the Department of National Revenue. Since provincial payments were based on tax assessed, the federal government bore the full cost of taxes not collected. To offset this cost, the federal government retained penalties and interest imposed on delinquent taxpayers.

6

Adjusting to a New Tax System: The Tax Collection Agreements and Tax Reform, 1967-1977

During the mid-1960s, the federal and provincial governments in effect suspended their negotiations concerning the appropriate shares of revenue and expenditure for each level of government while they awaited the report of the Royal Commission on Taxation (the Carter commission).[1] Both levels expected that the commission would recommend major changes in the tax system and that negotiations would then be required to reallocate the income tax and death tax fields. Additional uncertainty arose from the fact that five provinces (Newfoundland, Prince Edward Island, Quebec, Manitoba, and British Columbia) held general elections in 1966. Under these conditions, no firm decisions could be made on the allocation of tax sources, and though the debate continued with unabated vigour serious negotiations were limited to the topics of equalization, conditional grants, and shared-cost programs.[2]

The tabling of the Carter commission report in the House of Commons in 1967 did not immediately end the suspense.[3] The pause in serious negotiations continued as the provinces waited for the federal government to formulate its response to the far-reaching proposals presented in the report. The federal government finally issued a white paper, *Proposals for Tax Reform*,[4] on November 7, 1969 and then launched a long series of hearings and discussions about its proposals. It did not present legislation embodying its final plans until June 1971. During the interval, both Ottawa and the provinces repeatedly presented their own views on the appropriate form of income and death taxes.

The September 1966 Meeting

While the federal government and the provinces waited for the Carter report, the provinces continued to press for a share of the three shared tax fields more in line with their burgeoning expenditures. The federal government remained unmoved. Finance Minister Mitchell Sharp pointed out that the tax

---

[1] Canada, *Report of the Royal Commission on Taxation* (Ottawa: Queen's Printer, 1966).

[2] Parts III and IV of this book discuss these topics in detail.

[3] Although the Carter report was published in 1966, its contents were not widely known until it was formally tabled in the Commons in February 1967.

[4] Canada, Department of Finance, *Proposals for Tax Reform* (Ottawa: Queen's Printer, November 7, 1969).

collection agreements left the participating provinces free to raise personal and corporation tax rates as they saw fit. At the same time, he announced his intention to discontinue the abatement system and leave the provinces free to set their own rates on top of a suitably reduced basic federal tax—a threat that was not implemented for six years.

The issue of federal retention of the main levers of national fiscal policy came to a head at a meeting of the Tax Structure Committee in September 1966. At that meeting, Sharp announced an end to the transfer of tax room from the federal government to the provinces when such a transfer was not offset by an equivalent reduction in federal expenditures. The federal government felt itself pushed to the limit of its ability to give up revenue to the provinces.

The minister's justification for this step is worth considering in some detail. He began by noting that the periodic negotiations over tax shares since the war had become increasingly divisive and therefore increasingly less effective. The problem that faced the committee was how all three levels of government were to finance their continually increasing expenditures. Unless the provinces had adequate access to the available sources of revenue, Sharp argued, they would "not possess that measure of fiscal strength which is an essential element of twentieth century Canadian federalism."[5] He went on to argue that the provinces did in fact have sufficient access to the revenue re-sources; the real problem was their growing need to raise tax levels that were already considered high—the same problem faced by the federal government.

Sharp noted that the provinces had greatly increased their share of the major tax fields since the war; the federal government, he said, could not reduce its share any further, since the concession of additional tax room to the provinces would imply that federal spending represented a lower national priority than provincial spending. In any case, a loss of federal taxes in one area would merely mean increased federal taxation in some other area. Thus the finance minister held firm against the provinces' calls for increased tax room, citing the ancient duty "to tax no more than we need, and to reduce taxes when we can and should."[6]

In shutting the door to future provincial requests for more tax room, Finance Minister Sharp also questioned the concept that there was some particular share of income tax and estate taxes and succession duties that was rightly federal or rightly provincial, given that both levels had constitutional rights in those fields. He went on to suggest, however, that certain taxes had "national" as opposed to "provincial" characteristics. The corporation income tax, for example, should be predominantly federal by virtue of its peculiar value as an instrument of national economic policy. Since the personal

---

[5] Canada, *Federal-Provincial Tax Structure Committee*, proceedings of a meeting held in Ottawa, September 14-15, 1966 (Ottawa: Queen's Printer, 1966), 23.

[6] Ibid., at 25.

income tax was the principal tax for redistributing income, it too ought to remain predominantly a federal tax. The personal income tax was also one of the central instruments for regulating total demand in the economy, and "Canadian governments must not allow total federal income taxes to be abated so much that they can no longer be used for this purpose."[7]

The finance minister noted that the recent opting-out arrangements with Quebec, which had increased that province's tax room, had enabled Quebec to bring its individual income tax to the same level as the federal tax. He offered the other provinces a transfer of 17 points, which would produce substantially the same results, if they followed Quebec in opting out. This transfer would reduce the federal share to the minimum that the minister felt was essential for effective federal social and economic policy.

To allow the provinces more flexibility in setting their own income tax rates (as a percentage of the federal rates), the finance minister proposed to remove the concept of "standard rates" of provincial income tax, then 24 percent, from both tax and equalization legislation.

Finally, the finance minister proposed that the Tax Structure Committee meet again to consider the reports of the various federal and provincial royal commissions on taxation.

In response, the provincial leaders quickly made the point that they regarded the shares of tax resources as fully negotiable. In his opening remarks, Ontario premier John Robarts noted that although the provinces and municipalities were responsible for the fastest growing expenditure fields— education, health, highways, and water and sewage treatment facilities—the federal government dominated the tax sources with the highest automatic rates of growth. He rejected the argument that the federal government needed at least 50 percent of the individual income tax in order to carry out its fiscal policies effectively. He also made the point that if the provinces had to resort to raising rates in their own tax fields the level and incidence of all taxation could rise to inappropriate levels and the lack of coordination could produce serious impediments to economic growth. He further argued for retention of the abatement system in order to forestall tax competition and to continue the "uneasy truce" between the 11 tax systems. Although the provinces were not legally bound to personal income tax rates equivalent to the federal abatement, they clearly found it politically difficult to diverge significantly from the abatement level.

Quebec premier Daniel Johnson took an even stronger stand. He proposed that old age security, family allowances, and related federal programs be transferred to the provinces, along with the tax room to finance them. As an interim measure for 1967-68, he called for an extra 25 percent of succession duties and the remaining corporation income tax on natural resource

---

[7] Ibid.

companies (excluding the taxes earmarked for the old age security fund). He also wanted a transfer of three points of corporate taxable income over each of the next five years, to limits by 1971-72 of 100 percent for natural resource companies and 46 percent of the total tax on corporate income—24 points—for other corporations. When the functional transfers were complete, Quebec suggested, the federal government should transfer the balance of the personal income tax and 6 more points on the general corporate income tax, for a grand total of 30 points or 58 percent of the total tax.

Manitoba's premier, Duff Roblin, had wanted the Tax Structure Committee to study priorities in government spending; because it had not, his province would make no long-term commitment. Instead, he asked for 50 percent of the individual income tax in the 1967 tax year, while all parties awaited a study of spending priorities and the findings of the Carter commission.

Premier W.A.C. Bennett of British Columbia stated that "the provinces should receive, over the next five-year period, an additional two per cent per year of personal income tax and an additional one per cent per year of corporation income tax."[8]

Saskatchewan premier Ross Thatcher explicitly refrained from asking for tax room on the condition that Saskatchewan not lose equalization. Alberta's E.C. Manning introduced a novel proposal that involved the occupancy of the personal and corporate income tax fields primarily but not exclusively by a bi-level agency. The proposal is described in chapter 9. He also proposed that the existing arrangements be extended by one year, to December 31, 1967, and that the estate tax and succession duty field be abandoned by the federal government.

Interim Arrangements

After the September 1966 meeting, the federal government and the provinces agreed to extend the existing tax arrangements to the tax years 1967 and 1968. In the fiscal years 1964-65 and 1965-66, the provinces benefited from a speed-up in the collection of corporate income taxes instituted by the federal government in its 1963 budget. This was to be the only improvement in provincial tax collections enjoyed by the provinces for several years.

Serious negotiations on tax arrangements began, somewhat belatedly, at a meeting of ministers of finance and treasurers on November 4 and 5, 1968. The federal minister of finance, Edgar Benson, proposed an indefinite extension of the tax collection agreements scheduled to expire at the end of the current year. He offered to amend the agreements so that the withholding system would respond more promptly to a change in a province's rates. Under the proposed amendment, the system would introduce any change in rates as of either July 1 or January 1, given at least 2½ months' prior notice.

---

[8] Ibid., at 106.

Indeed, Benson offered to provide for collection at new rates as soon as it was administratively feasible to do so following the introduction of the necessary provincial legislation.

Benson also spelled out the federal position on general increases in income taxes. It was one of the weaknesses of the abatement system, he noted, that the federal government could not introduce income tax measures that would affect basic federal tax (BFT) without affecting the abatements of tax room to the provinces. In the past, Ottawa had routinely introduced minor changes in the personal and corporate income tax bases (that is, changes in exemptions and deductions) without concerning itself about their effect on provincial revenues. At the November meeting, Benson undertook that any future federal tax increases would be designed to minimize "crowding out"— that is, to have as little effect as possible on provincial collections and the provinces' freedom to change their own tax rates. Thus Benson's October budget had introduced changes in the estate tax, but the changes were designed to safeguard the total provincial revenue position. By the same token, the October budget had also proposed a new tax, the social development tax, to be levied on personal income after the calculation of BFT; the purpose of the tax was to finance the federal share of the new joint program for medical insurance. Benson acknowledged that he could have achieved the same result by increasing BFT rates, a step that would have increased the value of the abatement to the provinces. Given the federal resolve not to tamper with provincial revenue, however, it would have been inappropriate to ask Parliament to take this action.

Most of the provincial representatives at the conference expressed dissatisfaction with Ottawa's decision to finance medicare through the income tax system without increasing BFT rates, since it deprived the provinces of a way of financing their own share of medicare. Ontario's treasurer condemned the decision as an attempt to coerce the provinces into entering the federal medicare program. Nova Scotia's representative asked for changes in the new social development tax that would allow the provinces to share in the proceeds.

The participants in the November conference approved new tax collection agreements that would take effect on January 1, 1969. Unlike the old agreements, the new ones were to last indefinitely. The new agreements also incorporated the amendments offered by the federal government to provide for more rapid implementation of provincial rate changes. Otherwise the new agreements differed little from their predecessors.

At a conference held on June 5 and 6, 1970, Finance Minister Benson announced that payments to the provinces under the tax collection arrangements would be accelerated by one month, a change that gave the provinces a one-time increase in revenue of $167 million[9] (as estimated in February 1971).

---

[9] Canada, Department of Finance, unpublished estimate, February 1971.

The Federal Tax Reforms

On June 18, 1971, Finance Minister Benson introduced his revised proposals for tax reform, as embodied in Bill C-259.[10] The Bill was a landmark in the history of income taxation in Canada. It also created a number of new problems in federal-provincial fiscal relations and established several important precedents. The proposed reform was so extensive that the federal government could not honour its earlier commitment to avoid changes that would affect provincial revenues. The Bill affected all of the provinces—both those that had signed collection agreements and Quebec, which was to change its system to parallel the new federal system. Controversy over the federal proposals had begun with the publication of the federal discussion paper *Proposals for Tax Reform*[11] in 1969 and did not abate until Bill C-259 was finally passed late in 1971. It took effect on January 1, 1972. The Bill was the focus of the negotiations for the 1972-1977 fiscal arrangements.

The reformed tax structure included a new and broader definition of taxable income, which included, for the first time, capital gains. Equally important were changes in the federal rate structure for personal income tax. The old age security tax and the social development tax were special federal taxes calculated, after the determination of BFT, as a flat 4 percent of taxable income to a maximum of $240 and 2 percent of taxable income to a maximum of $120, respectively. The reform incorporated these two taxes into the federal progressive rate structure before the determination of BFT, but marginal rates at the middle and top end of the income scale were lowered significantly. These changes were the first federal initiatives in the history of the tax collection system to have a major impact on the provincial yield from the personal income tax.

The federal government recognized the need for compensating provincial changes, and the provinces were not slow to calculate the effects of the federal changes on their revenues and to react accordingly.[12] The incorporation of the two special taxes and the lower marginal rates for middle- and high-income taxpayers flattened the progressive rate structure of provincial personal income taxes; consequently, lower income taxpayers would pay more provincial tax under the new system. This change was offset to a certain extent by increases in exemption levels and allowable deductions. At taxable income levels above $8,000, the provincial marginal rates were lower than they had been before the reforms, although they now applied to a base that had been expanded to include capital gains enjoyed after December 31, 1971. The net effect was to reduce collections for some provinces, increase them for others, and change (and initially lower) the elasticities for all provinces; that is, the increase in tax resulting from increases in income or

---

[10] SC 1970-71-72, c. 63.

[11] Supra footnote 4.

[12] See the statement by W.D. McKeough to the meeting of ministers of finance in Jasper, Alberta, January 31, 1972 (mimeograph).

GNP. For the first time, federal-provincial financial discussions involved computer simulations of tax collections.

Tax Reform and Provincial Personal Income Taxes

A further outcome of the reforms—one whose importance was perhaps underestimated at the time—was that the federal government abandoned the abatement system and lowered its tax rates to "make room" for a provincial surtax. This meant that the personal income tax forms no longer showed a calculation of tax based on the rate schedule, a deduction from BFT for provincial taxes, and the calculation of provincial taxes as a percentage of BFT, which could easily be compared with the federal abatement. In 1971, the taxpayer calculated BFT, deducted 28 percent, and then calculated provincial tax, often at more than 28 percent; in 1972 and subsequent years, the taxpayer calculated BFT and then simply added the appropriate provincial tax. Thus the federal government was no longer seen to be offering direct relief for provincial taxation; nor was it setting a rate for "normal" or "standard" provincial taxes—the provinces could choose any rate they desired.

At this point, however, the change was a matter more of form than of substance. The federal government set its rates with a view to the effect on provincial rates, and it was necessary, for practical purposes, to strike an equivalent to the 28 percent abatement of 1971. The federal government suggested a provincial rate of 30 percent on the revised BFT, but in a finance ministers' conference on November 2, 1971 it bowed to provincial pressure and set it at 30.5 percent.

The 1972-1977 Fiscal Arrangements

Intense study and negotiations followed the introduction of Bill C-259, and revisions to the collection agreements and stabilization agreements were worked out in conferences held on July 13 and 14 and November 1, 2, and 15 to 17, 1971. The result was submitted to Parliament on March 1, 1972 as Bill C-8, The Federal-Provincial Fiscal Arrangements Act, 1972, to cover the period 1972 to 1977.[13]

Part III of the 1972 Act extended the tax collection agreements and increased provincial flexibility. Both Manitoba and Ontario were able to provide individual income tax credits, through the federal tax collection machinery, for residential property tax. Under tax reform, the federal government withdrew from the estate and gift tax fields, and most provinces moved in to fill the gap. Those without their own collection machinery—the Atlantic provinces, Manitoba, and Saskatchewan—entered into collection agreements under which the federal government acted as their collecting agent for three years, for a fee of 3 percent. The same provinces, plus British

---

[13] Federal-Provincial Fiscal Arrangements Act, 1972, SC 1972, c. 8.

Columbia and Ontario, entered into similar arrangements, but with no fee, for provincial gift taxes.

Under the 1972-1977 arrangements, federal guarantees of provincial revenues became much more important than they had been before. The net effect of federal tax reform, once again, was to decrease substantially the elasticity of provincial personal income taxation and thus to reduce provincial revenues in the short term.[14] In agreeing to a five-year guarantee for provincial personal and corporation income taxes, the federal government acted in the belief that after five years the capital gains tax would have matured and personal incomes would have risen sufficiently to offset the other reductions. Part IV of the 1972 Act provided that provinces would not suffer a loss of income tax revenue for the five years covered by the Act as a result of adopting the new federal model. Payments would be made to the provinces if their income tax revenue fell below what it would have been had the 1971 federal income tax system been extended without change. Later in the period, the federal government gave up its original method of calculation, representative sampling of returns, in favour of an elaborate computer simulation.

In order to qualify for the revenue guarantee, a province had to levy a rate under the new system equivalent to the rate it used under the old system. Nova Scotia introduced an increase in its individual income tax rates that took effect on January 1, 1972 and so did not qualify. The 1971 provincial rates on federal basic tax on individual incomes and the equivalents for 1972 were spelled out in section 15 of the 1972 Act; they are shown in table 6.1.

The 22-percentage-point abatement allowed to Quebec in 1971 for opting out was increased to 24 points in 1972, a change spelled out in part VII of the Act. Since Quebec adopted the main components of the federal reform, it was eligible for guarantee payments.

As table 6.2 shows, the revenue guarantee under the 1972-1977 arrangements soon grew to represent a significant source of revenue for all provinces. The change in the method of calculation caused some controversy when it was introduced. The negotiations for the 1977-1982 arrangements would be made more difficult by the provinces' desire to continue this important source of revenue and the federal government's adamant assertion that it was no longer needed.

Part V of the 1972 Act introduced a new but temporary form of revenue sharing. The provinces received 20 percent of the special federal 15 percent tax on distributions of corporate income surplus built up before January 1, 1972 and paid out after that date.

---

[14] See Douglas H. Clark, "Federal-Provincial Fiscal Arrangements for the 1972-1976 Fiscal Period," in *Report of Proceedings of the Twenty-Third Tax Conference*, 1971 Conference Report (Toronto: Canadian Tax Foundation, 1972), 271-78, and David B. Perry, "Tax Reform and Provincial Tax Revenues," Fiscal Figures feature (1972), vol. 20, no. 2 *Canadian Tax Journal* 138-43.

Table 6.1 Conversion of Provincial Individual Income Tax Rates, 1972

	1971 rates as percentages of basic federal tax	1972 specific converted rates as percentages of basic federal tax
Newfoundland	33	36.0
Prince Edward Island	33	36.0
Nova Scotia	28	30.5
New Brunswick	38	41.5
Ontario	28	30.5
Manitoba	39	42.5
Saskatchewan	34	37.0
Alberta	33	36.0
British Columbia	28	30.5

Source: Douglas H. Clark, "Federal-Provincial Fiscal Arrangements for the 1972-76 Fiscal Period," in *Report of Proceedings of the Twenty-Third Tax Conference*, 1971 Conference Report (Toronto: Canadian Tax Foundation, 1972), 271-78, at 274.

Table 6.2 Provincial Revenue Guarantee Entitlements for the Fiscal Years 1972-73, 1973-74, and 1974-75[a]

	Final	Preliminary	
	1972-73	1973-74	1974-75
	$ millions		
Newfoundland	1.9	5.7	8.8
Prince Edward Island	0.4	1.2	2.1
Nova Scotia[b]	—	8.8	14.0
New Brunswick	2.5	8.3	14.7
Quebec	13.4	58.1	93.0
Ontario	50.3	127.1	140.5
Manitoba	6.5	16.4	24.0
Saskatchewan	4.5	10.5	18.0
Alberta	5.7	23.8	42.5
British Columbia	3.1	11.5	21.0
Total	88.3	271.4	378.6

[a] Figures represent entitlements for the year shown. Actual payments, made in the same or subsequent fiscal years, are shown in table 7.1 below. [b] Nova Scotia excluded itself from the guarantee program when it imposed, for the year 1972, a provincial tax rate higher than the specified converted rate, as prescribed by the Act. The Act was later amended to limit Nova Scotia's ineligibility to the first year of the guarantee only.

Source: Canada, Department of Finance, unpublished data, various years.

Federal initiatives in personal income taxation continued to provoke controversy throughout the period. The indexation of exemptions and rate brackets in 1974, another unilateral federal change, reduced provincial yields[15] substantially below the level they presumably would have achieved in its absence; nor was Ottawa willing, despite considerable provincial pressure, to provide compensation for the change under the guarantee.[16]

Tax Reform and Death Taxes

The federal tax reform included the abolition of federal estate and gift taxes. A number of provinces—Newfoundland, Prince Edward Island, Nova Scotia, New Brunswick, and Manitoba—had been enjoying their 75 percent share of federal estate taxes under the terms of the tax-sharing arrangements, and the federal government offered to enter into agreements with them to collect, for a small fee, the equivalent provincial succession duties and gift taxes, beginning in 1972. Saskatchewan had withdrawn from the field in 1969 but reentered it under this collection arrangement. Since the federal government foresaw that the taxation of capital gains would soon compensate for (and make unnecessary) death taxes, it limited its offer to three years.

Subsequent Developments

Bill C-233, introduced in 1973 to amend the Federal-Provincial Fiscal Arrangements Act, 1972, also made concomitant amendments to the Federal-Provincial Fiscal Revision Act, 1964 and the Income Tax Act.[17] The bill provided legislative authority to restore Nova Scotia to the roster of provinces that qualified for the guarantee by reducing to one year the period of ineligibility for any province that had not adopted the breakeven rates as of January 1, 1972. It also amended the Income Tax Act to permit the continuation of the abatement of three percentage points of federal income tax to Quebec associated with youth allowances under the new family allowances program. The amendment to the Fiscal Revision Act provided for recovery by the federal government from the Quebec government of an amount equivalent to the three points of personal income tax originally provided to Quebec when it opted out of the federal youth allowances program. The integrated national system of family allowances, which applied to the residents of all provinces, including Quebec, replaced the youth allowances and made the special abatement superfluous. It was continued, however, to avoid a ma-

---

[15] In all provinces except Quebec. Instead of the automatic system used by the federal government, Quebec adopted discretionary indexing, so that cabinet could set the amount, if any, by which rate bracket and exemptions would be changed.

[16] See J.R. Allan, D.A. Dodge, and S.N. Poddar, "Indexing the Personal Income Tax: A Federal Perspective" (1974), vol. 22, no. 4 *Canadian Tax Journal* 355-69, and Brian Hull and Lawrence Leonard, "Indexing the Personal Income Tax: An Ontario Perspective" (1974), vol. 22, no. 4 *Canadian Tax Journal* 370-77.

[17] An Act To Amend the Federal-Provincial Fiscal Arrangements Act, 1972, the Federal-Provincial Fiscal Revision Act, 1964, and the Income Tax Act, SC 1973-74, c. 45.

jor redesigning of the Quebec personal income tax system, and the equivalent value of the abatement was deducted from other payments to the province.

The second piece of legislation was introduced in 1975. Bill C-57[18] established that there would be no compensation under the income tax guarantees for provincial losses attributable to indexation of the personal income tax system or to corporation income tax measures designed to offset the non-deductibility of provincial natural resource levies.

In December 1974, Finance Minister John Turner stated that in his view it was possible to relax somewhat the rigid federal guidelines imposed on the design of the personal and corporate tax systems of agreeing provinces without distorting or damaging the overall system. This concession enabled provinces such as Ontario and Manitoba to introduce personal income tax credit systems that were integrated with the income tax system. Turner's conditions for approving provisions were that they should not jeopardize the main features of the federal tax system, strain the tolerance of taxpayers, or overburden the capacity of the federal collection machinery. The federal government charged a fee of 1 percent of the value of provincial credits, which by 1975 it was administering for Ontario, Manitoba, Saskatchewan, Alberta, and British Columbia.

[18] An Act To Amend the Federal-Provincial Fiscal Arrangements Act, 1972, SC 1974-75-76, c. 65.

7

Revenue Sharing Reaches Its Limits: 1977-1997

The summer and fall of 1976 was a period of intense negotiation between Ottawa and the provinces on the shape of the fiscal arrangements that would take effect on April 1, 1977.

The federal government presented its basic position to a meeting of first ministers held on June 14 and 15, 1976. The federal position emphasized Ottawa's desire to revise its method of sharing the costs of established joint programs,[1] which principally involved the concession of additional tax room to the provinces. The provinces, however, expressed more interest in another matter—the income tax revenue guarantee that the federal government had introduced in 1972 to ease the provinces' adjustment to tax reform.

The revenue guarantee was scheduled to expire in 1977, and at the June meeting Prime Minister Pierre Trudeau made clear his government's determination not to renew it. The provincial premiers were equally strong in their opposition to the demise of the guarantee, which had become a significant source of provincial revenue. They were reinforced in their resolve by the fact that indexation of the personal income tax was reducing provincial revenues but was not included among the tax changes covered by the revenue guarantee. It was the first major unilateral federal tax change to affect the provincial tax base. British Columbia wanted full compensation for the revenue loss that had resulted from federal income tax changes since 1971. The province's 1977 budget noted that "[o]nly at the conclusion of the first ministers' meeting [in December 1976] did British Columbia yield on this point, and then only to safeguard the national tax collection system."[2]

Provincial feeling was so strong after the June meeting that at a meeting in Edmonton in August 1976 the 10 provincial premiers decided to explore the possibility of developing a provincial consensus. The provincial ministers of finance and treasurers, meeting on September 14 and October 20, formulated a single set of proposals for presentation at a federal-provincial conference of finance ministers and treasurers to be held in Ottawa on December 6 and 7, 1976. The presentation dealt with three major issues: equalization,[3] established programs financing,[4] and the revenue guarantee.

---

[1] The federal proposals are described in chapter 15.

[2] British Columbia, Ministry of Finance, Budget, January 24, 1977, 11.

[3] Discussed in chapter 9.

[4] Discussed in chapter 15.

The Revenue Guarantee Negotiations

There had been no expectation at the start that the income tax revenue guarantee provided under the 1972-1977 arrangements would involve substantial amounts of money. By 1973, however, it had become obvious that tax reform was producing large provincial revenue losses, and the cost of the guarantee, as table 7.1 shows, was rising commensurately. The federal minister of finance, John Turner, acknowledged publicly in May 1973 that all of the provinces would face a difficult problem of adjustment when the guarantee came to an end; he promised to consult with the provinces on some concrete proposals. No proposals emerged, however, until 1976: at a meeting of federal and provincial finance ministers and treasurers held on April 1 and 2, a new federal finance minister, Donald Macdonald, offered a form of budget-to-budget revenue guarantee and promised that he would try, wherever possible, to implement federal income tax policy in a way that would leave the provincial systems unaffected.

The provinces considered these proposals to be matters for further discussion; their attention was centred on the existing guarantee payments. They estimated that the value of the personal income tax component of the guarantee in 1976 was about $800 million—about 18 percent of provincial revenue from personal income tax—and stressed the rapid increase in entitlements since 1973.

At the June 1976 first ministers' meeting, the premier of British Columbia, William Bennett, reiterated his province's dissatisfaction with a federal decision to change, retroactively, the manner in which the guarantee was calculated for the years 1974 to 1976. Ottawa had made the change when it discovered that the original formula was biased—expensively—in the provinces' favour. Premier Bennett also pressed for the continuation of the guarantee beyond 1976—a matter that had already been discussed at a conference of western premiers in April. The premiers made it clear at the June meeting that revisions of the guarantee payments were "totally unacceptable," and they asked for fulfilment of the 1973 commitment to compensate provinces for changes in the new Income Tax Act. They also called for both increased provincial flexibility (under the tax collection agreements) in the design of the tax system and greater insulation from the effects of unilateral federal tax changes. All of the western premiers expressed dissatisfaction with the current income allocation formulas for corporation income taxes, a dissatisfaction shared by New Brunswick. At the June conference, Premier Allan Blakeney of Saskatchewan suggested that the provinces be given additional tax points to make up for deficiencies in past revenue guarantee payments and that the system continue with 1976 as the base year.

The revenue guarantee was a critical part of the bargaining that ended at the December first ministers' meeting, which gave final form to the first Established Programs Financing (EPF) agreement. The provinces recognized that the guarantee program could not continue in its present form, but they did not want to increase the total tax burden by increasing their own taxes.

Table 7.1 Revenue Guarantee Payments Under the 1972-1977 Arrangements

	1973-74	1974-75	1975-76	1976-77	1977-78	1978-79	1979-80	Total for period
				millions of dollars				
Newfoundland	0.8	10.7	10.1	18.6	13.3	3.2	2.2	58.9
Prince Edward Island	0.2	2.4	2.2	4.0	2.7	0.6	0.3	12.4
Nova Scotia	na	15.0	14.7	25.3	18.4	3.8	2.5	79.7
New Brunswick	1.2	16.3	14.1	21.3	16.4	3.2	2.7	75.2
Quebec	5.0	107.4	100.4	219.5	143.9	31.5	22.2	629.9
Ontario	22.3	206.9	192.1	379.4	210.4	43.6	9.5	1,064.2
Manitoba	3.9	29.3	26.5	41.2	31.4	5.4	5.7	143.4
Saskatchewan	2.3	20.9	18.3	39.0	38.2	2.5	3.8	125.0
Alberta	5.2	43.9	42.0	73.3	66.3	14.8	7.6	253.1
British Columbia	1.7	22.5	40.1	121.6	59.5	13.2	15.7	274.3
Total	42.6	475.2	460.5	943.1	600.4	121.6	72.1	2,715.5
As a percentage of provincial revenue from personal income tax	1.0	8.5	7.2	12.3	6.3	1.1	0.6	

Source: Public Accounts of Canada, various years, and Statistics Canada, *Public Finance Historical Data, 1965-66 to 1991-92*, catalogue no. 68-512, March 1992.

Their joint presentation called for an additional four-percentage-point abatement of personal income tax, equalized to the national average. They calculated that a four-point abatement would be equivalent to the personal income tax element of the guarantee in 1976, or to about 80 percent of the combined personal and corporate income tax guarantee entitlements. The federal government estimated that the proposed abatement would cost $860 million in 1977-78 and $5.5 billion over the five years of the proposed arrangements. The federal argument was that the revenue guarantee had been designed to protect the provinces against the uncertainties of the new income tax system, uncertainties that had now disappeared. The federal government offered a limited guarantee: if a change in federal legislation reduced a province's yield by more than 1 percent of federal basic tax, Ottawa would provide compensation equal to the amount in excess of 1 percent for the first year of the change—after which the provinces could amend their own income tax act to recapture the lost revenue.

In a compromise reached at the December meeting, the provinces accepted the limited guarantee and, in place of a continuation of the 1972 revenue guarantee, an additional federal withdrawal from the personal income tax of 1 percentage point plus the equivalent in cash. These two transfers were incorporated into the EPF formula; that is, the income-tax point was equalized to the national average and the cash ($7.92 per capita for 1977-78) was escalated by the EPF escalators. It was not possible to forecast the value of the limited guarantee, but it was forecast that the value of the additions to the EPF formula would be $400 million in 1977-78.[5]

The federal government retained the guarantee, albeit in a limited form, to encourage agreeing provinces to adhere to a relatively uniform tax system. For this reason, it extended the limited guarantee to Quebec's personal income tax. In the event, Ottawa made no payments to any province under the revised revenue guarantee program during the 1977-1982 period.

The Tax Collection Agreements—1977-1982

The tax collection agreements were extended for the period 1977-1982 with very few changes. One new development was the signing of agreements with the territories; the agreement with the Northwest Territories took effect beginning in 1978 and the agreement with the Yukon in 1980.

The federal government continued in this period to view the tax collection system favourably, though without overlooking its shortcomings—in particular, the constraints on federal revenue and federal flexibility occasioned by the fact that any changes in the definition of taxable income or the basic rate structure affected provincial taxes.

---

[5] Estimate developed from projections in Canada, Department of Finance, *Financial Assessment of EPF Proposals* (Ottawa: the department, November 1976).

The provinces too were aware of the constraints implicit in the collection agreements. As income taxes became increasingly important to the provinces, they became increasingly eager to use these taxes as instruments of social and economic policy. Since the early 1970s, Ottawa had responded to the provincial pressure for greater flexibility by allowing the provinces to introduce, under the tax collection agreements, a variety of special income tax provisions—surtaxes, credits, low-income relief, and dual rates for corporations. The federal government used three criteria in considering a provincial request for the introduction of a special provision: administrative feasibility, protection of the harmony of the national tax system, and the "efficient functioning of the Canadian economic union."[6]

By 1980, however, the federal government had become concerned about the cumulative effect of the special provisions. Revenue Canada was, in effect, called upon to administer several different tax systems simultaneously. The net effect of several special provisions within one province might be a pattern of tax incidence at odds with the goal of harmony in the national tax system. Special provisions introduced by one province might put pressure on other provinces to compete. The federal government steadfastly refused to administer tax measures that amounted to discriminatory tax treatment. Thus it rejected proposals by British Columbia in 1980 for special dividend tax credits for firms based in British Columbia and for small business venture capital. Revenue Canada agreed to administer Saskatchewan's mortgage interest tax credit but refused to accommodate its special exemption for provincial income tax on capital gains from certain non-rental residential properties, farms, and small businesses. The province had to refund the amounts directly to the taxpayers.

In a 1975 position paper, Alberta detailed its case for setting up its own corporate income tax system.[7] The province did not feel that the allocation formula treated Alberta's industries, or Alberta itself, equitably. It also noted that a flexible provincial system could take better account of problems and opportunities unique to the province. Alberta hoped to translate its non-renewable resources into long-term gains by using its ample revenue from the oil and gas industry to promote industrial diversification, and incentives delivered through the corporate income tax system could be an effective means of encouraging such diversification. The federal government did not respond favourably to suggestions for increased provincial flexibility within the collection agreements; Alberta took itself out of the agreement with respect to corporation income taxes and on January 1, 1981 began collecting its own tax.

---

[6] Canada, Department of Finance, *Federal-Provincial Fiscal Arrangements in the Eighties: A Submission to the Parliamentary Task Force on the Federal-Provincial Fiscal Arrangements* (Ottawa: the department, April 1981), 54.

[7] Alberta, Treasury Department, *Basic Objectives and Terms of Reference for Alberta's Business Taxation and Incentives: A Position Paper of the Government of Alberta Based on the Recommendations of the Provincial Treasurer's Tax Advisory Committee* (Edmonton: the department, January 1975).

Reciprocal Taxation

In summarizing the proceedings of the finance ministers' conference of January 18 and 19, 1973, Finance Minister Turner noted that the federal government was negotiating reciprocal taxation agreements with a number of provinces, to take effect by April 1, 1974. In fact, it was not until 1977 that six provinces agreed to end the established practice of exempting each level of government from consumption taxes levied by the other. Under the agreements, implemented in part VIII of the 1977 fiscal arrangements and EPF legislation,[8] federal and provincial consumption taxes would apply to the two levels of government in the same manner as they applied to the private sector. The aim was to eliminate the distortions in the economy and particularly in the allocation of resources that had been caused by the exemption of government from general taxation.

The original signing provinces in 1977 were Newfoundland, Prince Edward Island, Nova Scotia, New Brunswick, Quebec, and Ontario. Manitoba and British Columbia signed agreements in 1983. Alberta refrained from signing because it had no retail sales tax, and it dropped its tax on motor fuel for road vehicles in 1978. The agreement with Quebec differed from those signed with the other eight provinces in that it excluded provincial taxes on tobacco, meals, and hotel accommodation. The agreements required the provinces to refrain from claiming refunds of federal sales and excise taxes. For its part, the federal government agreed to pay, through its suppliers, provincial motor fuel taxes, tobacco taxes, amusement taxes, and sales taxes on building materials purchased by contractors working under federal contracts. It would also pay taxes on meals and accommodation purchased by federal employees in travel status. In making a purchase in a given province, Ottawa would maintain its exemption from the applicable ad valorem retail sales tax by quoting a provincial sales tax licence. The Intergovernmental Taxation Centre of the federal Department of Finance would then calculate the tax that would have been due had the purchase been made in the province of end use and remit an equivalent amount to that province. Motor vehicle registration fees would be calculated in the same manner, with adjustments for nominal amounts paid by individual departments.

The reciprocal taxation agreements covered only consumption taxes; there remained the contentious issue of the federal liability for provincial payroll taxes. The issue first arose in 1970, when Quebec began to finance hospital and medical insurance from taxes levied on individual incomes and employer payrolls rather than from general revenues. The federal government refused to pay taxes on its payroll, arguing that it had no constitutional obligation to do so; the province disagreed. Late in 1976, the federal government agreed to pay the provincial levy, including the amounts that the province claimed for 1975-76 and 1976-77, but continued to reject the notion that it had a con-

---

[8] Federal-Provincial Fiscal Arrangements and Established Programs Financing Act, 1977, SC 1976-77, c. 10.

stitutional obligation to pay. It refused to admit liability for the period 1970 to March 1975—a liability that the province estimated to be $19 million, as of 1976.

Quebec continued to push unsuccessfully for formal recognition of a federal obligation to pay. It was joined by Manitoba in 1982 and by Newfoundland and Ontario in 1990. After some consideration, the federal government agreed to pay the levies imposed by these three provinces on an interim basis, without conceding any legal obligation to pay. It agreed to undertake a review of its policy regarding provincial payroll taxes, but the review is not yet complete. Meanwhile, the interim arrangements continue.

The introduction of the federal goods and services tax (GST) in 1991 automatically terminated the reciprocal taxation agreements. The GST legislation specifically excludes provincial governments from the GST, and the federal government remains exempt from provincial retail sales taxes. Three new types of agreement have been negotiated. Under the first, the provinces and the federal government pay each other's specific commodity taxes (such as gasoline, tobacco, and alcohol taxes) but not the GST or retail sales tax. All indirect government purchases, such as travel and accommodation expenses incurred by employees, are subject to the GST, provincial retail sales taxes, and any relevant specific taxes. Newfoundland, Prince Edward Island, Nova Scotia, Quebec, Ontario, Manitoba, and British Columbia have concluded agreements based on this model. The second type of agreement provides that neither level of government will pay any commodity taxes, general or specific, imposed by the other level. Saskatchewan and the territories operate under this arrangement. The third type of agreement, unlike the first two, involves no formal arrangement: administrative decisions provide exemptions. In New Brunswick, each level pays the other's specific commodity taxes. In that province, and in Alberta, indirect purchases are taxable. Since the amounts payable by the two levels are approximately the same under all three arrangements, there are no federal payments. Table 7.2 summarizes the payments made under the reciprocal taxation agreements until their termination in 1991.

Transfers of Taxes on Public Utilities

The 1977-1982 arrangements continued the long-established transfer to the provinces of a share of the federal income tax on privately owned public utilities—a share that had increased from 50 percent to 95 percent as of January 1, 1966. In August and September 1978, the federal government introduced a series of austerity measures that included the elimination of the transfer of the federal tax. After negotiations with the provinces, it agreed instead to reduce the transfer from 95 to 50 percent. The necessary legislation encountered various delays, however, and in December 1980 the federal government withdrew it. The transfer was restored, retroactively, to 95 percent. Extra payments were made in 1980-81 to compensate the provinces for the payments made on the 50-percent basis in the two previous fiscal years.

**Table 7.2   Federal Payments to the Provinces Under
the Reciprocal Taxation Agreements**

Fiscal year	Total payments, $ millions
1977-78	46.6
1978-79	100.4
1979-80	105.3
1980-81	145.3
1981-82	141.4
1982-83	157.4
1983-84	197.9
1984-85	209.0
1985-86	242.8
1986-87	255.6
1987-88	261.1
1988-89	294.1
1989-90	319.1
1990-91	247.2
Total	2,723.3

Source: Public Accounts of Canada, various years.

At present, payments are made to eight provinces and the two territories. Nova Scotia and New Brunswick have no privately owned utilities. Alberta passes the federal money to the utilities along with a refund of its own corporation income tax and has legislation that requires the companies to pass these amounts to their customers, usually in the form of lower rates.

In 1990, another federal exercise in spending restraint froze the transfers of the income tax on privately owned public utilities at the 1989-90 dollar level until the end of 1995-96. The 1995 federal budget eliminated the transfers completely.

Transfers of Part V Taxes

The 1977-1982 arrangements continued the transfer to the provinces of 20 percent of the yield of a special federal tax of 15 percent on corporate distributions of income that a corporation had not distributed before the end of its 1971 taxation year. This section of the federal Income Tax Act was repealed effective December 31, 1978. Payments for the 1978 tax year were made in June 1980, and a smaller payment was made in June 1981 in respect of companies whose taxation year ended in 1979. Very small payments were made in subsequent years with respect to a few retroactive elections to distribute corporate income in this manner.

The 1978 Sales Tax Reduction Program

In his 1978 budget, the federal minister of finance, Jean Chrétien, introduced an innovation in federal-provincial tax sharing. To stimulate a flagging national economy, he proposed to finance a temporary reduction in provincial retail sales taxes.[9] He offered to provide full compensation for a reduction of 3 percentage points, to last six months, for the Atlantic provinces and a reduction of 2 percentage points, also for six months, for the other provinces that imposed retail sales taxes, provided that these provinces financed an additional 1-point reduction or extended the 2-point reduction for an additional three months. The compensation would take the form of a one-time abatement of 1978 federal personal income tax, to a maximum of $100 per taxpayer; the provinces would pick up the resulting amount directly through their own personal income tax systems. If this amount failed to cover the loss of sales tax revenue, Ottawa would make up the deficiency with cash grants.

Because the minister had chosen to introduce the measure in a budget, he had been constrained by secrecy rules from discussing it explicitly with the provincial governments before he introduced it. He claimed to have recruited provincial cooperation in informal discussions just before the budget speech, but this claim was disputed by Quebec. Bitter debate followed, since Quebec rejected an across-the-board reduction in its sales tax in favour of full exemptions for clothing, footwear, textiles, and some household furniture. The federal government initially refused to compensate the province but eventually settled on a special abatement of $85 for each Quebec resident who paid 1978 federal income tax. The province made no commitment to pick up that specific amount through its personal income tax, and in the event it chose to raise the revenue from other taxes.

The other provinces accepted the federal proposal, and the initiative worked smoothly outside of Quebec. In Quebec's case, however, the result of this bold experiment in federal-provincial tax coordination was increased tension between the province and the federal government. No similar measure has been introduced since.

The Tax Collection Agreements, 1982-1997

Much of the description of events to this point has turned on the changes effected through the tax agreements. The shift in resources between the federal government and the provinces in the 1960s and 1970s took the form of transfers of tax room from the former to the latter, and the tax collection agreements played a prominent role in this process. By the late 1970s, however, other collection arrangements were becoming far more important than the tax agreements, a change signified by the indefinite extension of the agreements in their existing form in 1977. Since then, debate about the tax agreements has centred on the procedures under which the federal government administers the income tax statutes of the provinces and the territories, and on the degree of flexibility permissible in provincial income taxes.

---

[9] For a full discussion of this measure, see Jean-Marie Dufour and François Vaillancourt, "Federal and Provincial Sales Taxes: Evidence of Their Effects and Prospect for Change," in Wayne R. Thirsk and John Whalley, eds., *Tax Policy Options in the 1980s*, Canadian Tax Paper no. 66 (Toronto: Canadian Tax Foundation, 1982), 408-36, at 413-15.

In recent years, the most important changes in the agreements have reflected the continuing effort by the provinces to modify their personal income tax systems, in order to promote various social and economic goals, by adopting special tax provisions (although as was noted above not all of these provisions have been successfully accommodated within the collection agreements). In some cases, a province has concluded that the incidence of the tax system adopted for the nation as a whole is inappropriate to its particular circumstances and has introduced special tax reductions to lower the tax on low-income taxpayers, surtaxes to increase the tax on high-income taxpayers, or flat taxes to flatten the overall incidence. In other cases, a province has adopted special credits designed to encourage, for example, contributions to political parties, investments in venture capital companies, or investments in companies with headquarters in the province. The result has been the complex set of provincial special measures, administered by the federal government, shown in tables 7.3 and 7.4. Ottawa has charged an administrative fee for some of these provisions.

The federal government has been willing to accommodate the various provincial innovations because none of them affect the definition, fundamental to the existing collection agreements, of provincial tax as a tax on basic federal tax. The tax-on-tax approach limits provincial flexibility in designing income taxation to suit particular provincial needs but preserves the fundamental harmony of the joint federal-provincial system.

This approach has not satisfied the provinces, however. In the past several years, the western provinces in particular have pressed for changes in the collection agreements that would allow them to levy their tax on taxable

Table 7.3 Provincial Rates, Reductions, and Surtaxes, 1990

Province	Basic tax rate percent	Low-income tax reductions	Surtaxes[a] Rate, percent	Surtaxes[a] Threshold, dollars
Newfoundland	62.0	—	—	—
Prince Edward Island	57.0	—	10	12,500
Nova Scotia	59.5	—	10	10,000
New Brunswick	60.0	—	—	—
Ontario	53.0	Yes	10	10,000
Manitoba	52.0	Yes	2[b]	30,000[c]
Saskatchewan	50.0	Yes	12[d]	4,000
Alberta	46.5	Yes	8	3,500
British Columbia	51.5	—	—	—
Yukon	45.0	—	—	—
Northwest Territories	44.0	—	—	—

[a] Unless noted otherwise, the surtax rate is applicable to basic provincial tax and the threshold is in dollars of basic provincial tax. [b] The Manitoba surtax rate applies to net income. [c] The Manitoba threshold refers to net income and varies with individual and family circumstances. [d] Saskatchewan's basic provincial tax includes amounts in respect of flat taxes.

Source: Canada, Department of Finance, *Personal Income Tax Coordination: The Federal-Provincial Tax Collection Agreements* (Ottawa: the department, June 1991), 20, table 1.

Table 7.4 Provincial Tax Credits, 1990

	Income-tested	Economic development	Other
Newfoundland		Stock savings plan Venture capital	
Prince Edward Island			Political contribution
Nova Scotia	Home ownership savings plan	Stock savings plan	Political contribution
New Brunswick		Stock savings plan	Political contribution
Ontario	Home ownership savings plan Property and sales tax		Political contribution
Manitoba	Property tax Cost of living		Political contribution Royalty tax rebate
Saskatchewan		Stock savings plan Venture capital Labour-sponsored venture capital	Royalty tax rebate
Alberta			Political contribution Royalty tax credit Royalty tax rebate
British Columbia	Renters' reduction	Venture capital Employee share ownership plan Employee venture capital	Political contribution Royalty tax rebate
Yukon			Political contribution
Northwest Territories			Political contribution

Source: Same as table 7.3, at 22, table 2.

income, as defined in the federal legislation, rather than on basic federal tax. In response to this increasing pressure, the federal government announced in its 1991 budget that it would study the possibility of changing the collection agreements. The resulting discussion paper, released in June 1991,[10] examined the possibility of changing the provincial personal income tax from a tax on the federal tax to a tax (or taxes) on taxable income, like the federal tax itself. Tax collection agreements constituted on this basis would allow the provinces to set their own rate schedules, within prescribed limits, and to

---

[10] Canada, Department of Finance, *Personal Income Tax Coordination: The Federal-Provincial Tax Collection Agreements* (Ottawa: the department, June 1991).

determine the levels of their non-refundable personal tax credits. The provinces would have more flexibility in their income tax structures than they have been able to achieve with their elaborate systems of flat taxes, surtaxes, tax reductions, and tax credits. By accommodating provincial needs, the adoption under the agreement of a tax-on-base approach might forestall the establishment of completely separate provincial income tax systems. Such a change would make the design of provincial tax systems more transparent, but it would keep the close coordination of the federal and provincial systems intact and maintain the advantages to taxpayers of joint collection. The discussion paper made no recommendations, however, and a subsequent report prepared by a group of tax practitioners concerned itself chiefly with identifying the technical difficulties inherent in such a change.[11] As of this writing, there is no indication whether any changes will be made in the collection agreements.

The GST

In 1991, Ottawa replaced its long-established and long-derided manufacturers' sales tax with a value-added tax—the goods and services tax (GST). For the first time, federal sales taxes appeared on invoices and receipts, at a rate of 7 percent, side by side with the retail sales taxes levied since the late 1950s and early 1960s by all of the provinces except Alberta. The provincial sales taxes gave Canadians a familiar standard against which to judge the new federal tax, and most of them found it wanting. The primary objection to the GST was that its coverage was broader than that of the provincial taxes. In particular, the latter generally exempted services; the GST did not.

It had been Ottawa's expectation that the provinces would quickly adapt their retail sales taxes to the new, state-of-the-art GST and accept federal administration of a harmonized federal/provincial sales tax. Nor did the federal authorities anticipate any great difficulty in persuading the provinces to take this step. Indeed, two provinces, Prince Edward Island and Saskatchewan, initially indicated a willingness to harmonize their sales taxes with the GST in a system administered by the federal government. When they saw the public reaction to the GST, however, they quickly changed their plans. Only Quebec accepted the federal proposal, and at a price: instead of agreeing to federal administration of a combined federal/provincial GST, Quebec prevailed upon Ottawa to allow it to collect both the GST and the province's own new tax, a form of partial VAT.

In April 1997, after years of coaxing and negotiation, Ottawa was able to welcome three provinces—New Brunswick, Nova Scotia, and Newfoundland—into participation in a "harmonized sales tax" (HST) administered by Revenue Canada. As in the case of Quebec, however, this compliance came

---

[11] Advisory Committee on Federal-Provincial Tax Collection Agreements, *Report*, January 1992.

at a price. In order to reconcile their constituents to the new arrangement, the three provinces in effect dropped their own sales tax rates from 11 percent (in New Brunswick and Nova Scotia) and 12 percent (in Newfoundland) to 8 percent. In combination with the GST rate of 7 percent, the result was a rate for the HST of 15 percent. The federal government agreed to provide the three provinces with a subsidy of almost $1 billion over four years to cushion the shock to provincial revenues. The subsidy was available to any province that by adopting an 8 percent provincial rate within the GST system would suffer a drop in provincial sales tax revenue of at least 5 percent.

News of this subsidy was not well received by the three provinces that did not qualify for it—Quebec, Ontario, and British Columbia—or by Alberta, which had no sales tax and no intention of introducing one.

Conclusion

After the conclusion of the negotiations for the 1977-1982 period, the federal government would no longer offer additional tax room to the provinces. In fact, Ottawa was not in a position to offer the provinces additional resources in any form. The federal government turned instead to fine-tuning the cash transfers to ensure that it was able to meet its minimum objectives in the most economical fashion. In subsequent years, therefore, concern about the provision of adequate assistance to the provinces focused not on taxes but rather on equalization, stabilization, and established programs financing. In the area of taxes, the emphasis in federal-provincial negotiations shifted from provincial demands for more tax room to increasingly technical discussions of the design of the tax system.

The years after 1977 also saw several new ventures in federal-provincial cooperation, including a joint effort to cope with the petroleum crisis of the late 1970s and early 1980s—an effort that began in acrimony and ended in reasonable harmony; the tax aspect of this episode is covered in the next chapter. Of more enduring importance was the development of the nascent equalization program into a full-scale effort to compensate for all of the major differences in revenue potential among the provinces. Equalization eventually became one of the largest items in the federal budget.

Ottawa and the provinces continued to share expenditures through the traditional method of jointly financed programs, and a new method of cost-sharing, one that involved the exchange of tax space for federal cash payments to finance established programs, was devised to meet the needs of Quebec and later modified and extended to all provinces. All of these subjects, of immense importance in the Canadian federal-provincial scene, are dealt with in the chapters that follow.

8

Natural Resource Taxation: A Special Case

The post-war evolution of the personal and corporation income tax systems proceeded within guidelines that both the federal government and the provinces respected, and competition for the tax dollar between the two levels of government was minimal. But there were no guidelines, and there was a great deal of competition, in the evolution of federal and provincial taxation of the natural resource industries—forestry, mining, and petroleum and natural gas. There were only two main speakers in the income tax debate—the federal government and the provinces; there were three and often four in the debate on the taxation of natural resources—the two levels of government, the companies, and, much of the time, the courts.

The problems that would have arisen in any case in the complex area of resource taxation were complicated by the dual status of the provinces vis à vis the natural resources within their boundaries. In addition to their normal taxing powers under the constitution, the provinces also possessed the rights associated with the ownership of these resources. Thus they could extract both taxes and a return as proprietors. This state of affairs resulted in provincial resource revenue systems that were usually part tax systems and part royalty systems, an arrangement that gave great flexibility to the provinces that had retained ownership of substantial resources but also complicated the relationship between the federal and provincial systems.

In the late 1960s, as each of the two levels of government sought to increase its resource revenues at the expense of the other, this relationship became increasingly contentious. In the 1970s, with the tenfold increase in international oil prices inspired by the Organization of Petroleum Exporting Countries (OPEC), the friction between the two levels became severe. The situation was further complicated by efforts at both levels to increase Canadian petroleum production and by federal measures to alleviate the effects of oil price rises in the consuming areas of the country. This state of affairs persisted until 1985, when the collapse of international petroleum prices produced a different set of problems.

The details of the resource-related programs developed by the two levels during the 1970s and early 1980s are beyond the scope of this book. This chapter provides a brief outline of these programs.

The Petroleum Battle

The battle between the federal government and the producing provinces—primarily Saskatchewan and Alberta—over control of petroleum
resources and revenues was joined in earnest with the OPEC price rise of
1973 and the ensuing general international price rise of 1974. At the outset,
the federal government and the major oil-producing provinces agreed to a
uniform price system for crude oil and natural gas that was designed to
shelter domestic consumers from the full effects of the rise in the world price.
The federal government froze the domestic price at a level below the
prevailing world price and introduced a subsidy for refineries in eastern
Canada, which used imported rather than domestic oil. The subsidy was
initially funded by a federal oil export tax (shared with the producing
provinces). This tax was later replaced by a charge (not shared), which was
eventually augmented by a tax on gasoline for personal use.

When the oil price freeze and import subsidies were introduced, Canada
was exporting more crude oil and refined products than it imported and
natural gas was significantly underpriced, in terms of its energy potential,
relative to oil. Thus any longer-term response to the energy situation would
inevitably involve a realignment of crude oil and natural gas prices and a
revision of the oil import compensation program. The price freeze made it
possible to conduct federal-provincial negotiations without severe pressure
of time.

As the price of oil rose dramatically, the producing provinces and the
federal government began to jockey for position in the energy field. Both
sides aspired to rate-setting and tax powers; each side was concerned about
the other's moves.

Saskatchewan took the position in late 1973 that it ought to receive the
proceeds of the oil export tax for oil extracted in Saskatchewan and pressed
Ottawa for the monies collected. It introduced a taxation bill of its own that
made the provincial oil tax equal to the difference between the going price
and a set wellhead price. To forestall a federal judicial challenge on jurisdiction, the bill would also have given the province control over oil production and ownership of all major oil and gas reserves (with compensation to existing owners). Producers would enjoy a reduction in the provincial tax of up to 50 percent for money spent on exploration and development
in Saskatchewan.

In late 1973, Premier Peter Lougheed of Alberta called a special "energy"
session of the legislature. The purpose of the session was to secure for the
province both an increase in revenues from oil production and firm control of
marketing. Legislation to set royalty rates was not yet ready for passage, but
the government did set up a new provincial marketing agency, the Alberta
Petroleum Marketing Commission, to establish wellhead prices and control
oil marketing in the province. The commission did not exercise its power to
set wellhead prices, but the threat remained.

At the insistence of the provinces, the first ministers met in Ottawa on January 22 and 23, 1974 to discuss the energy situation. This meeting, the first major conference on energy, and on crude oil and natural gas pricing in particular, failed to produce a consensus or any major conclusions, despite the fact that most provinces supported the federal government's basic energy strategy, as outlined by Minister of Energy, Mines and Resources Donald S. Macdonald. This strategy called for the establishment of domestic price levels for crude oil and natural gas that were both high enough to encourage national self-sufficiency and uniform (net of transportation costs) across the country. To ensure uniformity, Ottawa would provide subsidies for eastern users of imported oil. The "windfall" from the inevitable price increases would be divided between the producers, the producing provinces, and the federal government, which needed the funds not only for its import subsidies but also for the purpose of redressing, through its equalization program, the growing disparity between the revenues of the producing provinces and those of the non-producing provinces.

Disagreements arose over both the price level to be struck—the federal government and the eastern provinces hoped for prices well below international levels, whereas the West generally argued for higher prices—and the division of the "windfall" revenues from the higher oil and gas prices. Thus Alberta opposed the federal oil export tax as discriminatory, since no such tax was applied to other energy exports, such as electricity, and as contrary to the spirit and intent of Confederation. Saskatchewan argued that the oil import compensation program should be financed from general revenues, rather than from oil exports only. Most of the provinces were opposed to excluding the proceeds of the oil export tax from the equalization formula.[1]

The conference ended with little resolved. The price freeze, at $4 per barrel, was to continue until the end of March, but Saskatchewan was permitted to raise its price to $5 ($6 on exports) in accordance with revisions already enacted in provincial legislation. A continuing committee of the 11 energy ministers was to pursue the search for a longer-term solution.

Bilateral negotiations between the federal government and each of the producing provinces preceded an informal meeting of first ministers on March 27, 1974 that decided on a system of pricing and revenue-sharing for the period April 1, 1974 to June 30, 1975. It was agreed that the national uniform price would be $6.50 per barrel plus transportation costs. The federal government agreed to replace the oil export tax with an oil export charge (at rates to be set by the cabinet rather than enshrined in legislation), which Ottawa would use exclusively to finance compensation for the cost in excess of $10 per barrel of oil imported into eastern Canada. The increase in the wellhead price would go to the producing provinces, to be distributed at their

---

[1] Part III, below, discusses the implications of the oil export tax for the equalization formula.

discretion, but the bulk of the revenue retained by the provinces would be put into capital accounts. Only a much smaller portion would go into general revenue, and only this amount would be subject to equalization. An additional feature of the 1974 agreement was the participation of the federal, Alberta, and Ontario governments in a consortium to build a plant—the so-called Syncrude plant—to extract bitumen from the oil sands deposits in northern Alberta.

The agreement did not work well for the federal government. Oil exports declined as domestic demand increased, and they were soon exceeded by imports. Thus federal revenue from the oil export charge fell short of federal expenditure on oil import compensation. The producing provinces, meanwhile, increased their royalties and prices substantially, in some cases taking 100 percent of the price increase. These provincial charges substantially reduced taxable corporation income for federal tax purposes, and the federal government was not slow to halt the erosion.

Federal Protective Measures

The 1971 tax reform legislation[2] had included measures intended primarily to protect the federal tax base against growing provincial resource levies, which were deductible from federal taxable income. The 1971 legislation provided that after 1976 such levies would not be allowed as a deduction for federal corporate income tax purposes. In lieu of the deduction, taxpayers would be given an abatement of 15 percentage points of taxable income. Despite this measure, or perhaps because of it, the inroads made on the federal corporate income tax by increased provincial royalty and tax rates had become so extensive by 1974 that the federal government advanced the disallowance to 1974. The deduction of provincial natural resource taxes and royalties was disallowed, and the depletion allowance was replaced by a system of earned depletion. Effective May 6, 1974, Ottawa raised its corporation income tax rate on resource profits to 50 percent and introduced a system of abatements for oil and gas profits of 10 percentage points in 1974, 12 points in 1975, and 15 points thereafter.[3] Special provisions were introduced for specific non-conventional petroleum projects: thus Ottawa would allow full deductibility of provincial royalties and the resource allowance for the Syncrude project.

The Provinces Respond

The producing provinces were not pleased. On December 12, 1974, Alberta introduced two measures to ease the situation for the oil companies. The Alberta Petroleum Exploration Plan introduced a refund of the provincial

[2] SC 1970-71-72, c. 63.

[3] These rates were in addition to the general 10-percentage-point abatement for provincial income tax. A 15-percentage-point abatement was immediately available for mining production profits.

corporation income tax on the non-deductible royalties, granted small companies a full credit for the federal tax as well, raised the thresholds for the higher royalty rates, and reduced supplementary royalties from 60 to 50 percent. The Alberta Royalty Tax Credit Program increased subsidies for drilling. On December 30, 1974, Saskatchewan announced a program to rebate the provincial portion of corporation income tax on non-deductible levies and to lower "excess" royalties. At about the same time, British Columbia announced its intention of working out with the federal government a system of rebating the extra tax arising from non-deductibility.

For both Saskatchewan and Alberta, the primary goal of policy over the next few years was to gain control of the pricing of domestic oil production, take for themselves most of the difference between Canadian and world prices, and thus eliminate the basis for the federal oil export tax, which was designed to appropriate that difference for the federal fisc. The two provinces differed, however, in the policies they adopted in pursuit of this common goal. In Alberta, the production companies leased most of their gas and oil rights from the province; consequently, the provincial government relied primarily on the powers of ownership in making its case for the right to control pricing. Saskatchewan, by contrast, based its case for control on its constitutional right to tax and regulate its resource industries.

The federal government was not backward in challenging the two provinces' claims. In 1975, it intervened before the Saskatchewan Court of Appeal on behalf of Canadian Industrial Oil and Gas Limited (CIGOL) to argue that the Saskatchewan oil royalty was in fact an indirect tax and that the province had, therefore, no authority to levy it. Ottawa was unsuccessful in this instance but won its point a year later, when the Supreme Court overturned the Saskatchewan court's ruling and decided in favour of CIGOL.[4] Soon afterwards, the federal government supported the Central Canada Potash Company in a successful attack on Saskatchewan's potash prorationing scheme.[5]

For both Saskatchewan and Alberta, the federal move in 1974 to disallow provincial royalties as expenses under the Income Tax Act seemed to strike at the very heart of provincial ownership. From the federal government's perspective, the move was an eminently successful one; it had the desired effect of inducing the provinces to reduce their royalties and thus of protecting the federal tax base. From the provinces' perspective, however, the federal government's efforts to protect its position amounted to a dangerous assault on provincial rights. At a first ministers' conference held on December 13 and 14, 1976, Premier Alan Blakeney of Saskatchewan argued that in areas in which the constitution gave the provinces exclusive

---

[4] *Canadian Industrial Gas and Oil Ltd. v. Government of Saskatchewan et al.* (1977), 80 D.L.R. (3d) 449.

[5] *Central Canada Potash Co. Ltd. et al v. Government of Saskatchewan et al.* (1978), 88 D.L.R. (3d) 609.

authority, such as the ownership, control, and taxation of natural resources, the provincial interest was paramount. With the CIGOL case (as yet unresolved) in mind, he asked for an amendment to the British North America Act that would give the provinces the power to levy indirect taxes with respect to natural resources. The suggestion was eventually incorporated into the Constitution Act of 1982, which revised the British North America Act.

The establishment of a federally owned national petroleum company, the Energy Supply Allocation Board, and federal limits on petroleum export volumes were other federal moves that heightened federal-provincial tension. The 1974 pricing agreement, however, was due to expire at the end of June 1975, and the federal Petroleum Administration Act[6] called for negotiation in setting prices for crude oil and natural gas; only in the absence of consensus could the federal government act unilaterally.

The 1975 Conference and Its Aftermath

It was against this backdrop of confrontation and bitter debate that the first ministers met in Ottawa on April 9 and 10, 1975. Minister of Energy, Mines and Resources Macdonald intended to increase oil and gas prices gradually, in order to ease the burden on consumers and lessen the inflationary impact of the change. He proposed to raise prices to a level high enough to encourage the development of new, higher-cost resources and acknowledged that the producing provinces had a right to a fair return on their non-renewable resources. The federal government was looking for a higher price for crude oil, beginning July 1, 1975, and a still greater rise in the price of natural gas, to establish a more realistic relationship between the two energy sources and to encourage increased exploration for natural gas. It also wished to increase the tax on oil exports, which were rapidly declining, in order to meet the costs of compensating for oil imports, which were increasing in both quantity and price. When the price of $6.50 per barrel was set in 1974, the world price was about $10.50 per barrel. By April 1975, the world price had risen to $12 per barrel.

The provinces were adamant in upholding their own positions. British Columbia pressed for an increase in natural gas prices and proposed that the resulting revenue be divided equally between the federal, provincial, and local governments. Premier Lougheed of Alberta renewed his threat to set prices for Alberta oil production. Saskatchewan suggested that all of the proceeds of any increase in price above $6.50 (indexed) be placed in an "energy security fund" held jointly by the federal government and the producing provinces; it also pressed for deductibility of provincial royalties. The provinces east of Saskatchewan were less eager for increases in the uniform domestic price of crude oil, and many of them argued that there should be no change until the current recession ended.

---

[6] SC 1974-75-76, c. 47.

In view of the sharply conflicting positions presented at the conference, it is not surprising that the participants reached no conclusions about the extent and timing of increases in prices. Subsequent bilateral negotiations at the level of officials and ministers also failed to produce a consensus, and the federal government felt that it had no choice but to act unilaterally. In his 1975 budget,[7] Finance Minister John Turner announced that, effective for 12 months beginning July 1, the national price for crude oil and its equivalents would increase from $6.50 to $8 (excluding transportation charges). He asked the industry to refrain from increasing product prices for 45 days; that is, until the inventories of cheaper supplies had been consumed. At the same time, the minister announced an increase in natural gas prices effective November 1—a major step toward realizing his plan to price gas at parity with crude oil in Toronto within three to five years. To finance the increasing costs of oil import compensation, the June 1975 budget imposed a tax of 10 cents per gallon on gasoline for personal use.

Turner's 1975 budget also sought to resolve the issue of taxes by meeting in part the producing provinces' request for deductibility of provincial resource levies and for recognition of the provincial position. The budget provided for a resource allowance (or deduction from income) equal to 25 percent of production income, after related expenses, from petroleum or mineral resources. Ottawa would withdraw the resource abatement of 15 percent and reduce the basic corporation tax rate applicable to resource production profits to the general rate of 46 percent. This change was expected to stimulate exploration and development, since it would increase the value of the tax savings associated with exploration and development costs, and those associated with depletion as well.

Three years passed after the 1975 conference without the achievement of any fundamental agreement between Ottawa and the producing provinces and hence without any major changes in the federal-provincial revenue-sharing arrangements. The federal government and the producing provinces were able to agree on an increase to $9.05 in the wellhead price of oil as of July 1, 1976 and $9.75 as of the following January. In 1977, Ottawa and Alberta agreed to a price of $10.75 per barrel for six months beginning in July of that year and increases of $1.00 every six months until January 1979, when the price would reach $13.75.

The 1978 Conferences and the Neufeld Report

The federal and provincial resource ministers met on January 20, 1978 in preparation for a first ministers' conference in February. They could not agree on the deductibility of provincial royalties, and in any case their views did not necessarily represent the official positions of their governments. Although no consensus on oil and gas questions was possible, there was

---

[7] Canada, Department of Finance, Budget Papers, Budget Speech, June 23, 1975.

agreement that the mining industry was in crisis because of increases in provincial levies and declining world prices. The resource ministers recommended that the first ministers authorize a joint tax review by the federal and provincial finance ministers and resource ministers with a view to (1) leaving the mining industry with enough retained earnings to provide financial stability, maintain its competitiveness in international markets, and encourage investment in the exploration, development, and processing of mineral resources; and (2) providing the industry with a stable and predictable taxation regime that took into account the priorities of each province.

The first ministers' conference, held on February 13 to 15, took up the recommendation and enlarged upon it, directing the finance ministers and resource ministers to review the taxation of both the mining industry and the petroleum industry. A committee of federal and provincial officials chaired by Dr. E.P. Neufeld studied the matter, and the finance ministers and resource ministers met on November 3 to consider the committee's report.[8] The Neufeld report devoted less attention to the oil and gas industry than to the mining industry, where the problems were acute. The report examined economic conditions in the mining industry, the relevant federal and provincial taxation systems, and the question of the level of tax in the industry. It identified seven major objectives for future resource taxation policies and put forward recommendations for achieving these objectives. At their November meeting, the finance ministers and resource ministers undertook to consider carefully, before the preparation of the 1979 budgets, whether special economic conditions in the mining and petroleum industries justified changes to the resource-related aspects of the tax system.

As a part of a federal economic recovery program launched during the summer of 1978, Finance Minister Jean Chrétien suspended an increase in oil prices scheduled for January 1, 1979. Ottawa subsequently negotiated with the provinces to arrange for an increase in wellhead prices to $13.75 and an equivalent increase in the complementary natural gas price on July 1, 1979. An additional $1.00 per barrel and its equivalent for gas was to be added on January 1, 1980. The agreement expired on June 30, 1980. The finance minister proposed to negotiate with Alberta to deregulate natural gas prices and allow them to seek their own level.

The taxation of natural resources was a major topic at a first ministers' conference on the economy, held on November 27 to 29, 1978. The ministers arrived at few concrete decisions, but they made some progress. The report of the Neufeld committee was tabled, and there was general agreement that if one level of government moved to reduce taxes on resource industries the other level would not act to offset the reductions. The two levels also agreed to consult each other on the appropriateness of further measures to provide greater stability and opportunity for the mining industry through the tax system.

---

[8] *Federal-Provincial Resource Taxation Review—joint report by federal and provincial officials to Finance and Resource Ministers,* November 1, 1978.

The Continuing Oil-Pricing Dispute

By 1979, the debate over domestic oil prices had become primarily a dispute between Alberta, the biggest producer, and Ontario, the biggest consumer. The domestic price continued to hover at about 60 percent of the world price: by late 1979, in response to yet another major increase in world prices, it had reached $13.75 per barrel. Alberta characterized the lower domestic price as a subsidy for the consuming provinces that had amounted to billions of dollars over the six years since the first world oil-price shock. Ontario felt that the artificially high prices for domestic crude oil, relative to world prices, that it had paid under the national oil policy up to 1973 justified reciprocal treatment when the situation was reversed.

Alberta took the position that its ownership of resources gave it the power to determine when and how and how much oil to produce. The federal government had no jurisdiction over production or over sales within the province, but in the matter of sales outside the province Alberta could negotiate only with the federal authorities, not with other provinces. Alberta argued for a steady, but gradual, climb to the world price, in line with Canada's commitments to other countries (including the members of the International Energy Agency). The province was willing, however, to settle on a price slightly below the Chicago composite price in order to accommodate the major manufacturing provinces. It was, it said, searching for a "fairer" sharing of revenues between the two levels of government and among the provinces.

The government of Alberta put its strongest bargaining tool to use when, in May 1980, it introduced legislation that allowed the province to set maximum monthly levels for production from Crown-owned reserves, which represented about 85 percent of Alberta's total oil supplies.[9] The province maintained its demand that domestic prices be raised to world prices.

Nova Scotia, meanwhile, was attempting to assert its moral and legal claims to jurisdiction over off-shore drilling activities. An agreement signed by Ottawa and the governments of the four Atlantic provinces in 1977 had set up a joint board to manage the Atlantic off-shore natural resources. Any resulting revenues were to be divided between the provinces and the federal government on a 75-25 percent basis. Nova Scotia continued to claim ownership of off-shore resources and expressed its intention to control the extent and pace of development of these resources and to levy provincial royalties on production. It called for bilateral negotiations with the federal government to arrive at a resolution more favourable to itself than the 1977 agreement. Negotiations were also in progress between Newfoundland and the federal government, but the emphasis in this case was on pricing arrangements.

---

[9] Mines and Minerals Amendment Act, 1980, SA 1980, c. 32.

None of these bilateral negotiations were going well, however, and on May 13 the federal government let it be known that it was considering two new tax systems, both of which were unacceptable to Alberta. The first, a two-part natural gas export tax, would allow Ottawa to skim off up to one-third of the extra revenues on existing natural gas export sales and up to 100 percent of the export revenues on future sales. The second was a "refinery gate" tax on all oil products consumed in Canada; it would be designed to cover the full cost of the subsidy for foreign crude imported into eastern Canada. Alberta rejected the concept of an extended federal tax on natural gas exports and refused to discuss it with Marc Lalonde, the federal minister of energy, during negotiations for a new pricing agreement to replace the one that was to end on June 30, 1980.

Another federal initiative in May 1980 was the announcement of plans to extend the eastern end of the natural gas pipeline system from Toronto to Quebec City. The intention was to increase demand for natural gas, which was well below total potential production. Consequently, a number of firms were suffering from lagging revenue. One cause of the weak demand for gas was the existence of a surplus of residual (or heavy industrial) fuel oil, a by-product of the production of motor fuel. The federal government therefore linked its pipeline proposal with a plan for the construction of a major refinery to upgrade residual oils into motor fuel and other non-fuel products and thus ease the pressure of competition on natural gas.

On May 28, 1980, Energy Minister Lalonde called for a revision of the system of sharing oil and natural gas revenues that would give the federal government sufficient funds to carry out a national energy program, especially the subsidization of imported oil. Under the existing arrangement, each rise in the international price worsened the federal fiscal position and improved that of the producing provinces.

On June 18, 1980, less than two weeks before the expiration of the existing pricing agreement, Lalonde met with Alberta's energy minister, Mervin Leitch, in a final effort to negotiate a new domestic price for oil. The current price was $14.75 per barrel, less than one-half of the average price of imported crude landed in Montreal. Thirty-six hours of negotiation failed to produce an agreement; the ministers passed the problem of setting a price for domestic crude oil to their leaders, who were to meet in July, and the existing price agreement was extended to August 1.

The premiers and the prime minister were no more successful in achieving consensus on taxing and pricing policies. Shortly after the July meeting, Alberta unilaterally raised the wellhead price by $2.00, to $16.75 per barrel, as of August 1, 1980. The federal government made no move to counteract this measure and continued its negotiations with the producing provinces. Meanwhile, however, it also continued to prepare the ground for the introduction of a national energy policy.

The National Energy Program

The federal government was concerned with striking a balance between the national interest and regional interests. Late in 1980, it moved unilaterally to establish a new regime for all aspects of the oil and gas industry. In the paper, presented with the budget of October 28, that outlined the national energy program (NEP),[10] Energy Minister Lalonde noted that there was a national claim as well as a regional one to the wealth that the rise in world prices for crude oil had generated. This claim arose from three factors: the protection that the federal government had given the developing oil and gas industry when domestic prices were above world prices, the generous income tax concessions that Ottawa had provided for oil and gas exploration and development, and the federal responsibility for national economic and energy policies. The federal government also wished to maintain and eventually increase the proportion of the oil and gas industry that was owned by Canadians.

The NEP used pricing, tax measures, expenditure programs, and direct federal regulation to balance domestic energy supply and demand, increase the proportion of Canadian ownership in the energy industry, expand the public sector's role in that industry, and ensure greater industrial benefits from energy development. Ottawa planned to use the additional federal revenues raised by the program to subsidize imports of oil to those areas of Canada that did not have access to western oil supplies.

The program divorced the domestic industry from world oil prices. Ottawa set the domestic price for standard crude oil arbitrarily at the current level of $16.75 and planned to increase it by $1.00 per barrel semi-annually until the end of 1983, by $2.25 per barrel semi-annually until the end of 1985, and by $3.50 per barrel semi-annually until the end of 1990, when it was expected to approximate the price set for oil sands production. This formula would have increased the price of conventional crude over the decade from $16.75 per barrel to $63 per barrel. Prices for natural gas were set separately for consumers in Toronto, Montreal, Quebec City, and Halifax and were to rise roughly in step with oil prices.

The NEP introduced two new taxes. The natural gas and gas liquids tax (NGGLT) was set at 30 cents per thousand cubic feet as of November 1, 1980 and was to rise to 75 cents by mid-1983. The 8-percent petroleum and gas revenue tax (PGRT) was applied, beginning January 1, 1981, to net operating revenues from oil and gas production; federal incentive measures provided through the Income Tax Act for the oil and gas industry had seriously eroded

---

[10] Canada, Department of Energy, Mines and Resources, *The National Energy Program*, (Ottawa: the department, 1980). Although the federal government presented the NEP, as it was described in this document, as a fait accompli, the program was later modified on several occasions, as described below.

the federal income tax base, and the PGRT was intended to recapture the lost revenue.

The NEP also changed existing tax and incentive arrangements. Revenues from the oil export charge were shared equally with the producing provinces. The income tax incentives for exploration were reduced and supplemented by the petroleum incentives program (PIP), which provided federal grants for exploration activities. A completely different set of federal charges and incentives applied to the so-called Canada lands—oil and gas fields in the far north and off-shore.

Finally, Ottawa supplemented the NEP's pricing and tax provisions with a number of measures designed to reduce oil and gas consumption and encourage the development of alternative sources of energy.

Lalonde's paper included an analysis of the distribution of revenues under the program; it is reproduced in table 8.1. The federal share of revenues was to increase sharply, from 12 percent in 1979 to nearly 28 percent in 1983, at the expense of the industry, whose share would drop from 39 percent to 32 percent, and the provinces, whose share would drop from 49 percent to 41 percent.

Provincial Reaction

Not surprisingly, the three producing provinces, like the oil and gas industry, vehemently opposed the NEP, on the basis that it represented federal infringement of provincial jurisdiction. Alberta argued successfully in the Supreme Court of Alberta in 1981 that the NGGLT was unconstitutional when applied to exports of natural gas from provincially owned wells.[11] To emphasize its opposition, the province also introduced production cutbacks, beginning in March 1981, that were to reduce oil output by 15 percent over nine months. Saskatchewan was prepared to challenge the application of the PGRT to provincial Crown corporations. British Columbia withheld payment of taxes and prepared to take its case to the courts as well. Most of the other provinces were also against the NEP, and all except New Brunswick and Ontario indicated that unless the NEP were modified they would oppose the federal government's efforts to repatriate the constitution.

By September 1981, however, the federal government and Alberta were able to strike a compromise, embodied in the Canada-Alberta Energy Pricing and Taxation Agreement. By the end of the next month, Ottawa had signed similar agreements with Saskatchewan and British Columbia. Under the terms of these agreements, the federal government would (1) establish a two-tier price system for oil in which the higher price applied to newly discovered conventional oil, synthetic oil, and oil from the Canada lands; (2) set a revised schedule of price increases; (3) eliminate the NGGLT on exports of natural gas; (4) increase the PGRT from 8 percent to an effective rate of 12

---

[11] Reference re Proposed Federal Tax on Exported Natural Gas (1981), 122 D.L.R. (3d) 48 (Alberta Court of Appeal).

Table 8.1 Projection of Net Revenues from Oil and Natural Gas Production Under the National Energy Program

	Actual 1979 revenues		Projected 1983 revenues	
	$ billions	%	$ billions	%
Federal[a]	1.4	12.0	8.0	27.5
Industry[b]	4.6	39.3	9.2	31.6
Provincial[b]				
Saskatchewan	0.4	3.4	1.0	3.4
Alberta	4.8	41.0	9.7	33.3
British Columbia	0.5	4.3	1.2	4.1
Total provincial	5.7	48.7	11.9	40.9
Grand total	11.7	100.0	29.1	100.0

[a] Includes corporate income tax and federal share of oil export charge. [b] Assumes land bonus payments included in provincial share only.

Source: Canada, Department of Energy, Mines and Resources, *The National Energy Program* (Ottawa: the department, 1980), 108.

percent; (5) introduce an incremental oil revenue tax (IORT), effective January 1, 1982, that would divert 50 percent of the difference between new and old oil prices to the federal government; and (6) share the administration of incentive programs with the provinces. The compromise was expected to give 26 percent of oil and gas revenues to the federal government, 44 percent to the provincial governments, and 30 percent to the industry.

Although these new arrangements were acceptable to the producing provinces, who dropped their court challenges of NEP taxes, they were vigorously criticized by the oil and gas industry.

Both the original NEP and the subsequent compromises were predicated on the assumption that domestic prices would remain well below international prices. Within six months of the introduction of the original NEP, however, world prices began to decline.

In May 1982, the federal government reduced the PGRT from 12 to 11 percent for one year, suspended the IORT for a year, and increased some wellhead prices. Later in 1982, the federal and Alberta governments introduced a series of joint incentive measures for enhanced oil recovery projects. Ottawa extended its suspension of the IORT for 12 months in 1983 and again in 1984; it finally eliminated the tax at the end of 1984. The federal government also granted further concessions to the oil and gas industry in both 1983 and 1984.

In March 1985, the new Conservative government in Ottawa and the governments of the producing provinces signed the western accord, which struck down the provisions of the NEP. World prices for crude oil had fallen to approximately the level set in Canada. Consequently, the petroleum compensation charges (PCC), designed to fund the federal subsidy program for crude oil imported into eastern Canada, and the oil export charge were no longer operative and were dropped. The Canadian ownership special charge

(COSC), intended to fund the federal government's purchase of non-resident-owned oil companies, was also eliminated. The federal government ceased to regulate domestic oil and gas prices. The NGGLT too was eliminated, and the PGRT was to be phased out. This process was accelerated in 1986 in order to end the PGRT as of October 1986.

By October 1986, therefore, the federal government had withdrawn entirely from the direct taxation of oil and natural gas production, leaving the now sparse field to the provinces. Many of the federal incentive programs related to oil and gas were also dismantled. Federal tax reform in 1987 and 1988 reduced the value of many oil and gas tax incentives, and thus increased the federal tax revenue from this sector. The federal government also increased its excise tax rate on gasoline in 1987 and 1988.

The crisis in this specialized area of federal-provincial fiscal relations was triggered mainly by the dramatic rise during the 1970s in world oil prices. Both levels of government had the power to levy taxes in the natural resource field, and both took full advantage of that power. The federal government was concerned about the regional effects of the rise in prices, and it was prepared to assert the primacy of its regulatory and taxing powers over those of the provinces in order to cushion the impact of the rise on the non-producing provinces. The producing provinces took the matter to the courts, but Alberta's production cuts and the provinces' threat to oppose repatriation of the constitution forced a compromise before the legal questions were fully resolved. The issue was ultimately defused by a drop in world oil prices as dramatic as the earlier rise. The decline in prices made many of the new federal taxes non-productive and eliminated the associated federal spending on oil import compensation. A change in philosophy, in line with an international trend to deregulation, added to the pressure on the federal government to quit the game. Because the essential issues were never resolved, however, a new world oil crisis could raise them again.

The development of the oil and gas deposits off the shores of Newfoundland and Nova Scotia in the 1980s did not produce a quarrel over revenues analogous to the earlier dispute between Ottawa and the western provinces. One reason for the difference was the fact that prices were not as buoyant as they had been in the previous decade; another was the fact that the two provinces were more interested in getting the deposits into production, to stimulate their economies, than they were in asserting the superiority of their claims on income from the industry. Ottawa managed, without undue difficulty, to negotiate revenue-sharing agreements with both provinces.

Conclusion

The events described in this chapter stand in contrast with the relatively harmonious evolution of tax sharing outlined in the earlier chapters. The chapter has illustrated the problems that can arise when the federal government and the provinces share a tax field and national policy is at odds with regional interests.

The conflict over natural resource taxation has recently found its echo in another dispute over a shared tax field. A decline in the relative importance of corporate income tax collections over the past few decades, even in times of corporate prosperity, has led the provinces to follow the federal government in exploring other means of taxing corporations or business in general. In the late 1980s, the provinces began to increase their taxes on payrolls and corporate paid-up capital. Since these taxes are deductible for corporate income tax purposes, they have become a substantial drain on federal revenues. The 1991 federal budget included a plan to disallow such provincial taxes as a deduction; in lieu of a deduction, businesses would be granted an automatic allowance of up to 6 percent of taxable income. The proposed allowance, like the allowance granted in lieu of deductions for provincial natural resource levies, has met with a poor reception from the provinces, and from many taxpayers with capital- or labour-intensive operations as well. Although the federal government has since postponed implementation of the proposal, the underlying issue will persist as long as provincial governments fine-tune their own tax systems at the expense of the federal tax system.

Examination of the natural resource issue is also useful because it shows the volatility of provincial fortunes. The rise in oil and gas prices brought on by the world oil crises of the 1970s raised the wealth of the producing provinces partly at the expense of the consuming provinces. This change in the relative positions of the provinces had serious consequences for the evolution of the equalization system, which is discussed in the next section.

PART III

EQUALIZATION

Introduction

As a rule, the central government of a federal state tries to ensure that all regional goverments are able to provide their citizens with roughly the same level of public services without having to resort to unduly high rates of taxation. This motive was the rationale for some of the statutory subsidies to the provinces introduced with the establishment of the Canadian federation and for the explicit equalization system that Ottawa introduced in 1957. It was also one justification for some of the shared-cost programs and conditional grants described in part IV.

The equalization system is a formal recognition of the fact that the provinces vary in their capacities to derive revenue from taxation and other sources and therefore vary as well in their capacities to finance the services that fall within their areas of responsibility under the British North America Act. Of course, the demand for these services differs from province to province, and so does the cost of providing them. It has not yet proved practical, however, to measure these differences. For the purposes of negotiating equalization, therefore, all parties have assumed that both costs and demand are uniform across the provinces on a per capita basis.

The formulas described in this part of the book have attempted, in an increasingly comprehensive and complex way, to equalize, or bring up to an average, the per capita yields from a variety of taxes. The original formula developed in 1957 was based on only personal and corporate income taxes and death taxes; the extent of subsequent changes is indicated by the fact that the formula for the current equalization arrangements takes 37 different provincial revenue sources into account.

The equalization system has been subject to considerable stress during its 40 years of existence. The enormous increase in provincial oil revenues in the mid-1970s and again in the early 1980s threatened to raise total equalization payments to levels that the federal government could not afford. Even Ontario, traditionally one of the wealthiest provinces, would have qualified for equalization under the existing formula. Ottawa's solution was to change the formula so that it reflected the general sense of which provinces did and did not require federal assistance.

The equalization program is important not only for its primary function— the provision of additional resources to the "have-not" provinces—but also for its effect on other aspects of federal-provincial fiscal relations, notably the transfers of tax points under the contracting-out and established programs financing arrangements described in part IV. In the absence of equalization payments, it would be difficult to use tax transfers to arrive at fair compensation under these arrangements.

Chapter 9 discusses the initial working-out of the equalization scheme and its relatively smooth operation over the next 20 years. Chapter 10 describes the threat posed to the equalization system by the enormous rise in some provinces' natural resources revenues during the 1970s. Chapter 11 deals with the radical changes in the equalization formula imposed by Ottawa in the early 1980s and with the subsequent development of the program.

9

Equalization Takes Root, 1957-1977

Two factors have determined the evolution of federal-provincial fiscal relations. The first, which underlies the difficulties outlined elsewhere in this book, is the mismatch between the responsibilities and the revenue resources of each of the two levels of government. The second is regional economic disparity. The British North America Act recognized the need for additional federal aid for certain regions, and the structure of the statutory subsidies, described in chapter 1, reflected this need. The Rowell-Sirois report of 1940 also recognized the problem, but the emphasis during the war years and the post-war reconstruction period was on national rather than regional programs.

Many federal direct spending programs have implicitly or explicitly contained some special treatment for low-income areas. The federal government's desire to direct proportionately more funds to low-income areas influenced the development of many conditional grant programs, in particular the grants for provincial hospital and medical insurance programs.[1] The federal commitment to overcoming regional disparities increased during the 1960s and 1970s. In 1969, the federal government set up a new agency, the Department of Regional Economic Expansion (DREE), and made it responsible for coordinating all federal activities—regional tax incentives, efforts to decentralize federal operations, and a host of ad hoc programs—aimed at stimulating depressed regional economies. Intergovernmental transfers, however, were the preferred instrument for the purpose of ensuring that all citizens enjoyed access to equal levels of public services. The federal government summed up its philosophy in a statement published in 1969:

> The federal government remains committed to the view that equal opportunity for individual Canadians requires the equalization of public services, and to the view that the national interest sometimes calls for the harmonization of particular provincial programs through the use of federal grants.[2]

---

[1] See chapters 12 and 13 for further details.

[2] Canada, *The Taxing Powers and The Constitution of Canada* (Ottawa: Queen's Printer, 1969), as quoted in R.M. Burns, "Federal-Provincial Relations: The Problem of Fiscal Adjustment" (1972), vol. 20, no. 3 *Canadian Tax Journal* 246-55, at 252.

The First Decade of Equalization, 1957-1967

The first step toward equalization of the yields of provincial revenue sources came with the 1957 tax sharing arrangements.[3] Under these arrangements, the federal government provided grants that brought hypothetical per capita provincial revenues from the standard taxes—that is, federally defined personal and corporate income taxes and succession duties—up to the average of the two provinces with the highest per capita revenues. Table 9.1 shows the calculation of equalization and stabilization payments for the fiscal year 1957-58, and table 9.2 shows these payments as a percentage of all provincial revenues, including transfers from the federal government.

At a federal-provincial conference held on November 25 and 26, 1957, the Atlantic provinces argued for additional equalization to bring their per capita revenue from all provincial and local sources up to the national average. The federal government agreed instead to provide special annual grants for the four Atlantic provinces totalling $25 million. The four provinces agreed among themselves to the following division: $2.5 million to Prince Edward Island and $7.5 million each to Newfoundland, Nova Scotia, and New Brunswick.

By providing these grants—the Atlantic provinces adjustment grants—the federal government in effect conceded that the original equalization formula was too limited to overcome all regional disparities. The Atlantic provinces adjustment grants plus limited equalization represented a step between the old system—or non-system—of ad hoc, unconditional grants to less-favoured regions and the far more complex and inclusive equalization system to come.

The 1962 federal-provincial arrangements added 50 percent of natural resource revenues to the taxes subject to equalization. They also changed the equalization standard: equalization would now be based on the average per capita revenue of all 10 provinces rather than on the average for the two most revenue-rich provinces. This change reduced the relative importance of basic equalization to the Atlantic provinces, so the adjustment grants were increased to $35 million per year ($3.5 million to Prince Edward Island and $10.5 million to each of the other three provinces). Table 9.3 shows the calculations under the revised formula of payments for the fiscal year 1962-63, and table 9.4 shows the payments to each province as a proportion of total provincial revenues.

Equalization Expands: The 1966 Proposal

In 1967, the scope of the equalization program was considerably broadened—the beginning of a process that eventually made equalization the largest source of federal funding for the provinces.

This process started in September 1966, when the federal minister of finance, Mitchell Sharp, presented a proposal for fundamental reform of the

---

[3] Federal-Provincial Tax Sharing Arrangements Act, SC 1956, c. 29.

Table 9.1 Calculation of Equalization and Stablization Payments, Fiscal Year 1957-58

	Nfld.	PEI	NS	NB	Que.	Ont.	Man.	Sask.	Alta.	BC	Total
Population in 1957, in thousands	424	100	703	563	4,755	5,571	864	890	1,165	1,445	16,480
					dollar figures, except per capita, in thousands						
Standard taxes											
Individual income tax (10%)	1,425	210	3,113	2,100	34,276	71,487	6,330	4,830	10,585	18,193	152,549
Corporate income taxes (9%)	2,838	441	5,857	4,155	79,084	126,113	11,083	8,188	20,512	27,430	285,701
Succession duties (50% of 3-year moving average)	333	151	1,110	6,954	24,496	23,689	1,874	1,172	1,994	4,779	66,552
Total											
Amount	4,596	802	10,080	13,209	137,856	221,289	19,287	14,190	33,091	50,402	504,802
Per capita	10.85	7.99	14.34	23.45	28.99	39.72	22.31	15.95	28.41	34.89	
Equalization											
Per capita equalization to weighted average of top 2 provinces ($38.73)	27.88	30.74	24.39	15.28	9.74	—	16.42	22.78	10.32	3.84	
Payment	11,811	3,085	17,150	8,607	46,309	—	14,193	20,264	12,022	5,547	138,988
Stabilization[a]											
Amount	15,768	4,194	24,699	20,280	157,888	194,417	31,532	31,212	40,992	59,709	580,691
Payment	—	307	—	—	—	—	—	—	—	3,760	4,067
Other											
Transitional grant to Newfoundland	1,400										1,400
Additional grant to Newfoundland	6,600										6,600
Total equalization, stabilization, and other	19,811	3,392	17,150	8,607	46,309	0	14,193	20,264	12,022	9,307	151,055

[a] See the appendix to chapter 11 for a discussion of the stabilization provisions.

Source: A. Milton Moore, J. Harvey Perry, and Donald I. Beach, *The Financing of Canadian Federation: The First Hundred Years*, Canadian Tax Paper no. 43 (Toronto: Canadian Tax Foundation, 1966), 58, table 13.

Table 9.2 Equalization and Stabilization Payable in Fiscal Year 1957-58

Province	Amount, $ thousands	As percentage of provincial revenue
Newfoundland	19,811	50.8
Prince Edward Island	3,392	37.7
Nova Scotia	17,150	26.8
New Brunswick	8,607	13.9
Quebec	46,309	9.0
Manitoba	14,193	19.2
Saskatchewan	20,264	.14.9
Alberta	12,022	4.9
British Columbia	9,307	3.3
Total	151,055	10.6

Sources: Table 9.1 and Statistics Canada, *Provincial Government Finance*, catalogue no. 68-205.

equalization system to the Tax Structure Committee. In his opening statement to the committee, the minister defined the principle that underlay his proposal:

> [T]he fiscal arrangements should, through a system of equalization grants, enable each province to provide an adequate level of public services without resort to rates of taxation substantially higher than those of other provinces.[4]

The minister's aim was to develop a comprehensive "prosperity index" by measuring each province's revenue or fiscal capacity in its entirety; this comprehensive measure would replace the partial measure currently in use. The new system would take into account all of a province's revenues and equalize them to the national average. Equalization payments would be sensitive to provincial revenue requirements—they would rise as provincial revenue rose—and to changes in provincial tax capacity. The formula would use actual provincial tax levels, rather than the arbitrary "standard" rates used under the existing system.

This approach was not the result of a sudden inspiration on the part of the minister of finance. It had first been examined in a publication of the American Advisory Committee on Intergovernmental Relations, "Measures of State and Local Fiscal Capacity and Tax Effort,"[5] released in late 1965. The newly formed Tax Structure Committee had been charged with a number of studies when it began its deliberations in 1964, including an examination of "the relation of equalization grants to the fiscal requirements and fiscal capacities of the provinces, and the best equalization arrangements for the period 1967-72."[6]

---

[4] Canada, *Federal-Provincial Tax Structure Committee*, Proceedings of a meeting held in Ottawa, September 14-15, 1966 (Ottawa, Queen's Printer, 1966), 14.

[5] American Advisory Committee on Intergovernmental Relations, "Measures of State and Local Fiscal Capacity and Tax Effort" (1965).

[6] Supra footnote 4, at 6.

Table 9.3 Calculation of Equalization and Stablization Payments, Fiscal Year 1962-63

	Nfld.	PEI	NS	NB	Que.	Ont.	Man.	Sask.	Alta.	BC	Total
					dollar figures, except per capita, in thousands						
Population in 1962, in thousands	470	106	746	607	5,366	6,342	935	930	1,370	1,659	18,531
Standard taxes											
Individual income tax (16%)	2,921	562	6,760	4,476	77,154	142,321	13,746	10,403	21,693	34,055	314,091
Corporate income taxes (9%)	3,685	538	6,204	4,707	81,441	141,428	12,919	8,545	22,753	33,978	316,199
Succession duties (50% of 3-year moving average)	297	61	2,307	920	15,415	27,682	2,345	1,065	2,984	7,130	60,206
Resource revenue (50% of 3-year moving average)	619	9	705	1,885	16,846	20,756	2,036	10,131	64,577	28,494	146,058
Total											
Amount	7,522	1,170	15,976	11,988	190,856	332,188	31,046	30,144	112,007	103,657	836,554
Per capita	16.00	11.04	21.42	19.75	35.57	52.38	33.20	32.41	81.76	62.48	
Equalization											
Per capital equalization to national average ($45.14)	29.14	34.10	23.72	25.39	9.57	—	11.94	12.73	—	—	
Basic equalization	13,696	3,615	17,695	15,412	51,353	—	11,164	11,839	—	—	124,773
Guaranteed equalization—all provinces[a]	10,459	2,594	14,505	13,486	59,844	—	11,979	21,126	11,802	—	145,796
Guaranteed equalization—provinces below national average[b]	11,666	2,703	15,964	14,753	72,246	—	13,902	22,660	—	—	153,893
Payment[c]	13,696	3,615	17,695	15,412	72,246	—	13,902	22,660	11,802	—	171,028
Stabilization[d]											
Amount	18,933	4,482	30,589	24,778	216,895	262,438	38,175	38,429	54,732	67,791	757,242
Atlantic provinces and additional grants	18,500	3,500	10,500	10,500	—	—	—	—	—	—	43,000
Payment	18,500	3,500	10,500	10,500	—	—	—	—	—	—	43,000
Total equalization, stabilization and other payments	32,196	7,115	28,195	25,912	72,246	0	13,902	22,660	11,802	0	214,028

[a] Amount needed to bring current yield of standard taxes and additional grants to Atlantic provinces up to total for final year of last two years of 1957-62 arrangements. [b] Amount needed to bring current yield of standard taxes and additional grants to Atlantic provinces up to projection of previous arrangement to current year. [c] Greatest of above three amounts. [d] See the appendix to chapter 11 for a discussion of the stabilization provisions.

Source: Same as table 9.1, at 78, table 18.

Table 9.4   Equalization and Stabilization Payable in Fiscal Year 1962-63

Province	Amount, $ thousands	As percentage of provincial revenue
Newfoundland	32,196	39.7
Prince Edward Island	7,115	37.4
Nova Scotia	28,195	24.7
New Brunswick	25,912	27.3
Quebec	72,246	7.6
Manitoba	13,902	10.2
Saskatchewan	22,660	10.4
Alberta	11,802	3.7
Total	214,028	11.1

Sources: Table 9.3 and Statistics Canada, *Provincial Government Finance*, catalogue no. 68-205.

The minister's proposal had been discussed in a paper prepared by the federal department of finance in February 1966,[7] and it was fully reviewed at a meeting of the Continuing Committee on Economic and Fiscal Matters held in July 1966. Thus, when the federal government announced the formula publicly at a Tax Structure Committee meeting held on September 14 and 15, the provinces were in a position to respond.

Sharp's statement to the committee described the proposed system as follows:

> It would provide that any province in which average provincial tax rates (not its own tax rates) would yield less revenue per capita than the yield in Canada as a whole would be entitled to an equalization payment. The payments would be arrived at in this way. We would determine what it is the provinces generally tax—in technical terms the tax base for each revenue source—and the average level of the rates or levies which the provinces generally impose. Then we would apply this average tax level to the tax base in each province—again the incomes or sales or resource production which provinces generally tax—to find out whether the per capita yield in that province is below the national average. If the total yield of all provincial revenues, calculated in this way, were to yield less than the national average in any province, the federal government would make up the difference in equalization payments.[8]

Sharp's presentation included a table, reproduced here as table 9.5, that used calculations for fiscal year 1966-67 to illustrate the effect of the proposed changes on payments to the provinces. The table showed aggregate payments to the seven recipient provinces of $353 million under the old

---

[7] Unpublished paper prepared by the federal Department of Finance, February 1966, for the Tax Structure Committee on the representative tax method of equalization. It was never made public but was referred to by G.I. Smith, Nova Scotia's minister of finance, supra footnote 4, at 68.

[8] Ibid., at 16.

Table 9.5 Estimated Equalization Payments to Provinces Under Federal Proposals of September 1966 and Under 1962-1967 Arrangements (Using 1966-67 Figures for Illustrative Purposes)[a]

Province	Total payment, $ millions			Per capita payment, dollars			Payment as percentage of provincial revenues from own sources[c]		
	1962-1967 arrangements[b]	Proposed arrangements	Change	1962-1967 arrangements[b]	Proposed arrangements	Change	1962-1967 arrangements[b]	Proposed arrangements	Change
							%	%	%
Newfoundland	37.2	59.8	+22.6	73.96	118.89	+44.93	49.9	80.3	+30.4
Prince Edward Island	10.6	10.8	+0.2	98.15	100.00	+1.85	73.1	74.5	+1.4
Nova Scotia	50.2	69.0	+18.8	66.14	90.91	+24.77	46.7	64.1	+17.4
New Brunswick	44.6	60.3	+15.7	71.25	96.33	+25.08	46.6	62.9	+16.3
Quebec	149.5	235.3	+85.8	26.08	41.04	+14.96	10.7	16.9	+6.2
Ontario	—	—	—	—	—	—	—	—	—
Manitoba	27.5	29.1	+1.6	28.68	30.34	1.66	14.5	15.4	+0.9
Saskatchewan[d]	33.2	27.2	-6.0	34.84	28.54	-6.30	13.2	10.9	-2.3
Alberta	—	—	—	—	—	—	—	—	—
British Columbia	—	—	—	—	—	—	—	—	—
Total	352.8	491.5	+138.7	—	—	—	—	—	—

[a] All figures estimated. [b] The amounts shown for 1962-1967 arrangements include the Atlantic provinces adjustment grants. [c] "Provincial revenues from own sources" consists of provincial net general revenues less all transfers from the federal government (based on D.B.S. statistics); i.e., it includes all provincial revenues from taxes, licences, fees, fines, etc. [d] The payment to Saskatchewan under the proposed arrangements is a transitional payment that would be paid in 1967-68, and would decline during 1967-68 to 1971-72.

Source: Canada, *Federal-Provincial Tax Structure Committee*, proceedings of a meeting held in Ottawa, September 14-15, 1966 (Ottawa: Queen's Printer, 1966), 17.

system and $492 million under its proposed successor—a difference of 39 percent. Saskatchewan received less under the proposed formula, and Prince Edward Island and Manitoba received very little more. For the other four provinces, however, the new formula was substantially more generous than the old. In particular, as the federal finance minister noted, the proposed system would provide significantly more money to three of the four Atlantic provinces than did the existing system, which included the Atlantic provinces adjustment grants. Sharp objected to these grants in principle, since they were for fixed amounts and went to only four of the seven provinces receiving equalization. Accordingly, he proposed to drop them as of March 31, 1967. He would, however, continue both the adjustment grants and the old equalization formula for any of the Atlantic provinces that preferred to keep them.[9] As for Saskatchewan, the only loser under the prospective scheme, the blow would be softened by a phase-in provision: the reduction in payments would be accomplished gradually and would not be completed until 1971-72. Finally, the minister's proposals removed the link between equalization and provincial revenue stabilization.

The Provinces React

The provinces used the meeting of the Tax Structure Committee in September 1966 to present their first public reaction to the federal proposals. Premier John Robarts of Ontario endorsed both the general principle of equalization and the new proposals. He noted, however, that the proposed system made no effort to reflect differences in costs from province to province. He further suggested that only 50 percent of non-renewable natural resource revenues be taken into the formula.

Quebec and New Brunswick too supported the federal proposal; the other provinces did not. Nova Scotia's minister of finance and economics, G.I. Smith, delivered a detailed and unfavourable analysis of the proposed system, objecting in particular to its failure to take account of savings and local government revenues. He preferred the "total income method" also described in the federal Department of Finance technical paper that described the federal proposal.[10] This system would use personal and corporation income as the base for determining the equalization payable to each province. The base would be adjusted by adding back expenses of corporations, taking account of natural resource revenues, and removing a certain per capita amount to reflect the cost of necessities. The formula would determine entitlements by applying the percentage difference between the national average per capita base and the per capita base in each province to the aggregate of all provincial revenues to be equalized. As in the existing formula, no equalization would be payable if the per capita base in a province

---

[9] The minister also removed the link between equalization and provincial revenue stabilization. See the appendix to chapter 11 for a discussion of the stabilization provisions.

[10] Supra footnote 7.

exceeded the national average. Smith also argued for the retention of the Atlantic provinces adjustment grants, on the ground that the Atlantic provinces needed the grants in order to catch up to national levels of spending.

Premier W.A.C. Bennett of British Columbia was critical of the principle of equalization, which he felt did nothing to encourage fiscal responsibility. He was in favour of payments to individuals, not provinces, supported by strong federal regional development policies. Like Premier Robarts, he felt that cost differentials should be taken into account, but unlike most premiers Bennett favoured removing equalization from the tax sharing arrangements.

Prince Edward Island objected to the federal proposals on the ground that the Atlantic provinces adjustment grants, or a similar program not tied to per capita equality, could meet its special needs better than a formula. The province's smallness, lack of resources, and reliance on federal transfers made the choice of an equalization system a matter of serious concern to it.

Manitoba disliked the proposals to use a representative tax system in calculating per capita provincial revenues and to equalize revenues only to the national average. The representative tax system was "completely unacceptable" to Saskatchewan, the only province that stood to see its equalization entitlements drop. Premier Ross Thatcher called for an extension of the existing system until the Carter report[11] was published. If this suggestion was not acceptable to other participants, the premier was willing to accept the offer made to the Atlantic provinces—that is, to retain the old system if they wished.

Alberta too was in favour of an extension of the existing system for one year while further study was made of the problem. Premier E.C. Manning objected to the federal proposals on the ground that the increase in funding to "have-not" provinces and the consequent increase in the tax burden in "have" provinces would shift tax incidence and cause resentment. The premier outlined an alternative system of equalization that could be implemented after the extension period. He proposed the establishment of a federal-provincial "basic revenue fund" that would distribute to the provinces per capita payments based on the national average per capita cost of education, public health, and public welfare. The balance in the fund would be transferred to the federal government for its purposes. The fund would be financed by special federal-provincial taxes on personal and corporate income and retail "turnover." Both levels of government would levy the taxes, and the rates would be set through consultation, on the basis of the expenditures of the fund and federal revenue requirements. The federal government would collect the taxes. Both levels would have the option of adding taxes in the three fields. Alberta's position was that this system would provide sufficient equalization and more provincial freedom in the three functions. The present shared-cost programs would be discontinued.

---

[11] Canada, *Report of the Royal Commission on Taxation* (Ottawa: Queen's Printer, 1966).

Subsequent discussions produced an explicit guarantee for the Atlantic provinces and expanded stabilization provisions that would protect Saskatchewan from a drop in revenue. Generally speaking, however, the federal proposals discussed at the September 1966 meeting became the 1967-1972 arrangements.

The 1967-1972 Arrangements

The equalization system for the 1967-1972 period evolved logically from the basic system first used in 1957. It differed from the original system in two respects. First, it equalized per capita revenue for each province to the national average rather than to the average of the two most revenue-rich provinces; this change kept the total cost to the federal government down and directed money to the provinces where the need was greatest. Second, the new scheme used a broader representative tax system—one based on 16 revenue sources rather than 4—and hence provided a more precise reckoning of differences in provincial revenues. The formula was later revised to include an even broader array of provincial revenue sources; thus its growth roughly paralleled the growth of provincial revenue requirements. The 1966 report of the Tax Structure Committee had pointed out that under the old system provincial and local expenditures were growing faster than equalization payments.

Table 9.6 lists the 16 provincial revenue sources equalized under the 1967-1972 formula. For each revenue source, a base was chosen that was as close as possible to the actual base of that revenue source for all provinces. The provinces' total revenue from the source was then divided by the base to arrive at a "national average provincial revenue rate." Total revenue was also divided by national population to arrive at a national average per capita yield. The next step was to apply the national average provincial revenue rate to the base in each province and express the result in per capita terms. The equalization entitlement for a province from this source was the difference between the national average per capita yield and the per capita yield in that province at the national average rate. The sum of the differences, positive and negative, for all of the revenue sources, multiplied by the population of the province, gave the total equalization payment.

This formula conformed to the theoretical design of the equalization system, and under the current version of the system, introduced in 1982, no other formula is possible. Under the 1967-1972 system, however, it would have been possible to obtain exactly the same results, much more simply, by calculating percentage shares—the formula adopted under the 1972-1977 arrangements. This formula applied the difference between the province's percentage share of population and its percentage share of the base to the revenue for all provinces from that base to arrive at the equalization factor for that base. For example, a province with a relatively small income tax base—that is, low federal basic tax per capita—received equalization with respect to personal income.

**Table 9.6 Summary of Provincial Revenue Sources,
As Used in the Equalization Formula, 1967-1972**

1) Personal income taxes.
2) Corporate income taxes.
3) Succession duties and share of estate tax.
4) General sales taxes.
5) Motor fuel tax.
6) Motor vehicle revenues.
7) Alcoholic beverage revenues.
8) Forestry revenues.
9) Oil royalties.
10) Natural gas royalties.
11) Sales of Crown leases and reservations on oil and natural gas lands.
12) Other oil and gas revenues.
13) Metallic and non-metallic mineral revenues.
14) Water power rentals.
15) Other taxes.
16) Other revenues.

Source: Federal-Provincial Fiscal Arrangements Regulations, 1967, PC 1967-1934, SOR/67-520 (1967), 101 *Canada Gazette Part II* 1639.

For most recipient provinces, the use of national averages and aggregates minimized the effect on equalization payments of changes in tax rates, since the larger provinces had a greater weight than the smaller ones in establishing the national average.

With the introduction of substantially larger equalization payments, the Atlantic provinces additional grants were abolished, but the Atlantic provinces were guaranteed equalization of at least the equivalent amount. The 1967-1972 arrangements also contained stabilization provisions based on all provincial revenue sources, including equalization, to prevent undue hardship for Saskatchewan, which expected to lose equalization completely, and any province that experienced a drop of more than 5 percent in its revenues in any one year.

Total equalization payments for each province consisted of the sum of the entitlements, positive and negative, for each of the 16 revenue sources. If the total for a province was negative, no equalization was payable. Table 9.7 shows the payments for 1967-68, and table 9.8 compares these payments with total revenues for the recipient provinces.

At a meeting of finance ministers and treasurers on November 4 and 5, 1968, Nova Scotia pressed for the inclusion of municipal revenues in the equalization formula. It stressed the importance of this source of revenue, the size of local responsibilities, and the close relationship between the provincial and local governments. If equalization was intended to ensure that all provinces had the ability to provide at least a national average level of services, then it could not be restricted to services provided by provincial expenditures. Nova Scotia pointed out that the Tax Structure Committee had recognized the difficulty of separating the provincial and local levels when it

Table 9.7   Calculation of Equalization Payments, Fiscal Year 1967-68

	Nfld.	PEI	NS	NB	Que.	Ont.	Man.	Sask.	Alta.	BC	Total
Population in 1967, in thousands	499	109	756	619	5,854	7,115	961	955	1,483	1,938	20,289
Provincial revenues					*dollar figures, except per capita, in thousands*						
Individual income tax	11,439	2,328	25,782	17,953	306,701	549,816	55,353	49,926	77,965	137,248	1,234,511
Corporate income taxes	7,740	942	8,967	7,659	158,298	279,364	23,202	15,336	34,378	64,464	600,350
Estate tax (75% of 3-year moving average)	1,010	231	5,069	1,928	39,437	59,422	3,749	2,850	5,890	10,237	129,823
Estimated revenue from all sources in formula	86,802	16,597	123,451	157,698	1,617,122	2,154,014	236,689	279,221	478,473	646,497	5,796,564
Equalization											
Yields at national average											
rates	74,923	18,576	138,768	110,556	1,422,971	2,227,629	231,036	261,437	624,348	686,320	5,796,564
Per capita	150.00	170.78	183.63	178.58	243.07	313.07	240.47	273.83	421.08	354.06	285.70
Deficiency from national average	135.70	114.92	102.07	107.12	42.63	—	45.23	11.87	—	—	—
Equalization from above	67,781	12,500	77,133	66,317	249,560	—	43,456	11,333	—	—	528,080
Guaranteed equalization	48,159	14,071	60,672	55,228	—	—	—	26,438	—	—	204,568
Payment	67,781	14,071	77,133	66,317	249,560	—	43,456	26,438	—	—	544,756

Source: *The Natoinal Finances, 1967-68* (Toronto: Canadian Tax Foundation, 1967), 138, table 69.

Table 9.8 Equalization Payable in Fiscal Year 1967-68

Province	Amount, $ thousands	As percentage of provincial revenue
Newfoundland	67,781	29.3
Prince Edward Island	14,071	29.0
Nova Scotia	77,133	24.9
New Brunswick	66,317	23.7
Quebec	249,560	10.0
Manitoba	43,456	11.1
Saskatchewan	26,438	6.1
Total	544,756	13.0

Sources: Table 9.5 and Statistics Canada, *Provincial Government Finance*, catalogue no. 68-205.

decided to perform its detailed revenue forecasts on a combined provincial and municipal basis. The provincial minister of finance, W. S. K. Jones, also argued that the inclusion of local revenue would help to reduce regional disparities by increasing the equalization payable to low-income provinces.

Equalization received scant attention at the meeting, however, from the federal finance minister, Edgar Benson. Benson stated that the federal government did not intend to make any changes in the equalization system but proposed instead to attack the causes of regional disparities by providing aid for the economic and social development of lower-income regions.

The 1972-1977 Arrangements

Major federal-provincial conferences on July 13 and 14, November 1 and 2, and November 15 to 17, 1971 resulted in only minor changes in the equalization system introduced in 1967. Part I of Bill C-8[12] extended equalization to 1977. The list of provincial revenue sources was expanded from 16 to 19. Table 9.9 shows that the addition of health insurance premiums and racetrack taxes had almost no adverse effect on the recipient provinces. The inclusion of the provincial share of income tax on power utilities, however, reduced the equalization payable to Newfoundland, Prince Edward Island, and New Brunswick. Table 9.10 shows the relationship between equalization and total revenue in the recipient provinces in 1972-73.

Under part II of the 1972 Act, the federal government would provide stabilization payments to make up any shortfall from the previous year that a province might suffer, but only if the shortfall was not caused by provincial tax changes. The stabilization provisions were separate from the revenue guarantee, described earlier, and no payments were made under the provisions during the 1972-1977 period.[13]

---

[12] Federal-Provincial Fiscal Arrangements Act, 1972, SC 1972, c. 8.

[13] See the appendix to chapter 11 for a full discussion of the stabilization provisions.

Table 9.9   Estimated Equalization Entitlements by Revenue Source, Fiscal Year 1972-73

Revenue source	Nfld.	PEI	NS	NB	Que.	Ont.	Man.	Sask.	Alta.	BC	Total
					$ thousands						
Personal income taxes	41,302	9,341	38,480	42,457	117,219	(305,566)	21,988	56,354	11,657	(38,616)	327,141
Corporate income taxes	10,126	2,275	12,866	11,807	30,221	(74,296)	3,924	17,441	(9,912)	(4,452)	88,660
General and miscellaneous sales taxes	14,416	3,764	11,661	9,902	114,039	(106,739)	5,336	24,910	(28,751)	(52,164)	184,028
Motive fuel taxes	12,656	528	5,833	3,120	18,216	(31,893)	4,081	222	(13,660)	322	44,656
Motor vehicle licensing revenues	4,586	191	2,114	1,131	6,601	(11,557)	1,479	80	(4,950)	117	16,182
Alcoholic beverage revenues	7,216	153	1,842	5,374	40,237	(28,054)	(2,637)	3,048	(4,740)	(23,483)	55,233
Hospital and medicare insurance premiums	6,571	1,423	4,622	5,158	15,807	(38,432)	1,434	7,136	2,020	(6,466)	42,151
Succession duties and gift taxes	4,163	722	2,776	3,576	1,504	(23,950)	3,267	3,754	5,160	(972)	19,762
Race track taxes	1,048	47	911	943	(527)	(6,948)	976	1,582	(96)	1,855	4,980
Forestry revenues	(1,126)	749	4,548	(132)	10,856	33,688	4,901	2,763	4,885	(61,132)	22,559
Oil royalties	4,879	1,029	7,296	5,902	55,557	71,773	8,407	(18,832)	(143,558)	7,547	64,238
Natural gas royalties	1,226	258	1,833	1,483	13,958	17,731	2,279	1,208	(41,143)	1,167	22,245
Sales of Crown leases and reservations on oil and natural gas lands	1,487	314	2,224	1,800	16,936	21,514	2,765	1,465	(49,920)	1,415	26,991
Other oil and gas revenues	2,093	17	3,130	2,532	23,832	30,388	3,891	(5,169)	(59,090)	(1,624)	30,326
Metallic and non-metallic mineral revenues	(5,790)	348	1,940	978	3,500	(1,806)	(3,398)	(973)	5,037	165	(3,395)
Water power rentals	(295)	282	1,790	683	(10,857)	5,976	(234)	1,380	3,730	(2,455)	(7,251)
Other provincial taxes	4,470	860	4,376	4,372	12,127	(27,948)	900	5,095	(2,238)	(2,014)	32,200
Miscellaneous provincial revenues	5,757	1,108	5,636	5,630	15,618	(35,993)	1,159	6,562	(2,883)	(2,594)	41,470
Federal government revenues shared with the provinces	(1,604)	(263)	(1,212)	794	4,466	(1,955)	620	1,117	(3,827)	1,864	3,918
Total equalization payments	113,181	23,146	112,666	107,510	489,310	(514,067)	61,138	109,143	(332,279)	(181,520)	1,016,094

Note: A negative total indicates no equalization payable.

Source: *The National Finances, 1972-73* (Toronto: Canadian Tax Foundation, 1972), 144, table 10-2.

Table 9.10   Equalization Payable in Fiscal Year 1972-73

Province	Amount, $ thousands	As percentage of provincial revenue
Newfoundland	113,181	24.0
Prince Edward Island	23,146	20.3
Nova Scotia	112,666	17.9
New Brunswick	107,510	19.1
Quebec	489,310	9.1
Manitoba	61,138	7.3
Saskatchewan	109,143	15.0
Total	1,016,094	11.6

Sources: Table 9.8 and Statistics Canada, *Provincial Government Finance*, catalogue no. 68-205.

In 1973, Bill C-233[14] revised the equalization formula by adding to the list of revenue sources school-purpose taxes raised by local governments.

Equalization and the Oil Squeeze

The dramatic changes in energy supplies and values in the 1970s and 1980s changed many aspects of daily life in Canada. No less important, however, was the sudden shift in the relative revenue positions of provinces that produced oil and provinces that consumed it. This shift played havoc with the equalization formula, and drastic action was needed to restore a balance.

The automatic response of the equalization formula to the increases in provincial oil revenues was to increase the entitlements of the recipient provinces. Thus the federal government faced the prospect that one of its major spending programs would escalate uncontrollably. Oil prices continued to increase, and the oil and gas factors in the equalization formula eventually overshadowed all of the other factors, converting even Ontario into a province entitled to equalization. This outcome, in the federal government's view, was not within the spirit of the equalization system; changes were required to prevent relatively wealthy provinces from receiving equalization as a result of unusual circumstances. Such changes would also limit the growth of federal spending on equalization.

On the first occasion that oil revenues threatened to create a problem for the equalization formula, the federal government acted unilaterally and immediately to defuse the threat. The Oil Export Tax Act of 1974[15] excluded from the equalization formula the provincial share of the federal oil export tax levied between September 1, 1973 and March 31, 1974 (as described in chapter 8). The rationale for this step was that oil import compensation payments were in lieu of equalization payments. This interim measure

[14] An Act to Amend the Federal-Provincial Fiscal Arrangements Act, 1972; the Federal-Provincial Fiscal Revision Act, 1964; and the Income Tax Act, SC 1973-74, c. 45.

[15] SC 1973-74, c. 53.

was replaced by the Petroleum Administration Act of 1975,[16] which provided for a uniform pricing policy for crude oil sales and an import compensation program (also described in chapter 8).

An important part of the pricing agreement with the producing provinces was an understanding that most of their increased revenue would be put into capital accounts and thus kept out of the equalization formula. During the January 1974 first ministers' conference on energy, described in chapter 8, Saskatchewan sought a revision of the equalization system under which personal and corporation income taxes and a proposed federal-provincial estate tax system would each be equalized to the level in the province with the highest revenue from that source or to the average for the top two provinces. At that conference, most provinces indicated that they were opposed to such ad hoc adjustments to the equalization formula, especially to adjustments introduced by the federal government without provincial consultation.

The November 1974 budget introduced changes in equalization to take account of new provincial oil and gas revenues. These changes were discussed at a finance ministers' conference on December 9 and 10, 1974 and given legislative form, as Bill C-57, in 1975.[17] The Bill redefined oil and gas revenues as oil revenues from Crown lands, oil revenues from freehold lands, natural gas revenues from Crown lands, natural gas revenues from freehold lands, sales of Crown leases and reservations on oil and natural gas lands (already in the formula), and other oil and gas revenues (that is, those not included in any other oil and gas categories). This disaggregation increased the number of revenue categories from 19 to 22. For each oil and gas category, Bill C-57 established a distinction between "basic" revenues and "additional" revenues. Basic revenues were oil and gas revenues that were not attributable to the international oil-price disturbance of 1973 and 1974. Additional revenues were oil and gas revenues that were attributable to the disturbance—attributable, that is, to higher prices and higher levels of taxation but not to increases in production. The oil and gas revenues to be equalized would consist of all "basic revenues" plus one-third of "additional revenues." The new formula would apply to the fiscal years 1974-75 to 1976-77, inclusive.

At a first ministers' conference held on April 9 and 10, 1975 to discuss energy prices, Premier Allen Blakeney of Saskatchewan objected to the unilateral federal decision to exclude some natural resource revenue from the equalization formula; he especially objected to the exclusion as it applied to natural gas revenue. New Brunswick's Premier, Richard Hatfield, also objected to the changes. The federal authorities, on the other hand, were pushing for increased federal revenue from oil and gas to pay for the substantial increase in equalization costs that resulted from partial inclusion of "addi-

---

[16] SC 1974-75-76, c. 47.

[17] An Act to Amend the Federal-Provincial Fiscal Arrangements Act, 1972, SC 1974-75, c. 65.

tional" oil and gas revenues. Premier Frank Moores of Newfoundland had hoped for only temporary changes in equalization, and he argued that the federal changes failed to recognize that steady growth in oil revenues had been anticipated even before the oil crisis began. He also suggested that the sale of petroleum and natural gas leases and reservations be excluded from the equalization formula.

The provinces' objections and reservations did not deflect the federal government from its course: Parliament approved Bill C-57, without revision, in July 1975.

At the first ministers' conference of June 14 and 15, 1976, the subject of equalization was not a matter of urgent concern but was discussed by all provincial speakers. Although the "have" provinces supported the concept of equalization, most of them felt that there were upper limits to the acceptable level of payments. Saskatchewan reiterated its earlier suggestion that equalization be increased by exchanging the national average for a standard based on either the average revenues of the two most revenue-rich provinces or the revenues of the single province with the highest revenues per capita. Premier Blakeney was opposed to the arbitrary ceilings and penalties present in the system for provinces that increased their own taxes. He argued that if resource revenues continued to depress Saskatchewan's entitlement, some adjustment was in order for the implicit oil subsidy provided by Saskatchewan in selling below world prices. Premier Robert Bourassa of Quebec suggested that equalization should be based on an index of global wealth in order to equalize all or part of provincial, municipal, and school revenues where they fell below the national average. Premier Hatfield acknowledged the need for adjustments in the formula to take account of the very high natural resource revenues. He suggested the inclusion in the formula of municipal own-source revenue and agreed with Premier Blakeney that all revenues should be raised to the standard of the top one or two provinces.

Despite the problems of adapting the representative tax system of equalization to rising provincial oil and gas revenues, all parties were satisfied with the system's basic design. The provinces' submission to a conference of finance ministers and treasurers on December 6 and 7, 1976, stated that "[a]ll provinces recognize this program as the cornerstone of Canadian federalism."[18] In fact, the complex system had gained such general acceptance that when the first ministers met on December 13 and 14 the discussion of equalization centred on technical difficulties such as the definition of certain tax bases. The federal government had presented for discussion a proposal for revising equalization, called "formula B," under which a further disaggregation of revenue sources would increase the number of categories from 22 to 29

---

[18] British Columbia, Ministry of Finance, "Statement by the Honourable Merv Leitch, Provincial Treasurer of Alberta, on Behalf of All Provincial Ministers of Finance and Provincial Treasurers, at the Meeting of Ministers of Finance and Provincial Treasurers, Ottawa, December 6 and 7, 1976," in *British Columbia Budget*, January 24, 1977, at 36.

and only 50 percent of all revenue from non-renewable natural resources would be subject to equalization. The provinces were willing to accept formula B but wanted certain technical changes in it. In a speech to the conference, federal finance minister Donald Macdonald offered to review a federal proposal to limit the natural resource revenue entitlement to one-third of the total entitlement.

The 1977-1982 arrangements extended the existing equalization system to 29 separate categories of revenue—the formula B option. The new formula included only 50 percent of non-renewable natural resource revenues and set the further limit that entitlements with respect to natural resource revenues could not exceed one-third of the total equalization entitlement. This limit did not become operative immediately but might have applied to the 1982-83 payments had further changes not been introduced, as described in the next chapter.

Table 9.11 lists all the 29 revenue sources used under the new formula and shows the calculation of provincial entitlements for the 1977-78 fiscal year. Table 9.12 compares equalization payments and total provincial revenues in the same year.

Although the changes introduced after the price of oil began its rise were substantial, they did not resolve the problem, for oil prices continued to rise. The new equalization formula would be tested and found wanting very soon.

Table 9.11 Estimated Equalization Entitlements by Revenue Source, Fiscal Year 1977-78

	Nfld.	PEI	NS	NB	Que.	Ont.	Man.	Sask.	Alta.	BC	Total
						$ millions					
Personal income taxes	107.3	26.4	115.1	107.4	315.5	(515.4)	73.3	33.6	(80.2)	(186.5)	778.7
Business income revenues	31.8	8.1	43.6	32.3	102.1	(167.2)	17.1	22.3	(99.2)	9.2	257.3
Sales taxes	35.1	11.1	49.4	17.6	157.6	(53.0)	26.4	(1.8)	(149.3)	(95.2)	295.4
Tobacco taxes	2.9	0.3	4.2	(0.8)	(21.6)	6.6	3.1	3.7	(1.2)	2.8	(8.2)
Gasoline taxes	9.8	0.1	2.3	(0.5)	20.9	(17.8)	3.7	(3.6)	(18.7)	3.1	32.8
Diesel fuel taxes	0.4	0.9	4.1	0.9	(1.8)	2.4	1.0	(2.3)	(6.7)	0.9	3.3
Non-commercial vehicle licences	4.8	0.3	3.1	2.3	9.6	(10.4)	—	0.5	0.5	(10.8)	20.7
Commercial vehicle licences	2.0	0.4	2.6	0.6	24.5	12.6	(1.5)	(8.0)	(21.8)	(11.2)	20.5
Revenue from sale of spirits	4.8	(0.7)	0.8	4.0	65.6	(23.3)	(5.2)	(3.9)	(15.6)	(27.1)	65.5
Revenue from sale of wines	2.9	0.4	1.6	1.8	(1.7)	2.6	1.1	3.2	(1.4)	(10.6)	9.4
Revenue from sale of beer	(0.1)	0.3	1.9	1.4	(8.5)	(0.9)	0.6	2.1	2.5	0.8	(2.3)
Hospital and medicare insurance premiums	5.8	1.3	3.2	3.1	18.8	(27.7)	(0.1)	4.8	1.5	(10.7)	36.9
Succession duties and gift taxes	1.6	0.3	1.8	1.7	3.1	(6.9)	1.3	(1.7)	(0.8)	(0.3)	8.1
Race track taxes	2.1	0.1	1.9	1.7	3.0	(13.6)	1.4	2.7	(1.0)	1.7	13.0
Forestry revenues	(2.6)	0.8	5.0	(1.2)	4.0	35.5	3.8	3.9	8.9	(58.1)	13.8
Crown oil revenues	21.1	4.5	31.3	25.7	235.2	313.3	36.9	(54.5)	(680.2)	66.7	300.2
Freehold oil revenues	1.2	0.3	1.8	1.5	13.4	17.4	0.1	(5.3)	(35.5)	5.3	12.8
Crown gas revenues	13.9	3.0	20.6	16.9	154.9	205.7	25.4	12.0	(425.8)	(26.6)	246.8
Freehold gas revenues	0.8	0.2	1.2	1.0	8.8	11.6	1.4	0.5	(29.0)	3.5	13.9
Sales of Crown leases and reservations	2.5	0.5	3.7	3.0	27.5	36.6	4.5	(0.2)	(69.3)	(8.7)	41.4
Other oil and gas revenues	1.0	0.2	1.5	1.2	11.3	15.0	1.8	(1.0)	(31.4)	0.4	16.1
Mineral revenues	(10.2)	0.9	3.1	1.3	16.4	3.4	(0.3)	(10.2)	5.8	(10.2)	1.0
Water power rentals	(7.8)	0.3	1.6	0.7	(4.6)	8.9	(0.8)	1.4	3.6	(3.2)	(9.2)
Insurance premium taxes	1.4	0.2	0.2	(0.1)	(2.2)	(8.6)	2.3	3.0	(0.5)	4.4	4.7
Payroll taxes	3.7	0.9	3.4	3.1	8.5	(22.0)	0.9	4.7	0.8	(4.2)	25.3
Local property and school taxes	22.6	5.9	32.5	26.3	83.0	(115.7)	3.6	(1.6)	(26.7)	(29.8)	172.2
Lottery revenues	1.9	0.3	1.5	1.5	5.6	(8.6)	—	(0.5)	0.1	(1.8)	10.3
Miscellaneous provincial taxes	12.6	2.5	11.4	10.4	37.3	(58.2)	0.8	(1.6)	(6.5)	(8.8)	73.5
Shared revenues	0.2	(0.1)	0.3	0.2	0.6	(0.7)	0.2	0.1	(0.7)	(0.1)	1.5
Total entitlements	273.5	69.8	354.7	264.8	1,286.7	(378.5)	202.8	2.7	(1,677.9)	(405.4)	2,455.1

Note: A negative total indicates no equalization payable. A dash indicates an entitlement of less than $50,000.

Source: *The National Finances, 1977-78* (Toronto: Canadian Tax Foundation, 1977), 138, table 10-2.

Table 9.12 Equalization Payable in Fiscal Year 1977-78

Province	Amount, $ million	As percentage of provincial revenue
Newfoundland	273.5	25.9
Prince Edward Island	69.8	29.2
Nova Scotia	354.7	26.4
New Brunswick	264.8	23.4
Quebec	1,286.7	10.6
Manitoba	202.8	12.3
Saskatchewan	2.7	0.1
Total	2,455.1	12.7

Sources: Table 9.11 and Statistics Canada, *Provincial Government Finance*, catalogue no. 68-205.

10

The Equalization System on Trial, 1978-1981

The equalization arrangements introduced in 1977 were better designed to weather storms than the earlier formulas had been, but they proved to be vulnerable to the massive disruptions that the provincial revenue structure was to experience over the next few years.

Natural Resource Revenues Continue to Grow

The problem became visible in 1978, when the preliminary figures for tax bases and provincial revenues for fiscal 1977-78 became available. The calculations made then indicated that the total amount payable for equalization would be significantly higher than the original estimate—and, further, that the traditionally "have" province of Ontario qualified for equalization. This result offended the basic premise underlying the equalization system, namely that payments should go only to the needy provinces. Ontario was far from qualifying as a needy province, except in the technical sense as determined by the formula.

Two factors were working together to produce this unintended result. The first was the unparalleled increase in provincial revenues from oil and natural gas production and land sales in Saskatchewan, Alberta, and British Columbia. Total provincial revenues from these sources grew by an average of nearly 46 percent per year from fiscal year 1972-73 to fiscal year 1979-80. They amounted to approximately $397 million at the beginning of the period and more than $5.5 billion at the end of it. Since Ontario has virtually no revenue from these sources, its traditionally positive entitlements from oil-and-gas-related revenues increased very rapidly. The second factor was the relatively slow growth in revenue from the other provincial revenue sources. Provincial personal income taxes rose from about $2.8 billion in 1972-73 to $10.4 billion in 1979-80, an average annual rate of growth of 20 percent. (This growth includes significant expansion of provincial occupancy of the field at the expense of federal tax revenues.) Over the same period, provincial corporate income taxes rose from $893 million to about $2.2 billion, an average increase of only 13 percent per year. Thus Ontario's negative entitlements with respect to the traditional revenue sources were not sufficient to offset its rapidly growing positive entitlements with respect to oil and gas revenues. The formula therefore determined that equalization amounts were due to Ontario.

Correcting the Formula

Ontario agreed with the rest of the provinces and the federal government that
it should not receive an equalization payment, and its entitlement was put in
abeyance until enabling legislation could be enacted to give effect to this
exception to the general rule. Bill C-26,[1] introduced in Parliament in
December 1978, sought to amend the 1977-1982 arrangements by excluding
from equalization payments any province with per capita personal income
that was regularly above the national average.[2]

In addition to this "personal income override," Bill C-26 included amendments to limit the relative importance of oil and gas revenues in all equalization calculations. Revenue from the sale of Crown leases on oil and natural
gas lands was phased out of the formula over the fiscal years 1979-80 and
1980-81. In spite of this cutback, equalization entitlements to the recipient
provinces in respect of oil and gas revenues rose from 18 percent of total
equalization in 1972-73 to nearly 33 percent in 1979-80.

The arbitrary exclusion of Ontario created some problems for both the
concept of equalization and the equalization formula, for it seemed to indicate that the formula approach was acceptable only so long as it produced the
required results. The overall history of equalization, however, has made it
clear that the formula has always been subject to certain overriding axioms.
Furthermore, the cost to the federal government of making equalization payments to Ontario would have been substantial, at a time when the federal
government was hard pressed to find funding for other purposes, and it was
apparent that the province was able to finance an adequate level of services
without this additional assistance. To provide equalization payments to a
province as rich as Ontario, whose per capita income was traditionally well
above the national average, might have reduced the credibility of both the
concept of equalization and the operation of the program. Thus the damage
from allowing Ontario to receive such payments would have been greater
than the damage risked by modifying the formula to reflect a subjective
opinion of all the parties concerned.[3]

The Special Parliamentary Task Force

The original Bill C-26 had not been given third reading in both chambers of
Parliament before the election of 1979, and it died on the order paper. It was
only in late 1980, when the federal government and the provinces had begun
the negotiations for the 1982-1987 period, that the legislation was rein-

---

[1] Bill C-26, An Act To Amend The Federal-Provincial Fiscal Arrangements and Established
Programs Financing Act, 1977, first reading December 11, 1978.

[2] For a more detailed analysis of the situation at that time, see David B. Perry, "Equalization
and Shifting Provincial Revenues," Fiscal Figures feature (1979), vol. 27, no. 6 *Canadian Tax
Journal* 730-36.

[3] See Ontario, Ministry of Treasury and Economics, Budget Papers, *Equalization and Fiscal
Disparities in Canada*, April 22, 1980, 10.

troduced in the House of Commons as Bill C-24.[4] Parliament was not disposed to give the Bill the necessary quick passage until the government agreed to set up the Special Parliamentary Task Force on Federal-Provincial Fiscal Arrangements, chaired by Liberal MP Herb Breau. After this action by the government, Parliament gave the Bill speedy passage.

The government charged the task force with examining "the programs authorized by the Federal-Provincial Fiscal Arrangements and Established Programs Financing Act, 1977 focusing, in particular, on fiscal equalization."[5] This examination was to take place "within the context of the government's expenditure plan as set out in the October 28, 1980 budget."[6] The task force was unique in the history of federal-provincial fiscal relations in that it brought the full attention of parliamentarians of all parties to bear on all of the key issues under negotiation. It also heard representations from the provinces, interest groups, and academics, so the proceedings of its hearings provide a good summary of current thinking on the issues.

The task force upheld the basic principle of equalization, which had been incorporated into the proposed constitution. In addition, it resisted the arguments presented by some provinces and academics for changing the system to one of direct payments to individuals, or to one of provincial sharing of a revenue pool or other forms of interprovincial equalization, and recommended the continuation of the present system:

> [T]he Task Force interprets equalization payments as a continuing feature of Canadian federalism. They take the form of direct, unconditional payments by the federal government to provincial governments and are designed to be sufficient to guarantee that all provincial governments have the fiscal capacity to ensure comparable levels of public service at comparable levels of taxation.[7]

At a more detailed level, the task force considered ways of avoiding the distortions that arose from the disparity across provinces in oil and gas revenues. The Economic Council of Canada, which had been conducting basic research on this question, had concluded that the inclusion in the formula of resource rents from hydroelectricity generation would do much to alleviate the problem. The task force rejected this approach, on the ground that there was not sufficient experience in measuring these rents, but recommended that further research be carried out in this area with a view to incorporating the rents into the formula for the 1987-1992 arrangements.

The task force also discussed the perennial problem of trying to adjust the equalization system to reflect disparities in the costs of standard provincial

---

[4] An Act To Amend Laws Relating to Fiscal Transfers to Provinces, SC 1980-81-82-83, c. 46.

[5] Canada, *Fiscal Federalism in Canada: Report of the Parliamentary Task Force on Federal-Provincial Fiscal Arrangements* (Ottawa: Supply and Services, August 1981), iii.

[6] Ibid.

[7] Ibid., at 158.

services, but its members could see no way at that time of taking this aspect of regional inequality into account. They suggested that the formula continue in its present form but that the technical committees of officials continue to search for a solution.

Another recommendation put before the task force was that the representative tax system be replaced by a macroeconomic measure of fiscal capacity. The parliamentarians rejected this suggestion as well, on the ground that because firm data were lacking a macroeconomic formula would have to rely on estimates and approximations. In addition, as table 10.1 shows, the adoption of such a formula would have reduced the total amount of equalization payable and changed the relative distribution of federal assistance. Neither result was seen as desirable at the time.

The task force also brought to light a problem that had hitherto not received much attention. The basis of the formula was population, as measured by intercensal estimates provided by the Chief Statistician of Canada and actual census data. The census, however, always misses some residents, and the 1976 census had missed some 477,000. The proportion of residents overlooked was highest in British Columbia and Quebec and higher than average in New Brunswick. The subsequent correction of population figures produced significant changes in the amounts of equalization owed to certain provinces: some enjoyed unexpected gains; others found it necessary to surrender large overpayments. The problem had not been serious up to that point, but the 1981 census was expected to create some difficulties.

Another problem arose from the fact that the 1977-1982 formula included municipal property taxes used for school purposes but not property taxes used for other purposes. In 1980, Quebec reduced school taxes and increased the room available for other municipal taxes; as a result, the six provinces with entitlements for school taxes saw these entitlements shrink substantially. The task force recommended that the equalization system be made neutral with respect to changes in the structure of municipal property taxes by taking all such taxes into the formula. Calculations in the task force report, summarized in table 10.2, indicated that this modification would increase the equalization payable to all recipient provinces by $307 in fiscal 1979-80 and by $530 million in 1984-85.

A large share of the task force's attention went to the problems that provincial natural resource revenues had created for the equalization system. The task force's report pointed out the rapid increase in equalization payable with respect to provincial oil and gas revenues during the 1970s, the result of both the tremendous increases in these revenues and their uneven distribution across the country. As the report noted, the formula was based

> on the assumption that provinces collect revenues only with a view to
> financing public services, and that the revenues accruing to them
> constitute an adequate measure of their expenditure needs. To the extent
> that natural resource revenues accruing to the three western-most
> provinces reflect good fortune, rather than a desire on the part of their

Table 10.1 Estimates of Equalization Payments Calculated Under a Macro-Economic Formula and Under a Representative Tax System Formula When All Provincial and Municipal Revenues Are Equalized (Based on 1980-81 Data)

	Nfld.	PEI	NS	NB	Que.	Ont.	Man.	Sask.	Alta.	BC	Total
						$ millions					
Entitlement under macro-economic formula[a]	469	97	548	475	1,107	(−230)	243	74	(−2,117)	(−592)	3,013
Entitlement under representative tax system formula	512	122	659	568	2,885	(1,433)	509	(−401)	(−5,193)	(−739)	5,255[b]

[a] Based upon adjusted net provincial income at factor cost. [b] Excludes Ontario's entitlement.

Source: Canada, *Fiscal Federalism in Canada: Report of the Parliamentary Task Force on Federal-Provincial Fiscal Relations* (Ottawa: Supply and Services, August 1981), 163, table VII-1.

Table 10.2 Estimated and Projected Costs of Equalizing Property Taxes for Municipal Purposes, 1979-80 to 1984-85

	Nfld.	PEI	NS	NB	Que.	Ont.	Man.	Sask.	Alta.	BC	Total
						$ millions					
1979-80 (estimated)	47.7	9.7	54.0	47.1	141.1	−132.0	7.4	−1.4	−118.8	−54.7	307.0
1980-81 (estimated)	58.3	11.8	64.8	57.1	157.2	−164.7	4.8	−2.2	−132.0	−55.3	354.1
1981-82 (estimated)	64.6	12.9	70.8	62.7	160.8	−193.2	1.6	−2.4	−129.2	−48.5	373.4
1982-83 (estimated)	75.3	14.8	82.2	74.5	175.2	−157.0	10.3	0.3	−205.9	−69.7	432.6
1983-84 (projected)	85.6	16.5	92.6	85.0	184.3	−147.2	14.0	2.1	−254.8	−78.0	480.0
1984-85 (projected)	96.7	18.4	103.7	96.6	192.2	−131.5	18.3	4.4	−312.3	−86.6	530.4

Note: Since Ontario, Alberta, and British Columbia did not receive equalization payments, the negative values shown for these provinces did not reduce the federal outlays for equalization purposes.

Source: Same as table 10.1, at 163, table VII-2.

governments to provide services to their citizens, the above assumption
no longer holds, and it has proven necessary to impose limitations on
the treatment of those revenues.[8]

The limitations described above prevented "over-equalization" to the
recipient provinces, which might then have been able to offer levels of
service above a "reasonable" level at the expense of the federal treasury.

The task force examined the measures introduced in 1978—the personal
income tax override and the exclusion of certain resource revenues from the
formula—in the light of the long-term future for oil and gas revenue, the
treatment of these revenues by the provinces, and the federal government's
ability to fund increased equalization. The task force recognized that there
were too many unknowns (not the least of which was the federal-provincial
sharing of oil and gas revenues in the future) to arrive at a solution that
would stand for more than a short time, and so it refrained from making any
concrete recommendations. The task force's report did contain four general
rules that were designed to guide future decisions in this difficult area of
the formula:

> 1) The maximum portion of natural resource revenues that should be
> included in the equalization formula should be that portion of these reve-
> nues that are used for budgetary purposes, that is, as a minimum, the
> portion sequestered to non-budgetary heritage funds should be excluded.

> 2) To the extent that resource-rich provinces use their resource
> revenues to provide special services to their citizens that they would not
> normally offer if they were rich non-resource producing provinces, it
> would be reasonable to exclude from the formula a portion of resource
> revenues that find their way into provincial budgets. For example, if a
> resource-rich province decides to retire most municipal debts, as Alberta
> did in 1979, the federal government need not assume that the retiring of
> municipal debts is a normal provincial expenditure. In short, resource
> revenues should be included in the formula only to the extent that they
> are used to finance what might be considered normal provincial services.

> 3) All resource revenues should be treated in the same manner. That
> is, no particular type of resource revenue should be excluded from the
> equalization formula and all resource revenues should be included to
> the same extent. (Under the current formula, revenues from land sales
> are excluded, non-renewable resource revenues are included to the
> extension of 50 per cent, and renewable resource revenues are included
> in full.)

> 4) There should continue to be some kind of ceiling or safety net
> relating to the share of total equalization that may be paid out on
> account of resource revenues in order to protect the federal treasury
> against runaway increases in the cost of equalization.[9]

---

[8] Ibid., at 164.
[9] Ibid., at 164-65.

The report went on to suggest that resource revenues should be treated as income to the residents of the province or to corporations operating there. The assumption would then be that the revenues would otherwise have accrued to taxpayers and could therefore be included in the personal or corporate income tax calculations, at an arbitrary percentage, and then automatically equalized at less than full value.

The members of the task force recognized the difficulty of dealing with the effects on the formula of large and unevenly distributed resource revenues, and they were prepared to sacrifice some theoretical purity in order to limit these effects. Like the Ontario government, they accepted the personal income override as a short-term expedient but stressed the need for a long-term solution in the shape of a new formula—one that would not yield unintended results. Indeed, Ontario had agreed to the override on the condition that the formula be so revised.

In the course of its hearings, the task force heard a number of academic observers recommend that the producing provinces' "additional revenues" from oil and gas be used to establish an interprovincial equalization fund. The members of the task force rejected this idea on the grounds, first, that it would be unacceptable to the provinces and, second, that as federal parliamentarians they could not accept the idea that the provinces should assume a function traditionally reserved for the central government. They did, however, see merit in the idea of an "energy bank,"—that is, an interprovincial capital fund financed by "additional" revenues from natural resources that would make loans to the less wealthy provinces. But although the report endorsed the idea, it did not develop it to the point of making specific recommendations.

The task force recommended that the existing formula be continued for the following five years, with modifications to correct the problems identified. It recognized that these modifications would reduce the equalization payments to one or two particular provinces. In order to maintain revenue stability for those provinces, the task force recommended that

> if any province whose equalization entitlement in 1981-82 is more than
> $5 per capita sees its equalization entitlement reduced by more than 5
> per cent as a result of the implementation of a revised formula, it should
> continue to receive 95 per cent of its 1981-82 entitlement until 1984-85
> or until the formula yields more than 95 per cent of its 1981-82 entitle-
> ment, whichever comes sooner.[10]

Provincial Positions

The provinces, meanwhile, had been putting their views about the future of the equalization formula on the record in a number of forums. Their concerns ranged from worry about their own revenues as recipient provinces to more

---

[10] Ibid., at 171.

general concerns about the level of transfers. Almost all of the provinces were willing to agree that the federal government had to take some action to reduce spending and control the growth of its deficit; all of them were concerned that the thrust of federal restraint would be to reduce their own revenues from federal transfers. All aspects of the fiscal arrangements were up for renegotiation, and the established programs financing (EPF) transfers were perhaps more vulnerable than equalization. Traditional "have" provinces such as Ontario were concerned that the cuts would primarily be in EPF transfers, with offsetting enrichment of the equalization formula to limit the damage to the "have-not" provinces. In this case, Ontario and the three western provinces would bear the brunt of the federal cost-cutting measures. Thus these four provinces were even more interested than the others in the shape of the equalization formula for the next five-year period.

While Parliament and the task force were examining these issues, a committee of federal and provincial officials was established in late 1980 to explore possible reforms to the equalization system. In addition, Ontario's treasurer, Frank Miller, included in his 1980 and 1981 budgets special papers that considered the problem of the increased burden on the federal government created by the link between provincial resource revenues and equalization payments.[11] The papers noted that the "over-equalization" provided to recipient provinces might exceed growth in the demand for services (and consequently the cost of providing a uniform standard). In a prescient comment in the 1980 budget paper, Miller noted that the national average was the agreed-upon target for equalization and that until

> the early 1970s, it was reasonable to assume that the national average would be determined by British Columbia, Ontario and Quebec, given that these provinces collectively account for nearly three-quarters of the total population of the country. However, when the norms can be so radically skewed by a province with less than 9 per cent of the population, the real objectives of the program begin to lose their focus. . . . To address the extreme inequality created by a super-rich province with a small share of the population, all provinces could in theory be equalized to the revenue raising capacity of the wealthiest province. However, with the present formula, this would require a doubling of the federal government's total revenues."[12]

The paper went on to illustrate its contention that over-equalization had occurred by examining the revenue positions of the provinces.

This analysis was all in aid of Ontario's position that the formula needed a thorough reform. The 1980 paper pointed out that the federal government had proposed significant changes during the negotiations of 1976, but that its

---

[11] Supra footnote 3 and Ontario, Ministry of Treasury and Economics, Budget Papers, *Renegotiation of Federal-Provincial Fiscal Arrangements: An Ontario Perspective*, May 19, 1981.

[12] Supra footnote 3, at 13.

proposals had not been accepted by the recipient provinces because of uncertainty over the new EPF arrangements and general concern over the long-term implications of the changes. The paper went on to describe four proposals for reforming the system.

The first proposal involved a change in the method of calculating entitlements. The existing formula calculated the equalization for a given province by applying the difference between its share of population and its share of the revenue base for all provinces to the revenue of all provinces. The proposed formula would substitute the province's share of gross domestic product for its share of the total revenue base. Natural resource revenues would continue to be discounted by 50 percent. Although this scheme would not address the problem of oil and gas revenues directly, it would severely limit the growth of federal equalization payments.

The other three proposals were for variations on a two-tier system. Under the second proposal, the federal government would finance basic equalization in the normal fashion and the producing provinces would provide additional equalization directly to the non-producing provinces out of natural resource revenues. The third proposal was similar in intent: the provinces would contribute 25 percent of their natural resource revenues in excess of the national average per capita to a special fund, and the federal government would contribute to the same fund its savings from excluding natural resource revenues from the equalization formula. The proceeds from the fund would be distributed to all provinces on an equal per capita basis. Under the fourth proposal, the formula would include all revenues (including natural resource revenues at full rates or at 50 percent). Again, the federal government would provide a basic level of equalization. The base amount would be increased by an agreed-upon factor, and the shortfall would be paid by the oil-and-gas-producing provinces on the basis of their shares of oil and gas revenues.

As was mentioned earlier, although the concept of provincial participation in the funding of equalization or the sharing of natural resource revenues, outlined in the Ontario paper, had gained a good deal of support in academic circles, it was not acceptable to either the producing provinces or the federal government. The federal government was at this time developing the idea that the equalization function, defined in general terms, was an essential element of the proposed constitution and, further, that it should be solely a federal responsibility.

The debate continued, but no consensus emerged. The radical solutions were rejected, and there seemed to be too little common ground to provide a basis for compromise or evolutionary change. The importance of equalization to the Atlantic provinces, Quebec, and Manitoba made it difficult for them to agree to revisions to the formula that would reduce their entitlements.

The issue of equalization was complicated by two other major issues that absorbed the energies of the federal government and the provinces during 1980 and 1981. The first was the problem of the regulation and taxation of the oil and gas industry in western Canada, discussed in detail in chapter 8. Until the pricing structure for oil and gas and the division of oil and gas revenues between the federal government and the producing provinces had been settled, it was not possible to settle the problem of equalizing natural resource revenues. The second problem was that of constitutional change. This broader issue concerned all of the provinces and involved matters on which agreement was proving to be even more elusive than agreement on the principles of equalization.

11

The Federal Government Seizes the Initiative, 1981-1997

The Federal Government Makes the First Move

The tone of federal-provincial negotiations to determine fiscal arrangements for the period 1982-1987 was set early. The federal minister of finance, Allan MacEachen, announced in his October 1980 budget that he planned to achieve significant savings in social services expenditures during the 1982-83 fiscal year, mainly by limiting the growth of established programs financing (EPF) transfers. The minister's November 1981 budget was more precise: he hoped to spend $1.5 billion less than the projections of the existing system called for. Although he provided no specific figures on equalization, the implication was that the minister was looking for savings in this area as well.

Federal-provincial negotiations had produced no solution for the 1982-1987 period by the time that Finance Minister MacEachen brought down his federal budget of November 1981. In an accompanying paper,[1] MacEachen spelled out the federal position in detail for the first time. The federal government did not waver from its position that the basic elements of the equalization formula were sound, and it agreed with the provinces that the formula should include all provincial and local government revenues, including all property taxes.

The problem was how to deal with provincial oil and gas revenues under an inclusive formula. The federal government and the oil-producing provinces had only recently reached agreement on price and revenue-sharing policies, and the effects of this agreement had not yet been felt in the equalization formula. It was likely, however, that the inclusion of all oil and gas revenues would continue to disrupt the equalization formula.

The critical issue, according to the minister's November budget paper, was the definition of an appropriate standard of equalization. To what level should revenues in the low-income provinces be raised? The paper pointed out that the standard could be set by reference to one or more of the provinces that were able to provide an adequate level of provincial and local services. Ontario and the western provinces were the obvious candidates, but the western provinces had been able to provide high levels of public services

---

[1] Canada, Department of Finance, Budget Papers, *Fiscal Arrangements in the Eighties: Proposals of the Government of Canada*, November 12, 1981.

while accumulating surpluses and maintaining low levels of taxation. As the minister pointed out, equalization

> to the level of British Columbia's or Saskatchewan's fiscal capacity would require payments of $16.7 or $14.7 billion respectively in 1982-83, and would more than triple the cost of the program. Equalization to the level of Alberta, the top province, would cost a staggering $98 billion, considerably more than total federal outlays planned for that year. Equalization to the national average with a comprehensive measure of capacity would require total payments in 1982-83 of $10.2 billion [an increase of 150 percent over 1981-82], with Ontario receiving $2.6 billion.[2]

The minister concluded that on the basis of either the level of public service or the level of taxation, Ontario was the logical choice as the standard for a comprehensive equalization formula. He estimated that if the next highest province, Quebec, were chosen, total equalization payments would drop to less than $1 billion and Quebec would no longer qualify for payments:

> The basic premise underlying the adoption of an Ontario standard with a comprehensive measure of fiscal capacity is that this province is able and will continue to be able to provide its residents with a satisfactory level of public services by imposing average rates of taxation upon its own bases as defined in the representative tax system.[3]

To support this change from the concept of national averages to the concept of a representative province, the minister pointed to the general acceptance of the override clause and the fact that Ontario had the highest fiscal capacity of all the provinces, with the exception of the oil-producing provinces. He further noted that Ontario's revenue structure more closely approximated the revenue structures of the traditional recipient provinces than did either the national average or any other average that included any of the oil-producing provinces.

The provincial reaction, predictably, was negative. Because the federal proposal had come so late in the negotiations, less than five months before the current arrangements expired, the provinces mounted their assault almost immediately. The recipient provinces not only stood to lose considerable sums; they would be further disadvantaged by the fact that a formula based on only one province would be subject to the fluctuations in revenue that any province may experience.

The first opportunity for serious bargaining occurred at a meeting of federal and provincial finance ministers and treasurers held on November 23, 1981.[4] By that time, the constitutional talks had been concluded and the

---

[2] Ibid., at 18.

[3] Ibid.

[4] It is important to note that negotiations on fiscal arrangements had fallen behind the normal schedule: by the third week of November in 1976, for example, the parties were only three weeks away from complete agreement.

federal government had signed agreements with the western provinces for sharing oil and gas revenues. Agreement before the expiration of the existing arrangements appeared impossible, and the provinces pushed for a one-year extension of the existing arrangements, with a provision for minimum payments to protect the recipient provinces. The federal government rejected this proposal.

The finance ministers and treasurers met again on December 14 and 15, 1981. A confidential report prepared by provincial officials and supported by all of the provinces except Quebec characterized the federal proposal as an even more important departure from the existing system than had been originally understood—as, in fact, the most significant change in the formula in at least a decade and a half. At the meeting, Finance Minister MacEachen presented revised estimates of equalization entitlements based on new data on personal and corporate income taxes. He offered to consider, in general terms, some modifications to his proposal, including the provision of a floor under the payments. Some provinces presented counterproposals, but no consensus of the provincial positions on equalization emerged, other than the request for a one-year extension of the existing formula.

The next meeting of the finance ministers and treasurers, on January 22, 1982, followed two significant developments. First, changes in the federal budget after its introduction in November had reduced the additional personal and corporate income tax revenue that flowed automatically to the provinces. Second, revised population data based on the 1981 census, issued in early January, indicated that the Atlantic provinces and Manitoba had received substantial overpayments over the previous four years. The law was clear on the necessity for recovery by the federal government. These developments made the fiscal squeeze on the provinces implied by the federal proposal more severe and the necessity for compromise more compelling.

At the January meeting, Finance Minister MacEachen offered several concessions. He was willing to set a floor under equalization equal to 85 percent of the previous year's entitlement; move the base year for the cap on equalization from 1981-82 to 1982-83; provide a minimum annual increase in equalization that would particularly benefit Manitoba, which stood to be hit hard by the proposed move away from the national standard; and review the revenue sources and tax bases used in the formula. No firm conclusions emerged from this meeting.

At the conclusion of a first ministers' conference on the economy held on February 4, 1982, Finance Minister MacEachen proposed a change in the equalization standard from Ontario levels to a representative average standard—that is, per capita average revenues over five provinces, excluding Alberta (the highest) and the Atlantic provinces (the lowest), which like Alberta had 9.2 percent of the total population in 1981. He presented further details to a meeting of finance and treasury officials in late February. The representative average standard would apply to the previously proposed group of revenues plus local government revenues from the sale of goods and services. The latter amounts, which included revenues from water sales, had risen substantially in recent years as local governments turned increasingly to user charges. The new proposals also described in detail the "floor" provisions and minimum increase provisions that the finance minister had put forward at the January meeting. These provisions are discussed below.

Although the provinces did not accept the revised proposals at the February meeting and continued to press for an extension, the federal government went ahead with them. On March 19, 1982, it introduced the proposals to Parliament in the form of Bill 97,[5] which received royal assent on April 7, 1982 with effect retroactively to April 1.

The Mechanics of the 1982-1987 Arrangements

The 1982 legislation extended the equalization system to March 31, 1987. It implemented the federal proposals of November and February and expanded the list of revenue sources subject to equalization from 29 items to 33. The new list appears in table 11.1.

The changes in the list reflected changes in provincial revenues. Because provincial capital taxes on corporations had grown in importance, the legislation separated item 3 from the miscellaneous tax item. It substantially revised the oil and gas revenue items (numbers 17 to 22) to reflect current tax practice in the oil-producing provinces and included these items at full values, without the special limits imposed by earlier legislation. The 1982 legislation also restored Crown leases (item 23) and separated potash revenues from the residual natural resource category (25). It expanded item 30 to include all local government property taxes, not just school-purpose taxes. Finally, it modified the residual category (item 32) by excluding capital taxes on corporations and adding local government revenues from sales of goods and services (including water revenues) and miscellaneous local government taxes. The formula continued to exclude local licence revenue.

Bill 97 also spelled out the new representative average standard. The new formula was based on the concept of a national average rate of tax, as developed in 1967, which was determined for each revenue source in the list by expressing the revenue collected by all provinces as a percentage of the relevant revenue base for all provinces. The per capita yield for a single revenue source for a single province was calculated by applying the national average rate of tax to the province's tax base and dividing the result by its population. The equalization entitlement for each province was determined by subtracting the per capita yield in the province from the average per capita yield for each revenue source for the five provinces in the standard (Quebec, Ontario, Manitoba, Saskatchewan, and British Columbia). The per capita

---

[5] An Act To Amend the Federal-Provincial Fiscal Arrangements and Established Programs Financing Act, 1977 and To Provide for Payments to Certain Provinces, SC 1980-81-82-83, c. 94.

Table 11.1 Summary of Provincial Revenue Sources, As Used
in the Equalization Formula, 1982-1987

1) Personal income taxes.
2) Corporation income taxes, revenues derived from government business enterprises not included in any other paragraph of this definition, and revenues received from the Government of Canada pursuant to the Public Utilities Income Tax Transfer Act.
3) Taxes on capital of corporations.
4) General and miscellaneous sales and amusement taxes.
5) Tobacco taxes.
6) Motive fuel taxes derived from the sale of gasoline.
7) Motive fuel taxes derived from the sale of diesel fuel.
8) Non-commercial motor vehicle licensing revenues.
9) Commercial motor vehicle licensing revenues.
10) Alcoholic beverage revenues derived from the sale of spirits.
11) Alcoholic beverage revenues derived from the sale of wine.
12) Alcoholic beverage revenues derived from the sale of beer.
13) Hospital and medical care insurance premiums.
14) Succession duties and gift taxes.
15) Race track taxes.
16) Forestry revenues.
17) Conventional new oil revenues.
18) Conventional old oil revenues.
19) Heavy oil revenues.
20) Mined oil revenues.
21) Domestically sold natural gas revenues.
22) Exported natural gas revenues.
23) Sales of Crown leases and reservations on oil and natural gas lands.
24) Oil and gas revenues other than those described in items 17 to 23.
25) Metallic and non-metallic mineral revenues other than potash revenues.
26) Potash revenues.
27) Water power rentals.
28) Insurance premium taxes.
29) Payroll taxes.
30) Provincial and local government property taxes (including grants in lieu of such taxes from the federal and provincial governments).
31) Lottery revenues.
32) Miscellaneous provincial taxes and revenues including miscellaneous revenues from natural resources, concessions and franchises, and sales of provincial goods and services; and local government revenues from sales of goods and services and miscellaneous local government taxes.
33) Revenues from the Government of Canada from any of the sources referred to in this definition that are shared by Canada with the provinces other than revenue shared under the Public Utilities Income Tax Transfer Act.

amounts, positive and negative, for all 33 sources were added together, and a net per capita deficiency was multiplied by the provincial population to produce the province's total equalization payment.

Although the basic mechanics of the new arrangement were almost the same as those of previous representative tax measures, the switch from a national average to the five-province average changed the size and relative distribution of equalization significantly. The adoption of a more restrictive standard made possible the adoption of a less restrictive formula—one that included the oil and gas revenues excluded under the two previous arrangements; nor was there any further need for the override clause.

The exclusion of Alberta's revenues from the representative average standard and the fact that oil and gas revenues in Quebec, Ontario, and Manitoba were very low served to hold down equalization entitlements arising from these sources. As a result, total entitlements were smaller under the new system than they would have been under a continuation of the old one.

Tables 11.2 and 11.3 provide detailed estimates of the equalization calculations for 1982-83. These estimates were prepared by the Department of Finance in July 1982, before the regulations had been revised to define the new provisions relating to oil and gas revenues. The dollar effect of the revisions was expected to be relatively small, since the per capita tax base for these revenues in the representative average standard was very close to the per capita base in the recipient provinces with no such revenues. In Manitoba, the difference was so small that it did not have any effect on payments during the transitional phase. The two new revenue sources, municipal tax revenues and local government revenues from the sale of goods and services, were included with similar provincial revenues in the legislation but calculated separately in the estimates to show their effects on total equalization.

Table 11.2 shows for each of the 33 revenue sources the average per capita yield, at the national rates, for the five provinces in the representative average standard and the difference between that yield and the per capita yield, at the national rate, for each province. The sum of the differences, positive and negative, for all 33 sources was multiplied by the province's population to produce the province's basic equalization entitlement. If a province had a negative total—that is, a net excess—no equalization was payable. Table 11.3 shows the provincial entitlements for the 1982-83 fiscal year, and table 11.4 shows the relative importance of equalization to each of the provinces in 1982-83.

The new legislation set maximum and minimum equalization payments and provided transitional relief. The minimum payment to a recipient province was 95 percent of the previous year's payment if the province's per capita revenue was 70 percent or less of the national average, 90 percent if the per capita revenue was more than 70 but no less than 75 percent of the national average, and 85 percent if the per capita revenue was over 75 percent of the national average. This provision was designed to protect Newfoundland and Nova Scotia from a sudden drop in equalization if their offshore oil and gas deposits should produce significant provincial revenue.

A second minimum provision ensured that the 1982-83 equalization would be at least equal to its 1981-82 payment plus five-thirds of the average annual change over the last four years of the previous agreement. In 1983-84, the minimum was the 1981-82 payment plus five-thirds of the average annual change; in 1984-85, the minimum was the 1981-82 payment plus twice the average annual change. This provision was inserted to assist Manitoba,

Table 11.2 Calculation of Equalization for 1982-83: Average Per Capita Yield for the Representative Average Standard and Per Capita Deficiency or Excess by Province[a]

Revenue source[b]	Average per capita yield, representative average standard	Average per capita yield, deficiency (+) or excess (−)									
		Nfld.	PEI	NS	NB	Que.	Ont.	Man.	Sask.	Alta.	BC
		dollars									
Personal income taxes	703.09	330.83	358.84	236.54	284.48	88.51	−56.27	154.90	112.49	−149.04	−126.61
Business income revenues	116.60	59.97	66.38	43.75	30.88	19.33	−10.87	24.18	2.96	−131.52	−20.95
General sales taxes	352.75	104.47	140.56	69.55	71.88	58.61	−13.04	59.68	−22.19	−244.41	−109.37
Tobacco taxes	46.57	12.85	3.41	−1.26	1.17	−6.18	2.40	3.97	7.12	−11.20	2.90
Gasoline taxes	105.63	27.52	4.72	4.62	−10.00	10.91	−5.13	7.79	−8.18	−39.52	−9.36
Diesel fuel taxes	26.84	7.81	17.23	7.02	−9.57	4.80	−1.71	−0.26	−8.04	−16.23	−2.90
Non-commercial vehicle licences	34.59	13.18	2.37	−1.24	4.40	1.51	−0.84	−2.42	1.22	−6.56	−0.45
Commercial vehicle licences	19.40	1.01	3.86	2.46	−2.28	5.07	1.56	−8.17	−15.67	−31.18	−8.10
Revenues from the sale of spirits	49.73	6.12	−10.58	−4.09	8.74	16.01	−4.33	−12.45	−4.01	−15.99	−17.65
Revenues from the sale of wine	13.42	9.40	7.27	5.55	7.42	−0.52	0.92	3.78	6.56	0.68	−5.34
Revenues from the sale of beer	21.09	−1.56	2.87	2.73	2.10	−1.35	0.01	2.05	3.96	3.28	0.95
Hospital and medical insurance premiums	76.79	7.60	4.30	−1.28	1.70	4.80	−4.85	4.83	8.76	3.67	−0.92
Succession duties and gift taxes	1.90	1.33	1.17	0.85	1.13	0.43	−0.34	0.66	0.25	−0.87	−0.27
Race track taxes	5.80	5.60	1.76	3.95	4.39	1.52	−1.77	1.35	4.40	−1.85	−0.06
Forestry revenues	12.20	2.44	12.20	11.11	−1.24	6.73	7.66	10.01	9.55	10.03	−46.31
Crown oil revenues	18.87	18.87	18.87	18.87	18.85	18.87	18.87	13.60	−262.01	−1,255.77	−15.68
Freehold oil revenues	1.96	1.96	1.96	1.96	1.96	1.96	1.78	−5.20	−26.59	−83.22	1.16
Crown gas revenues	15.66	15.66	15.66	15.66	15.54	15.66	15.66	15.66	−25.31	−912.04	−81.66
Freehold gas revenues	0.21	0.21	0.21	0.21	0.21	0.21	−0.12	0.21	−0.60	−31.97	0.03
Sales of Crown leases	5.28	5.28	5.28	5.28	5.28	5.28	5.23	5.28	−45.87	−228.58	−14.35
Other oil and gas revenues	1.02	1.02	1.02	1.02	1.02	1.02	1.02	0.90	−7.68	−58.86	−3.19
Mineral revenues	10.05	−27.35	10.05	4.56	−1.39	3.97	−0.31	−4.09	−0.27	6.17	−6.62
Water power rentals	9.07	−57.48	9.07	7.89	4.37	−4.51	5.29	−5.83	6.35	8.32	−6.04
Insurance premium taxes	13.64	6.90	4.91	3.93	2.65	−0.47	−0.33	2.51	1.77	−1.54	0.58
Payroll taxes	61.55	25.94	26.49	14.49	19.39	6.26	−5.95	7.08	14.56	−1.15	−3.71

(Table 11.2 is concluded on the next page.)

Table 11.2 Concluded

Revenue source[b]	Average per capita yield, representative average standard	Average per capita yield, deficiency (+) or excess (−)									
		Nfld.	PEI	NS	NB	Que.	Ont.	Man.	Sask.	Alta.	BC
		dollars									
Property school taxes	201.99	66.86	62.65	52.21	53.14	23.89	−12.39	2.21	−7.00	−56.27	−15.25
Lottery Revenues	16.00	6.26	4.51	3.04	4.35	1.66	−1.11	0.81	0.70	0.20	−0.93
Miscellaneous provincial taxes	89.34	35.94	35.07	27.63	26.90	11.09	−5.35	8.21	−10.20	−47.21	−8.55
Shared tax on undistributed income	0.07	0.06	0.07	0.07	0.07	0.03	−0.06	0.05	0.07	0.05	0.06
Shared oil export charge	8.26	8.26	8.26	8.26	8.26	8.26	8.26	7.56	−159.79	−37.12	8.26
Municipal tax revenues	342.49	113.38	106.22	88.53	90.11	40.50	−21.01	3.75	−11.87	−95.42	−25.86
Potash revenues	9.35	9.35	9.35	9.35	9.35	9.35	9.35	9.35	−181.64	9.35	9.35
Capital tax	32.76	13.58	20.19	13.27	11.65	7.79	−3.31	2.52	0.11	−42.46	−8.73
Local government sales of goods and services	120.04	48.30	47.13	37.12	36.15	14.90	−7.18	11.03	−13.71	−63.43	−11.48
Total	2,544.03	881.60	1,003.35	693.63	703.06	375.91	−78.24	325.50	−629.80	−3,521.67	−527.05

[a] The calculations were performed to five decimal places; for the sake of simplicity, they have been rounded here to two. [b] The classification of revenue sources in this table does not agree in all particulars with table 11.1. This is so because not all revenue sources and bases had been redefined in the regulations when the calculations were made. Until this was done, the calculations had to conform to existing regulations, even though changes had been made internally. Later calculations reflect the revised classification shown in table 11.1.

Source: Canada, Department of Finance, Second Estimate of Equalization Payments for 1982-83, July 5, 1982.

Table 11.3   Calculation of Equalization for 1982-83: Equalization Entitlements by Revenue Source and Province

Revenue source[a]	Nfld.	PEI	NS	NB	Que.	Ont.	Man.	Sask.	Alta.	BC	Total, six recipient provinces
					millions of dollars						
Personal income taxes	188.3	44.1	201.0	198.6	573.5	-488.3	159.5	110.0	-344.8	-354.6	1,364.9
Business income revenues	34.1	8.2	37.2	21.6	125.2	-94.4	24.9	2.9	-304.3	-58.7	251.1
General sales taxes	59.5	17.3	59.1	50.2	379.8	-113.2	61.4	-21.7	-565.4	-306.4	627.2
Tobacco taxes	7.3	0.4	-1.1	0.8	-40.0	20.9	4.1	7.0	-25.9	8.1	-28.5
Gasoline taxes	15.7	0.6	3.9	-7.0	70.7	-44.5	8.0	-8.0	-91.4	-26.2	91.9
Diesel fuel taxes	4.4	2.1	6.0	-6.7	31.1	-14.9	-0.3	-7.9	-37.5	-8.1	36.7
Non-commercial vehicle licences	7.5	0.3	-1.1	3.1	9.8	-7.2	-2.5	1.2	-15.2	-1.3	17.1
Commercial vehicle licences	0.6	0.5	2.1	-1.6	32.9	13.6	-8.4	-15.3	-72.1	-22.7	26.0
Revenues from the sale of spirits	3.5	-1.3	-3.5	6.1	103.8	-37.6	-12.8	-3.9	-37.0	-49.4	95.7
Revenues from the sale of wine	5.4	0.9	4.7	5.2	-3.4	8.0	3.9	6.4	1.6	-15.0	16.7
Revenues from the sale of beer	-0.9	0.4	2.3	1.5	-8.8	0.1	2.1	3.9	7.6	2.7	-3.4
Hospital and medical insurance premiums	4.3	0.5	-1.1	1.2	31.1	-42.1	5.0	8.6	8.5	-2.6	41.1
Succession duties and gift taxes	0.8	0.1	0.7	0.8	2.8	-3.0	0.7	0.2	-2.0	-0.7	5.9
Race track taxes	3.2	0.2	3.3	3.1	9.8	-15.4	1.4	4.3	-4.3	-0.2	21.0
Forestry revenues	1.4	1.5	9.4	-0.9	43.6	66.5	10.3	9.3	23.2	-129.7	65.4
Crown oil revenues	10.7	2.3	16.0	13.2	122.3	163.8	14.0	-256.1	-2,905.2	-43.9	178.5
Freehold oil revenues	1.1	0.2	1.7	1.4	12.7	15.4	-5.4	-26.0	-192.5	3.2	11.7
Crown gas revenues	8.9	1.9	13.3	10.8	101.5	135.9	16.1	-24.7	-2,110.0	-228.7	152.6
Freehold gas revenues	0.1	..	0.2	0.1	1.3	-1.1	0.2	-0.6	-74.0	0.1	2.0

(Table 11.3 is concluded on the next page.)

Table 11.3 Concluded

Revenue source[a]	Nfld.	PEI	NS	NB	Que.	Ont.	Man.	Sask.	Alta.	BC	Total, six recipient provinces
					millions of dollars						
Sales of Crown leases	3.0	0.6	4.5	3.7	34.2	45.4	5.4	-44.8	-528.8	-40.2	51.5
Other oil and gas revenues	0.6	0.1	0.9	0.7	6.6	8.9	0.9	-7.5	-136.2	-8.9	9.8
Mineral revenues	-15.6	1.2	3.9	-1.0	25.7	-2.7	-4.2	-0.3	14.3	-18.6	10.1
Water power rentals	-32.7	1.1	6.7	3.1	-29.2	45.9	-6.0	6.2	19.2	-16.9	-57.1
Insurance premium taxes	3.9	0.6	3.3	1.9	-3.1	-2.9	2.6	1.7	-3.6	1.6	9.2
Payroll taxes	14.8	3.3	12.3	13.5	40.5	-51.7	7.3	14.2	-2.7	-10.4	91.7
Property school taxes	38.1	7.7	44.4	37.1	154.8	-107.5	2.3	-6.8	-130.2	-42.7	284.3
Lottery revenues	3.6	0.6	2.6	3.0	10.7	-9.7	0.8	0.7	0.5	-2.6	21.3
Miscellaneous provincial taxes	20.5	4.3	23.5	18.8	71.9	-46.4	8.5	-10.0	-109.2	-23.9	147.3
Shared tax on undistributed income	..	..	0.1	..	0.2	-0.5	0.1	0.1	0.1	0.2	0.4
Shared oil export charge	4.7	1.0	7.0	5.8	53.6	71.7	7.8	-156.2	-85.9	23.1	79.8
Municipal tax revenues	64.5	13.0	75.2	62.9	262.5	-182.3	3.9	-11.6	-220.7	-72.4	482.0
Potash revenues	5.3	1.1	7.9	6.5	60.6	81.1	9.6	-177.6	21.6	26.2	91.2
Capital tax	7.7	2.5	11.3	8.1	50.5	-28.7	2.6	0.1	-98.2	-24.5	82.7
Local government sales of goods and services	27.5	5.8	31.5	25.2	96.6	-62.3	11.4	-13.4	-146.8	-32.2	198.0
Total	501.8	123.2	589.4	490.8	2,435.8	-679.0	335.0	-615.6	-8,147.4	-1,476.3	4,476.1

[a] See table 11.2, note b.　.. Less than 0.1.

Source: Same as table 11.2.

Table 11.4   Equalization Payable in 1982-83

	Amount, $ millions	As a percentage of provincial revenue
Newfoundland	501.8	28.5
Prince Edward Island	123.2	30.9
Nova Scotia	589.4	25.3
New Brunswick	490.8	24.4
Quebec	2,435.8	11.0
Manitoba	335.0	11.7
Total	4,476.1	14.2

Sources: Table 11.3 and Statistics Canada, *Provincial Government Finance*, catalogue no. 68-205.

the only recipient province whose revenues were closer to the five-province average than to the national average and, consequently, the province that otherwise would have lost the most in relative terms. The transitional payments were expected to produce a higher fiscal capacity in Manitoba than in Ontario in 1982-83 and 1983-84. At the time of the legislation's passage, the federal government forecast that Manitoba would receive $165 million over the three-year transitional period and that Quebec, which would also benefit briefly from the arrangements, would receive $85 million in the first year. Table 11.5 shows the provisional calculations for transitional and supplementary equalization payments during the 1982-1987 period. The figures represent the estimates made during each fiscal year, not the final calculations of entitlements made several years later.

All of the equalization provisions were subject to an overriding limit on total federal equalization, which was not to increase over the fiscal year 1982-83 at a rate greater than the rate of increase shown by the gross national product over the calendar year 1982. Individual recipient provinces would have their entitlements reduced accordingly. The federal government's adoption of this arrangement represented a change in the position it had maintained in earlier negotiations, when it had proposed to use as the base the lower equalization payments made in 1981-82.

Throughout the negotiations leading up to the new arrangements and even following their enactment, the federal government had failed to release any estimates of the amounts due under the various proposals, or under an extension of the previous arrangements—a sharp contrast to its practice in earlier negotiations. Finance Minister MacEachen's argument was direct: the old formula was deficient and could not be maintained. Because it excluded some natural resource revenues and municipal property taxes and because it arbitrarily denied payments to Ontario, it had to be changed in any event.

The provincial governments, however, were not uninterested in comparisons of the old formula with the new one. The 1982 Quebec budget included a table that showed the provincial finance department's estimates of the effects the new formula for each province; it is reproduced here as table 11.6.

Table 11.5   Basic and Supplementary Equalization Payments, Fiscal
Years 1982-83 to 1986-87; Estimates Made During Each Fiscal Year

	1982-83	1983-84	1984-85	1985-86	1986-87
	millions of dollars				
Basic equalization					
Newfoundland	502	535	568	626	673
Prince Edward Island	123	115	122	132	142
Nova Scotia	589	536	542	571	609
New Brunswick	491	489	538	600	638
Quebec	2,436	2,476	2,663	2,744	2,779
Manitoba	335	291	343	420	432
Saskatchewan	—	—	—	—	147
Total	4,476	4,441	4,776	5,093	5,420
Supplementary					
Newfoundland	—	—	—	15	—
Prince Edward Island	—	11	7	5	—
Nova Scotia	—	67	78	20	—
New Brunswick	—	28	—	20	—
Quebec	175	474	411	110	—
Manitoba	89	177	136	50	65
Saskatchewan	—	—	—	—	—
Total	264	756	633	220	65

Sources: *The National Finances, 1982-83 to 1986-87* (Toronto: Canadian Tax Foundation),
chapter on general payments.

Table 11.6   Effect of the Changes in Equalization Contained in Bill C-97[a]

	Old act, $ millions	New act, $ millions	Difference	
			$ millions	Percentage change
Newfoundland	1,710.2	1,824.2	+114.0	+ 6.7
Prince Edward Island	404.8	450.3	+ 45.5	+ 11.2
Nova Scotia	2,091.3	2,261.5	+170.2	+ 8.1
New Brunswick	1,648.8	1,789.0	+140.2	+ 8.5
Quebec	8,691.8	8,039.6	−652.2	− 7.5
Manitoba	1,586.8	1,327.8	−259.0	− 16.3
Saskatchewan	274.4	—	−274.4	−100.0
Total	16,408.1	15,692.4	−715.7	− 4.4

[a] Based on information for the five-year period 1977-1982.

Source: Québec, Ministère des Finances, *1982-83 Budget*, Additional Information, May 25,
1982, appendix IV, 4.

According to the Quebec calculations, Newfoundland's equalization entitlement would have been little different had the new formula been in place for
the period 1977 to 1982, and the entitlements for the other three Atlantic
provinces would have been from 8 to 11 percent larger. Quebec's total
equalization for the period would have been well over 7 percent smaller, and
Manitoba's over 16 percent smaller. Saskatchewan would have received no

equalization during the 1977-1982 period under the new formula, whereas it had received $274 million under the old formula in the first four years of the period; by 1981-82, it had ceased to qualify under the old formula.

There were two technical provisions in the 1982 equalization legislation that affected the size of payments. The first related to the federal-provincial sharing of the proceeds from the oil export charge imposed under the national energy program, which was expected to receive parliamentary passage after the end of the 1981-82 fiscal year. Saskatchewan was anxious to credit its share to its 1981-82 accounts; the equalization legislation accommodated this desire and included the amount in the calculations for 1981-82.

The effects of the second technical provision were more substantive. As was noted earlier, revisions to the intercensal estimates of population as a result of the 1981 census substantially changed the equalization entitlements of certain provinces. In 1977, it had been agreed that these revisions would affect only those years not finalized[6] when the figures were released. The first pre-census estimates had underestimated the shifts in population, and the census revealed substantial overpayments of equalization to the four Atlantic provinces and Manitoba for the fiscal years 1980-81 and 1981-82.

These potential debts of the provinces were no doubt a factor in the bargaining for the 1982-1987 period. In any event, the federal government agreed to forgive the amounts, estimated at $68 million for Newfoundland, $8 million for Prince Edward Island, $49 million for Nova Scotia, $61 million for New Brunswick, and $31 million for Manitoba. The benefit conferred by this measure may have been enough to offset the worst effects of the reduction in these provinces' equalization payments and established programs financing (EPF) transfers. The original estimates of Quebec's equalization entitlements for 1980-81 and 1981-82 proved to be too low, and large adjusting payments were provided to the province. Saskatchewan was to repay the overpayment it had received for 1980-81, the last fiscal year for which it had qualified for equalization. The federal government took the position that the province's fiscal capacity was sufficient to permit repayment and restricted forgiveness to provinces that had equalization entitlements in 1982-83.

Subsequent Developments

The original minimum and transitional payment provisions under the 1982-1987 arrangements provided additional payments to all of the recipient provinces through 1984-85. In April 1985, the federal government modified the equalization system by introducing two types of supplementary

---

[6] The calculations of equalization payments are revised regularly to reflect up-to-date information on provincial revenues. The entitlements for a given fiscal year are not fully determined and paid until several years after the end of that year.

payments. Payments of the first type were for Nova Scotia, Quebec, and Manitoba, the richest of the recipient provinces and consequently the provinces that faced the largest reductions in their equalization payments when the original transitional payments ended with the 1984-85 fiscal year. The supplementary payments for these provinces were calculated to ensure that their 1985-86 equalization payments would be no less than 95 percent of their 1984-85 payments. Total equalization payments for 1986-87 were similarly guaranteed at 95 percent of the 1985-86 level. Payments of the second type were for the poorer recipient provinces, which would lose relatively little with the ending of the original transitional provisions and therefore stood to gain relatively little from a payment scheme designed to compensate for the lapse of those provisions. These provinces, Newfoundland, Prince Edward Island, and New Brunswick, would receive payments based on the average of the per capita supplementary payments to Nova Scotia, Quebec, and Manitoba.

The 1987-1992 Arrangements

Although the negotiations that preceded the 1987-1992 arrangements were sometimes bitter, they usually centred on technical issues rather than on matters of principle. The supplementary payments introduced in 1985 were one source of controversy: the federal government made some technical modifications that increased entitlements to the recipient provinces, but it adamantly refused either to continue the special payments in their existing form or to incorporate them into the basic calculations. Bill C-44[7] extended the existing equalization system, including the provisions for setting maximum and minimum payments, until March 31, 1992 and provided that the technical changes, to be spelled out in regulations, would be implemented over the first two years of the new arrangements. Since no province was now levying succession duties or gift taxes, these revenue sources were eliminated from the formula. Table 11.7 shows the revenue sources and bases used in the 1987-1992 formula, and table 11.8 shows the calculation of the 1991-92 entitlements. Bill C-44 also provided for forgiveness of amounts owed by recipient provinces under the 1982-1987 equalization formula as a result of the recalculation of entitlements on the basis of revised population data from the 1986 census. Table 11.9 shows the relative importance of equalization to each province in 1991-92.

The overall limitation on equalization payments, which held total payments to a rate of growth no higher than that of the gross national product, cut in during the 1987-1992 period. It became effective for entitlements in the 1988-89 fiscal year but did not show up in calculations until 1990-91, when revised figures were available for earlier years. As the last line of table 11.8 shows, the 1991-92 entitlements were reduced in total by an estimated

---

[7] An Act To Amend the Federal-Provincial Fiscal Arrangements and Federal Post-Secondary and Health Contributions Act, 1977, SC 1987, c.14.

**Table 11.7 Summary of Provincial Revenue Sources,
As Used in the Equalization Formula, 1987-1992[a]**

Source[b]	Base[b]
1) Personal income taxes (collections less credits and Quebec abatement).	Federal basic tax as determined in each province.
2) Business income revenues (corporate income tax, remittances from provincial government business enterprises (excluding liquor and lottery agencies and the BC Petroleum Company), and the provincial share of the tax on privately operated public utilities, less income tax credits).	Taxable profits, profits of provincial government business enterprises. Adjustments to eliminate effect of provincial oil and gas levies and other natural resource taxes, and to reflect deductions for small business and manufacturing and processing profits.
3) Capital tax revenues (includes debt guarantee fees imposed on borrowings of provincially owned electrical utilities).	Total paid up capital and equity of deposit-taking institutions, as adjusted. Also adjusted for sectoral differences.
4) General and miscellaneous sales taxes.	Sales of main commodities subject to provincial sales taxes (excluding sales of food, children's clothing, tobacco, gas, construction, and services).
5) Tobacco taxes.	Volume of tobacco sales.
6) Gasoline taxes.	Volume of gasoline sales adjusted for preferentially treated sales.
7) Diesel fuel taxes.	Volume of diesel fuel sales adjusted for preferentially treated sales.
8) Non-commercial vehicle licences.	Registrations of passenger vehicles.
9) Commercial vehicle licences.	Sales of commercial vehicles.
10) Revenue from the sale of spirits.	Volume of spirits sold.
11) Revenue from the sale of wine.	Volume of wine sold.
12) Revenue from the sale of beer.	Volume of beer sold.
13) Hospital and medical insurance premiums.	Number of individual income tax returns adjusted for special low-income relief measures.
14) Race track taxes.	Pari-mutuel betting.
15) Forestry revenues.	Value-added by forestry industry from activity on Crown lands, plus stumpage.
16) New oil revenues less rebates and credits.	Value of production, excluding heavy oil.
17) NORP[c] oil revenues less rebates and credits.	Value of production, excluding heavy oil.
18) Old oil revenues less rebates and credits.	Value of production, excluding heavy oil.
19) Heavy oil revenues less rebates, credits, and oil export charge.	Value of production, all heavy oil.
20) Mined oil revenues less rebates and credits.	Value of production of synthetic crude.
21) Domestically sold natural gas revenues less rebates and credits.	Volume of production for domestic market.
22) Exported natural gas revenues less rebates and credits.	Volume of production for export market.
23) Sales of Crown leases less rebates and credits.	Provincial revenues from new NORP and heavy oil, plus domestic and exported natural gas.
24) Other oil and gas revenues less rebates and credits.	Volume of marketable crude, synthetic crude, condensate, and oil equivalent of natural gas.

(Table 11.7 concluded on the next page)

Table 11.7 Concluded

Source[b]	Base[b]
25) Minerals—iron.	Value of production of iron ore and iron remelting.
26) Minerals—uranium.	Value of production.
27) Minerals—asbestos.	Value of production.
28) Minerals—coal.	Volume of production adjusted for different types of coal.
29) Minerals—other.	Value of production of metal and non-metal mining industry less items above and revenue from potash, sulphur, and part of sand and gravel.
30) Potash revenues.	Value of production.
31) Water power rentals.	Electricity generated by publicly and privately owned companies from hydro sources.
32) Insurance premium taxes.	Property, casualty, and life insurance premiums, plus fraternal benefit contributions and dues, less dividends paid to insured.
33) Payroll taxes.	Wages and salaries, plus military pay.
34) Provincial and local property taxes less regular property tax credits and related income tax credits.	Constructed from data on capital stocks to reflect residential, farm, commercial, industrial, and federal land and building values using personal disposable income, net provincial income, and provincial GDP.
35) Lottery revenues.	Personal income adjusted to eliminate provincial and local transfers, federal income tax, and UIC, CPP, and QPP contributions.
36) Miscellaneous provincial and local taxes and revenues from the sale of goods and services, including local water revenues.	Revenues from the foregoing revenue sources, excluding natural-resource-related revenues.
37) Shares revenues: off-shore activities.	Offshore activities.

[a] See note b, table 11.2. [b] Consumption tax revenues include, where appropriate, provincial revenue from reciprocal taxation agreements. [c] New oil reference price, as established in 1976-78.

Source: Canadian Tax Foundation *The National Finances 1991* (Toronto: the foundation, 1991), 16: 11-13.

$679 million—about 7.4 percent less than the amount that would otherwise have been payable. The comparable amounts for earlier years were $499 million in 1988-89, $1,087 million in 1989-90, and $1,283 million in 1990-91.[8] These ceilings were cutting in at a time when provincial finances were already strained by reductions in tax revenue as a result of the 1990-1992 recession and slow growth in other federal transfers;[9] they were, therefore, a matter of grave concern to the recipient provinces.

---

[8] As given in Québec, Ministère des Finances, *1991-92 Budget*, May 2, 1991, appendix E, 18.

[9] See chapter 17, below.

Table 11.8 Estimate of Equalization for 1991-92: Equalization Entitlements by Revenue Source and Province

Revenue source[a]	Nfld.	PEI	NS	NB	Que.	Ont.	Man.	Sask.	Alta.	BC	Total
					millions of dollars						
Personal income taxes	390.6	77.4	357.7	371.4	1,968.2	-2,873.3	443.0	501.6	181.7	-39.5	4,110.0
Business income revenues	83.9	19.0	119.0	86.6	43.0	-390.4	143.5	119.2	-164.7	84.6	614.3
Capital tax revenues	17.5	4.1	25.1	17.2	43.5	-120.9	19.8	21.2	-171.4	36.3	148.4
General and miscellaneous sales taxes	93.2	22.9	57.7	103.7	521.6	-582.7	97.8	86.8	-379.4	-123.5	983.6
Tobacco taxes	7.9	-0.9	-1.2	12.2	-26.4	-31.4	14.3	22.5	-7.4	21.0	28.5
Gasoline taxes	9.5	-1.1	-4.4	-7.7	115.2	-112.8	4.9	-4.1	-101.1	-3.3	112.5
Diesel fuel taxes	10.1	2.7	6.0	-1.4	61.6	-26.1	1.2	-23.1	-69.8	-13.6	57.0
Non-commercial vehicle licences	8.6	0.1	8.1	3.9	42.0	-8.9	-4.2	0.9	-1.3	-29.8	59.3
Commercial vehicle licences	2.5	0.9	1.1	-2.9	32.0	-30.1	-1.5	-4.8	-35.4	4.3	27.4
Revenue from the sale of spirits	-5.7	-0.3	-11.3	9.1	158.3	-101.5	-11.2	-10.9	-49.5	-34.7	127.9
Revenue from the sale of wine	8.6	1.6	7.6	7.9	-23.2	32.7	10.3	11.9	9.2	-31.7	24.7
Revenue from the sale of beer	-3.8	0.9	4.8	5.1	-2.8	-19.6	4.5	8.7	13.9	9.3	17.3
Hospital and medical insurance premiums	1.2	0.2	0.9	1.3	-1.2	-9.8	2.4	4.0	-0.1	4.7	8.7
Race track taxes	3.3	0.2	4.4	3.5	16.3	-26.5	2.2	5.1	0.8	2.9	35.1
Forestry revenues	10.0	4.7	28.6	-15.7	97.2	240.7	30.0	26.5	72.8	-394.3	181.1
New oil revenues	—	—	—	—	—	—	—	—	—	—	—
NORP oil revenues	4.4	1.0	6.8	5.5	51.7	71.2	2.6	-118.2	-728.2	-7.3	-46.3
Old oil revenues	1.8	0.4	2.8	2.3	21.2	29.7	0.6	-38.2	-493.1	-13.3	-9.1
Heavy oil revenues	0.9	0.2	1.4	1.1	10.5	15.5	1.7	-32.7	-19.2	4.9	-16.8
Mined oil revenues									-146.2		—
Domestically sold natural gas revenues	3.4	0.8	5.4	4.3	40.9	55.7	6.6	-43.9	-583.2	-59.2	17.5

(Table 11.8 concluded on the next page.)

Table 11.8 Concluded

millions of dollars

Revenue source[a]	Nfld.	PEI	NS	NB	Que.	Ont.	Man.	Sask.	Alta.	BC	Total
Exported natural gas revenues	1.9	0.4	2.9	2.3	22.0	32.3	3.5	3.2	–574.6	–61.1	36.3
Sales of Crown leases	2.5	0.6	3.8	3.1	29.1	40.6	3.4	–44.5	–442.8	–28.5	–2.2
Other oil and gas revenues	1.0	0.2	1.6	1.3	11.8	16.5	1.1	–18.1	–195.4	–11.3	–1.2
Mineral resources—iron	–9.2	0.1	0.4	0.4	–5.8	3.3	0.5	0.5	1.2	1.5	–13.1
Mineral resources—uranium	1.2	0.3	1.8	1.5	14.0	–0.6	2.3	–22.3	5.2	6.6	–1.2
Mineral resources—asbestos	—	—	—	—	—	—	—	—	—	—	—
Mineral resources—coal	1.3	0.3	–0.6	0.9	15.3	22.5	2.5	–14.1	–12.2	–26.2	5.7
Mineral resources—other	2.5	1.0	4.2	–5.4	28.6	–11.2	–15.5	5.8	17.7	–7.6	21.1
Potash revenues	1.6	0.4	2.5	–3.0	19.0	28.0	3.1	–59.1	7.1	8.9	–35.5
Water power rentals	–8.6	2.3	14.5	9.3	–109.7	120.7	–7.1	13.6	42.2	–17.5	–85.7
Insurance premium taxes	8.1	1.4	7.7	3.6	3.2	–29.1	5.9	4.4	5.9	15.7	34.2
Payroll taxes	47.1	10.9	44.5	44.5	176.9	–333.1	47.3	71.2	12.5	37.7	442.4
Provincial and local property taxes	209.0	45.4	222.4	218.0	639.4	–584.4	109.4	8.6	–434.1	–173.0	1,452.2
Lottery revenues	14.4	3.1	16.2	14.4	–54.6	53.1	13.7	16.3	28.0	–28.5	23.5
Miscellaneous provincial and local taxes and revenues	85.9	17.9	82.1	84.4	351.8	–492.2	85.6	79.6	–110.1	–24.7	787.1
Shared revenues: off-shore activities	—	—	—	—	—	—	—	—	—	—	—
Entitlement adjustment[b]	–34.7	–7.9	–54.2	–43.8	–411.7	—	–66.4	–60.6	—	—	–679.3
Total	971.8	210.9	970.3	938.9	3,898.8	–5,022.2	957.7	517.0	–4,321.3	–890.1	8,465.5

[a] See note b, table 11.2. [b] The entitlement adjustment line consists of an equal per capita constraint, applicble to provinces eligible for equalization.

Source: Canada, Department of Finance, Estimate of Equalization, February 28, 1991.

Table 11.9 Equalization Payable in 1991-92

Province	Amount, $ millions	As a percentage of provincial revenue
Newfoundland	971.8	28.4
Prince Edward Island	210.9	27.5
Nova Scotia	970.3	22.0
New Brunswick	938.9	22.9
Quebec	3,898.8	10.1
Manitoba	957.7	15.5
Saskatchewan	517.0	9.1
Total	8,465.5	13.4

Sources: Table 11.8 and Statistics Canada, *Provincial Government Finance*, catalogue no. 68-205.

Conclusion

The massive upheaval in world oil markets in the 1970s produced changes on a similar scale in the relative revenue positions of the Canadian provinces, and these changes, in turn, created serious problems for the equalization system. The federal government took immediate action to correct some of these problems, but at the cost of the theoretical purity of the equalization formula. It had become obvious by the late 1970s that nothing short of a major overhaul would remedy the system. In the absence of a consensus among the provinces, the federal government introduced changes that preserved the flavour of the old system but departed in significant and worrisome ways from the concept of equalization as it had emerged over the previous 15 years. The changes were designed to produce a system that gave the desired results without resorting to special exemptions. Although this ad hoc approach may have offended the purists, it reinforced the contention of others that the whole basis of federal-provincial fiscal relations was the art of discovering a systematic method of expressing the compromise between what the federal government felt it could afford and what the provinces felt they must have from the federal government.

In the 1990s, the "have-not" provinces were finding that the automatic ceiling on equalization payments, coupled with the decline in other transfer programs, imposed serious constraints on their financial positions. Tables 11.10 and 11.11 show the status of the equalization program in the middle of the decade. As a comparison of tables 11.9 and 11.11 makes clear, equalization payments as a share of total revenue for the "have-not" provinces had fallen by 1.3 percentage points, or nearly 10 percent, between 1991-92 and 1996-97. The result of this state of affairs was that for the first time since the early 1980s federal-provincial negotiations on equalization were again centred on basic principles, and on the objectives that should underlie the system, rather than on the technical details of the formula.

Table 11.10 Estimate of Equalization for 1996-97: Equalization Entitlements by Revenue Source and Province

Revenue source[a]	Nfld.	PEI	NS	NB	Que.	Ont.	Man.	Sask.	Alta.	BC	Total
							millions of dollars				
Personal income taxes	325.7	69.5	333.5	320.6	1,568.5	-2,021.4	336.5	413.3	-213.6	-296.9	3,367.6
Business income revenues	101.1	18.1	153.0	101.9	-93.5	-80.6	146.6	52.6	-512.5	-25.1	479.9
Capital tax revenues	37.6	10.2	61.0	27.6	63.5	-196.5	45.2	36.4	-166.1	51.4	281.4
General and miscellaneous sales taxes	92.1	7.9	56.6	89.6	501.5	-55.1	110.3	58.4	-553.6	-615.1	916.3
Tobacco taxes	11.8	-0.2	-7.0	4.7	-63.4	-40.3	18.8	10.5	4.6	74.5	-25.0
Gasoline revenue	7.6	-4.2	-16.5	-11.9	101.1	-46.9	-8.3	-23.0	-136.7	-22.8	44.8
Diesel fuel revenue	13.0	3.4	10.9	-8.2	79.6	-18.6	-11.0	-50.0	-98.9	..	37.7
Non-commercial vehicle licences	5.9	-0.4	4.4	2.3	30.6	-2.7	-5.1	5.9	-39.5	-28.6	43.5
Commercial vehicle licences	4.5	1.3	6.2	-2.6	37.9	-8.1	-2.8	-4.7	-56.6	-22.3	39.7
Alcoholic beverage revenues	-3.4	1.4	2.3	13.3	85.6	5.4	-6.9	8.8	-40.3	-92.9	101.2
Hospital and medical insurance premiums	0.6	-0.5	-3.0	-1.5	-12.8	15.8	-1.5	2.9	-13.5	-4.5	-15.6
Race track taxes	1.2	0.1	1.7	1.5	10.3	-14.4	2.1	1.9	0.6	0.1	18.9
Forestry revenues	31.8	10.2	60.9	-9.8	109.8	539.9	60.0	14.1	-21.5	-723.8	277.1
NORP oil revenues	5.7	1.4	9.4	7.6	73.6	110.3	6.6	-190.7	-689.3	0.2	-86.4
Old oil revenues	0.7	0.2	1.1	0.9	8.6	13.0	-0.1	-18.1	-240.9	-3.4	-6.7
Heavy oil revenues	1.7	0.4	2.8	2.3	22.1	33.6	3.4	-70.6	-31.0	11.5	-37.9
Mined oil revenues	—	—	—	—	—	—	—	—	-243.0	—	—
Domestically sold natural gas revenues	3.2	0.8	5.3	4.3	41.6	61.1	6.4	-45.0	-422.1	-64.2	16.6
Exported natural gas revenues	1.9	0.5	3.2	2.6	25.2	38.3	3.9	1.4	-588.5	-68.8	38.7
Sales of Crown leases	3.0	0.7	5.0	4.1	39.3	58.8	4.9	-73.7	-418.3	-29.3	-16.7
Other oil and gas revenues	1.3	0.3	2.1	1.7	16.8	24.7	1.9	-27.2	-237.6	-16.2	-3.0
Mineral resources—asbestos	..	..	0.1	0.1	-1.5	1.0	0.1	0.1	0.2	0.3	-1.1
Mineral resources—coal	0.7	0.2	-0.1	0.7	8.9	13.5	1.4	-8.7	-8.6	-15.1	3.0
Mineral resources—other	-14.0	1.3	6.2	-9.2	18.4	2.5	-9.2	-1.9	25.5	-9.8	-8.3

(Table 11.10 is concluded on the next page.)

Table 11.10 Concluded

Revenue source[a]	Nfld.	PEI	NS	NB	Que.	Ont.	Man.	Sask.	Alta.	BC	Total
					millions of dollars						
Potash revenues	1.8	0.4	3.0	-8.2	23.2	35.3	3.6	-74.2	8.8	12.1	-50.4
Water power rentals	-10.1	2.5	15.9	10.0	-138.9	149.4	-21.1	12.7	47.8	-2.2	-128.9
Insurance premiums revenues	7.4	0.7	6.6	1.0	19.4	-17.6	5.7	4.9	—	-12.3	45.7
Payroll taxes	40.5	6.7	47.1	35.2	174.9	-225.4	35.2	56.1	-34.4	-40.8	395.7
Provincial and local property taxes	212.6	36.1	239.8	244.1	810.3	-689.2	201.7	133.4	-473.9	-456.3	1,878.1
Lottery revenues	-17.6	3.1	12.3	23.8	-78.9	46.2	46.1	41.7	80.0	-55.2	30.6
Miscellaneous provincial and local taxes and revenues	92.8	17.0	100.6	93.1	358.1	-371.6	100.4	82.8	-248.8	-169.8	844.8
Shared revenues: preferred share dividend	1.3	0.4	2.5	2.6	11.3	-18.4	-2.3	1.9	-0.8	7.6	17.7
Total	962.2	189.6	1,127.0	944.3	3,851.1	-2,658.1	1,072.4	352.1	-5,322.4	-2,617.5	8,498.7

[a] See note b, table 11.2.

Source: Canada, Department of Finance, Estimate of Equalization, October 1996.

Table 11.11   Equalization Payable in 1996-97

	Amount, $ millions	As a percentage of provincial revenue
Newfoundland	962.2	26.6
Prince Edward Island	189.6	22.7
Nova Scotia	1,127.0	22.7
New Brunswick	944.3	19.2
Quebec	3,851.1	9.0
Manitoba	1,072.4	15.5
Saskatchewan	352.1	5.6
Total	8,498.7	12.1

Source: Table 11.10 and unpublished material from Statistics Canada.

Appendix: Stabilization

Although formal stabilization provisions have been an element in federal-provincial fiscal relations since 1957, it is only in the last decade that stabilization payments have been made. The 1957-1962 arrangements provided for stabilization payments to bring a province's yield from the standard taxes and equalization up to a minimum that was the greatest of (1) the previous year's financial arrangements extended to the current year, (2) the last payment under the previous arrangements adjusted for population changes, and (3) 95 percent of the average payment for the two previous years under the current arrangements. For the 1962-1967 arrangements, the stabilization level was changed to 95 percent of average receipts from the standard taxes, equalization, and stabilization over the two preceding years.

The present stabilization system, which provides insurance against any sharp drop in a province's total revenues, dates from the introduction of the representative tax system of equalization in 1967. The 1967 legislation provided stabilization payments to provinces whose total revenues from the sources enumerated in the equalization formula (at the previous year's provincial tax rates), equalization, and other general purpose federal transfers dropped below 95 percent of the previous year's revenues. The level was raised in 1972 from 95 percent to 100 percent.

For the 1977-1982 period, the federal government modified the stabilization formula to limit the payment with respect to declines in natural resource revenues to the amount in excess of 50 percent of the previous year's revenues. It also made adjustments to prevent provincial revenue initiatives from triggering stabilization payments. Otherwise, the system remained unchanged, and no stabilization payments were made during the period.

In approaching the negotiations for the 1982-1987 period, the federal government proposed to continue the program without changes, and there was little discussion of stabilization during the negotiations themselves. The legislation extended the stabilization provisions indefinitely, rather than, as in the past, for five years. The formula was modified specifically to exclude the local government revenues added to the equalization formula. The limitations on natural resource revenues were retained in the form adopted in 1977.

The basic stabilization provisions had long been seen as important to the Atlantic provinces; the guaranteed floor on revenue made their securities more attractive in the United States bond markets. It was not, however, one of the Atlantic provinces that made the first claim under the provisions. In 1982, British Columbia suffered more than the rest of the country from the international recession. The demand for its exports decreased, and prices plummeted. The province's revenues declined so precipitously that it qualified for stabilization payments. There was a protracted period during which the province's claim was examined in detail. A payment of $80 million was made in 1983-84, a payment of $94 million in 1984-85, and a final payment of about $400,000 in 1986-87.

The stabilization provisions were changed for the 1987-1992 period. Technical adjustments were introduced to correct problems that had arisen when the first claim was made and processed. Entitlements in excess of $60 per capita were to be regarded not as grants but as interest-free loans for five years.

Once again, a western province made a claim under the stabilization provisions. Reductions in world prices for oil and gas sharply reduced Alberta's natural resource revenues for the fiscal year 1986-87, so it filed a claim for $539 million. The federal government honoured the claim in part by making a payment of $75 million in June 1989. Under the legislation, it had until December 31, 1990 to settle the claim. By that date, it had agreed to pay an additional $148 million and to submit the question of its liability for another $196 million to arbitration. The arbitration was to determine whether the $196 million, which arose from Alberta's resource royalty credit against income taxes, represented a reduction in income taxes (which could be fully compensated) or a reduction in natural resource revenues (which could be compensated to the extent that the reduction exceeded 50 percent). The issue was resolved in Alberta's favour on June 18, 1991, and the federal government immediately transferred $196 million to Alberta, bringing the total stabilization payment to $419 million.

As a result of the recession of 1990-91, a number of provinces, including Ontario, became eligible for stabilization payments. Over the four years ending March 31, 1995, the federal government paid out $1.2 billion, and some claims were still outstanding. Finance Minister Paul Martin announced in his 1995 budget that the federal government would provide stabilization payments only when a province's revenue fell below 95 percent of its previous year's revenue.

The stabilization arrangements have had a long and previously inactive role in federal-provincial fiscal relations. To most observers, they were for many years chiefly of benefit to provincial borrowers, especially in the Atlantic provinces, whose prospectuses were made more attractive to foreign lenders by the implied floor on provincial revenues. Not all observers saw this "letter of comfort" aspect as the chief advantage of stabilization. The federal Department of Finance has argued that stabilization is in fact more important to those provinces that do not regularly receive equalization.[10] Recipient provinces are cushioned from declines in their own revenues, since their equalization payments will automatically increase if their revenues decline relative to the average used in the equalization formula. Provinces that do not receive equalization lack the same protection, but, as the past decade has shown, stabilization provides a cushion.

---

[10] Canada, Department of Finance, *Federal-Provincial Fiscal Relations in Canada: An Overview* (Ottawa: the department, 1975).

PART IV

CONDITIONAL GRANTS

Introduction

The first three parts of this book have explored two distinct but closely related developments: the evolution of tax-sharing between the federal government and the provinces, and the growth of Ottawa's program of unconditional transfers to the provinces under the equalization formula. This part discusses the evolution of the federal government's complex system of conditional grants.

The enormous transfer of fiscal resources to the provinces through tax-sharing and equalization increased the provinces' independence of Ottawa in determining public policy within their jurisdictions. During the same period, however, the federal government developed a number of new and important national policy objectives in areas of provincial responsibility, such as post-secondary education, hospitalization insurance, and medical care. In order to maintain some approximation of national standards in these areas, the federal government passed over the alternatives of giving the provinces more tax points or larger unconditional grants in favour of a system of grants and shared-cost programs that obliged the provinces to satisfy federal criteria if they wished to receive federal funding.

In the long run, however, close federal supervision of provincial activity in these policy areas proved untenable. The cost-sharing arrangements gave the federal government some control over how the money was spent but no control over how much was spent. Since the federal government matched provincial spending on these programs dollar for dollar, provincial spending drove federal spending and every provincial dollar spent was in effect worth two dollars—a bargain that the provinces found hard to resist. On the other hand, the provinces were resentful of an arrangement that obliged them to accept federal standards in areas of provincial jurisdiction. Moreover, the flow of federal money attracted provincial funds that might otherwise have been spent in other areas and thus distorted provincial priorities.

The fact that both levels of government had objections to the cost-sharing arrangements made it relatively easy for them to achieve a compromise. The result was the established programs financing (EPF) scheme, introduced in 1977. Under this scheme, the federal contribution to provincial spending on the major shared-cost programs would grow only at a rate determined by the growth rates of per capita GNP and income tax collections; half the contribution would consist of a further surrender of tax points to the provinces, and half would be in cash. In achieving more control over the level of spending, however, Ottawa lost some control over how the money was spent, since the

173

funds were no longer allocated to specific spending areas. The provinces could distribute the money among the so-called established programs— hospital insurance, medicare, and post-secondary education—according to their own priorities, subject to a requirement that they maintain loosely defined national standards in these areas.

By 1982, the federal government was concerned that even the reduced transfers under the EPF system were growing more rapidly than its means to pay for them. Its response was to change the formula, unilaterally, so that the value of the tax points was deducted from the total value of its contribution, now determined by GNP growth alone, and the cash payment was equal to the residual. This subtle change dramatically reduced both the long-term projections of federal direct spending and the total resources available to the provinces, since the value of the tax component was growing more rapidly than the value of the total entitlement.

With the breaking of the direct link between federal standards and federal funding under the EPF, the provinces felt increasingly less constrained by those standards—all the more so as the cash component of the federal trans- fers became smaller. The federal government fought hard to maintain a share of control over the established programs, particularly in the area of health care, where it felt that national standards were compromised by the prov- inces' imposition of user fees and their toleration of extra billing for medical services. In 1984, Ottawa introduced legislation that reduced the EPF trans- fers to provinces that followed these practices. After a prolonged struggle, the provinces fell into line, and in 1988 the federal government released to them the last of the funds it had withheld on the ground of non-compliance.

The federal government was, however, rapidly losing the fiscal clout it needed in order to win victories of this kind. During the later 1980s and the early 1990s, as part of a broad effort to reduce its expenditures in the face of large deficits and weak revenues, Ottawa imposed a series of ever less generous limits on the EPF program. Finally, it took the major step of combining the EPF program with the last major shared-cost program, the Canada assistance plan (CAP) for social welfare.

The new arrangement, the Canadian health and social transfer (CHST), was introduced in 1996. It blended the CAP into the EPF arrangements and retained the combination of cash and tax transfers. Like the EPF arrange- ments, the CHST system ensured that the value of the tax transfers would grow more rapidly than the value of the total package, and thus that the cash component would gradually decline.

Equalization, the transfers of ever more tax points to the provinces, and the decline in the cash value of conditional grants all worked to shift the balance of power and responsibility from the federal government to the prov- inces. By 1997, fifty years after the federal government entered into the first set of post-war tax agreements with the provinces, the relative positions of the two levels of government were well on their way to becoming reversed.

Chapter 12 begins the section by examining the basis of the conditional grants and shared-cost programs. Chapter 13 follows the development of a comprehensive national program of hospital and medical insurance. Chapter 14 looks at the early development of national welfare programs and a number of special shared-cost initiatives. Chapter 15 traces the later development of these joint efforts and discusses the "contracting-out" arrangements under which Ottawa offered the provinces greater autonomy in the administration of national programs. Chapter 16 examines, among other matters, Ottawa's abortive attempt in the 1970s to reform social welfare services, an episode that demonstrates the difficulty in this period of establishing new national programs financed by federal transfers. Chapter 17 describes the transformation of shared-cost programs into established programs financing, and chapter 18 deals with the broadening of the EPF principle under the rubric of the Canadian health and social transfer.

12

Overview and First Steps

The concentration to this point on the sharing of tax revenue and equalization should not be taken to mean that these are the only important elements in the financial arrangements between the federal government and the provinces. Of at least equal importance are the arrangements under which the federal government provides funding for provincial programs that meet particular conditions.

Arrangements of this type—grants-in-aid, conditional grants, shared-cost programs, joint programs, and specific purpose transfers—have been an integral part of Canadian government finance since the beginning of the century. The federal government and the provinces have shared the responsibility for a wide variety of undertakings: the introduction of specific recovery programs after the First World War; the development of a system of pensions for the aged; promotion of the health sciences, hospital insurance, and medical insurance; the encouragement of post-secondary education; the building of the Trans-Canada Highway; and a variety of economic development programs. Shared-cost programs have ranged from programs that provide federal grants in order to cover a portion of certain carefully defined and quite specific provincial expenditures to programs that provide a federal payment that is completely unrelated to actual provincial expenditures and made only on the condition that the province supply the indicated services in some form.

The theoretical justification for shared-cost programs is well established.[1] When a provincial function is of national interest and the exercise of that function produces "spillover" benefits that should properly be financed by the federal government, the shared-cost approach is justified. This approach is also indicated when it is appropriate to impose minimum national standards and eligibility criteria in provincial spheres in order to discourage migration to high-benefit provinces and eliminate artificial barriers to mobility. The shared-cost approach is also appropriate when the provinces cannot afford to undertake necessary programs in areas within their jurisdiction. Finally, shared cost programs are appropriate when an activity is seen as essential from a national perspective but is constitutionally the prerogative of the provinces. For example, federal assistance for bilingualism provides money to the provinces to undertake training in the second official language, an area— education—that is not within the jurisdiction of the federal government.

---

[1] See George E. Carter, *Canadian Conditional Grants Since World War II*, Canadian Tax Paper no. 54 (Toronto: Canadian Tax Foundation, 1971), chapters 1 and 4.

The theoretical and practical problems inherent in the shared-cost approach are also well known.[2] This chapter and the six chapters that follow it show how the federal government and the provinces have repeatedly adapted the device first used in the early 1900s. The extent to which shared-cost programs have changed can be seen from the change in terminology. Under the grant-in-aid and conditional grant programs common until the mid-1960s, the federal government imposed specific conditions on the design of the provincial program, its eligibility criteria, and its accounting and auditing procedures. The federal-provincial medicare program, however, introduced a new approach to cost-sharing, one that involved far less precise conditions for provincial access to federal funding. With the development of contracting-out and, later, established programs financing (EPF), federal grants often ceased to be in aid of specific expenditures, since they were no longer conditional on provincial adherence to detailed regulations and, indeed, did not even represent a sharing of the actual costs. At this point, Statistics Canada adopted the phrase "specific purpose transfers" to cover all transfers that were identified with a specific category of provincial expenditure. This convention is the one used in the statistical analyses provided in this and the following chapters.

Table 12.1 indicates the importance of specific purpose transfers to both the federal government and the provinces. In 1950, federal transfers to the provinces accounted for about 10 percent of federal spending but covered 20 percent of provincial spending, as determined for national accounts purposes; specific transfers accounted for three-fifths of total transfers. In the immediately following years, as the first peace-time federal-provincial fiscal arrangements matured, federal general purpose transfers increased in relative importance; by 1955, they accounted for four-fifths of all transfers. This state of affairs was short-lived, however: although the arrangements in effect from 1952 to 1962 involved large federal general purpose transfers, specific purpose transfers rose again in relative importance. They exceeded 50 percent of total transfers in 1961, by which time most provinces had joined the hospital insurance program. Largely because of the introduction of contracting-out,[3] health transfers declined to 29 percent of all transfers in 1965, down from a peak of 42 percent the year before.

In 1980, as table 12.1 shows, all transfers amounted to nearly 21 percent of federal spending and covered 21 percent of provincial spending. The change shown in the table for the period 1950 to 1980 understates the increase in the importance of federal transfers of resources, since the figures do not include the federal government's unconditional transfers of tax room to the provinces, including transfers of tax room associated with contracting-out and the EPF arrangements. The decade after 1980 saw a decline in all transfers relative to tax room and an increase in the proportion of transfers provided unconditionally—especially transfers under the equalization system.

---

[2] Ibid.

[3] See chapter 15.

**Table 12.1 Federal Cash Transfers to Provinces, National
Accounts Basis—Selected Calendar Years, 1950 to 1995**

Year	As a percentage of federal spending	As a percentage of provincial spending	As a percentage of total transfers			
			General purpose transfers	Specific purpose transfers		
				Health	All social	Total
1950	10.5	20.3	40.4	8.8	51.2	59.6
1955	9.2	24.4	78.8	7.7	13.3	21.2
1960	14.3	27.2	54.9	22.7	33.8	45.1
1965	15.8	21.5	34.6	29.3	50.3	65.4
1970	21.6	23.3	33.5	34.8	59.3	66.5
1975	21.1	23.8	38.7	31.9	49.6	61.3
1980	20.4	21.0	30.1	32.0	59.2	69.9
1985	18.5	20.7	27.3	32.6	62.6	72.7
1990	17.0	18.2	34.0	24.2	52.9	66.0
1995	17.6	18.1	30.0	24.6	56.1	70.0

Source: Richard M. Bird, *Financing Canadian Government: A Quantitative Overview*, Financing Canadian Federation no. 1 (Toronto: Canadian Tax Foundation, 1979), 57 and appendices, as updated.

The Early Years

Conditional grants had a late start and grew slowly at first. Federal payments made in 1900 for assistance to 4-H clubs can be identified as a form of conditional grant to the provinces, but the first experiment with a nationwide program—a program for agricultural education—did not occur until 1913. The federal grants for this program in fiscal 1913-14 represented the entire funding; no provincial contributions were required, and there was very little federal supervision of provincial expenditures.

The stress on building social capital that followed the First World War and the lack of provincial resources for this purpose led to a number of joint projects. As a rule, the provinces assumed half the cost of the undertaking and were required to meet at least general standards set by the federal government. The first real shared-cost programs began in 1919 and covered vocational education, highway construction, employment offices, and venereal disease prevention.

In 1927, the federal government adopted the Old Age Pension Act, which provided for provincial administration of income-tested pensions and federal funding for 50 percent of the cost. Under the terms of the program, individuals who passed a means test, met residency requirements, and were aged 70 or more were entitled to pensions paid by the participating province. British Columbia joined the program in 1927, Saskatchewan and Manitoba in 1928, Alberta and Ontario in 1929. Federal concern about the lack of uniformity among provincial means tests, increases in spending with the onset of the Great Depression, and a lack of federal powers of audit led to the introduction in 1931 of a provision that gave the federal government the right to audit all expenditures of federal money by a province. In the same year, the federal government increased its share of the program's cost to 75 percent. Prince Edward Island joined the program in 1933, Nova Scotia in 1934, and New Brunswick and Quebec in 1936. Newfoundland joined when it entered Confederation in 1949. In some provinces, the municipalities bore a part of the cost not met by federal contributions. The program wound up at the end of 1951, when the federal government assumed full responsibility for Old Age Security.[4]

The shared-cost approach had much to recommend it in a period when provincial and local governments faced heavy demands and lacked the resources to meet them. At the same time, there was some concern about the fact that the federal government was taking initiatives, on a national basis, in areas of provincial jurisdiction. In general, the shared-cost approach failed to establish itself as a successful means of transferring funds. There were four main reasons for this failure. First, only a limited number of programs suitable for joint action of this kind were of equal interest to all of the provinces. Second, shared-cost programs encouraged provinces to undertake certain functions that they found difficult to maintain when the federal grants were withdrawn. Third, problems of control and administration made the grants ineffective as a means of transferring large amounts of funds to the provinces. Fourth, the grant structure of the shared-cost programs was uniform across the provinces, so the programs could not be adapted to regional differences.

Unemployment Relief

Relief to the unemployed was originally a municipal function. As the depression of the 1930s took hold, however, the costs of providing relief became too great for local authorities, which saw their property tax bases shrink even as their unemployment rolls grew. Provincial authorities gave help as municipal resources became exhausted, but the demand for relief soon drained provincial revenues as well. As an emergency measure, the federal government provided $317 million in grants and $175 million in loans to provinces and municipalities for unemployment relief during the worst years of the Depression. Many of the loans were later written off. In total, the federal grants and loans covered about 40 percent of the cost of relief. This aid was provided because the provinces were in extremis, not because the federal government saw unemployment relief, at this time, as a field of shared jurisdiction, or as one in which it wished to establish national standards. Indeed, the federal government attached few conditions to its aid. There were marked regional differences in eligibility criteria, and local relief restrictions frequently impeded labour mobility.

---

[4] For a full history of this program, see Kenneth Bryden, *Old Age Pensions and Policy-Making in Canada* (Montreal: McGill-Queen's University Press, 1974).

The situation was examined carefully by the Royal Commission on Dominion-Provincial Relations (the Rowell-Sirois Commission).[5] The commission rejected the alternative of strengthening the existing conditional grants mechanism and recommended instead that the federal government assume direct responsibility for unemployment relief and other welfare services provided by the provinces. The introduction of federal unemployment insurance in 1940 was a response to this recommendation.

Conclusion

The tendency toward decentralization that characterized Canadian fiscal federalism during the depression of the 1930s was reversed during the Second World War and the first decade of the ensuing peace. The federal government's primacy during the war years is easily explained by the requirements of the war effort. Meanwhile, public sentiment was laying the groundwork for action by the federal government to ensure that the transition to peacetime would occur without a recession. Memories of the depression and its consequences were still fresh, and most Canadians agreed that only action at the national level could prevent a recurrence of those consequences.

The federal government introduced a number of programs designed to ease the transition to peacetime and, riding on the sentiment described above, ventured into areas of provincial jurisdiction to correct the problems brought to light during the depression. The next two chapters illustrate this trend by examining shared-cost programs in health care and social welfare—responsibilities originally assigned to the provinces.

---

[5] Canada, *Report of the Royal Commission on Dominion-Provincial Relations* (Ottawa: King's Printer, 1940). See in particular A. E. Grauer, *Public Assistance and Social Insurance*, a study prepared for the Royal Commission on Dominion-Provincial Relations (Ottawa: King's Printer, 1939).

13

Health-Care Programs

The possibility of providing some form of health insurance had been under discussion at the federal level since the First World War, but no definitive steps were taken until the Second World War was in progress. In 1941, the federal minister of pensions and national health called a meeting of the Dominion Council of Health and other interested agencies to consider the question of health insurance. In 1942, the federal Advisory Committee on Health Insurance was set up, and in 1943 the House of Commons appointed a committee to study social security. This committee heard the submission of the advisory committee and examined its draft bill. The provinces endorsed the idea of a public health insurance system at a federal-provincial conference in 1944, and the speeches from the throne in 1944 and 1945 announced the federal government's intention to proceed with a plan. Ottawa and the provinces began negotiations to devise a detailed system of provincial health insurance with federal financial assistance—a process that would in the end take more than a decade.

The federal government set out its formal proposals for initiatives in the area of health care just as the war was ending. Its "green book" studies, prepared for the Conference on Reconstruction in August 1945, included plans for the establishment of provincially run hospital insurance systems, with a federal subsidy of 60 percent, and for a variety of federal grants in aid of public health services and hospital construction.[1] The provinces failed to endorse these proposals, but by 1948 the federal government had put eight health services grant programs into effect on its own initiative. The funds allocated for these programs were distributed among the provinces under a variety of formulas:

1) *General public health grants*. Funds were distributed on a per capita basis. To qualify for funding, a province had to maintain its existing level of support for local public health services.

2) *Tuberculosis control grants*. The distribution of grant money was based partly on population and partly on the incidence of deaths from tuberculosis.

3) *Mental health grants*. Funds were distributed on a per capita basis.

4) *Venereal disease control grants*. Distribution was based on both population and incidence.

---

[1] The green book studies examined a wide range of topics, as described in chapter 14. Dominion-Provincial Conference on Reconstruction, 1945. *Dominion and Provincial Submissions and Plenary Conference Discussions*. Ottawa, Queen's Printer, 1946.

5) *Aid for crippled children.* Funds were distributed on a per capita basis.

6) *Professional training grants.* No mode of distribution was specified.

7) *Public health research grants.* Again, no mode of distribution was specified.

8) *Aid for the civilian blind.* Only this program, whose costs were split evenly between the federal government and the provinces, provided conditional grants as such.

In May 1948, the federal government introduced legislation for a modified and more ambitious system of health services grants. The new system, which became effective with the 1949-50 fiscal year, comprised 10 separate grant programs, and again the method of funding varied from program to program:

1) *Hospital construction grants.* This program, the largest of the 10, provided the lesser of one-third of total costs or $1,000 per bed or equivalent space ($2,000 after 1957) for the construction of active-treatment hospitals; the provinces were required to match the federal contribution, but the remainder could come from local or private sources. The program ended in 1970.

2) *Cancer control grants.* This was the only other program that required matching provincial outlays (based on the per capita cost of the existing program in Saskatchewan). The funds allocated for the program were distributed among the provinces on a per capita basis. The purpose of the grants was to promote the expansion of clinics, laboratory services, and treatment facilities.

3) *Health survey grants.* This program, which ended with the 1952-53 fiscal year, funded surveys of health services and facilities. It consisted of a flat amount and an amount calculated on a per capita basis.

4) *General public health grants.* The grant monies were originally distributed on a per capita basis. In 1960, the program was enriched and put on the same basis as the health survey grant program. The purpose of the program was to help support local public health services.

5) *Tuberculosis control grants* consisted of a flat amount and an amount based on the number of deaths from tuberculosis. Their purpose was to promote the detection and treatment of tuberculosis.

6) *Mental health grants*, for research, prevention, and care, consisted of a flat amount and a per capita allotment.

7) *Professional training grants.* These grants too consisted of a flat amount and a per capita allotment. They were intended to provide bursaries and to subsidize short courses in new or expanded training programs.

8) *Public health research grants* were awarded for specific research projects, not on a provincial basis.

9) *Venereal disease control grants* consisted of a flat amount and a per capita allotment. In the 1960-61 fiscal year, the program was absorbed by the general public health grant program.

10) *Crippled children's grants* . These grants were for prevention, correction, rehabilitation, and training; they consisted of a flat amount and a per capita allotment. The program was replaced in 1953 by a program of child and maternal health grants, which consisted of a flat amount and an amount based on live births and infant deaths. The new program provided monies for training, equipment, immunization, and research.

The surveys funded by the health survey grants revealed a serious shortage of laboratory and radiological facilities. In 1953-54, accordingly, the federal government introduced a program of per capita grants to the provinces for training, equipment, and facilities. The program ended in 1959-60, but the hospital insurance program included regular funding for these purposes.

The national health grants program was an example of the use of a package of grants to encourage or assist the development of specific provincial or local services. As noted, few of the grants were matching grants; most of them consisted of both a flat amount and an amount based either on provincial population or on actual or potential caseload. The flat payment gave relatively more assistance to the smaller provinces, for which the basic start-up and minimum operating costs were disproportionately high. The balance of the grants provided a uniform level of assistance across the country.

The federal government restructured the general health grants program when it introduced the hospital insurance program in 1958 and restructured it again, more drastically, soon after it introduced medicare in the late 1960s. It announced the details of the second restructuring at a conference of federal and provincial health ministers held in November 1968. Only the professional training and public health research grants were to continue; the other grants would be phased out over a three-year period ending March 31, 1972. The federal government initially proposed to adopt some form of enrichment of other health grants to compensate the provinces for this loss, but it subsequently dropped the idea.

Hospital Insurance

In the early post-war period, discussion of a national health insurance plan centred on insurance for hospital care. At a federal-provincial conference in October 1955, the 11 governments agreed to set up a subcommittee of federal and provincial ministers of health and finance to study such a program. The subcommittee met in January 1956 to discuss proposals from the federal government and the provinces. The federal government offered to pass legislation for hospital insurance when a majority of the provinces (at least six), representing more than 50 percent of the total population, signified their intention of joining the scheme. Ottawa would provide a grant calculated by multiplying the insured population of a province by 25 percent of the per capita shareable costs in that province plus 25 percent of the national average per capita shareable costs.

The federal Hospital Insurance and Diagnostic Services Act[2] was passed in 1957 and took effect on July 1, 1958. Initially, as table 13.1 shows, only five provinces participated in the program;[3] two others, Ontario and Prince Edward Island had indicated their acceptance of it and joined within a few months. Two more years passed before all of the remaining provinces and the two territories had joined. In signing agreements under the Act, the provinces undertook to make insured hospital services available to all of their residents under uniform terms and conditions. The services covered by the provincial insurance programs varied widely from province to province, but the provinces were required at a minimum to provide coverage for in-patient services; accommodation and meals at the standard or public ward level; necessary nursing services; laboratory, radiological, and other diagnostic procedures; drugs; operating rooms; radiotherapy; and physiotherapy. All of these services (except accommodation, meals, and drugs) were also to be available to out-patients. The federal government deducted any co-insurance or deterrent charges (as used in Alberta and British Columbia) before it calculated the grants. Capital charges and debt charges were also excluded from the grant calculations, as were services to anyone who qualified under other federal or provincial legislation, such as veterans, injured workers, and tuberculosis and mental patients. The provinces had pressed for inclusion in the grant formula of the costs of care for tuberculosis and mental patients, and they continued to press for it after the passage of the Act. In 1957, the new Conservative government agreed to include these costs, provided that it was allowed the option of offsetting the amounts against adjustments in other federal-provincial payments. This arrangement was not acceptable to the provinces, and the offer was dropped. It did not cease to be a point of discussion, however.

The method of determining the federal share resulted in a built-in form of equalization, since the payment was proportionately larger for provinces whose costs were less than the national average. It was the first time that a form of equalization appeared in a conditional grant program. As table 13.1 shows, the federal payments varied widely as a proportion of eligible provincial expenditures during the program's first year (1958-59). In applying for federal payments, the provinces had to satisfy detailed reporting requirements; indeed, the final payments were not made until all provincial audit reports had been received. Thus the final payment came some 27 months after the end of the relevant calendar year.

---

[2] SC 1975, c. 28.

[3] The Conservative government, elected after the passage of the Act, amended it to allow start-up with any number of provinces.

**Table 13.1   Federal Contributions to Hospital Insurance As a
Percentage of Provincial Costs, Calendar Years 1958 and 1968**

		Federal contributions as a percentage of provincial costs	
	Date of entry	1958	1968
Newfoundland	1/7/58	59.9	54.8
Prince Edward Island	1/10/59	na	66.5
Nova Scotia	1/1/59	na	54.4
New Brunswick	1/7/59	na	52.3
Quebec[a]	1/1/61	na	na
Ontario	1/1/59	52.8	47.9
Manitoba	1/7/58	44.8	53.1
Saskatchewan	1/7/58	40.5	50.9
Alberta	1/7/58	50.9	47.2
British Columbia	1/7/58	45.3	53.4
Yukon	1/7/60	na	53.9
Northwest Territories	1/4/60	na	53.9
Average		47.8	49.8

[a] Information on Quebec, which opted out of the program in 1965, is not available in the source.

Source: Canada, Department of National Health and Welfare, *Annual Report*, under the Hospital Insurance and Diagnostic Services Act (various years).

The departments of health administered the program in Newfoundland, Saskatchewan, Alberta, and British Columbia; special, separate commissions were set up in Prince Edward Island, Nova Scotia, New Brunswick, Quebec, Ontario, and Manitoba. Membership in the insurance program was optional only in Prince Edward Island and Ontario and then only for individuals not in designated groups (such as employees of firms with more than a minimum number of employees). In the other provinces, membership was either automatic or compulsory. Funding methods varied widely across the provinces and over time. They included premiums alone, a combination of premiums and user charges, earmarked taxes, and appropriations from general tax revenues to cover all or a part of the provincial share.

The Hospital Insurance and Diagnostic Services Act, which created what was then a completely new type of shared-cost program, set the pattern for joint federal-provincial undertakings in the post-war period. The hospital insurance program began on the initiative of the federal government, and several years passed before all provinces had agreed to participate in it. The terms of the program set out both detailed standards for eligible expenditures and detailed reporting requirements. The program's financing was not directly related to provincial spending, it had a significant equalization element, and its design made it very difficult for either level of government to control expenditures. From the federal viewpoint, the program was a means of providing a minimum level of services in a given area to all Canadians regardless of their province of residence. It represented for many provinces both a financial boon, since it helped them to fund an expensive program, and a fiscal snare, since it committed them to large and rapidly increasing outlays. In all of these respects, the hospital insurance program served as a paradigm for the major shared-cost programs that followed it.

The Health Resources Fund

At the July 1965 federal-provincial conference at which Prime Minister Lester Pearson unveiled his medicare proposals (described later in this chapter), he also announced his intention to establish the Health Resources Fund. Legislation was passed and the fund was set up as of January 1, 1966 to help the provinces meet the capital costs of planning, acquiring, constructing, renovating, and equipping health training and research facilities. The fund was intended to help the provinces provide the extra personnel and facilities that would be needed when medicare became fully operational.

The original proposal was to set up a fund to facilitate the transfer to the provinces of $500 million over 15 years. The initial offer contained no details about the allocation of the fund, but subsequent negotiations determined that $400 million would be assigned to the provinces and territories on a per capita basis, $25 million would go to regional projects in the Atlantic provinces, and $75 million would be for projects of national significance. Federal participation was determined on a project basis, after a careful review of the value of the project in terms of the objectives of the fund and a detailed analysis of the structure of the projected buildings.

Federal funds usually covered 50 percent of a project's cost; the federal share was higher for regional projects in the Atlantic provinces. Eligible facilities included schools, hospitals, and other institutions for the training of health personnel for research. Costs incurred after December 31, 1980 were not eligible.

In 1968, the federal government announced its intention to limit annual payments under the program to $37.5 million. In 1978, it closed off the fund by limiting its support to provincial projects that had been approved for the program before November 3, 1978. By the end of March 1981, the fund had transferred a total of $418 million to the provinces. Thereafter, the federal payments were minimal and the program gradually disappeared.

National Medicare

In 1961, the federal government appointed the Royal Commission on Health Services, under the chairmanship of Chief Justice Emmett Hall of Saskatchewan. The commission's report, issued in 1965,[4] called for a comprehensive health services program. The provinces would administer the program, and the federal government would draw on general revenues to

---

[4] Canada, *Report of the Royal Commission on Health Services* (Ottawa: Queen's Printer, 1965).

meet 50 percent of its costs. The program would cover physical and psychiatric care, prescription drugs (with a cost in excess of $1.00), optical services, and, for children under the age of 18, dental care and eyeglasses. The commission indicated that the federal government should proceed as soon as at least two provinces containing at least 50 percent of the national population indicated their willingness to enter an agreement.

At a federal-provincial conference in July 1965, Prime Minister Pearson outlined the extent to which the federal government proposed to implement the recommendations of the Hall commission. His proposal called for a federal contribution in support of provincial medicare programs that met four basic conditions. The federal contribution, which would become available on July 1, 1967, would amount to approximately one-half of the national cost of a comprehensive medicare program that covered all physicians' services.

The four basic conditions, which were eventually embodied in the legislation that enacted the program, were as follows:

1) *Comprehensive scope.* At a minimum, the provincial plan had to cover all services provided by physicians, both general practitioners and specialists, regardless of where the services were made available. The provinces were not restricted to these services, and many did expand benefits to cover dental services, prescribed drugs, and other important services.

2) *Universal coverage.* Provincial plans had to provide insured services on uniform terms and conditions to all insured residents and to cover not less than 95 percent of insurable residents. In addition, the plan could not impose a minimum period of residence or any waiting period in excess of three months before coverage began.

3) *Public administration.* Provincial plans had to be administered and operated on a non-profit basis by a public authority—that is, by the provincial government or a provincial government agency.

4) *Portability.* The benefits under any provincial plan had to be available to both insured persons temporarily absent from the province and to persons who moved to another participating province until they qualified for medicare benefits in that province.

The federal government later granted minor concessions with respect to coverage and administration, as detailed below.

No formal federal-provincial agreements were necessary under the federal proposal, nor did the proposal specify how many provinces had to indicate an intention to introduce medicare plans before the federal program went into effect. The prime minister's proposal failed to indicate what form the federal compensation would take.

The initial reaction of most provinces was favourable. Only Alberta took issue with the proposal, on the basis of its coverage (which was virtually compulsory) and its administrative features.

The federal proposals were further discussed at a special meeting of federal and provincial ministers of health in September 1965. Federal legislation was introduced in July 1966, and the program was to begin on July 1, 1967. On September 8, 1966, however, the federal minister of finance, Mitchell Sharp, citing the program's potential to increase inflation, announced a deferral of the start-up date to July 1, 1968, when, it was hoped, price pressures would have subsided. At the time of the announcement, no province had officially indicated its intention to participate, and only Saskatchewan already had a plan in effect that met the terms of the legislation. Alberta and British Columbia had entirely voluntary plans, and Newfoundland and Ontario had voluntary programs that were available only to certain segments of their populations. By the time the provinces had digested the full details of the federal proposal and analyzed its cost implications, most of them were less enthusiastic about the federal program than they had been when Ottawa first proposed it. Only Saskatchewan and British Columbia joined the program on its start-up date.

Provincial misgivings deepened when the federal finance minister, Edgar Benson, introduced his October 1968 budget, which imposed the Social Development Tax—a tax of 2 percent to a maximum $120—on the taxable income of individual taxpayers. The design of the tax was such that the revenue went only to the federal government, which advanced the rationale that it needed the revenue to pay its share of medicare. At a meeting of ministers of finance and treasurers on November 4 and 5, 1968, the eight provinces that had not joined the plan expressed outrage. Ontario's treasurer, Charles MacNaughton, called the tax a premium for medicare that coerced the Ontario taxpayer into pushing for provincial participation. He called for the collections to be turned over to the provinces. Quebec's premier, Jean-Jacques Bertrand, wanted a formal declaration that the federal government would not apply the new tax to Quebec residents; he described the tax as a means of obliging Quebec residents to finance programs outside Quebec that were in fact within provincial jurisdiction.

At the November conference, Ontario presented a detailed explanation of its position on medicare. It noted that such a large new program would exacerbate the already serious imbalance between revenue and expenditure at the provincial level. Ontario, where over 95 percent of the population was already covered by some form of private medical insurance, assigned a lower priority to medicare than to a number of other, unrelated provincial functions. The program seemed to contradict both the federal government's position that provincial revenues and expenditures should be brought into line and its efforts to contain the costs of other major shared-cost programs. The province argued that the federal cost estimates were too low and that the real costs were too high to be incurred at a time when governments in Canada were trying to restrain expenditure. Ontario also expressed concern that a shift away from premium-financed medicare would break the link between costs and benefits. Finally, Ontario criticized the federal program's lack of flexibility, its timing, the coverage it provided, and its basic sharing formula, which in

Ontario's view undercompensated high-cost programs and overcompensated low-cost programs. If, for example, British Columbia, Saskatchewan, and Newfoundland were the only provinces in the plan, Newfoundland would receive $12 per capita in addition to the total cost of its plan. Ontario was opposed to such implicit equalization.

The federal government modified two of its criteria when the legislation was introduced.[5] A provincial plan would be acceptable if it provided coverage for at least 90 percent of insurable residents in the first year and 95 percent by the third year. After much public dispute with Ontario, the federal government modified the plan to allow administration by a private authority designated by the province. These concessions proved sufficient: the eight provinces that had failed to join the plan at the start had all come in by the beginning of 1971. Table 13.2 shows both the dates when each of the provinces joined the plan and the total amount that each province received under the cost-sharing arrangements that ended on March 31, 1977.[6]

As in the case of hospital insurance, the provinces followed a variety of methods in financing their shares of the cost of medicare. Some provinces imposed special charges or added to existing taxes. Quebec imposed a special tax on personal income and required a matching contribution from employers; the self-employed were required to contribute the equivalent of the combined amount.

Conclusion

The history of medicare illustrates much of what provinces and theoreticians have criticized about shared-cost programs. As Carter noted, "the provinces regarded medicare as a fait accompli; participation in the program by all provinces was inevitable."[7] The program had been a part of the Liberal election platform in 1963, and the federal government was clearly and publicly committed to it. The difficulty that provincial governments faced in trying to limit their residents' access to a federal program was exacerbated when the federal government imposed its special tax in the 1968 budget.

Medicare now stands as the last major national shared-cost program to be introduced in a long history of such initiatives. Building on popular demand and provincial precedents, the federal government introduced the program in order to encourage the extension of medicare to the residents of all provinces. The federal medicare program was significant for its unique design. The conditions attached to it were more general and less restrictive than those

---

[5] Medical Care Act, SC 1966-67, c. 64.

[6] The provinces received smaller amounts in subsequent fiscal years to cover adjustments in the payments for prior years. See chapters 17 and 18 for breakdowns of the cash payments associated with the medicare element of established programs financing.

[7] George E. Carter, *Canadian Conditional Grants Since World War II*, Canadian Tax Paper no. 54 (Toronto: Canadian Tax Foundation, 1971, 76.

Table 13.2   Contributions to the Provinces Under the Medical Care Act, 1968-69 to 1976-77

	Date of entry	Contributions, 1968-69 to 1976-77, $ millions[a]
Newfoundland	1/4/69	129.6
Prince Edward Island	1/12/70	23.7
Nova Scotia	1/4/69	190.6
New Brunswick	1/1/71	133.8
Quebec	1/11/70	1,269.8
Ontario	1/10/69	1,834.3
Manitoba	1/4/69	245.5
Saskatchewan	1/7/68	235.8
Alberta	1/7/69	408.1
British Columbia	1/7/68	579.8
Northwest Territories	1/4/71 ⎫	
Yukon	1/4/72 ⎭	10.7
Total		5,061.7

[a] Small adjustments for this period made in subsequent years are excluded.

Source: Public Accounts of Canada, various years.

associated with any previous shared-cost program. The administrative provisions were much simpler than the provisions of any earlier program. Even the federal payment system was relatively straightforward. In spite of this simplicity, or because of it, the program suffered no major administrative problems. There were other problems associated with medicare, however, and the effort to deal with them led to the concept of established programs financing, which is discussed in chapters 17 and 18.

14

Welfare and Other Programs

During the first eight decades of confederation, welfare was the major area of cooperation between the federal government and the provinces. Both levels sought to provide for the aged and the unemployed within the bounds of their respective jurisdictional and financial constraints.

Relief for the unemployed and the unemployable was a serious problem for provincial and local governments during the depression of the 1930s, and a number of ad hoc federal programs were introduced. Unemployment relief was a matter of particular concern to the Rowell-Sirois commission, whose report criticized the federal government for its insistence that relief of the unemployed was primarily a provincial and local responsibility.[1] The results of this federal aloofness, the report noted, were marked differences across localities in standards of relief and eligibility criteria, differences that created serious barriers to labour mobility; severe financial distress at the provincial and municipal levels; and inadequate control by the federal government over its grant and loan programs. The commission recommended that responsibility for the relief of unemployed employables be transferred to the federal government. In 1941, the federal government moved on this recommendation and with the agreement of the provinces passed legislation to set up a federal system of compulsory unemployment insurance for those workers most vulnerable to layoff.

In 1945, the federal government passed further legislation to advance social welfare in Canada and to fulfil its commitment to maintain a high or stable level of income and employment, as spelled out in its White Paper on Employment and Income tabled in April 1945.[2] In the same year, the federal government introduced a program of universal family allowance payments and price support for farmers and the fisheries.

One of the federal "green book"[3] proposals presented to the Conference on Reconstruction in 1945 was that the federal government assume complete financial and administrative responsibility for pensions to persons aged 70 or over, at $30 per month with no means test, and provide a 50-percent subsidy

---

[1] See Canada, *Report of the Royal Commission on Dominion-Provincial Relations*, book II (Ottawa: King's Printer, 1940), 15-24.

[2] Canada, Department of Reconstruction, *Employment and Income, with Special Reference to the Initial Period of Reconstruction* (Ottawa: the department, April 1945).

[3] Canada, *Health, Welfare, and Labour*, reference book for the Dominion-Provincial Conference on Reconstruction (Ottawa: King's Printer, 1945).

for a provincial means-tested pension of $30 per month to persons aged 65 to 69. The federal government also offered to extend unemployment insurance to all employees in Canada and to provide assistance benefits equal to 85 percent of insurance benefits to those not yet or no longer eligible for unemployment insurance benefits. Not all of the provinces accepted these proposals, but only Ontario presented counterproposals. It called upon the federal government to pay 75 percent of provincial aid to unemployables and to adopt a national plan of universal pensions for individuals 65 or older. In the absence of an agreement with the provinces, the federal government shelved its welfare proposals.

In the early post-war years, discussion of welfare programs centred on old age pensions. In 1950, about 45 percent of persons aged 70 or more were receiving either full or partial pensions under the shared-cost, means-tested program introduced in 1927 (see chapter 12); the proportion of recipients ranged from 35 percent in Ontario to 77 percent in Newfoundland. In the same year, a joint committee of the House of Commons and the Senate recommended that the federal government institute a universal old age pension of $40 per month for individuals aged 70 or more and that the federal government and the provinces contribute jointly to a similar pension to be paid to needy individuals aged 65 to 69.[4] At a 1950 federal-provincial conference, Prime Minister Louis St. Laurent accepted this plan. He noted that it would require an amendment to the British North America (BNA) Act, and that in the opinion of Cabinet this amendment ought to have the unanimous consent of the provinces.[5]

The federal government offered at the conference to continue to pay 75 percent of the provincial pensions to blind persons aged 21 to 69, as provided under the existing old age pension legislation. The conditions inherent in the means tests were to be liberalized at the same time. The conference ended with agreement that the federal government would draft an amendment to the BNA Act for universal pensions: the amendment would be submitted to the provinces, and the two levels would then jointly determine the appropriate assistance for individuals aged 65 to 69. The provinces welcomed the federal proposals; Alberta and Saskatchewan felt that they did not go far enough.

All of the provincial legislatures accepted the proposed amendment to the BNA Act, and by mid-1951 the amendment had received approval from the Parliament of the United Kingdom. Federal old age pension payments for all persons aged 70 or more began on January 1, 1952. The Old Age Security Act[6] imposed a special tax of 2 percent on personal income (to a maximum of $60), an additional tax of 2 percent on corporations, and an increase of 2

---

[4] Canada, *Report of the Joint Committee of the Senate and House of Commons on Old Age Security* (Ottawa: King's Printer, June 28, 1950).

[5] Canada, *Proceedings of the Constitutional Conference of Federal and Provincial Governments*, held at Ottawa, December 4-7, 1950 (Ottawa: King's Printer, 1951), 8.

[6] SC 1951, c. 18.

percentage points in the manufacturers' sales tax. The revenues were earmarked for the fund from which the pensions were to be paid.

Although the Old Age Security Act relieved the provinces of responsibility for those aged 70 or more, for other groups the practice of providing assistance on a shared-cost basis continued. The Old Age Assistance Act,[7] which also took effect on January 1, 1952, provided for equal federal and provincial sharing of the cost of means-tested pensions for individuals aged 65 to 69. The Blind Persons Act of 1951[8] extended federal assistance (at 75 percent of total costs) to blind persons through similar tests of means. All of the provinces adopted the new system, and uniform regulations and means tests were used across the country. Supplemental provincial assistance, not qualifying for federal contributions, varied considerably from province to province.

In 1949, Newfoundland introduced assistance for disabled persons, and in 1952 Ontario and in 1953 Alberta introduced similar programs. The federal government announced its intention to establish a joint program in the November 1953 speech from the throne. A federal-provincial conference was convened to discuss the proposal in January 1954, and the Disabled Persons Act[9] was passed in the same year. Under it, the federal and provincial governments shared equally the costs of a means-tested pension for persons who met medical tests for total and permanent disability. The basic pension and the medical and income tests were uniform, but the level of provincial supplementation varied.

As noted earlier, the federal "green book" proposals for aid to unemployed employables were not implemented, and for nearly 10 years no action was taken in this area. Support was growing, however, for the concept of a federal grant-in-aid program under which the administration of aid to the unemployed would be a provincial or local responsibility.

In May 1955 and again in June, federal and provincial officials met to develop a mutually acceptable plan for federal assistance for unemployed employables. The administrative details of the plan were completed at a federal-provincial conference in October 1955, and Parliament passed the federal Unemployment Assistance Act in 1956.[10] Under the terms of the Act, the federal government would reimburse a province for payments within the existing provincial framework of general assistance, as determined by the province and its municipalities. The Act set no ceiling on the amount of assistance for which the federal government would share responsibility.

In an attempt to ensure that assistance to unemployables, estimated at 0.45 percent of the total population, remained a provincial responsibility, the Unemployment Assistance Act provided that the federal contribution would

---

[7] SC 1950-51, c. 55.
[8] SC 1950-51, c. 38.
[9] SC 1953-54, c. 55.
[10] SC 1956, c. 26.

apply only to the proportion of the recipient population in excess of 0.45 percent of the total population. Several provinces objected to this provision, which excluded the hard core of provincial and municipal welfare cases, and did not immediately enter agreements. The legislation was amended later in 1956 to lower the threshold in Nova Scotia's case and again in 1957 to remove it altogether, whereupon the remaining provinces joined the program (see table 14.1). The federal government had now made itself partially responsible for assistance to all unemployed persons except those in receipt of mothers' allowances, those in certain institutions, and those in receipt of other jointly funded assistance.

In 1965, the federal government began to lower the starting age for the old age security pension on a schedule that by 1970 would give a pension all persons aged 65 or more. In 1967, it moved to end the old age assistance program over the next three years by adding the guaranteed income supplement (based on income) to the basic old age security payment. The introduction of the Canada assistance plan (CAP) in 1966[11] marked the end of the other categorical welfare programs (those for the blind and the disabled) and the unemployment assistance program. In some cases, however, recipients could continue to receive assistance under the earlier programs, if it was more generous than the assistance available to them under the CAP.

The Canada Assistance Plan

In April 1965, after an extensive joint federal-provincial review of existing programs, Prime Minister Lester Pearson proposed a comprehensive public assistance program—the Canada assistance plan (CAP), whose details would be developed in consultation with the provinces. The CAP was originally intended to supplement the categorical programs described earlier so that social assistance could be better integrated with social insurance plans such as the Canada and Quebec pension plans and medicare schemes. Legislation was enacted in July 1966 to take effect retroactively to April of that year. All of the provinces joined immediately, although, as was noted earlier, some recipients stayed with the categorical programs.

In addition to replacing some existing programs, the CAP extended federal assistance to cover provincial assistance to needy mothers with dependent children and children in child welfare agencies. The federal government agreed to pay 50 percent of the cost of providing recipients with basic requirements and 50 percent of certain costs of improving and extending welfare services. Like unemployment assistance but unlike assistance under other welfare programs, CAP entitlements were based on measures of need, not on measures of income. The program was open-ended, and provinces were free to set their own rates of assistance. The CAP also made funds available for provincial expenditures on administration and research.

---

[11] SC 1966-67, c. 45.

**Table 14.1 Implementation of Federal-Provincial Agreements
on Assistance to Unemployed Employables**

	Date of initial agreement	Effective date
Newfoundland	December 21, 1955	July 1, 1955
Prince Edward Island	February 3, 1956	July 1, 1955
Nova Scotia	February 14, 1958	January 1, 1958
New Brunswick	February 3, 1956	January 1, 1956
Quebec	July 1, 1959	July 1, 1958
Ontario	December 30, 1957	December 1, 1956
Manitoba	May 30, 1956	July 1, 1955
Saskatchewan	March 28, 1956	July 1, 1955
Alberta	April 22, 1958	January 1, 1958
British Columbia	December 21, 1955	July 1, 1955
Yukon	November 1, 1959	January 1, 1959
Northwest Territories	December 30, 1958	January 1, 1958

What distinguished the CAP from earlier federal programs was the open-ended nature of the federal assistance it provided and the freedom it gave provinces to set benefits and rates of assistance. Although payments to the provinces under the CAP were not without conditions, the plan was flexible enough to cover a variety of experimental or non-traditional activities and forms of assistance. The administration of the federal grants, however, continued to involve detailed accounting and auditing.

Vocational Training

As was noted in chapter 12, one of the first federal shared-cost programs, introduced in 1919, was designed to stimulate provincial activity in technical and vocational education. The federal government extended and supplemented this program on a number of occasions, and in 1939 it introduced a separate program for training unemployed youth. The Vocation Training Coordination Act of 1942[12] and its subsequent amendments enlarged and consolidated the federal role in the area of vocational training. Federal assistance under the Act eventually covered vocational correspondence courses, retraining of unemployed persons, training of the disabled, and the capital and operating costs of provincial technical and vocational schools. In 1960, the federal Technical and Vocational Training Assistance Act[13] superseded the earlier legislation. The new Act was in large part a response to rising rates of unemployment among unskilled workers: its purpose was to encourage the provinces to both expand and intensify their training programs, and to help cover the costs of building the necessary facilities.

Under the earlier programs, federal aid usually represented 50 percent of the total approved costs. Under the 1960 legislation, however, the federal

---

[12] SC 1942-43, c. 34.
[13] SC 1960-61, c. 6.

government provided 75 percent of approved provincial expenditures on technical and vocational school facilities, alterations and repairs to facilities for retraining the unemployed, and programs for retraining employed persons for industry. It also met 90 percent of living allowances for unemployed persons who were taking training. The legislation provided that the capital grants would expire on March 31, 1967. When the expiry date arrived, however, several provinces were still involved in extensive vocational-school building programs. The federal government agreed to transitional arrangements under which per capita grants were available, without time limit, until each province had received in total the equivalent of $800 for each of its residents aged 15 to 19, as of June 1961. Payments under this grant program were finally completed on March 31, 1972.

The rest of the Technical and Vocational Training Assistance Act also expired on March 31, 1967 and was replaced by the Adult Occupational Training Act,[14] which provided complete reimbursement for provincial expenditures on specific training or retraining programs whose costs had previously been shared. Training allowances became a direct federal expenditure. At the same time, the federal government made available a greatly broadened and enriched federal system of aid for post-secondary education, including technical education.

In no other instance did federal-provincial cooperation develop quite as it did in the case of technical and vocational training. As in the case of old age security, the federal government assumed an increasingly large role in the financing and administration of programs in an area of provincial spending and ultimately eliminated provincial participation. In the earlier case, however, the federal assumption of sole responsibility had required an amendment to the constitution, whereas in the case of vocational training no amendment was needed. This was so because the programs in question had to do not with education as such—unequivocally a provincial responsibility— but with manpower retraining and labour-force problems, an area in which some federal activity was accepted. Moreover, the 1967 legislation avoided the constitutional issue by treating the federal payments as purchases by the federal authorities of training services from the provinces. The provinces received significant financial compensation for their loss under the new legislation of conditional grants for some programs related to vocational training, since the change occurred at the same time as the introduction of the tax abatements and cash payments for post-secondary education—a more generous system of unconditional transfers for a more broadly defined area of provincial spending. In addition, the extension of the capital grants ensured that no province would lose access to federal assistance for an expensive part of its capital program because its rate of building had been slower than the national average.

---

[14] SC 1966-67, c. 94.

Development Programs

The post-war programs of federal assistance for regional development of resources and industry began in 1962. In that year, the federal government introduced the Agricultural Rehabilitation and Development Act,[15] which was designed to facilitate the economic growth of rural areas and to increase rural incomes, employment opportunities, and living standards. The federal government signed agreements that ran from April 1, 1962 to March 31, 1965 with all 10 provinces for joint projects to promote non-agricultural uses of low-productivity land, increase rural employment opportunities, or encourage the development and conservation of water and soil resources. Federal assistance for approved projects was limited to $20 million in any fiscal year and $50 million over three-and-a-half years. The federal government paid 50 percent of the costs of projects of national interest and 33-⅓ percent of the costs of projects of provincial or local interest. It also paid 66-⅔ percent of the cost of land to be used for community pastures. Each province was given an initial allotment of $750,000, and the balance was distributed according to a formula based on rural population, the number of small farms, and agricultural production.

In 1965, new, five-year agreements expanded the joint program to include fishing and mining projects. The federal government made additional assistance available for comprehensive rural development plans, research, and projects in special areas. In 1966, it made the assistance for special areas available to all rural areas. The agreements were renewed for another five years in 1970.

From 1966 to 1969, the federal government provided grants for major rural development projects, without requiring a matching provincial contribution, through the fund for rural economic development (FRED). On April 1, 1969, the federal government united its many programs for the stimulation of provincial and local economies under the Department of Regional Economic Expansion (DREE).

As of April 1, 1970, 22 districts were designated as "special areas" eligible for federal assistance. Under agreements with the provinces, the federal government undertook to provide long-term loans and grants of up to 100 percent of the cost of provincial or local programs in these areas for water and sewer systems, industrial parks, schools, roads and highways, the servicing of residential land, housing, harbour development, training facilities, and similar projects. Agreements under the Agricultural and Rural Development Act and the fund for rural economic development were also extended, but in 1974 most federal programs were combined under the 10-year general development agreements signed with all of the provinces except Prince Edward Island. The goal of the agreements was to identify obstacles to

---

[15] SC 1960-61, c. 30, later changed to the Agricultural and Rural Development Act.

development and to encourage economic and social development projects in slow-growth areas. Subsidiary agreements were used to cover specific programs such as manpower training, the development of sites for industrial facilities, and the improvement of transportation networks. The federal government would pay up to 90 percent of the cost of a subsidiary agreement with Newfoundland. The figure was 80 percent for Nova Scotia and New Brunswick; 60 percent for Quebec, Manitoba, Saskatchewan, the Northwest Territories, and the Yukon; and 50 percent for Ontario, Alberta, and British Columbia.

In Prince Edward Island, federal aid for economic development was coordinated under the comprehensive development plan set up earlier under the fund for rural economic development. The federal government agreed to meet 100 percent of agricultural research costs, 50 percent of costs for the school construction program, and 90 percent of costs for all other programs covered under the plan.

By 1984, the last of the general development agreements had expired; the subsidiary agreements continued to the end of their terms. The general agreements were replaced by the economic and regional development agreements (ERDAs), 10-year umbrella agreements that set out a general statement of objectives and the division of responsibilities between the federal government and the province. Subsidiary agreements were again signed for the commitment of resources to specific projects or areas.

Only five years later, however, the pressure of deficits led the federal government to reduce its spending on joint projects for regional development. As the ERDAs were being renegotiated, the federal government eliminated some programs and left others to the provinces alone. More than three decades of effort to reduce regional disparities, using a variety of approaches, had in fact had little direct success.[16] Table 14.2, which examines changes in per capita personal income in each province since 1961, provides one indication of changes in regional disparities since the introduction of federal development programs in the early 1960s.

The Municipal Winter Works Incentive Program

During the recession of 1957, the provinces suggested that the federal government provide their municipalities with some incentive to change the timing of their capital projects in order to limit the usual loss of construction jobs in the winter months. Ontario introduced a program of provincial grants to local governments for this purpose during the winter of 1957-58. On October 27, 1958, Prime Minister John Diefenbaker announced a federal program to provide, through the provinces, grants to local governments equal to

---

[16] The changes in the federal government's regional development activities are described in *The National Finances, 1988-89* (Toronto: Canadian Tax Foundation, 1990), chapter 1.

Table 14.2 Per Capita Personal Income (Excluding Government Transfers to Persons) as a Percentage of the National Average, Selected Calendar Years, 1961 to 1990

	Nfld.	PEI	NS	NB	Que.	Ont.	Man.	Sask.	Alta.	BC
1961	53.2	54.3	74.2	63.3	89.4	121.0	93.3	68.8	100.1	113.8
1966	53.3	57.8	70.3	65.9	89.7	118.9	90.4	89.1	97.4	110.0
1971	54.9	55.4	72.3	67.6	89.7	119.4	91.6	76.9	96.3	107.7
1976	56.1	63.4	72.3	68.1	91.6	113.0	90.0	95.3	103.8	109.5
1981	55.1	62.5	70.0	64.6	91.3	108.5	91.1	93.8	117.7	113.4
1986	57.5	66.3	79.5	69.0	90.7	114.5	89.8	86.7	106.5	99.0
1989	59.1	65.2	76.9	70.5	89.7	117.4	84.7	77.4	100.6	101.0
1990	59.0	65.6	77.4	70.5	90.1	117.0	84.8	76.6	100.7	101.0

[a] Data for Newfoundland not applicable before 1949.

Sources: Statistics Canada, *National Income and Expenditure Accounts*: Annual Estimates, 1926 to 1986 and Annual Estimates, various years, catalogue nos. 13-201 and 13-531.

50 percent of direct labour costs incurred from December 1 to April 30 on approved capital projects. Grants under the municipal winter works incentive program required provincial approval, but matching or complementing provincial expenditures were not obligatory; however, five provinces provided grants equal to 25 percent of the direct labour costs of projects approved under the program. The federal government reviewed the program, year by year, for 10 years.

On August 30, 1968, Prime Minister Pierre Trudeau announced that the program would not be adopted for the coming winter. There were no strong provincial objections.[17] All three levels of government found that the uncertainty of the program limited their ability to carry out long-term planning. The employment provided was not necessarily suitable for those who suffered most from seasonal unemployment. Finally, the program did nothing to solve the underlying problems in the regional labour markets.

The winter works program typified relations between the federal government and local governments in Canada. Little or no direct, formal contact occurs between the two levels. Federal grants intended for the local level are channelled through the provinces. Often, as in the case of winter works, the provinces supplement the federal grants—an arrangement that creates complications for the municipalities, since the provincial requirements for accounting and accountability generally differ from the federal requirements.

Municipal Development and Loan Plan

The municipal development and loan plan provides another example of the relationship between the federal government and municipalities. The federal

---

[17] For a full evaluation of the program, see Lawrence J. Close and Ronald M. Burns, *The Municipal Winter Works Program: A Study of Government Decision-Making*, Canadian Tax Paper no. 53 (Toronto: Canadian Tax Foundation, 1971).

government put the plan forward in July 1963 at a federal-provincial conference called for that purpose. The plan was designed to encourage municipalities to accelerate their public works projects and thereby create additional employment; it would provide federal loans for this purpose directly to municipalities on a first-come, first-served basis. After discussion with the provincial representatives, the federal government agreed instead to distribute the loan funds, on a per capita basis, among the provinces, which would in turn lend the funds to their municipalities at their discretion. By August 2, 1963, Parliament had passed the Municipal Development and Loan Act,[18] which created a loan fund of $400 million. Ottawa would forgive one-quarter of the value of loans for projects completed by March 31, 1966 (a deadline subsequently extended by six months). Quebec, Ontario, Manitoba, and Saskatchewan administered the fund in their provinces, but the other six provinces permitted the federal government to make the loans directly to their municipalities.

The Community Services Contribution Program

At a meeting on June 13, 1978, the provincial ministers responsible for municipal affairs and the federal minister of state for urban affairs worked out the basis for a new grant program, the community services contribution program, to replace existing federal grant programs for urban research, local works, and water and sewage projects. The initial allocations under the program were set at $150 million for 1978 and $250 million for 1979, and the funds were to be distributed to local projects by the provinces. Delays in implementing the program and in executing agreements with the provinces caused the provinces to delay eligible local projects. Finally, the federal austerity program introduced in August 1978 formally deferred the program to January 1, 1979.

The original agreements signed under the community services program were intended to be temporary; they called for their own replacement by new agreements, designed to provide long-term certainty, before December 31, 1980. New agreements could not be agreed upon, however, and in November 1980 the federal government ended the program, though it agreed to continue to finance projects for which a commitment had been made before December 31, 1980.

The Trans-Canada Highway

The first federal grants for provincial or local road construction and other capital projects in the field of transportation were grants for railway grade crossings under a program that began in 1909. Most such programs have been small and have provided grants for specific projects such as a bridge or a particular section of road. In the case of the Trans-Canada Highway

---

[18] SC 1963, c. 13.

program, however, the emphasis was national rather than local, since the highway was to link all of the provinces and play a part in the national economy. Only Quebec abstained from joining the program upon its inception in 1950; it did not participate until 1960.

The agreements that became effective in 1950 provided for federal grants equal to 50 percent of the cost of constructing a paved, two-lane highway from St. John's to Victoria. The costs of acquiring rights-of-way and constructing interchanges were not shareable, but the provinces were reimbursed for half the costs of roads constructed between 1928 and 1949 that were incorporated into the Trans-Canada Highway system. The federal legislation specified a maximum of $150 million in grants and set December 9, 1956 as the date for completion of the highway.[19] In that year, however, the first of many extensions was enacted, the federal maximum was raised to $250 million, and the federal government agreed to pay 90 percent of the construction costs for one-tenth of the mileage in each province. Subsequent amendments raised the federal limit to $400 million in 1960, $625 million in 1963, and $825 million in 1966. In 1963, the federal government assumed responsibility for 90 percent of the construction costs incurred in the Atlantic provinces after April 1 of that year.

The progress of the Trans-Canada Highway program shows how a uniform, nationwide, federally inspired program gradually became less uniform and more expensive as the poorer provinces found it increasingly difficult to finance their share and still address their other priorities.

Conclusion

This chapter and its predecessor have provided examples of the various ways in which the federal government sought during the post-war period to achieve national objectives in areas of solely provincial jurisdiction. In some cases, the federal government simply transferred a given area of responsibility from the provinces to itself—either through an amendment to the BNA Act, as in the case of unemployment insurance and old age pensions, or through a less formal process, as in the case of retraining programs. In other cases, such as that of hospital insurance, the federal government provided partial funding for provincial programs that met certain conditions. The conditions were intended to establish minimum standards of service and full portability between provinces, and the programs were often undertaken with a view to persuading provinces to provide services not previously available.[20]

---

[19] The Trans-Canada Highway Act, SC 1949, c. 40.

[20] The account in this chapter and chapters 12 and 13 of conditional grant and shared-cost programs is far from being exhaustive. See appendix A to this book for a comprehensive list of these programs.

The provincial premiers spelled out the weaknesses of the shared-cost and conditional grant programs at a federal-provincial conference in July 1960. Premier Louis Robichaud of New Brunswick submitted that such programs were unfair to provinces that found it difficult to pay the uniform provincial share of costs; the low-income provinces could afford neither to accept nor to reject such grants. Robichaud called for a form of conditional grant that took into account the relative capacity of each province to pay its share of the cost of programs such as the Trans-Canada Highway. The premiers of Saskatchewan and Prince Edward Island, for their part, complained of the administrative and budgetary rigidity of the shared-cost programs.

Other provincial leaders criticized the very concept of cost-sharing. Premier Ernest Manning of Alberta argued that the trend toward shared-cost programs should gradually be reversed and the funds channelled instead into unconditional grants. Premier Leslie Frost of Ontario described cost-sharing as a system under which the federal government whetted the appetites of the provinces with their own money—that is, the money lost to the provinces as a result of the federal pre-emption, ever since the wartime tax agreements, of the provinces' share of the major tax fields. The newly elected premier of Quebec, Jean Lesage, requested that the federal government abandon shared-cost programs and provide instead additional tax room and equalization.

Four years later, when Quebec and the federal government began serious negotiations for contracting-out (see chapter 15), the shortcomings of shared-cost programs and conditional grants were still very much on Lesage's mind. In his statement at a federal-provincial conference held March 31, 1964, Lesage enumerated the familiar disadvantages of inefficiency, duplication, and high administrative costs—the consequences of the need to maintain staffs at both the federal and provincial levels devoted only to administering the grants. He noted further that the federal government generally proposed its cost-sharing programs without first consulting the provinces, as if it felt it were better able to judge needs than were the provincial administrations that dealt with the relevant areas. He referred to conditional grant programs as "unconditional gifts to the rich provinces,"[21] which would have provided the services even if the grants had not been available. In the case of less wealthy provinces, the subsidized program was often undertaken at the expense of other programs that the provincial administration might feel were more important but for which funding was not available. This element of coercion or compulsion, in Lesage's view, subordinated the provinces to the federal government and allowed the federal government to influence matters assigned to the provinces. Both situations violated the terms of the British North America Act.

---

[21] See "Extract from the Statement by Premier Lesage to the Federal-Provincial Conference, March 31, 1964," in A. Milton Moore, J. Harvey Perry, and Donald I. Beach, *The Financing of Canadian Federation: The First Hundred Years*, Canadian Tax Paper no. 43 (Toronto: Canadian Tax Foundation, 1966), appendix E, at 134.

The conditional grant and shared-cost programs provided by the federal government were successful in achieving federal aims and objectives. The post-war health care system in Canada was built in large part on the national health grants, the hospital insurance and medicare programs, and the health resources fund. The level of health services in the poorer provinces is well above what it would be if these provinces were obliged to rely solely on their own resources. Similarly, the development of the Canada assistance plan in place of ad hoc federal grants for unemployment relief largely solved the serious problem created by the fact that many provinces lacked the resources they needed to meet the provincial responsibility for welfare.

Prime Minister Pearson's statement at the 1964 conference spelled out his government's position on cost-sharing. According to Pearson, the use of shared-cost programs had been necessary in order "to remove the obstacles created by the uneven fiscal capacity of the provinces and the competing demands on provincial treasuries."[22] The programs had made an essential contribution to the economic and social progress of Canada, and in the process they had reduced regional disparities.

Yet however useful cost-sharing had been in the past, its future was by no means assured. Conditional grant programs of the type exemplified by the hospital insurance program—programs that involved detailed accounting and reimbursement procedures, equally detailed definitions of allowable expenses, and auditing by both levels of government—were clearly not satisfactory in the long run. The later conditional grant programs were less restrictive than the earlier ones; thus the medicare plan was less detailed, and more tolerant of provincial variation, than was the hospital insurance program designed a decade earlier. By the mid-1960s, however, more fundamental changes were at hand.

[22] See "Statement by Prime Minister L. B. Pearson to the Federal-Provincial Conference, March 31, 1964," ibid., appendix F, at 138.

15

Contracting-Out: Accommodating Provincial Autonomy

The last two chapters have described the development under a strong federal government of programs intended to establish uniform minimum standards of social welfare across Canada. The same period, however, also brought developments in federal-provincial financial relations that established the basis for what could eventually become a substantial measure of provincial autonomy. The most prominent of these developments was the introduction of contracting-out. Under this arrangement, a province withdrew from a shared-cost federal program but agreed to maintain the service covered by the program in exchange for increased tax room, cash payments, or a combination of the two. In its final form, block funding, the federal transfer was only remotely related to any specific area of provincial activity.[1]

These changes in transfer arrangements arose in large part because of change in the roles of the two senior levels of government. In the late 1940s and the 1950s, the requirements of post-war reconstruction and nation-building tended to encourage the dominance of the federal government. By the end of the 1950s, however, reconstruction was an accomplished fact and pressures for decentralizing began to mount. As was noted in chapter 4, the provinces applied pressure on the federal government during this period for changes in the tax-sharing arrangements. The provincial and municipal sectors were growing faster than the federal sector, and by 1963 they had together become larger than that sector.[2] In addition, provincial politicians were providing more vigorous leadership than they had in the past, thanks in part to the backing they received from a more assertive and sophisticated provincial public service. This last point is best illustrated by the increased assertiveness of the Quebec government after the election in 1960 of the Liberals under Jean Lesage, but similar, if less dramatic, changes occurred in the behaviour of other provinces as well. The growing provincial demand for decentralization naturally ran counter to the existing system of conditional grants and shared-cost programs, which, in the provinces' view, compromised provincial authority. Second thoughts about these programs, at both

---

[1] Described in chapter 16.

[2] Based on expenditures cast in a national income and expenditure accounts framework. See Richard M. Bird, *Financing Canadian Government: A Quantitative Overview*, Financing Canadian Federation no. 1 (Toronto: Canadian Tax Foundation, 1979), 113.

levels of government, were further encouraged by their rapid growth: total federal grant payments rose only slowly from 1945 to 1955, but during the next 10 years they increased more than tenfold.[3]

Contracting- or opting-out took three main forms.[4] In the first, a province contracted out of a wholly federal program financed from general federal revenues in return for a higher rate of federal tax abatement (as in the case of university grants). In the second, a province contracted out of a federal contributory scheme in favour of one of its own (as in the case of the Quebec pension plan). In the third form, a province contracted out of a federal conditional grant or shared-cost program in return for a higher rate of federal tax abatement or a transitional cash grant (as in the cases of hospital insurance, vocational training, health care, and a number of welfare grants).

The implications of the third form were especially important. In the past, when a province that failed to participate in a given joint program did not receive compensation, non-participation was, unsurprisingly, relatively rare. Now, however, a province that did not wish to participate in a federal initiative, as a matter of principle or because the function did not coincide with its own priorities, would not necessarily find itself penalized relative to provinces that did participate. Yet in the event only one province, Quebec, took advantage of contracting-out in any form.

The First Programs

The Rowell-Sirois commission put forward the notion of federal per capita grants to universities in 1940,[5] and in 1951 the Massey commission revived the idea.[6] The federal government responded by providing cash grants of 50 cents per capita directly to universities, distributed according to enrolment within each province. Although not all of the provinces were enthusiastic about this intrusion into an area of provincial jurisdiction, they all agreed to accept the grants in their first fiscal year, 1951-52. Quebec, however, had reserved its agreement until it obtained a promise from the federal government to consult with the province before the payment of the grants. In the absence of satisfactory arrangements with the federal government, Premier Maurice Duplessis in effect ordered Quebec universities to refuse the money offered for 1952-53.

Partly in order to finance provincial assistance to universities, Quebec then enacted its own personal income tax, to take effect as of January 1,

---

[3] Ibid., at 133-34.

[4] Described in J. Stephan Dupre, "Contracting Out: A Funny Thing Happened on the Way to the Centennial," in *Report of Proceedings of the Eighteenth Tax Conference*, 1964 Conference Report (Toronto: Canadian Tax Foundation, 1965), 205-18.

[5] Canada, *Report of the Royal Commission on Dominion-Provincial Relations*, (Ottawa: King's Printer, 1940).

[6] Canada, *Report of the Royal Commission on National Development in the Arts, Letters, and Sciences*, (Ottawa: King's Printer, 1951).

1954, at rates that averaged about 15 percent of federal rates—a figure 10 percentage points higher than the current federal tax credit. Duplessis called on the federal government to enrich this credit, a request that he justified by pointing to the money that Ottawa was willing to give for university grants. The compromise, as chapter 4 noted, was a federal credit of 10 percent, which was sufficient to offset the loss of the grants for three years. The new tax-sharing arrangement introduced in 1957 gave all provinces the equivalent, in the form of an abatement or a grant, of 10 percent of federal income tax. As a result, Quebec argued that it had lost its special compensation in lieu of university grants.

A revision of the university grant scheme in 1957 increased the federal grants to $1 per capita and designated the National Conference of Canadian Universities (NCCU) as the federal government's agent for the purpose of distributing the grants. The federal government stipulated that the NCCU retain grants not distributed (that is, those for Quebec universities) until they were claimed. Neither these changes nor a further increase in the per capita amount, to $1.50, in 1958 moved Quebec to change its position. At this point, however, the universities in Quebec broke ranks: in 1957-58 one university and in 1958-59 two accepted the grants offered by the NCCU. Subsequent negotiations achieved a long-term solution, and all Quebec universities were able to accept the grants for 1959-60.

The long-term solution, which took effect in 1960, included the granting to Quebec of an additional abatement of corporation income tax equal to 1 percent of taxable income. Quebec, for its part, agreed to raise its corporation income tax rate from 9 to 10 percent and to use the additional revenue to provide financing for its universities equivalent to its forgone entitlement under the grant scheme. If the value of the additional abatement fell short of the entitlement of $1.50 per capita, Ottawa would increase Quebec's equalization payment to cover the shortfall. On the other hand, if the value of the abatement exceeded the value of the grant entitlement, the federal government would recover the excess from the province's equalization payment. The agreement also permitted Quebec universities to collect the unclaimed amounts for 1957 to 1959 held by the NCCU.[7]

The federal government increased the per capita amount to $2 on September 1, 1962 and to $5 on September 1, 1966. Whenever the abatement fell short of the required amount for Quebec, Ottawa made up the deficiency with cash payments to the province. Whenever the abatement exceeded the required amount, the federal government recovered the excess.

---

[7] In fiscal 1960-61, the abatement exceeded $1.50 per capita by $1.6 million, which the federal government recovered from equalization payments. In 1961-62, the abatement again exceeded the equivalent grant and $1.2 million was recovered. In 1962-63, the grants were raised to $2.00 per capita, with the result that the abatement fell short by $1.7 million; the difference was added to the equalization payments.

This experience firmly established the principle of contracting-out and established it, moreover, in the context of a program of unconditional per capita grants. Neither the grants nor the contracting-out agreements involved any guarantees of program standards. The federal payments were not tied to provincial expenditures, and no auditing or requisition procedures were imposed. There was no requirement that the resources transferred, or their equivalents, be applied to spending in the relevant area.

Contracting Out of Shared-Cost Programs

By the time of the July 1960 federal-provincial conference, as was noted in chapter 14, the provincial leaders were prepared to advance serious criticisms of shared-cost programs and conditional grant programs: the programs had become too expensive and too complex, and they distorted provincial priorities. Quebec's Premier Lesage suggested a remedy, the first contracting-out proposal involving conditional grants. He proposed that the federal government allow a province to refuse, without penalty, direct federal patronage of programs to which the province's commitment was well established. Ottawa would compensate the province fully for the lost funding with additional tax room specifically reserved for the province and corresponding equalization. A province that chose this option would then be free to use its revenues as it saw fit in the jurisdictions that belonged to it.[8]

Lester Pearson, the leader of the federal Liberal opposition, endorsed Lesage's proposal. A pamphlet issued by the Liberals during the April 1963 federal election adopted a complementary position:

> If some provinces wish, they should be able to withdraw, without financial loss, from joint programs which involve regular expenditures by the federal government and which are well established. In such cases, Ottawa will compensate the provinces for the federal share of the cost, by lowering its own direct taxes and increasing equalization payments. This will be done also if some provinces do not want to take part in new joint programs.[9]

The Liberal party won the election and Pearson became prime minister.

At a federal-provincial conference that began on November 26, 1963, a majority of the provincial representatives observed that conditional grants and shared-cost programs could be replaced by either increased provincial access to jointly occupied tax fields or by increased unconditional assistance. Quebec continued to press for contracting-out and greater tax room, but Ontario felt that the existing system should be retained with relatively minor adjustments. The delegates agreed to convene a further general meeting on March 31, 1964.

---

[8] Canada, *Dominion-Provincial Conference, 1960*, held at Ottawa on July 25-27, 1960 (Ottawa: Queen's Printer, 1960), 130.

[9] National Liberal Federation, "Policies of the Liberal Party," quoted in A. Milton Moore, J. Harvey Perry, and Donald I. Beach, *The Financing of Canadian Federation: The First Hundred Years*, Canadian Tax Paper no. 43 (Toronto: Canadian Tax Foundation, 1966), 80.

At the opening of the 1964 meeting, Prime Minister Pearson presented his proposals for contracting-out or opting-out (both phrases were coined during the federal election campaign).[10] He began by emphasizing the value of conditional grant programs in removing the obstacles created by the uneven fiscal capacity of the provinces and competing demands on provincial treasuries. Conditions had changed, however, especially with the development of equalization, and offered "more alternatives than we had in the past."[11] The prime minister distinguished between conditional grants and shared-cost programs for capital projects and those for current services. The former were effective for a limited time only, and their number and extent depended on a continuing series of decisions. Although they might continue for some time, they were not perpetual—they ran down as the related capital expenditure tapered off. For the present, the federal government proposed not to touch grants for capital projects. In the case of well-established programs that involved regular expenditures, however, the federal government was willing to transfer to the provinces full responsibility and to alter the fiscal arrangements

> in such a way that the size of the [federal] expenditure transferred would be closely matched by the extra room made available for provincial taxes.
>
> Such a change cannot be made by our decision alone. The existing programs are covered by agreements which in the major cases run for several years ahead. For the period of the agreement, we can completely withdraw from the program concerned only if all provinces so wish.
>
> Therefore the only early change that we can make by federal policy, without the unanimous consent of the provinces, is to allow contracting-out. That is to say, the federal government would withdraw in the case of provinces that so wished but maintain the program for provinces wishing it to continue.[12]

Pearson qualified his offer further. The federal government determined its contribution to the program on the basis of national per capita cost; if a province set up a separate system of hospital insurance that differed from the national system, this basis would be undermined. Accordingly,

> for this particular program [hospital insurance], there is only one kind of contracting-out which it is directly in our power to implement, pending renegotiation of the agreements with all provinces. It would be a revision not in the program but in the related fiscal provisions.[13]

Thus provinces that contracted out would have to maintain a program of hospital insurance identical with the program provided by all of the other provinces; interprovincial reciprocity, standards, administration, auditing,

---

[10] See "Statement by Prime Minister L. B. Pearson to the Federal-Provincial Conference, March 31, 1964," ibid., appendix F.

[11] Ibid., at 138.

[12] Ibid., at 139.

[13] Ibid.

and the calculation of compensation would all stay the same—only the form of the federal contribution would change.

Under the prime minister's proposal, the compensation for provinces that opted out of the hospital insurance program would take the form of a transfer of percentage points of equalized personal income tax room; it was judged that 12 or 13 points would be sufficient. As long as the contracting-out province left its program unchanged, Pearson noted, any shortfall or excess in compensation could be adjusted for by adding to or subtracting from the equalization due to the province. He was apparently assuming that neither Ontario nor British Columbia, which did not receive equalization, would choose to contract out. If a contracting-out province later changed its program, its compensation would be based on historic costs escalated in accordance with current results.

The tax-point proposal applied only to hospital insurance. The prime minister did not offer the categorical welfare programs as candidates for contracting-out, since they were under review by the federal government and the provinces. He did offer some smaller programs as candidates, but compensation would take the form of cash, not tax points. He stressed that his government proposed to examine programs individually, rather than to lump a group together and then work out compensation and conditions.

The federal proposal was more than matched by Premier Lesage's statement to the conference. His proposals for contracting-out were more detailed and specific than the federal proposals. Quebec should be able to contract out of well-established programs—those formally or informally recognized as permanent—such as unemployment assistance, disability and blindness allowances, old age assistance, winter works, hospital insurance, hospital construction, and grants for public health. Compensation would be in the form of personal income tax points. During an interim period, positive or negative adjustments to equalization payments would bring total compensation to the amount that would have been provided under the conditional grant programs. After the interim period, compensation would be limited to abatements to each province of sufficient personal income tax points to transfer the equivalent of that province's share of the total compensation under the old program. If a majority of the provinces contracted out, however, there would be a uniform abatement set to the level necessary to compensate fully the province with the highest level of personal income tax; full equalization would complete the compensation to the others. The contracting-out provinces would then be free to alter their programs as they saw fit.

Quebec was not prepared to contract out of a small number of joint programs of a temporary nature that it had recently joined, such as capital assistance to technical education, the Trans-Canada Highway, programs under the Agricultural Rehabilitation and Development Act (ARDA),[14] and the Centennial of Confederation.

---

[14] SC 1960-61, c. 30.

In the case of future shared-cost programs, and of existing programs in which Quebec did not participate at present, the premier asked for financial equivalence, based on the province's share of total population, initially in cash but eventually in the form of additional tax points. He also called for retroactive compensation for programs in which his province had not participated. If the federal government later changed a program after Quebec contracted out, the compensation should be adjusted up or down to maintain the relationship between regular federal support and compensation for contracting-out.[15]

The other provinces' reactions to Quebec's proposals ranged from mild disapproval to strong objection, but subsequent negotiation proceeded on a bilateral basis between Quebec and the federal government. At Quebec's request, federal and provincial representatives met on June 8 and 9, 1964 specifically to discuss contracting-out. Prime Minister Pearson presented the final federal proposals to Premier Lesage in a letter dated August 15, 1964.[16] The letter outlined an interim or transitional arrangement under which Quebec or any other province that wished to contract out would continue to provide the relevant services according to the agreements then in force, furnish the federal government with an accounting of the expenditures incurred, and continue to participate in federal-provincial consultation and coordination. The form of the transfer and the length of the interim period would vary from program to program. More durable contracting-out arrangements would be worked out on the basis of the experience acquired during the early years of the transition and the recommendations of the Tax Structure Committee, which had been set up at the June 1964 conference.

Compensation for the well-established social programs, which the subsequent legislation would refer to as Schedule I programs, would consist of personal income tax points equalized to the level of the top two provinces, with cash adjusting payments or recoveries as required. Pearson's letter specified the expiry date of the interim period and the number of personal income tax points for each of these programs:

1) Hospital insurance (December 31, 1970), 14 points.

2) Old age assistance and blind and disabled persons allowances (March 31, 1970), 2 points.

3) Welfare portion of unemployment assistance (to unemployables) (March 31, 1970), 2 points.

4) Vocational training (March 31, 1967), 1 point.

5) Health grants (March 31, 1967), 1 point.

---

[15] See "Extract from the Statement of Premier Jean Lesage to the Federal-Provincial Conference, March 31, 1964," ibid., appendix E.

[16] Ibid., appendix G.

Thus a total of 20 tax points were available to provinces that contracted out. The agreements for items 2 and 3 above were to expire before the indicated date if the federal government established a comprehensive program of public assistance. With the establishment of the Canada assistance plan, the two abatements were merged.

The federal government offered cash compensation in lieu of conditional grants for the following programs, later referred to as Schedule II programs; it reserved the right to terminate any of the programs at the expiration of the interim period indicated in parentheses:

1) Agricultural lime assistance (March 31, 1967).

2) Pure-bred sires (March 31, 1967).

3) Forestry agreements (March 31, 1967).

4) Hospital construction (March 31, 1968).

5) Roads to resources (exhaustion of entitlement).

6) Campgrounds and picnic areas (March 31, 1967).

The federal government deemed the following joint programs to be not eligible for opting-out:

1) Capital programs:

a) Trans-Canada highway.

b) Railway grade crossing.

c) Vocational training (capital assistance).

d) The Agricultural Rehabilitation and Development Act.

e) Municipal winter works.

2) Current programs:

a) Grants to 4H clubs.

b) Grants to special fairs.

c) Compensation for animal disease losses.

d) Crop insurance.

e) Farm labour agreements.

f) Health grants (research and demonstration projects).

g) Public health research grants.

h) Training of unemployed.

i) Training in cooperation with industry.

j) Fisheries industries development.

3) Emergency measures.

4) Centennial of Confederation.

Quebec agreed to these proposals, and they went into effect, following the passage of the Established Programs (Interim Arrangements) Act,[17] on April 1, 1965. Provinces had until October 31, 1965 to contract out of eligible programs. Only Quebec took advantage of the legislation, and it limited its contracting-out to the Schedule I programs and the forestry agreements. The other Schedule II programs were never part of contracting-out agreements.

In 1966, the federal government replaced the categorical welfare grants with the Canada assistance plan (CAP).[18] The contracting-out option was transferred to the new program, and Quebec maintained its independent status. The 2-point abatement for old age, blind, and disabled allowances and the 2 points for unemployment assistance thus became 4 points for the CAP. The termination date, March 31, 1970, stayed the same.

The contracting-out arrangement and the 1-point abatement for vocational training were allowed to expire on March 31, 1967, when the grants to the other provinces ended. Similarly, the contracting-out arrangement and cash payments for forestry agreements were allowed to expire as scheduled, when the agreements with the other provinces ended. The agreements with Quebec for the other Schedule I programs were subsequently extended, in several stages, to March 31, 1973, not by formal legislation but by means of special enabling votes in federal supplementary estimates. When new fiscal arrangements were put into effect with the passage of the Federal-Provincial Fiscal Arrangements Act, 1972,[19] the temporary contracting-out provisions were extended to March 31, 1977 for hospital insurance and the Canada assistance plan. The health grants were allowed to expire.

The new approach to tax sharing and a new federal rate schedule required the revision of the personal income tax abatements for Quebec in 1972. The 14 points for hospital insurance became 16, and the 4 points for the Canada assistance plan became 5. The 3-point abatement for youth allowances, which is discussed below, did not change. Part VII of the Federal-Provincial Fiscal Arrangements and Established Programs Financing Act, 1977[20] superseded the Established Programs (Interim Arrangements) Act, extended contracting-out agreements indefinitely, and once more changed the tax base. Quebec's abatement for the established programs (in this case, hospital insurance) was reduced to 8.5 points; the province continued to receive abatements of 5 points for the Canada assistance plan and 3 points for youth allowances.

---

[17] SC 1964-65, c. 54.
[18] SC 1966-67, c. 45. See chapter 14.
[19] SC 1972, c. 8.
[20] SC 1976-77, c. 10.

The Canada Pension Plan

During the 1963 federal election campaign, the Liberal party committed itself to implementing a number of programs that overlapped provincial jurisdiction. Thus the party proposed the establishment of a comprehensive contributory pension scheme to complement the old age security pensions. The proposal called for a non-funded plan, under which contributions would match benefits. The Liberals also proposed to provide benefits to disabled contributors and the survivors of contributors, arrangements that would require a constitutional amendment.

The new Liberal government brought up its pension proposal at the federal-provincial conference in July 1963. Several provinces had implemented or proposed pension legislation of their own, and there was far from unanimous support for the federal plan. Quebec had earlier specifically stated its intention of staying out of such a plan. The provinces, which faced extensive capital programs for hospitals, schools and universities, and city-building, were loath to lose their pension funds or the right to make use of them.

Protracted and often bitter discussion followed between the federal government and the provinces. By the time of the March-April 1964 federal-provincial conference, it was reported that Quebec had decided to produce a proposal of its own. Negotiations between Quebec and Ottawa resulted in a compromise, as outlined in a letter from Prime Minister Pearson in mid-April 1964. The Canada and Quebec plans would be modified to bring their terms into substantial agreement. Any province could choose between permitting its residents to participate in the Canada pension plan (CPP) and providing them with a similar pension plan under provincial administration. The federal government would lend the funds collected under the CPP to the participating provinces for investment, and the funds accumulated by the provincial plans would remain under the control of the provinces concerned. Provinces that borrowed investment funds from the federal plan would guarantee an interest rate at least equal to the rate on long-term federal securities—a rate significantly below the rate available to the smaller provinces on the open market. Each participating province's share of the federal funds would be proportionate to the share of total contributions paid by its residents. In April 1965, after more discussion and controversy, and after public hearings by a special committee of the Senate and the House of Commons, federal legislation was passed that embodied the essential features of the scheme outlined a year earlier in Pearson's letter. The legislation took effect January 1, 1966.[21]

Only Quebec did not become a party to the Canada pension plan. Instead, it set up its own plan, the Quebec pension plan (QPP), which used a more generous indexing factor than did the CPP and therefore provided for a slightly larger base for contributions and benefits. In 1974, an amendment to the federal plan changed the indexing system to make it agree with that of the QPP.

---

[21] Canada Pension Plan, SC 1964-65, c. 51.

No integration of the two plans or transfer between them is possible. QPP funds are not committed to specific provincial uses, as CPP funds are, but are instead turned over to a provincial agency, the Caisse de dépôt et placement, which has a mandate to invest them in any secure and high-yielding securities that will contribute to the development of the provincial economy—not necessarily in securities of the province or its local governments. In fact, the QPP has consistently enjoyed a higher rate of return on its investments than has the CPP.

Although the essential features of the CPP and QPP are identical, there have been periods when the two plans have diverged in terms of contributions and benefits. The differences have not been sufficient, however, to put the participants in one plan at a disadvantage relative to the participants in the other. Consequently, the existence of two separate plans has not hindered interprovincial labour mobility.

During the 1980s, it became necessary to increase contributions to the CPP fund (and the QPP fund as well) if it was not to disappear completely,[22] an outcome that would have forced the provinces to retire many of the securities they had issued to the fund and raise the money from the private capital market, often at much higher rates. Once again, the situation required a collective decision by all 10 provinces (including Quebec) and the federal government. At meetings of finance ministers and treasurers in 1985, it was agreed to increase rates gradually over the 25 years following 1986 to ensure that the fund remained intact. In 1989, a second agreement provided for additional increases in the rates sufficient to ensure that over a 15-year period the fund would always be large enough to cover 2 years' worth of benefits.

Table 15.1 shows the size of the CPP investment fund in 1991 and provides an indication of its importance to the participating provinces.

Youth Allowances

During the campaign for the 1963 federal election, the Liberals also proposed an extension of the family allowance system to cover children aged 16 and 17 who were still attending school or incapacitated. Once in office, Prime Minister Pearson moved to introduce these allowances. Quebec, which already had a similar plan in operation, wished neither to relinquish the function to the federal government nor to forfeit the federal funds involved.

Ottawa and Quebec agreed at the spring 1964 federal-provincial conference to harmonize their programs, and subsequent negotiations led to a compromise presented in the prime minister's letter of mid-April 1964. According to the agreement, the federal allowances would not be payable in Quebec but Quebec would receive a compensatory payment equivalent to the federal allowances that otherwise would have been payable. Later, the federal

---

[22] Neither plan was fully funded, so by the late 1980s, when they began to mature, benefits and expenses would have been greater than contributions and investment income.

**Table 15.1   Provincial and Federal Securities Held by the Canada
Pension Plan Investment Fund on March 31, 1991**

	Holdings, $ millions
Newfoundland	781.2
Prince Edward Island	168.2
Nova Scotia	1,428.8
New Brunswick	1,058.4
Quebec[a]	136.1
Ontario	17,042.7
Manitoba	2,031.1
Saskatchewan	1,686.1
Alberta	4,534.8
British Columbia	5,298.5
Yukon	3.8
Canada	3,492.2
Total	37,661.7

[a] Amounts available to Quebec relate only to the contribution of some federal employees in that province (for example, armed forces personnel and RCMP officers).

Source: Public Accounts of Canada for the fiscal year 1990-91.

minister of finance, Mitchell Sharp, offered to extend the opportunity to contract out to any other province that had introduced a similar system of allowances before the effective date of the federal plan, September 1964. Only Quebec qualified. The finance minister also revised the method of compensation: beginning with the 1965 tax year, instead of a cash payment, Quebec would receive a personal income tax abatement of 3 percentage points of federal tax, with adjusting payments or recoveries in cash as required.

As of January 1, 1974, the universal federal family allowances were increased and extended to all children under 18, a change that obviated the need for youth allowances. The federal government recognized, however, that the 3-point abatement had become an integral part of the Quebec personal income tax system and that to withdraw it would require a complete revision of the provincial rate structure. The abatement was therefore left in place, but its equivalent was recovered from other payments to Quebec.

As of January 1, 1974, the provinces were free to vary the amounts of the allowances, on the basis of the number of children in a family or their age, and to provide supplementary payments. Initially, Alberta, Prince Edward Island, and Newfoundland provided graduated systems through the federal administration, but by 1979 Prince Edward Island and Newfoundland had eliminated their graduated allowances. Quebec provided supplementary payments and administered the program itself.

Student Loans

The Liberal campaign of 1963 also produced a commitment to a federal program of loan guarantees for post-secondary students. Quebec wished to contract out of the federal plan, and the resulting negotiations culminated in another proposal by Prime Minister Pearson in his letter of April 1964. He offered equal fiscal compensation for any province that chose to rely on its own program rather than participate in the federal plan. The Canada Student Loans Act,[23] passed later that year, provided that the compensation for a contracting-out province would be proportional to its share of the population aged 18 to 24. The compensation would take the form of cash payments. The participating provinces would administer the loan plan, specify the institutions that qualified students for loans, and assume responsibility for reviewing applications for loans (which would be based on need). The federal government would pay service fees to the participating provinces for administration and cover the interest charges until the borrower was able to assume the expense.

The Continuing Debate on Contracting-Out

The debate on contracting-out continued after the passage of the original Act and the signing of the first agreements with Quebec. By late 1966, when negotiations for the 1967-1972 fiscal arrangements began, it had become apparent that contracting-out was not a solution to the problems associated with cost-sharing. Only Quebec found contracting-out attractive, and the non-participation of the other provinces created a gap between the federal laws and tax rates that applied in Quebec and those that applied in the rest of the country. Meanwhile, the rapid growth of the traditional shared-cost programs continued to distort the participating provinces' spending programs and aggravate their desire for more responsibility and autonomy.

Mitchell Sharp, the federal finance minister, recognized these problems. At a meeting of the Tax Structure Committee on September 14-15, 1966, he proposed major changes in the federal government's approach to shared-cost programs that would have gradually ended the cumulative influence of past federal initiatives in provincial jurisdictions on provincial decision making. His government was prepared to remove the federal conditions that applied to certain well-established and continuing shared-cost programs and turn over full responsibility for these programs to the provinces. The shared-cost approach would be retained in some form for projects with a limited duration and in contexts that involved important federal responsibilities.

The finance minister made a distinction between "economic" and "social" shared-cost and conditional grant programs. Economic programs, which dealt with agriculture, regional development, and resources, were designed to encourage employment and economic development where and when they were needed. Three specific economic programs would be discontinued— agricultural lime, roads to resources, and forestry grants—but the others would continue and were not candidates for contracting-out.

---

[23] SC 1964-65, c. 24.

In the case of the major social programs—hospital insurance, the Canada Assistance Plan, and the continuing portion of national health grants—the minister proposed the transfer to the provinces of 17 points of the personal income tax, the associated equalization up to the national average (which would be automatic under the new equalization formula proposed at the same time—see chapter 9) and an adjustment grant for each of the first three years of the new system, 1967-68 to 1969-70. The adjustment grant would bring total compensation up to the federal share of actual costs. The minister provided a table that compared this proposal with a projection of the existing grants; it is reproduced here as table 15.2.

During the first three years of the new system, the shared-cost programs would continue in their current form; only the method of transferring resources would change. The federally imposed conditions of the programs would be removed on April 1, 1970, and thereafter the adjustment payment would be increased on a basis unrelated to program costs. It remained to determine what this basis would be, and one purpose of the extended transition period was to allow time in which to make this determination. In particular, the three-year delay would allow time for the publication of the various government and royal commission studies of taxation then in progress; the results of these studies would presumably determine how far the

Table 15.2 Comparisons of Actual Federal Costs for Continuing Programs with Alternative Form of Federal Transfer (Tax Abatements), 1967-68[a]

	1) Actual federal share of program costs (1967-68)[b]	2) Yield of 17 points of personal income tax (including equalization)[c]	3) Additional federal compensation required (col. 1 – col. 2)
		$ thousands	
Newfoundland	35,377	16,767.2	18,609.8
Prince Edward Island	6,231	3,653.6	2,577.4
Nova Scotia	37,677	25,384.2	12,292.9
New Brunswick	29,426	20,790.3	8,635.7
Quebec[a]	360,353[d]	196,790.4	163,562.6
Ontario	341,531	305,236.5	36,294.5
Manitoba	48,998	32,284.6	16,713.4
Saskatchewan	46,623	32,119.2	14,503.8
Alberta	80,632	49,956.1	30,676.0
British Columbia	95,490	77,863.7	17,626.3
Total[e]	1,082,338	760,845.7	321,492.3

[a] Program costs are for fiscal 1967-68, whereas tax revenues pertain to the 1967 taxation year. [b] Figures pertain to the cost of the "continuing" programs: hospital insurance, Canada Assistance Plan, and the continuing portion of the health grants (professional training and public health research). [c] Per capita yields are equalized to the national per capita average ($33.53). [d] As noted, the federal contribution to Quebec was in the form of equalized tax abatements. [e] Columns may not add to totals owing to rounding.

Source: Canada, Department of Finance, unpublished data, September 1966.

federal government could go in supplementing the abatement of tax points and the associated equalization with cash grants. The delay would also allow time in which to see how well the new transfer arrangements worked and to make any necessary changes before the system as a whole came into effect. In subsequent discussions during the fall of 1966 about the final basis for increasing the adjustment payments, the federal government proposed an escalation factor of 1.5 times the annual growth on personal income.

Finance Minister Sharp was confident that the provinces would continue the programs after the federal government relinquished its control:

> Once major programmes like these have been established no government would discontinue them, because of the needs they fill and the public support they command.[24]

To ensure national integration, the finance minister proposed a general intergovernmental agreement with three provisions:

> First, all governments would agree to continue the intergovernmental machinery that has been developed for the purpose of reviewing programme developments and discussing programme improvements, and to continue to participate in these consultations. Secondly, the federal government would undertake to continue to provide technical assistance, to any province that wants it, for the purpose of maintaining and improving programme standards. Thirdly, the provinces would agree to maintain uniform residence requirements in respect of all health and social security measures where benefits to individuals and families are involved.[25]

"Portability grants" would be provided to any province that was experiencing net immigration.

The finance minister proposed that research and demonstration projects within the health grants and the Canada assistance plan continue to be funded by the existing shared-cost system. Certain grants of capital funds on a project basis would also continue. Similarly, joint economic programs, such as ARDA agreements, the Trans-Canada Highway, and municipal winter works, would continue unchanged, in recognition of the overriding federal responsibility for employment and economic stability and development. A number of shared-cost programs were under review, and the minister did not discount the possibility of additional proposals.

The provinces did not respond favourably; none of them accepted the federal offer. Ontario criticized a number of aspects of current conditional grant and shared-cost programs, calling for an end to implicit equalization and a system of regular reviews, but it did not support the 17-point proposal. Two provinces came out against contracting-out, the 17-point federal offer,

---

[24] Canada, *Federal-Provincial Tax Structure Committee*, proceedings of a meeting held in Ottawa, September 14-15, 1966 (Ottawa: Queen's Printer, 1966), 21.

[25] Ibid.

and federal retrenchment in general: Manitoba was opposed to federal withdrawal of a number of major and minor programs; Saskatchewan argued for some form of block grants with an appropriate escalator instead of contracting-out. In addition, Alberta called for the establishment of a definite order of priorities for all levels of government, and for no further federal initiatives or expansion of existing programs or projects without prior consultation and concurrence.

The newly elected premier of Quebec, Daniel Johnson of the Union Nationale, noted that his government would take a more independent stand than its Liberal predecessor had and would seek legal and political recognition of the French Canadian "nation" in a new constitution. His government was opposed to shared-cost programs in the long run and looked forward to making the contracting-out arrangements permanent. Quebec intended to enter no new cost-sharing arrangements; instead, it would seek unconditional compensation with which to provide its people with services appropriate to their particular needs. Premier Johnson stressed that Quebec should not be treated like other provinces:

> Let this point be understood once and for all: for social and cultural reasons, Quebec absolutely insists on full respect for its fields of jurisdiction within the constitution; federal interference in these fields, direct or indirect, will not be tolerated . . . . Canada is not made up of ten identical territories known as provinces, but of ten separate entities, none really like any other, including one—Quebec—which is the heartland of a nation.[26]

Soon after that conference, it became apparent that tax reform would be delayed, making the tax element of contracting-out less certain. Constitutional discussions promised to change the division of responsibilities between the federal government and the provinces. Studies of cost controls in the shared-cost programs also indicated that the quantum of the total transfer could change in the medium term. The situation was thus too fluid to produce a consensus between the federal government and the provinces. By 1968, the federal government was anxious to postpone the second stage of its contracting-out scheme—that is, the unconditional transfer of tax points and cash adjustment payments, increased according to a factor not directly related to the growth in program costs. At a conference of finance ministers and treasurers on November 4 and 5, the federal finance minister, Edgar Benson, reaffirmed the basics of the 1966 scheme but proposed that the second stage be postponed to 1973-74. He did not provide detailed proposals for the second stage.

The offer to the provinces remained open, but once again there were no takers. In refusing the offer, Prince Edward Island's treasurer, T.E. Hickey, argued that the loss of 17 points of personal income tax would impair the federal government's ability to use it as a fiscal device.

---

[26] Ibid., at 51.

Proposals for Tax Reform, the federal government's white paper on tax reform, was released on November 7, 1969.[27] It rescinded the contracting-out offers of 1966 and 1968. Only when the value of tax points under the proposed system and the potential growth of that value had been determined could the government begin to reconsider the use of tax points in lieu of conditional grants.

The issue continued to occupy some provincial and federal leaders. In November 1971, Prime Minister Pierre Trudeau stated that his government wished to see every province tax "as much as possible for its share of these programs," which would be transformed "from shared-cost programs to programs which are paid much more by the provinces themselves by their own form of taxation."[28] At a first ministers' conference in May 1973, Ontario asserted a preference for "clean" contracting-out—that is, for contracting-out in substance as well as in form.

As the federal tax system became more complex, with the introduction of special reductions and tax credits that applied after the calculation of basic federal tax, a technical problem arose for Quebec taxpayers. If a Quebec taxpayer's net federal tax payable before deduction of the abatement was less than the value of the abatement, no federal tax was payable. There was no mechanism, however, for providing the taxpayer with the value of the "unused" portion of the abatement, despite the fact that the taxpayer was required to pay at least the full equivalent of the abatement in provincial tax. At first, the loss to Quebec taxpayers was not significant. In a statement to a federal-provincial meeting of first ministers in November 1978, Premier René Levesque estimated that the loss for 1973 had been $5.5 million but forecast that the loss for 1978 would be at least $35 million. The federal Income Tax Act[29] was subsequently amended so that, beginning with the 1980 tax year, any part of the federal abatement that could not be used to reduce federal tax payable by Quebec residents would be refunded to them.

Conclusion

When contracting-out of joint programs was proposed in the early 1960s, it was praised as a means of providing greater provincial freedom in the operation of shared-cost programs. It was also condemned as being destructive of the federal system and the concept of nationwide minimum standards. It also evoked, for a time, serious political and emotional reactions not related to the basic principle of contracting-out.

---

[27] Canada, Department of Finance, *Proposals for Tax Reform*, (Ottawa: the department, November 7, 1969).

[28] Statement by the Hon. P. E. Trudeau to the Federal-Provincial Conference, Ottawa, November 15, 1971.

[29] RSC 1952, c. 148, as amended by SC 1970-71-72, c. 63, and subsequently amended.

To this point, the principle has proved to be neither as useful as its supporters had hoped nor as destructive as its critics had feared. The existing form of contracting-out for joint programs was originally intended to be a temporary measure, the precursor to some more advanced and more permanent arrangement that would apply to all of the provinces. Instead, contracting-out continues to apply only to Quebec, and no more advanced form of the scheme has replaced the original form. The "temporary" contracting-out arrangements have in fact been integrated with the permanent arrangements for established programs financing.[30]

The federal government's 1966 contracting-out proposals indicated the form that a mature scheme of contracting-out might take. Ottawa proposed to introduce contracting-out in two stages. In the first or interim stage, the form of the federal transfer for a given joint program would change but the substance of the program would not; that is, the amount of the transfer would continue to be determined by the federal government's assessment of program costs and federal conditions governing the program would continue to apply. In the second stage, the substance too would change; that is, increases in the federal contribution would be based on some factor other than costs and the provinces would be free to administer the program as they saw fit. In the event, no contracting-out arrangements went beyond the first stage. The form of payment for some programs was indeed altered from direct reimbursement to the transfer of tax room and adjusting payments, but the adjusting payments were designed to make the total reimbursement equal to the grants that would have been payable had the original programs been extended. Even more important, a province that contracted out was required to maintain the relevant services without change during the interim period. Thus, because contracting-out of joint programs has not advanced beyond the interim stage, the sole contracting-out province, Quebec, has had no greater flexibility in administration or program design than the other provinces.

The principle of contracting-out has been important in the evolution of federal-provincial fiscal relations. As chapter 17 will show, the federal government's 1966 offer set a precedent for the established programs financing arrangements introduced in 1977. Quebec's contracting-out of wholly federal programs, such as the youth allowances and the Canada Pension Plan, has been successful. Moreover, it has provided opportunities for testing alternative program designs. The contracting-out arrangements and other developments that have sprung from the same principle, like the shared-cost programs that they have replaced, represent a compromise between the federal government's desire for direct action and the provinces' need for greater control within their own jurisdictions. Increased provincial autonomy and financial flexibility have characterized federal-provincial programs since the acceptance of the principle of contracting-out.

---

[30] See chapter 18.

16

The Continuing Evolution of Joint Programs: 1966-1981

Chapter 15 has shown that contracting-out, although widely endorsed in principle, in practice appealed only to Quebec and did not prevent the continued development of existing federal-provincial joint programs and the introduction of new ones. The principle did, however, have some influence on the form of both new and existing programs.

Another approach to the problem of reconciling federal and provincial concerns, the use of block grants, emerged in the 1960s and early 1970s, when both levels of government were rapidly introducing new programs and enlarging existing ones. Block funding was useful both as a means of developing national standards and as a means of transferring resources from the federal government to the provinces. The latter purpose became particularly significant after the Tax Structure Committee established that, as time went on, financial pressure was likely to be more severe at the provincial and local levels than at the federal level.[1]

The principles behind contracting-out and block grants, developed and tested over a period of years, led to the federal program of assistance for post-secondary education and later to the established programs financing system. The form of a number of new programs and an abortive reform of the welfare system were also strongly influenced by the development of contracting-out and block grants.

Post-Secondary Education

Chapter 15 described the early history of federal grants to universities and the evolution of the special position of Quebec. At a meeting of the Tax Structure Committee in September 1966, Premier John Robarts of Ontario noted that universities were expected to make urgent demands for additional capital funds over the years 1966 to 1969. He referred to the problem as a temporary national emergency and noted that the Bladen Commission[2] had recommended federal-provincial sharing of capital costs. He also asked that the

---

[1] Canada, *Federal-Provincial Tax Structure Committee*, Proceedings of a meeting held in Ottawa, September 14-15, 1966 (Ottawa, Queen's Printer, 1966), 14. The work of the Tax Structure Committee is described in chapter 5.

[2] Association of Universities and Colleges of Canada, *Financing Higher Education in Canada; Being the Report of a Commission to the Association of Universities and Colleges of Canada* (Toronto: University of Toronto Press, 1965).

provinces, not the universities, receive the grants for university operating costs, and he wanted the grants to be calculated on the basis of enrolment, not total population.

In October, during the negotiations for the new fiscal arrangements, the federal government proposed to end the per capita grant for universities, by then $5, and programs of aid for the operating costs of vocational training, subject to certain transitional provisions. The capital grants for technical and vocational schools, however, would be extended until each province received the equivalent of $800 for each person aged 15 to 19 in 1961. At the same time, the federal government assumed complete financial responsibility for adult retraining.

The per capita grants for universities would be replaced by a federal-provincial cost-sharing program of aid for post-secondary education. Under this program, the federal government would cover 50 percent of the provinces' approved operating costs. The federal financing would consist of a reduction of 4 percentage points of basic individual income tax and a reduction equal to 1 percentage point of taxable corporate income, with the associated equalization, and a cash payment sufficient to bring the total transfer up to the 50-percent level.

Negotiations with the provinces produced a modification of this formula. Federal assistance would be equal to the greater of 50 percent of eligible operating costs of post-secondary educational institutions and $15 per capita of provincial population. The per capita amount would be increased after the 1967-68 fiscal year in accordance with the increase in eligible costs in all provinces. Once a province's per capita entitlement fell short of 50 percent of eligible costs, its transfers would be converted permanently to that basis. Provinces that began the arrangement on the 50-percent option would not be allowed to change. Assistance to Newfoundland, Prince Edward Island, and New Brunswick was initially based on the per capita option.

The proposal was implemented in part II of the Federal-Provincial Fiscal Arrangements Act, 1967,[3] which fixed the system for a five-year period. A province's entitlement was based on the operating expenditures incurred for post-secondary education by or in respect of each of the educational institutions in the province. What distinguished this arrangement from the true shared-cost programs was the fact that the federal government paid its share whether it was the province or the institution that met the actual cost; thus it matched not only provincial expenditures but also those financed by the institutions themselves from tuition fees and other non-governmental funds. The expenditures eligible for federal matching included expenditures for academic instruction, libraries, administration, and plants. Excluded were expenditures for student financial aid, capital assets (except as defined), rent, interest, debt repayment, and certain ancillary enterprises. Eligible expendi-

---

[3] SC 1966-67, c. 89.

tures were reduced by institutional revenues from contract or sponsored research and from other federal departments. Provincial returns were required and would be audited before the federal payments were made final.

In 1972, when the original five-year period ended, the federal government extended the payments to March 31, 1974 but limited their annual rate of growth to 15 percent. At the same time, it increased the personal income tax abatement to 4.357 points—the equivalent of 4 points under the pre-reform income tax system; the corporate income tax abatement did not change. In 1973, Ottawa extended the 1972 arrangements, including the limit on growth, to March 31, 1977. In 1977, the post-secondary education payments were brought under the established programs financing system, described in chapter 17.

The development of federal assistance for post-secondary education shows how fundamentally traditional forms of conditional grant and shared-cost programs were changing. The program introduced in 1967 provided what was in effect a form of block grant—an unconditional grant not tied to specific provincial spending. The federal government has no jurisdiction in the field of university education, and in recent years it has been careful not to intrude directly into this provincial sphere. The original grants to universities (and to the National Conference of Canadian Universities) had been entirely without conditions, and it was this circumstance that prepared the ground for the introduction of a system of grants to the provinces. At no time after 1967 did the program require the provinces to match federal contributions or to direct the grants specifically to post-secondary education. In any event, the program's definition of post-secondary education was broad: it covered any approved course that required junior matriculation (grade 11 or 12, depending on the province) for admission and lasted 24 weeks or longer.

The use of tax points for the grants to Quebec universities predated any other form of federal compensation by means of tax points and established a principle that was easily extended to all provinces. It was also a logical step in the progression from the conditional grants of pre-war Canada and the immediate post-war period to established programs financing.

Attention Turns to Block Grants

The concept of block grants emerged in federal-provincial meetings beginning in 1960. Block grants are determined on a per capita basis, or as a set amount subject to escalation, and are provided for broad policy areas. They have a minimum of detailed conditions. The recipient provinces are usually free to allocate all funds, both their own and the grants, as they wish within the policy area, provided certain minimum standards are met.

At a federal-provincial conference in 1960, the premiers of Prince Edward Island and Saskatchewan spoke in favour of a form of grant that would be unconditional within specific areas of government activity. At a similar conference three years later, Premier John Robarts of Ontario was more specific:

We suggest that the use of general purpose or departmental grants might help to overcome undesirable aspects of the present system of conditional grants. There are fields of governmental activity in which the federal government could specify a broad range of programs, the costs of which it would agree to share up to a maximum total contribution. Each province would be free to decide the particular programs in the broad range which it would implement, and the federal government would still have some control over the general purposes for which its funds were being employed.[4]

New Brunswick endorsed a similar system at a federal-provincial conference in the spring of 1964. It proposed general schedules of types of programs with some form of equalization or recognition of provincial ability to pay.

Attempts at Welfare Reform

During the early 1970s, federal and provincial ministers of welfare focused their attention on a major reform of the social security system and the federal-provincial sharing and funding of that system. The provinces had found that they were providing a number of social services, such as day care, meals on wheels, family planning, and counselling, that could be of use to people with incomes above the need thresholds. Any extension of such services to the non-poor would not qualify for grants under the Canada assistance plan (CAP), which was not structured to incorporate a fee system, although some services could be financed partially by a user-fee structure. Other items on the reform agenda were revision of family allowances; an income support plan for single parents, the handicapped, and those otherwise unable to work; and an income supplementation program designed to ensure that those who could work would be better off working than receiving public assistance.

Late in 1970, the federal government published *Income Security for Canadians,*[5] a white paper that dealt with certain aspects of federal welfare policy. The paper proposed a major revision of the family allowance system to restrict net benefits to lower-income recipients. Legislation to implement the family income security plan was introduced in 1971 and eventually contained provisions that allowed a province to contract out of the federal program at a later date and receive equivalent compensation if its plan met certain negotiated conditions. The legislation received a very hostile public reaction, mainly from parents who stood to lose their family allowances; it died on the order paper and was never reintroduced.

---

[4] As quoted in Donald V. Smiley, "Federal Block Grants to the Provinces: A Realistic Alternative?" in *Report of Proceedings of the Eighteenth Tax Conference*, 1964 Conference Report (Toronto: Canadian Tax Foundation, 1965), 218-22, at 219.

[5] Canada, Department of National Health and Welfare, *Income Security for Canadians* (Ottawa: the department, 1970).

The white paper also proposed changes in the Canada Pension Plan, which were not enacted, and changes in the old age security and guaranteed income programs, which were introduced in 1970. The paper offered certain general comments on the CAP but made no specific recommendations. Finally, the white paper proposed discussions between the federal government and the provinces for the purpose of changing entitlements to assistance, introducing more effective incentives for return to self-sufficiency, revising benefit levels in order to ensure adequate assistance, and devising new programs.

Federal-provincial negotiations produced little agreement on the white paper proposals that required provincial concurrence, and very few of these proposals were put in place. After a meeting of provincial welfare ministers in November 1971, the delegates called upon the federal government to convene a federal-provincial conference in the spring of 1973 to discuss social security on a comprehensive basis. In January 1972, the federal government responded with its own call for a joint federal-provincial review of the whole Canadian social security system, to begin in April 1973. Its contribution to the process was a document called *Working Paper on Social Security in Canada*, known as the orange paper.[6]

The orange paper contained two specific proposals that the federal government hoped to implement quickly. The first involved the extension of family allowances to children up to age 18, with an increase in the amount; the provinces would be allowed to vary the payments according to age or family size. The second specific proposal was to increase the pensionable earnings under the Canada Pension Plan and thereby increase both contributions and benefits.

The document also proposed that the provinces play a greater part in the design and administration of social security programs. To this end, it contained two important statements. Proposition 12 was as follows:

> That the levels of income guarantees and supplementation should be chosen by the individual provinces, and that the provinces should further be given the power to vary the levels of universal and other allowances paid under federally administered programmes (excepting wage-related social insurance measures). Where any province were to seek a reduction in the federal allowances under one particular programme, the moneys saved by such a reduction would be transferred to increase the allowances paid under another federal or federally-financed income support programme, as requested by the province.

> This provincial flexibility in setting the income support levels within each province would be subject to three conditions. First, the provinces would be bound to observe the minimum standards set by the Parliament of Canada in respect of the income support programmes administered or financed by the Government of Canada. Secondly, the provinces would

---

[6] Canada, Department of National Health and Welfare, *Working Paper on Social Security in Canada* (Ottawa: the department, April 18, 1973).

not be free to use this flexibility in such a way as to increase net federal payments to any province—whether to the people or to the government of the province, and whether by increases in federal payments or reductions in federal tax revenues—beyond what would have been paid under the "programme norms" legislated by Parliament to determine total federal contributions to the programme. Thirdly, the provinces would be required to contribute to the social security system the amount they would otherwise have contributed prior to any changes in the system, and before any changes in the levels of federal allowances or income support payments under any new "flexibility formula."[7]

Proposition 13 was as follows:

> That in the interest of combatting poverty by way of a fair distribution of income between people across Canada, and in the interest of promoting national unity through avoiding extremes in income disparities, national minimums should be set by the Parliament of Canada in the levels of the allowances administered and financed by the Government of Canada. Further, that "norms" should also be legislated by Parliament in respect of the payments under which such programmes, when such norms are required in order to determine the total contributions Parliament is prepared to make under the programmes.[8]

The federal and provincial ministers of welfare met again in Ottawa on April 25-27, 1973 to review the orange paper proposals. The ministers displayed a surprising degree of unanimity on general principles. They agreed to set up a system of task forces and sub-committees of federal and provincial deputies to examine the document and conduct a review of the entire Canadian social security system. The deputies were also to study changes required in the Canada Pension Plan, particularly with a view to keeping it parallel to the Quebec Pension Plan; they were to report on this matter in five weeks.

The ministers also agreed on the need for early legislation to revise the federal family allowances. At the April meeting, the minister of national health and welfare, Marc Lalonde, signified his intention to bring in a new family allowance measure by January 1, 1974. For the benefit of the provincial welfare ministers, he expanded upon the orange paper's proposal to provide $20 per child per month while allowing the greatest possible flexibility to provinces that wished to vary the allowance according to the child's age, the number of children, and family income.

Provincial reactions to the orange paper proposals began to emerge at the April conference and the first ministers' conference in May. Before the federal government announced its intention to introduce a family allowance system with provision for provincial flexibility, Quebec had been preparing to assert its constitutional right to determine the size of payments. At the

---

[7] Ibid., at 26-28.

[8] Ibid., at 28.

April meeting, however, Quebec's representative downplayed this aspect of the province's presentation and supported the federal proposals. British Columbia fully supported the proposed review; at the May meeting, Premier David Barrett stressed the legislative priority of the provinces and called for both increased federal funding and a maximum of provincial discretion in the use of this funding in the social welfare area. He also called for a program of public sector job creation at the community level. Both British Columbia and Saskatchewan called for an enriched family allowance system under which the allowances would be taxable, indexed, and subject to provincial determination.

At a meeting held on October 11, 1973, the federal and provincial welfare ministers agreed that Ottawa should remove the 2 percent limit on annual changes to the Canada Pension Plan and thus bring the federal plan into line with the Quebec plan.

The only major program change to emerge from the orange paper and the subsequent discussions was the revision of the family allowance system. Bill C-211, the Family Allowances Act, 1973,[9] was passed in December 1973 and went into effect on January 1, 1974. It provided for an allowance of $20 per month for every child under 18 years of age, including foster children and children in institutions. The allowance was included in the taxable income of the parent and would increase annually in accordance with the rise in the consumer price index. Provinces were free to vary the allowance according to the age of the child or the number of children in the family, but the minimum per child was $12 per month and the provincial average had to be $20 per month. Newfoundland, Prince Edward Island, Quebec, and Alberta indicated that they planned to vary the allowance. As was noted in chapter 15, the Act also discontinued the youth allowance program but continued the 3-point abatement provided to Quebec in order to avoid disrupting the province's tax structure. The federal government recovered the value of the abatement in full.

The federal-provincial working party on the review of the social security system delivered its report late in 1974. The overall federal review of the system was expected to be completed within 18 months.

At a conference of federal and provincial ministers of welfare held on February 18 and 19, 1975, the ministers instructed the continuing committee of officials to develop guidelines for income support and supplementation schemes and for alternative modes of federal-provincial financing of the reformed system. The ministers' aim was to have agreement on a reformed social security system by the summer of 1975, and the operational details were to be worked out by the end of that year. The federal government proposed the introduction of a social services act, which would separate federal aid for social services from federal aid for social assistance and treat it in a different manner. The first ministers agreed to this separation at a conference held on June 14 and 15, 1976.

---

[9] SC 1973-74, c. 44.

The provinces did not unanimously support the proposed reforms. The western premiers, meeting in April 1976, urged that the review of welfare programs by provincial ministers and officials be merged with broader discussions of fiscal arrangements. At the June meeting of first ministers, Ontario suggested a moratorium on proposals in the social security area pending further study. New Brunswick too was dissatisfied with the federal proposals, which could have resulted in a shift of support for unemployed employables to the provinces.

In June 1977, after two years of negotiation, the federal government tabled Bill C-57, the Social Services Act, in the House of Commons. The Bill defined social services as

> services having as their object enabling persons to lead useful, satisfying and independent lives, preventing personal and social conditions that cause disadvantage or disability, raising individuals, families and groups to a higher level of participation in social and economic life, protecting those whose personal or social well-being is at risk, or developing individual, group and community capacity for growth, enrichment and social participation.[10]

This broad definition included the provision of information, referrals, counselling, protective services, and preventive services. The restrictions that the Bill imposed on users were not all related to income or needs, and the shareable costs allowed under the Bill included administration costs and subsidies to private agencies that provided eligible services. The Bill specified income-tested user fees for certain services, such as day care, homemakers, meals on wheels, counselling, and employment-related services. It also provided federal assistance in the traditional form of sharing of approved costs, as agreed to by all provinces before its introduction.

During the summer of 1977, several governments, including Quebec, objected to Bill C-57 as an unwarranted intrusion into an area of exclusively provincial jurisdiction. In addition, a number of administrative difficulties inherent in the Bill came to light: it would be difficult in practice to distinguish between social services and other services such as health, recreation, and education, and the calculation of federal contributions under the terms of the Bill would be very complicated.

In September 1977, the federal government withdrew Bill C-57 and proposed a block-funding system of financing for social services, using the established programs financing system (by then operational) as a model. The social assistance system would continue unchanged under the CAP. Effective April 1978, each province would receive a per capita cash payment based on the national average federal contribution in 1977-78 for social services financed under the CAP, the Vocational Rehabilitation of Disabled Persons

---

[10] Bill C-57, Social Services Financing Act, first reading June 20, 1977.

Act,[11] and the vocational rehabilitation of young offenders program. Beginning April 1, 1979, the provinces would receive an additional payment of $5 per capita to finance new services that had been proposed under Bill C-57. Both payments would be escalated by a three-year moving average of gross national product per capita, as used in established programs financing. The equal per capita payments would be phased in over 10 years. Ottawa attached three conditions to the payments: (1) the provinces could not make eligibility contingent upon a minimum period of residence, (2) they had to acknowledge the federal contribution in all informational literature, and (3) they had to provide specified data on costs and programs to the federal government.

The plan had two apparent shortcomings. First, the proposal to base the per capita payments on a uniform national formula failed to take into account the wide variation—from $16 for Ontario to $32 for Quebec—in provincial per capita spending on the relevant services.[12] Second, the abandonment of cost-sharing meant that the concept of "50-cent dollars" would no longer hold, with the result that the provinces would have to pay the entire cost of any improvements in services; on the other hand, they would enjoy all of the savings that resulted from any reductions in services. Thus organizations that represented "client" groups (such as the National Council of Welfare) opposed the plan on the ground that it would make their task of persuading provinces to adopt new programs or enlarge old ones more difficult.

In spite of these problems, the provincial welfare ministers agreed at a meeting in March 1978 to endorse the federal proposals. They were introduced in the Commons formally on May 12, when Bill C-55, the Social Services Financing Act, was given first reading.[13] The Bill provided for the introduction in 1979-80 of an additional payment, of $5.07 per capita in the first year, to assist the development of new services; it also provided for a special five-year, $50-million rehabilitation fund for building or improving training centres for the handicapped and for making community facilities more accessible to them. The fund would be distributed among all of the provinces, and the projects would be funded on the traditional cost-sharing basis. When introducing the Bill, the minister of health and welfare, Monique Begin, estimated that in 1978-79 total payments would be $577 million, or $61 million more than the disbursements in 1977-78 under the CAP, the vocational rehabilitation of disabled persons program and the young offenders program. Payments under the Act were expected to be $798 million in 1979-80 and almost $2 billion by the end of the 10-year phase-in period. The Bill died on the order paper when Parliament was prorogued.

---

[11] RSC 1970, c. V-7.

[12] The figures for all of the provinces were as follows: Newfoundland, $19; Prince Edward Island, $29; Nova Scotia, $17; New Brunswick, $17; Quebec, $32; Ontario, $16; Manitoba, $28; Saskatchewan, $20; Alberta, $17; British Columbia, $22. The national average was $22.

[13] Bill C-55, Social Services Financing Act, first reading May 12, 1978.

The federal economic recovery program introduced in August and September 1978 called for general cuts in federal payments to the provinces, but Ottawa could not reach an agreement with the provinces on which federal-provincial programs to reduce. Since Bill C-55 had not been enacted and no agreements had been signed, the federal government decided to delay the implementation of the block-funding system for one year, thus saving the funds tentatively allocated for enrichment in 1979-80. There have been no moves since to reintroduce the proposal. Table 16.1 shows the payments under the existing programs during the period 1977-78 to 1981-82, and table 16.2 provides projections, released by the federal government in May 1981, of the federal grants that would have been payable over the same period had Bill C-55 become law. A comparison of the two tables shows that the block-funding arrangement would have provided substantially more than the provinces actually received.

Social services financing was the only area in which the joint review of the social security system produced a consensus for reform. It proved impossible to obtain the concurrence of the 11 governments for any major overhaul of the social assistance system. The federal government had entered into an agreement with Manitoba in 1973 to provide an experimental guaranteed annual income system for selected individuals and one community in the province. The federal government agreed to pay 75 percent of the experiment's estimated cost of $17 million. It was decided in 1978 to phase out the experiment, and no further experiments or permanent new programs have emerged to build on that experience.

The Parliamentary Task Force on Federal-Provincial Fiscal Arrangements examined the federal welfare grants in its 1981 report[14] and put forward some reflections on the experience to that time. It took the position that in the area of social welfare the federal government should be considered to have joint jurisdiction with the provinces and thus should continue to use open-ended cost-sharing rather than block funding to provide assistance. A further argument for continued cost-sharing, at least in the short term, was the fact that it would be too expensive to provide additional federal assistance through block funding, since it was impossible with block funding to direct funds to the areas of greatest need. The report therefore recommended that some of the restrictions on the CAP be loosened for certain "high-priority" areas and that the CAP arrangements recognize the differences in costs across provinces that arose from differing levels of need for social assistance payments. It also suggested measures to improve reporting and federal accountability under the CAP.

Although these views were constructive, it is apparent that in total the social services review had left no significant changes to mark its passage.

---

[14] Canada, *Fiscal Federalism in Canada: Report of the Parliamentary Task Force on Federal-Provincial Fiscal Arrangements* (Ottawa: Supply and Services, August 1981).

Table 16.1   Social Services Payments to the Provinces, 1977-78 to 1981-82[a]

	1977-78	1978-79	1979-80	1980-81[b]	1981-82[c]
	millions of dollars				
Newfoundland	8.9	9.6	9.3	11.4	13.5
Prince Edward Island	2.1	2.7	4.3	3.5	3.9
Nova Scotia	14.2	14.2	15.2	12.3	26.6
New Brunswick	8.6	9.5	11.5	19.0	16.0
Quebec[c]	207.1	229.3	226.4	165.0	182.3
Ontario	114.2	122.6	149.0	319.4	312.5
Manitoba	24.5	25.5	27.1	27.6	30.9
Saskatchewan	17.5	19.8	17.7	26.1	26.2
Alberta	30.7	38.8	44.5	49.1	62.2
British Columbia	46.2	55.7	76.8	93.3	94.2
Yukon	1.1	1.6	1.1	2.3	2.8
Northwest Territories	2.8	4.3	2.9	3.6	5.1
Total	477.9	533.6	585.8	732.6	776.2

[a] That is, payments under the Canada assistance plan (CAP), the Vocational Rehabilitation of Disabled Persons Act, and the young offenders program. [b] Source: CAP Supplementary Estimates 1980-81. [c] Source: Canada Treasury Board, 1982-83 Multi-Year Operational Plan. [d] The amounts given include the value of 5 tax-abatement units related to social-service-type costs.

Table 16.2   Estimated Social Services Payments to the Provinces If the Social Services Financing Act (Bill C-55) Had Gone into Effect[a]

	1977-78	1978-79	1979-80	1980-81	1981-82
	millions of dollars				
Newfoundland	8.9	10.2	15.7	17.8	20.6
Prince Edward Island	2.1	2.4	3.6	4.0	4.6
Nova Scotia	14.2	16.2	24.1	27.3	31.2
New Brunswick	8.6	10.2	16.8	19.7	23.2
Quebec[b]	207.1	227.3	308.0	342.4	382.4
Ontario	114.2	128.2	186.6	211.0	239.3
Manitoba	24.5	26.8	36.1	40.3	44.7
Saskatchewan	17.5	19.8	28.9	32.5	37.1
Alberta	30.7	36.0	56.1	62.3	72.2
British Columbia	46.2	52.6	77.8	89.0	102.9
Yukon	1.1	1.2	1.4	1.6	1.7
Northwest Territories	2.8	2.9	3.3	3.6	3.8
Total	477.9	533.8	758.4	851.5	963.7

[a] An escalation factor of $5.07 (escalated by the growth in the gross national product) has been added to 1979-80 and subsequent years in accordance with section 8 of Bill C-55. All provinces have been levelled up or down by 10 percent per year in accordance with the formula in section 7 of Bill C-55. [b] The amounts given include the value of 5 tax-abatement units related to social-service-type costs.

Source: Canada, House of Commons, *Debates*, May 20, 1981, 9737.

17

Established Programs Financing

Chapter 15 made the point that the option of contracting out of shared-cost programs, which Ottawa introduced in order to accommodate Quebec, had by 1969 been converted into a general offer to all of the provinces. There were no takers, and the federal government subsequently announced that it would suspend the offer until tax reform had been put in place.

Beginning in 1969, however, both the federal government and some provinces advanced proposals for alternatives to the traditional shared-cost program, a device that was causing increasing difficulty in the health care field. The two major programs, hospital insurance and medicare, were growing at alarming rates as new technology, wider coverage for medicare, and rapidly rising price levels created pressures that neither the federal government nor the provinces were able to resist, since neither had full responsibility for funding the programs.

The search for alternative ways of financing the joint health programs proved to be a lengthy one; it eventually encompassed a search for a new basis for financing post-secondary education as well. The negotiations for the 1972-1977 fiscal arrangements did not touch significantly on this area, except to limit the annual growth of federal assistance for post-secondary education to a maximum of 15 percent in 1972-73 and 1973-74. It was not until 1977 that the federal government and the provinces were able to agree on a revised system of financing for hospital insurance, medicare, and post-secondary education. The new system, established programs financing (EPF), was incorporated into the fiscal legislation for the 1977-1982 period.

First Steps

In 1969, the joint committee on health care costs presented its report to a meeting of federal and provincial health ministers.[1] The committee had established that the shared-cost system for financing hospital insurance and medicare was contributing to the rapid rise in health care costs; its chief recommendation was that a more economical system be found. A system that set federal contributions independently of current provincial spending and attached relaxed conditions to those contributions would give the provinces both an incentive to impose more effective cost controls and the flexibility to do it.

---

[1] Report of the joint federal-provincial committee on health care costs, 1969. Department of National Health and Welfare, mimeo, 1969.

Efforts to devise a more effective formula began with a conference of ministers of health in December 1970 and a series of conferences of federal and provincial health officials in 1971. At the December meeting, the federal government suggested a program of per capita grants based on 1970-71 contributions and unrelated to the subsequent increase in health costs; the program would begin in 1972-73 and run for five years. The annual percentage increase in the per capita grants would match the percentage increase in gross national product (GNP) per capita and the grants would be "levelled"—brought to the same level per capita for all provinces—over the five-year period. The provinces were reluctant to accept this proposal: they felt that the GNP escalator alone would not be sufficient and that provision should be made for additional growth factors to produce more federal assistance in the event of excessive growth in provincial costs.

The Lalonde Proposal

The minister of national health and welfare, Marc Lalonde, submitted a firm proposal to a meeting of health ministers held in December 1971. He proposed per capita payments for the five years beginning 1973-74, using the base year 1971-72 (adjusted to include an optometry benefit); the escalator— the annual increase in GNP per capita—would be raised by 1 percentage point in 1973-74 only. Provinces would be guaranteed as a minimum in the first year the amount they would have received under an extension of the existing arrangements. Ottawa would also provide a "thrust" fund of $640 million to finance new cost-saving measures: the distribution of the fund, on a per capita basis, would begin in 1972-73. Estimates indicated that the proposal would make more assistance available to the provinces over the five-year period than would an extension of the existing system.

Provincial reaction came at a meeting of provincial finance ministers in January 1972. Newfoundland and Prince Edward Island accepted the proposal, but most of the other provinces continued to argue that a per capita system would fall short of anticipated cost increases. Some argued for the inclusion of a risk-sharing provision—that is, a provision that would link federal contributions more directly with related cost increases. Discussions continued at the ministerial and official levels in 1972.

Lalonde put forward a revision of his proposal in January 1973. The per capita scheme would be introduced in 1974-75 rather than 1973-74 and would use a higher base year, 1972-73. Levelling would take place over 10 years. Ottawa would begin distributing thrust funds to provide risk-sharing in 1973-74. The level of support, based on 1972-73, would be increased each year by the percentage increase in a five-year moving average of GNP. The level of support would be enriched in the first year by the addition of 1 percentage point to the percentage increase in GNP. This figure would drop to three-quarters of a point in the second year, half a point in the third year, a quarter of a point in the fourth year, and zero in the fifth year. In addition, if a province's costs rose faster than the GNP, the federal government would cover a portion of the first 3 percentage points over the GNP rate of increase—that is, three-eighths of the first point, two-eighths of the second, and one-eighth of the third.

The thrust funds would be available to the provinces to use as they saw fit within the overall objectives of the federal program. Provincial projects would not require prior approval, nor would they be subject to federal audit, but a forecast of cash flow would be obligatory.[2] The thrust funds would not be incorporated into the base or subject to escalation. They were intended to provide seed money for measures designed to reduce escalation in the costs of basic health services. For example, a province might use some of its thrust funds to build nursing homes—a less costly alternative to providing chronic care in active treatment hospitals and under home-care programs.

Immediately after the January 1973 Lalonde proposals had been circulated to the provinces, the federal finance minister, John Turner, wrote to his provincial counterparts to suggest discussion of the method of financing the federal contribution. Two conferences were held in May 1973. The first, on May 8, was a joint meeting of federal and provincial ministers responsible for finance, post-secondary education, and health. The second, on May 23-25, was a full first ministers' conference.

Provincial sentiment before the two conferences did not favour the revised proposals, which most of the provinces felt still failed to provide them with adequate financial protection. Lalonde attempted to assuage these misgivings in a letter to his provincial counterparts, dated April 18, 1973, in which he presented further modifications to provide a larger per capita grant, greater risk-sharing, and increased flexibility. The letter also offered the provinces a guarantee that Canada assistance plan (CAP) contributions would not drop if cases were transferred from a needs-tested basis under the CAP to universal coverage under a broader definition of health care that included, for example, nursing home care previously covered under the CAP.

In the view of some provinces, however, the solution was not to enrich the Lalonde proposal but to discard it in favour of another approach. Ontario, Quebec, and Alberta all preferred some form of tax transfer for health care to Ottawa's per capita scheme. Ontario suggested a federal personal income tax cut of 9 percent; the provinces would pick up 4 percent immediately and assume the remainder gradually as the tax cut helped to reactivate the national economy. Quebec's proposal, originally put forward at a meeting of finance ministers in January 1973, was for a 28-percentage-point abatement to replace the major shared-cost programs—hospital insurance, medicare, and post-secondary education; the abatement would be equalized to the level of the province with the highest per capita revenues. Both provinces claimed to have widespread provincial backing for their compatible proposals.

---

[2] These conditions were less rigorous than those spelled out in the original thrust fund proposal. The federal government offered the more moderate terms to a conference of finance, health, and education ministers held on May 8, 1973 and discussed below.

The Turner Proposal

The federal government did not find the Ontario and Quebec proposals acceptable, but neither did it wholly reject the idea of a tax transfer. At the May 8 conference, Finance Minister Turner presented a specific proposal for tax transfers based on the assumption that the provinces would accept the proposed per capita formula for federal contributions to health care programs. The proposal reflected the federal government's expectation that the yield of tax transfers would grow faster than related provincial spending or anticipated federal spending. Thus Turner rejected as too expensive Quebec's proposal to substitute a 28-point personal income tax abatement for the federal contributions to hospital insurance, medicare, and post-secondary education. An abatement of that size would, moreover, leave the federal government with a share of the personal income tax insufficient to permit it to continue to use the tax as a fiscal instrument and as a source of revenue for the equalization program. The federal government could not allow the provinces to contemplate changes in the services provided under the existing programs.

Turner's proposal was contingent on its acceptance by all of the provinces. It consisted of (1) a transfer of 6 points of personal income tax, equalized to the national average, effective January 1, 1977 (cash payments would be made in the interim), and (2) the abolition, effective January 1, 1975, of federal excise taxes and duties on domestic and imported tobacco products, spirits, brandy, wine, and beer. The federal withdrawal from the field would leave the provinces free to move into it. These revenues too would be equalized to the national average. Cash adjustments would make up any amount by which the value of the tax room fell short of the federal obligation, as determined by the GNP-escalated formula, but the value of the tax transfers would eventually exceed the federal obligation. The personal income tax transfer would be accomplished by a federal tax reduction in a new rate schedule, as had been done in 1972,[3] rather than by an abatement. The change would be deferred until January 1, 1977 in order to give the new federal and provincial tax systems time to settle down after tax reform and the introduction of various provincial credits. By 1977, Turner estimated, the tax room would provide, on average, about 85 to 90 percent of the total compensation. The proposal combined excise duties and taxes with the personal income tax cuts in order to provide a rate of growth in total tax room that approximated growth in the related provincial expenditures.

The Faulkner Proposal

At the joint meeting on May 8, the secretary of state, Hugh Faulkner, proposed a new formula for aid to post-secondary education, to replace the arrangements scheduled to expire on March 31, 1974. Under the proposed formula, federal assistance would take the form of per capita grants based on

---

[3] See chapter 6.

the 1973-74 federal transfers per person aged 18 to 24. The rate of increase for the per capita allowance would be 7 percent per year. Given the projected growth rate for the 18-to-24 age group, total transfers would increase by 9.4 percent per year. Levelling provisions would adjust per capita entitlements that were greater or less than the national average by one-tenth of the disparity each year. By the end of 10 years, therefore, all of the provinces would be receiving the same entitlement per person aged 18 to 24. The new formula, expected to take effect on April 1, 1974, would use the previous combination of tax and cash transfers.

In discussing this proposal at the May 8 meeting, Finance Minister Turner turned down a request from Manitoba's minister of colleges and university affairs, Saul Miller, for an additional transfer of tax points, equalized to the level of the province with the highest per capita revenue, in order to give the provinces more autonomy in this field. In Turner's view, the value of these extra tax points would increase faster than the shareable costs, to the point where the provinces would be receiving an "overpayment." The Faulkner proposal was intended to provide administrative autonomy while limiting federal contributions to a "reasonable" rate of growth—that is, one close to the growth rate for the national economy. Turner also rejected the concept of equalization to the level of the highest province, since it ran counter to the generally accepted principle of equalization to the national average.

The Provinces Respond

Provincial reaction at the May 8 conference to the full package of federal proposals, including the Faulkner proposal, was unenthusiastic. According to Ontario Treasurer John White, spokesperson for the provincial representatives, all of the provinces favoured far-reaching change. They were unanimous in seeking 9 points of individual income tax in lieu of the federal grants for post-secondary education, and some of them wanted similar arrangements—tax room in lieu of grants—for the health programs. Several provinces supported Quebec's January proposal for federal withdrawal from all three programs in exchange for 28 points of individual income tax. Quebec welcomed the moves made by the three federal ministers as steps in the right direction but did not feel that they went far enough.

Newfoundland and Prince Edward Island stressed the point that the compensation provided under the proposals was not sufficient. New Brunswick felt that the Quebec proposal was too expensive and likely to endanger other federal assistance, such as regional development; it supported a strengthened version of the Lalonde proposal. Manitoba was concerned that the provincial demands for additional tax room and greater flexibility in shared-cost programs would limit the federal government's ability to influence national standards and, indeed, reduce federal influence generally.

The federal representatives at the May 8 conference responded to the provincial demands for large abatements of tax room by pointing out that whereas income tax collections were increasing by 19 percent annually health costs were rising by only 14 percent, and that the federal government hoped to reduce this figure to 10 percent. The federal ministers argued that the amount of tax room sought by Quebec and its allies represented a redistribution of income that went beyond the terms of the present conference and referred the discussion to the first ministers' conference scheduled for May 23-25. The meeting of finance, health, and education ministers, scheduled to last two days, ended after one.

The provinces refined their objections to the federal proposals at the first ministers' conference. British Columbia felt that the risk-sharing proposals were inadequate. Saskatchewan felt that equalization of tax points to the national average was inadequate and discriminatory, and that the total compensation package was inadequate. Manitoba's premier, Edward Schreyer, speaking for a number of provinces, rejected both the health care proposals and those for post-secondary education. Most of the provinces welcomed the increase in provincial autonomy and flexibility implicit in the federal proposals but felt that the compensation package was inadequate. Quebec, although it set aside its earlier specific request for a 28-point abatement in order to evaluate the federal proposal, noted that the value to it of the existing opting-out arrangements was greater than the value of the federal offer. Nova Scotia and New Brunswick were anxious to maintain a federal presence in the nationwide programs. In their view, a tax transfer would be inequitable for the poorer regions, and they stressed the importance of federal funds to any improvement in program standards in their provinces.

The provinces unanimously rejected the federal proposal for financing post-secondary education, on the ground that it based provincial entitlement on population instead of actual enrolment, a better measure of the program load. They also argued that the federal scheme did not take into account the growth in the relevant expenditure and that certain technical aspects of the proposal were unacceptable. Nothing conclusive was said about the other federal proposals, which the provinces took home for further study. In fact, however, the Turner proposal died at that meeting, in large part because of the opposition of the provinces, such as New Brunswick, that regarded the transfer of tax points as a transfer of federal power to the detriment of the nation.

The federal government extended the existing arrangements for financing post-secondary education to the end of March 1977. The limit on annual growth of 15 percent was retained for the new three-year period.

The discussion continued, without resolution, at a provincial premiers' conference held on August 9 and 10, 1973. Newfoundland, Quebec, Ontario, and Alberta continued to favour a federal withdrawal from the joint programs and a commensurate abatement of tax points. Nova Scotia, Prince Edward Island, New Brunswick, Saskatchewan, and British Columbia continued to oppose any federal withdrawal that threatened national standards and a uniform financing plan. Manitoba was uncommitted at this point. In the fall of 1974, the provinces formally rejected the Lalonde-Turner formula.

Early in 1975, in an attempt to break out of the deadlock produced by this rejection, the federal government and the provinces set up a working committee of officials with a mandate to develop targets for cost-saving in health care that could form the basis for further negotiations. The committee's work came to an abrupt end, however, with the federal government's austerity budget of June 23, 1975, which in effect set these targets unilaterally and presumed that negotiations to implement them would follow.

Among the programs affected by the budget were hospital and medical insurance, whose combined cost had increased in 1974-75 by 19.8 percent. In anticipation of a successful conclusion to the federal-provincial negotiations on cost controls and increased efficiency in these programs, Finance Minister Turner gave the required formal five-year notice to terminate the hospital insurance and diagnostic services agreements; he also indicated his intention to begin negotiations immediately with the provinces for new arrangements. In addition, he imposed ceilings on the rate of growth in federal per capita contributions for medicare of 13 percent in 1976-77, 10.5 percent in 1977-78, and 8.5 percent in 1978-79 and subsequent years. Since the projected rate of annual growth in population was 1.5 percent, the federal government anticipated rates of increase in the total contributions of 14.5 percent in 1976-77, 12 percent in 1977-78, and 10 percent in 1978-79.

The first provincial response did not come until the western premiers' conference in late April 1976, at which the premiers criticized the unilateral federal cuts in health and education transfers. They called for greater flexibility for the provinces and for an examination of the feasibility of using equalized tax points instead of federal grants to transfer resources to the provinces.

Established Programs Financing Moves Forward

Prime Minister Pierre Trudeau outlined the established programs financing (EPF) proposals at a first ministers' conference held on June 14 and 15, 1976.

The proposals applied to three joint programs—hospital insurance, medical insurance, and post-secondary education. They were considered "established programs" because they had been in place for a number of years, because public demand for the services they financed had continued during this period to be both high and predictable, and because their total annual cost of about $10 billion was shared more or less equally by the two levels of government. It was the characteristic of stability in the long term that led policy makers to look for alternatives to cost-sharing as the method of financing these programs. It was clear that the programs would be around for a long time to come, and it was no less clear that cost-sharing was not tenable in the long run.

That the existing cost-sharing arrangements were inadequate was a point on which the federal government and the provinces could agree. The costs of the established programs were increasing much more rapidly than other government spending, and both levels of government were anxious to find a method of controlling and stabilizing their contributions. It was hard for the provinces to control their spending when the federal requirements were inflexible and they were dealing in "50-cent dollars." The federal government faced equal uncertainty, since it had no choice but to match provincial spending levels. The provinces advanced the additional complaint that the carefully designed and rigidly enforced federal definitions of eligible expenditure distorted provincial spending priorities. As was noted earlier, the federal government had imposed ceilings on its contributions for medicare and post-secondary education. This step had increased the provinces' uncertainty without giving them any more control over the spending process. Cost-sharing also offended the principle of equity and worked against the establishment of national standards, since some provinces were able to spend more per capita—and therefore received more per capita—than other provinces. Finally, the existing system was creating ever greater auditing and administrative difficulties for both levels of government.

The proposals for reforming the system that Ottawa had advanced in 1973 had not been acceptable to the provinces because the level of funding implicit in these proposals was insufficient to meet rising program costs. It was the growing need for expenditure restraint at the federal level and the prospect of the expiry, on July 15, 1980, of the agreements made under the Hospital Insurance and Diagnostic Services Act[4] that prompted the federal government to put forward new proposals in 1976. Prime Minister Trudeau spelled out the basic principles underlining the EPF proposals in letters given to the provinces a week before the first ministers' meeting in June: (1) The federal government should continue to pay a substantial share of program costs, in order to maintain national standards. (2) Federal payments should be calculated independently of provincial program expenditures, in order both to avoid distortions of provincial priorities and to provide greater certainty for both levels of government. (3) The per capita federal payments should be more nearly equal across the provinces (a change that would work to the advantage of poorer provinces). (4) The arrangements should be put on a more permanent footing, in order to facilitate long-term planning by both levels of government. (5) There should be provision for continuing federal-provincial consultation and cooperation in health care and post-secondary education.

The EPF proposals themselves, as presented at the first ministers' meeting and in more detail at a meeting of finance ministers and treasurers in July, did not generate as much enthusiasm as had the prime minister's exposition of general principles. The federal contribution would be based on extension of its present contributions for the three programs, and it would be divided into two parts, cash and tax room, each of which would grow independently of the other and of the program costs. The cash payment would increase at the same rate as the GNP, whereas the tax room was expected to grow faster than the GNP. Consequently, the total compensation would also grow faster than the GNP but not as quickly as the tax component alone.

---

[4] RSC 1970, c. H-8.

The cash transfers would increase at the same rate as the GNP. They would be brought to the same level, in per capita terms, for all provinces, over a period of five years. The payments would be calculated independently of provincial expenditures. The provinces would agree to spend the federal funds in the fields in question, giving public acknowledgement of their source, but they would not be required to make matching expenditures of any kind from their own resources. Thus, although the earlier block-funding proposals had not found general acceptance, their key features were incorporated into the established programs financing proposals.

The federal government proposed to transfer an amount of tax room that was uniform across the provinces and equalized to the national average as part of the main equalization system. The amount of the tax transfer would be calculated with reference to the province or provinces with the highest per capita yield. A province whose cash and equalized tax transfer fell short of the amount that it would have received had the whole entitlement been paid in cash would receive transitional payments to make up the difference.

Because of the contracting-out arrangements, Quebec's position under the proposed scheme would differ from that of the other provinces. Quebec would receive no additional tax room for any portion of the tax transfer that consisted of personal income tax points. To the extent that the other provinces received increased personal income tax room, Quebec's interim transfer under the contracting-out legislation would become permanent.

The EPF proposals provided for early notice of any federal intention to change the contemplated arrangements. The legislation would require three years' notice of changes, and to ensure that changes were not imposed without public debate it would include the provision that the notice had to be authorized by a resolution of the House of Commons. No notice of change was to be entertained during the first two years of the arrangement, so at least five years would pass before any change became possible. Contributions for post-secondary education would begin on April 1, 1977 and contributions for health care in 1981-82, after the expiry—for which notice had already been given—of the agreements made under the Hospital Insurance and Diagnostic Services Act.

Because the federal government could not change the hospital insurance program for four years, it proposed a federal-provincial review of health care legislation and programs, during which time the basis for federal participation in hospital insurance and medicare could be developed. The federal government also promised to maintain its contributions under the two programs at the existing level, expressed as a proportion of the GNP.

The federal government refused to consider providing the entire compensation in the form of tax points. It argued that this approach would eliminate federal influence on the programs, to the detriment of national standards, and create inequities between provinces; moreover, equalizing to the province with the highest level of per capita revenue would be too expensive. The proposed compromise of combined tax points and block funding, Prime

Minister Trudeau noted, marked a shift in the federal position from an insistence on a narrow definition of national standards, which implied homogeneity, to an acceptance of a broad definition, or one that could accommodate a variety of provincial approaches.

Federal Minister of Finance Turner presented more details and five options for federal financing to a meeting of his provincial counterparts held in July. The total federal contribution would be based on the national average per capita contribution in an unspecified base year (the federal examples used a projection for the year 1976-77). The five options examined were: (1) the whole contribution in cash, subject to the conditions on cash payments noted above; (2) 66 percent in cash plus 8 points of personal income tax and 1 point of corporate taxable income; (3) 50 percent cash, 8.5 points of personal income tax, 1 point of corporate taxable income, and 50 percent of federal excise duties and taxes on tobacco and alcohol; (4) 50 percent cash, 12.5 points of personal income tax, and 1 point of corporation taxable income; and (5) 33 percent cash, 12 points of personal income tax, 1 point of corporation taxable income, and 50 percent of federal excise duties and taxes on tobacco and alcohol. The taxes would be equalized to the national average in all cases. The tax points included 4.357 points of personal income tax and 1 point of corporation taxable income already provided under the federal program of assistance for post-secondary education.

The provinces' reaction at the June meeting was, as usual, mixed. British Columbia disliked the federal proposal. It argued for an expansion of eligible costs under the three programs and objected to the use of the GNP as an escalator, since in the early 1970s the GNP had not increased nearly as quickly as health care costs. The province was in favour of retaining the matching or equal-sharing feature of the existing arrangement. If that was out of the question, then it wanted a straight transfer of tax points, with some form of adjustment to the associated equalization to reflect variations in provincial costs.

Alberta's position on shared-cost programs was still basically what it had been in 1971. Premier Peter Lougheed proposed that the cost-sharing system be replaced by tax transfers. Saskatchewan's premier, Alan Blakeney, criticized the federal government's imposition of ceilings on the three programs, a move that placed an unfair burden on provinces that controlled their own programs and raised doubts about the reliability of future federal commitments. Although Saskatchewan had been opposed to the replacement of conditional grants by tax transfers, it was willing to reconsider its position, given an adequate level of equalization. The premier stopped well short of embracing the federal proposal, however; he wanted a direct link between federal transfers and program costs and increases in federal contributions as national costs rose. He also called for new federal cost-sharing arrangements for provincial programs of aid for prescription costs and dental costs.

Manitoba's premier, Edward Schreyer, noted that a reinterpretation of the legislation in 1976 had reduced federal payments for post-secondary education and that the federal government had withdrawn certain support services for treaty Indians. He reiterated his province's position that, at a minimum, any new federal proposal should promote financial flexibility, should have no adverse revenue implications, and should not diminish long-term guarantees of federal financial support. Premier William Davis of Ontario welcomed the federal proposals for their similarity to his early suggestions for deconditionalization. He suggested that the agreements under the Hospital Insurance and Diagnostic Services Act be terminated four years early, as of March 31, 1977, to facilitate the introduction of the new proposals.

The offer was under discussion for the rest of the summer of 1976. At the annual premiers' conference held in August, it was decided that provincial ministers of finance and treasurers should meet to try and develop a provincial consensus on the appropriate arrangements. These ministers met on September 14 and October 20 and developed a position that all of the provinces supported. The joint provincial brief was submitted to a federal-provincial conference of finance ministers and treasurers, held on December 6 and 7, by Alberta's treasurer, Merv Leitch.[5] Table 17.1 shows the value for each province of the provincial proposal.

The provincial brief proposed that the traditional 50:50 sharing of costs for the established programs be replaced by a system that used national average federal contributions in fiscal 1975-76 as a base. The federal contribution would consist of two parts. The first would be a transfer of 1 point of corporate taxable income and 12.5 points of personal income tax, equalized to the level of the province with the highest yield. (The 1 point of corporate taxable income and 4.357 points of the personal income tax represented tax room already transferred for post-secondary education under the 1967-1972 arrangements.) The equalization of these tax points to the level of the province with the highest yield, rather than to the national average, was essential to the proposal, since it would provide all of the provinces with the potential to achieve the same standard of per capita program expenditure as the province with the highest standard. The provinces endorsed the federal government's aim of making federal transfers more nearly equal, on a per capita basis, across the provinces. The difference between the provincial proposal and the federal proposal was subtle: the federal proposal called for transitional payments to bring the cash transfers and tax transfers up to the level of a purely cash arrangement; thereafter the mix of tax room and equal per capita cash transfers would be relied upon to provide an approximate per capita equality across the provinces. The provinces wanted strict equality in per capita terms.

The provinces proposed that the second part of the federal EPF contribution consist of equal per capita cash payments, escalated in accordance with the three-year moving average of the increase in per capita GNP until 1980-

---

[5] The brief was reproduced as an appendix to British Columbia Ministry of Finance, *British Columbia Budget*, January 24, 1977, 35-39.

Table 17.1 Value of the Provincial Proposal for Established Programs Financing (Cash and Tax Transfer), 1978-79 to 1986-87

	1977-78	1978-79	1979-80	1980-81	1981-82	1982-83	1983-84	1984-85	1985-86	1986-87
	millions of dollars									
Newfoundland	151.2	169.4	190.4	211.9	234.3	275.5	282.8	310.2	340.2	373.3
Prince Edward Island	32.8	36.7	41.4	46.2	51.1	56.4	62.0	68.2	75.0	82.3
Nova Scotia	225.5	252.1	282.7	314.0	346.3	379.9	416.3	455.7	498.4	545.6
New Brunswick	187.7	211.3	238.1	266.0	295.0	325.6	358.8	395.1	434.9	478.7
Quebec	1,686.5	1,879.8	2,099.7	2,323.9	2,554.4	2,792.5	3,049.1	3,325.5	3,626.8	3,955.0
Ontario	2,272.2	2,554.7	2,878.6	3,213.0	3,562.5	3,928.5	4,326.9	4,760.4	5,237.0	5,760.9
Manitoba	277.8	309.8	346.2	383.5	421.8	461.4	504.1	550.1	600.7	655.4
Saskatchewan	254.7	286.3	322.4	359.8	398.8	439.6	483.9	532.2	585.3	643.5
Alberta	505.5	571.2	646.5	725.2	807.9	879.2	995.2	1,102.6	1,221.6	1,353.4
British Columbia	685.7	779.0	886.9	1,000.4	1,120.8	1,248.9	1,389.8	1,545.0	1,717.5	1,908.8
Total	6,279.6	7,050.2	7,933.0	8,844.0	9,792.9	10,787.4	11,868.9	13,045.0	14,337.4	15,756.8
	dollars per capita									
Newfoundland	268.92	298.32	331.66	365.24	399.14	434.28	472.02	512.63	556.77	604.20
Prince Edward Island	268.92	298.32	331.66	365.24	399.14	434.28	472.02	512.63	556.77	604.20
Nova Scotia	268.92	298.32	331.66	365.24	399.14	434.28	472.02	512.63	556.77	604.20
New Brunswick	268.92	298.32	331.66	365.24	399.14	434.28	472.02	512.63	556.77	604.20
Quebec	268.92	298.32	331.66	365.24	399.14	434.28	472.02	512.63	556.77	604.20
Ontario	269.00	298.39	331.72	365.26	399.14	434.28	472.02	512.63	556.77	604.20
Manitoba	268.92	298.32	331.66	365.24	399.14	434.28	472.02	512.63	556.77	604.20
Saskatchewan	268.92	298.32	331.66	365.24	399.14	434.28	472.02	512.63	556.77	604.20
Alberta	271.46	300.45	333.24	366.11	399.14	434.28	472.02	512.63	556.77	604.20
British Columbia	268.92	298.32	331.66	365.24	399.14	434.28	472.02	512.63	556.77	604.20
Average	269.15	298.52	331.81	365.34	399.14	434.28	472.02	512.63	556.77	604.20

Source: Joint provincial submission to federal-provincial conference of December 6 and 7, 1976, as reproduced in an appendix to British Columbia, Ministry of Finance, *British Columbia Budget*, January 24, 1977, 35-39.

81. Since hospital expenditures were likely to be the source of the largest cost increases, the provinces called for a re-examination of the escalation factor, and renegotiation to reflect actual costs, before the expiry on July 15, 1980 of the agreements under the Hospital Insurance and Diagnostic Services Act. The provinces accepted the principle of levelling down above-average per capita contributions over five years but proposed that levelling-up for below-average provinces be accomplished in the first year.

On November 26, 1976, Health and Welfare Minister Lalonde wrote to the provincial ministers of health, noting that an agreement had been reached between the federal and provincial governments to use 1975-76 as the base year for the hospital insurance and medicare programs. His letter also proposed a scheme for financing extended health care, under which the provinces would receive a transfer of 1 point of individual income tax and a grant of $10 per capita, escalated in accordance with GNP growth. The benefits could be either universal or income-tested. The aim was to broaden federal assistance for health care in exchange for a provincial commitment to meet certain targets for the provision of acute care beds and the ratio of physicians to population. Some of the relevant services were already financed under the Canada assistance plan, and were to have been transferred to the proposed Social Services Act in the absence of this proposal. The offer was valid only until January 1, 1977.

The federal and provincial finance ministers and treasurers could reach no agreement at the December 6 and 7 meeting, and all of the proposals were referred to a first minister's conference scheduled for the following week. In the interval, Lalonde offered to increase the proposed per capita grant for extended health care to $20, the rough equivalent of 2 points of personal income tax. The minister also removed the deadline for agreement, provided that all of the provinces agreed to incorporate the hospital insurance program into the established programs financing system as of April 1, 1977.

The 1977-1982 fiscal arrangements were completed at a meeting of first ministers in Ottawa on December 13 and 14, 1976. It was agreed that the tax transfer would take effect on January 1, 1977 (to coincide with the beginning of the tax year for individuals) but that the other aspects of EPF would not be introduced until April 1, 1977. The federal finance minister, Donald Macdonald, successfully solicited provincial approval for the recovery of the tax transfer for the period January 1 to March 31, on the ground that it represented a second payment of amounts that were already covered under the old arrangements. The provinces also yielded to the federal government's argument that equalization of the tax points to the level of the highest province would create an unacceptable precedent for the main equalization system. They agreed, accordingly, to equalization to the national average. The federal government offered to supplement the tax transfer with a transitional cash payment designed to ensure that each province would receive no less than it would have received had the entire federal payment been made in cash. In addition, instead of levelling-up below-average per capita payments over five years, as originally intended, it would accomplish the levelling in three years, at a lower cost.

All of the provinces readily accepted these arrangements. They were less amenable to changing the agreements signed under the Hospital Insurance and Diagnostic Services Act, and to secure their acquiescence Ottawa had to agree, in negotiations on December 13 and 14, to increase the total EPF financing by 1 more percentage point of personal income tax (to 13.5 points) and its cash equivalent. The enlarged federal offer of $20 per capita for extended health care covered residential care (excluding short-term stays in facilities associated with social services programs, such as halfway houses, that were already financed under the Canada assistance plan), nursing intermediate home care, converted mental hospitals, the health aspects of home care, and ambulatory health services.

At a press conference following the meeting of December 13 and 14, Prime Minister Trudeau noted that the Hospital Insurance and Diagnostic Services program now had the same general standards as medicare (universality, portability, and so forth) but that there were still no federal conditions on post-secondary education provided in the provinces. Ontario's treasurer, Darcy McKeough, reviewed the proposals to date and the compromise eventually reached. He noted that the provinces had moved down $400 million (in 1977-78 values) from their consensus position and that the federal government had moved up $600 million from its June offer.

Tables 17.2 and 17.3 summarize the federal analysis of the established programs financing system that emerged from the December 1976 meeting.[6]

Part VI of the Federal-Provincial Fiscal Arrangements and Established Programs Financing Act, 1977[7] defined the cash payment element of the established programs financing system. A province's cash payment consisted of a basic cash contribution, a transitional adjustment payment, and, in some cases, a levelling payment. The basic cash contribution consisted of 50 percent of the federal national per capita contributions for the three established programs in 1975-76 plus $7.63, multiplied by provincial population and adjusted by an escalator that represented the average increase in gross national product per capita over the previous three years. The definition of this escalator, in section 22(2)(a) of the Act, enshrined the cube root in federal legislation for the first time. The $7.63 represented the equivalent of 1 point of personal income tax in 1975-76 and was part of the arrangement that replaced the 1972 income tax revenue guarantee (see chapter 7).

The transitional adjustment payment compensated for the wide variation from province to province in the value of the tax transfer. It was defined as

---

[6] For a detailed analysis of the established programs financing system, see George E. Carter, "Financing Health and Post-Secondary Education: A New and Complex Fiscal Arrangement" (1977), vol. 25. no. 5 *Canadian Tax Journal* 534-50.

[7] SC 1976-77, c. 10.

Table 17.2 Comparison of Total Amounts Payable Under the Existing Shared-Cost Arrangements and the Established Programs Financing Proposal, Plus Additions Negotiated on December 13 and 14, 1976

	Existing shared-cost arrangements		Original EPF proposal[a]		Added during negotiations[b]		New total	
	1977-78	1981-82	1977-78	1981-82	1977-78	1981-82	1977-78	1981-82
	millions of dollars							
Newfoundland	133.3	197.4	137.1	231.6	12.6	16.0	149.6	247.7
Prince Edward Island	26.7	39.3	28.5	50.5	2.9	3.5	31.4	54.0
Nova Scotia	208.4	300.4	214.2	342.5	17.2	23.7	231.3	366.2
New Brunswick	161.5	239.8	170.0	291.6	15.7	20.2	185.6	311.8
Quebec	1,625.6	2,337.3	1,665.2	2,525.6	117.6	174.7	1,782.8	2,700.3
Ontario	2,194.5	3,251.0	2,272.3	3,562.2	162.7	256.0	2,435.0	3,818.2
Manitoba	255.4	368.6	263.2	417.1	21.2	28.9	284.5	446.0
Saskatchewan	223.0	324.7	234.4	394.2	20.6	27.3	255.0	421.5
Alberta	471.0	707.6	502.3	798.7	34.4	55.2	536.7	854.0
British Columbia	600.7	920.1	634.5	1,108.1	54.9	76.6	689.4	1,184.7
Total	5,900.1	8,686.2	6,121.7	9,722.2	459.8	682.1	6,581.5	10,404.3

[a] 12.5-point abatement of personal income tax (PIT) and 1-point abatement of corporate taxable income, cash payment of 50 percent of payments in 1975-76, escalated by GNP growth and five-year levelling. [b] One percentage point added to the PIT abatement plus the equivalent in cash of the extra equalized tax point (distributed on an equal per capita basis) and levelling-up over three years. The estimated values of these adjustments, in millions of dollars, were as follows:

	1977-78	1981-82
1-point PIT equalization	215.5	339.5
Cash equivalent	215.6	334.8
Transitional adjustment	6.7	7.8
3-year levelling-up	22.0	—
	459.8	682.1

Source: Canadian Intergovernmental Affairs Secretariat, documents from first ministers' meeting of December 13-14, 1976.

Table 17.3 Comparision of Per Capita Amounts Payable Under the Existing Shared-Cost Arrangements and the Established Programs Financing Proposal, Plus Additions Negotiated on December 13 and 14, 1976

	Existing shared-cost arrangements		Original EPF proposal		Added during negotiations		New total	
	1977-78	1981-82	1977-78	1981-82	1977-78	1981-82	1977-78	1981-82
Newfoundland	237.19	336.29	243.90	394.62	22.36	27.30	266.26	421.92
Prince Edward Island	218.85	307.03	233.41	394.62	24.11	27.30	257.52	421.92
Nova Scotia	248.39	346.08	255.27	394.62	20.47	27.30	275.74	421.92
New Brunswick	231.38	324.49	243.52	394.62	22.43	27.30	265.94	421.92
Quebec	259.23	365.20	265.54	394.62	18.76	27.30	284.29	421.92
Ontario	259.80	364.26	269.01	399.13	19.26	28.68	288.27	427.81
Manitoba	247.24	348.72	254.83	394.62	20.54	27.30	275.37	421.92
Saskatchewan	235.48	325.03	247.53	394.62	21.76	27.30	269.28	421.92
Alberta	252.95	349.60	269.76	394.62	18.48	27.30	288.24	421.92
British Columbia	235.57	327.67	248.83	394.62	21.54	27.30	270.37	421.92
Total	252.89	354.03	262.38	396.26	19.71	27.80	282.09	424.06

Source: Same as table 17.2.

the amount by which the basic cash contribution exceeded the value of the tax transfer and the associated equalization. In this way, the federal government ensured that the basic cash contribution would be at least equalled by the tax transfer and the associated payments, and that the provinces would receive as much in tax revenues and cash as they would have received had the entire federal contribution been in the form of cash.

The levelling payments compensated for the variation across the provinces in the per capita payments under the previous cost-sharing arrangements. One aim of the legislation was to ensure that the per capita payments would be the same for all of the provinces at the end of five years. Thus provinces that received per capita payments above the national average would have their payments levelled down over five years and provinces that received per capita payments below the national average would have their payments levelled up over three years.

In the federal accounts, the financing was to be attributed to the three existing programs according to the distribution of the three programs in 1975-76.[8] The cash payments attributable to post-secondary education would be made by the Department of the Secretary of State on the basis of figures provided by the Department of Finance. Similarly, the cash payments attributable to hospital insurance, medicare, and extended health care would be paid by the Department of National Health and Welfare.

There was no specific time limit on the established programs financing, but the federal government could alter or terminate the arrangement on three years' notice. The Act provided that April 1, 1982 was the earliest possible date for change or termination; thus the program was guaranteed for at least five years.

Part VI of the Act also provided for the introduction of an extended health care service program, although not all of the provinces had committed themselves to participation. Under the program, the Department of National Health and Welfare provided $20 per capita in 1977-78, an amount to be increased thereafter by the GNP escalator, for extended health care. The provincial reaction to this offer varied; some provinces, such as Manitoba and Saskatchewan, had hoped for more assistance from the federal government than that represented by $20 per capita. By the end of 1977-78, all of the provinces had accepted the federal offer.

The Act reduced the federal personal income tax rate schedule to reflect the federal withdrawal of 9.143 percentage points (13.5 points minus the 4.357 already provided). Since Quebec had opted out of the special welfare program (allowances for the blind and the disabled, unemployment assistance, and the Canada assistance plan) and hospital insurance, this change meant that the Act had also to establish certain equivalencies for that province.

---

[8] The allocation among the three existing programs was arbitrary, as described above, but the calculation of the amount to be allocated to extended health care, as described below, was done according to the formula.

Part VII of the Act provided for an indefinite extension of the opting-out arrangements. The personal income tax abatement was reduced to 8.5 points of the new federal base for the established programs and to 5 points for the special welfare program; the existing 3-point abatement for the provincial youth allowances did not change. As under previous opting-out arrangements, adjustments were made so that the net compensation was the same as it would have been had the province not opted out. Since the new federal base less the 16.5-point abatement was equal to the old base less the previous 24-point abatement, no changes were required in the Quebec Income Tax Act.[9]

The new legislation provided authority for the continued operation of assistance for post-secondary education, but the hospital insurance and medicare agreements continued to operate under the Hospital Insurance and Diagnostic Services Act and the Medicare Act.[10] The financing and auditing provisions in those acts were withdrawn, but the main reporting and statistical sections remained.

As noted, payments during the 1977-1982 period were based on federal payments for 1975-76. The provinces subsequently sought numerous revisions in the federal payments for the base year, and the federal government usually granted them. These changes had the effect of increasing the entitlements for subsequent years, but the timing and the size of the revisions were not predictable. The result was provincial uncertainty about the transfers under EPF, just as there had been provincial uncertainty about the transfers under the previous arrangements.[11]

Just how much room was available for unilateral federal changes in the EPF administration was to become even more evident as the pressure on the federal budget increased.

---

[9] RSQ 1977, c. I-3.

[10] RSC 1970, c. M-8.

[11] In the fall of 1978, Quebec asked the federal government to incorporate the revised estimates of federal obligations for 1975-76 in the estimates for 1978-79. The federal government acknowledged the validity of the claims but did not commit itself to immediate adjustment of current payments.

18

From Established Programs Financing to the Canadian Health and Social Transfer

The Task Force Report

Chapter 10 discussed the role of the Parliamentary Task Force on Federal-Provincial Fiscal Arrangements in relation to equalization. The task force's report, released in 1981,[1] also reviewed the operations of the established programs financing (EPF) arrangements.

The report concluded that EPF had been "successful in attaining its fiscal goals."[2] The provinces were now able to act on their own priorities, to introduce measures to increase the efficiency of service delivery, and to control more carefully provincial spending on hospital insurance, medicare, and post-secondary education. For the federal government, EPF meant that it knew with greater certainty what its spending in the three areas would be. It no longer faced the unpredictable increases in its spending estimates that had occurred regularly under the old cost-sharing regime.

The task force also pointed out a significant shortcoming of the new arrangements from the federal point of view. Established programs financing drastically restricted the ability of federal officials, and, ultimately, federal parliamentarians, to account for money spent by the federal government. Under the cost-sharing arrangements, federal funds had been requisitioned for specific policy areas, such as hospital care, and could be identified with specific provincial expenditures undertaken in accordance with federal legislation and federal regulations that were designed to achieve a given level of uniformity across the country. In the case of hospital insurance and medicare, the federal government had been able to assure itself that, in aggregate, the provinces were "matching" its expenditures. The new arrangements required the provinces to maintain standards that would ensure the same level of uniformity, but there was no mechanism to "match" federal and provincial spending.

The problem of accountability was more than a theoretical one. Its practical aspects had become evident by the time the task force began its deliberations. Parliament was voting vast sums of money to the provinces for

---

[1] Canada, *Fiscal Federalism in Canada: Report of the Parliamentary Task Force on Federal-Provincial Fiscal Arrangements* (Ottawa: Supply and Services, August 1981).

[2] Ibid., at 71.

the three main EPF programs, but it had no control over how the provinces spent the money or over a number of aspects of the programs themselves. Post-secondary educational institutions in several provinces alleged that their governments had not passed on the full amount obtained for post-secondary education under the EPF. From a broader perspective, however, the rights and wrongs of the issue were unclear. For one thing, the allocation among the programs of both cash and tax points was arbitrary, based as it was on the national average allocation in 1975-76. For another, the very point of the new arrangements was to allow the provinces to allocate the funds according to their own priorities, not according to a formula set by the federal government. As a federal body, the task force noted, it was powerless to remedy the situation described by the complaining post-secondary institutions.

A further problem had arisen with respect to standards, particularly in the context of the medicare arrangements. As was noted in chapter 13, the standards for provincial programs were loosely defined and the 1977 arrangements contained no enforcement or penalty provisions. From the beginning of medicare, some provinces had allowed doctors to "opt out" of the program and bill their patients directly. The patients were subsequently reimbursed by the provincial plan, but the reimbursement might cover only part of the bill. Other provinces did not allow opting-out but did allow doctors to practise "extra billing" or "balance billing"—that is, to charge patients amounts above the standard fees payable under the provincial plans. Both practices, the critics argued, violated the principle of comprehensive coverage. There were no clear-cut rules for either the federal government or the provinces to follow, and the latter were often engaged in contentious negotiations with the provincial medical associations in an effort to establish fair schedules of fees while keeping the growth of the relevant expenditures to a minimum.

The EPF arrangement was new, and it was not surprising that some problems should arise in the sensitive areas of post-secondary education and medicare. There was also confusion, however, about the significance of both the growth in dollar figures and the figures themselves. The levelling provisions in the 1977 legislation led to a rate of increase in the cash payments to some provinces well above the rate in per capita gross national product (GNP). The levelling payments were never earmarked for particular functions, nor were they related in any way to the programs included in EPF. The result was that provincial expenditures did not necessarily follow the growth patterns of the cash payments, a state of affairs that caused some concern to interested members of the general public.

Even more confusing was the inclusion in the EPF formula of the compensation in lieu of the revenue guarantee, in the form of 1 percentage point of personal income tax and its equivalent in cash—$7.63 per capita in 1975-76. As the task force noted, the provinces had at first excluded this compensation from their calculations of federal transfers received under the two health care programs and for post-secondary education. The federal government, on the other hand, had lumped it in with the compensation for the three programs, the approach favoured by the task force. In 1981, however, the two levels of government reversed their stands. The federal government announced that the compensation in lieu of the revenue guarantee would end on March 31, 1982 but that this change did not imply a change in the funding for the health programs and post-secondary education. The provinces now adopted the position that this compensation was in fact part of the EPF system and that its elimination would reduce the assistance provided for the three programs.

The federal position prevailed, and the compensation in lieu of the revenue guarantee was removed as of April 1982. Ottawa accomplished its removal by revising the 1977 Act[3] to define the total EPF entitlement as the national average per capita federal contribution for the three programs in 1975-76, escalated as before according to the growth in per capita GNP and multiplied by provincial population. This formula eliminated the cash portion of the compensation—the equivalent in cash of 1 percentage point of personal income tax. The cash transfer would hereafter be the total entitlement less the value of the equalized tax transfer, which would continue to be what it had been under the 1977 arrangements. The tax portion of the compensation in lieu of the revenue guarantee was matched in the cash payment because of the provision that the tax portion of the total compensation would be supplemented to make it equal to the basic cash payment. Thus the elimination of the cash portion of the compensation in lieu of the revenue guarantee automatically eliminated the tax portion as well. Under the 1982 amendments, therefore, the abatement of personal income tax "room" continued to be 13.5 points but the cash compensation was, in effect, lowered by the equivalent of 2 points (as determined in 1975-76 and since escalated according to the formula).

The task force's report was concerned primarily with accountability and the maintenance of national minimum standards. It noted, however, that the basic premise behind the EPF arrangements was that the provinces should be able to adjust their spending to fit their own priorities. Consequently, neither the provinces nor the system could be faulted if provincial spending failed to match the artificial allocation of federal assistance. The report then had this to say:

> [W]e are also concerned that funding levels for these programs be maintained and that adequate standards be assured. It can be argued that some provinces took the opportunity offered by introduction of EPF to practice spending restraint with an enthusiasm that threatens the maintenance of adequate standards.
>
> It is to redress any imbalance of this sort that the Task Force argues for a return to separate transfers for health and post-secondary education. Provincial governments must explain to their own electorates their

---

[3] Federal-Provincial Fiscal Arrangements and Established Programs Financing Act, 1977, SC 1976-77, c. 10.

decisions to practice expenditure restraint in relation to programs falling under EPF. But we would like to ensure that in future there is no lack of clarity as to the degree of federal support for these programs. It is for this purpose—and not to attach blame for past alleged "errors" in provincial expenditure decisions—that the Task Force makes recommendations for modifications to the EPF arrangements.[4]

In the task force's view, the establishment of two separate programs would also be a partial solution to the problem of defining an appropriate degree of federal control over program activities and standards:

> Hospital and medical care insurance have been the subject of federal legislation and conditional cost-sharing arrangements for many years. There is country-wide acceptance of the need to maintain and, if appropriate, to enforce national standards in the delivery of services. Moreover, satisfactory hospital, medical and extended health care require management decisions, technical knowledge and service delivery that are in large part similar in all of Canada. The health system is most efficient and effective if it is partly organized on a Canada-wide basis.

> Post-secondary education, on the other hand, is very different. The services provided and the role of higher education may vary from one language group to another, from province to province, and from one institution of higher learning to another. Among French-speaking Canadians, higher education is seen as critical in nurturing and developing the French language and culture. This is true for all French language institutions but has found, and continues to find, its strongest expression in Quebec where a succession of provincial governments has maintained a constant vigil against the possibility of outside interference. Quebec does not, of course, stand completely alone among the provinces in this determination to control education services.

> Although the post-secondary sector must serve broad Canadian purposes, the federal government's influence in this regard can only be indirect and complementary to the responsibility of the provinces. In this connection, *the Task Force believes that any federal attempt to legislate national standards for post-secondary education would be unacceptable.*[5]

By separating health care and post-secondary education, the task force reasoned, the federal government could legislate quite different roles for itself in each.

The task force suggested that the division of EPF funds between the two proposed programs approximate the division that had prevailed in 1977—that is, 32.1 percent for post-secondary education and 67.9 percent for hospital insurance and medicare; the cash grant for extended health care would continue to be a separate matter. The exact proportions, and the subsequent

---

[4] Supra footnote 1, at 76.

[5] Ibid., at 77-78 (emphasis in original).

allocation of the revenue guarantee compensation, would be subject to negotiation, but once the proportions were determined, the provinces would be required to use the funds for a given program area only in that area, and not for other purposes.

The task force also called for a fundamental change in the method of calculating compensation. The existing formula calculated the cash portion of a province's entitlement independently of the tax portion, on the basis of GNP growth. GNP, however, tended to grow less rapidly than tax revenues. The result was that a province's cash entitlement often fell short of the value of its tax entitlement. Since the degree of difference between the two entitlements varied from province to province, the value of the total per capita entitlement varied across the provinces as well.

The task force's proposed reform was designed to ensure that the total per capita federal contribution, and not just the cash portion, would be the same for every province. The per capita entitlement for each of the two proposed programs would be calculated on the basis of the 1977 data, scaled up according to the formula in the 1977 Act, and multiplied by provincial population to arrive at each province's total entitlement. This amount would then be reduced by the value to the province of the tax points and associated equalization, and the balance would then be the amount of the province's cash transfer.

The report also noted that the extended health care provisions of EPF were not, in practice, uniformly generous. Before April 1, 1977, when the provisions came into effect, the costs of extended care were covered under the Canada assistance plan (CAP) when the recipients were deemed needy; thereafter, CAP funding for this purpose ceased. For many jurisdictions, however, the extended health care grants proved to be smaller than the relevant CAP reimbursements had been—substantially smaller in the cases of Newfoundland, Prince Edward Island, and the Yukon, somewhat smaller in the cases of Quebec, Nova Scotia, and New Brunswick.

The point was made during the task force hearings that the 1981 census would inevitably reveal some errors in the population estimates used to calculate provincial entitlements under the 1977-1982 federal-provincial agreements.[6] The question was whether the base-year calculations and entitlements for 1977 to 1982 should be revised on the basis of the corrected population figures. The task force felt that the revisions should be made, but it advised against making any special allowances under the EPF arrangement to cushion the shock to any province or to the federal government that the revisions might cause.

Finally, the task force's report devoted considerable attention to the operating conditions of each program. It recommended consolidation and

---

[6] See ch. 10.

revision of the legislation to develop program standards and a system of enforcement, including withdrawal of federal funding if certain conditions were not met.

The EPF Arrangements for 1982-1987

Federal-provincial discussions on revisions of the 1977-1982 fiscal arrangements for the period 1982 to 1987 began late in 1980 but had few concrete results. The federal finance minister, Alan MacEachen, called for a reduction in the rate of growth in cash transfers to the provinces under what was then called the social affairs envelope (mainly the hospital insurance and medicare components of the EPF arrangement). The federal government, as already noted, was also concerned about its visibility in all three of the fields covered by EPF.

The provinces were generally satisfied with the EPF element of the 1977-1982 arrangements. The provincial finance ministers prepared a report for the provincial premiers' annual meeting in Victoria in the summer of 1981. The resulting communiqué argued that no changes should be made in EPF for the 1982-1987 period. It did address, with resolution, the question whether the provinces had maintained their commitment to retain the three EPF programs. The communiqué did not treat the compensation in lieu of the revenue guarantee as an integral part of EPF.

On November 12, 1981, Finance Minister MacEachen presented with his budget a major statement on federal-provincial fiscal relations. The only change specifically proposed was the ending of the compensation in lieu of the revenue guarantee by removing it from the EPF calculations, as recommended by the task force. The change was duly carried out in the 1982 legislation,[7] to the manifest displeasure of the provinces. All of the provinces had combined the compensation for the loss of the revenue guarantee with their cash entitlements under EPF in their own accounts; consequently, all of them showed decreases in their EPF transfers when they received their entitlements for 1982-83.

Even more controversial was the budget statement's emphasis on the question of the federal role in the established programs. Ottawa had several related goals in mind: greater visibility for the federal contribution to established programs, increased accountability to Parliament for this federal spending, a greater emphasis on minimum levels of performance and services (a goal promoted by both the federal government and various client groups), a greater federal voice in provincial administration, and guarantees of adequate provincial funding. None of these goals were acceptable to the provinces.

The financial arrangements had to be settled quickly, since the expiry date for the 1977-1982 agreements was close, but the question of the federal role

---

[7] SC 1980-81-82-83, c. 94.

in the EPF programs could not be resolved as easily. Accordingly, the budget paper called for an extension for one year of all aspects of EPF apart from the removal of the revenue-guarantee compensation. Ottawa and the provinces would use the time to negotiate clear standards and effective controls for health care, and the arrangements would be incorporated into new legislation that would come into effect on April 1, 1983. Similar legislation would be introduced for post-secondary education one year later, and in the absence of agreement on new arrangements in this area the federal government would freeze its future contributions at the per capita level provided in 1982-83.

In the provinces' view, a major advantage of the system introduced in 1977 was its long-term stability, which allowed the provinces to make their own long-range plans. This stability now seemed to be in question. All of the provinces' 1982 budgets expressed uncertainty over the future of financing for the established programs, and many provinces joined Ontario in condemning the ultimatum implicit in the federal budget. They feared that cash funding would be reduced in 1983 if negotiations failed to produce new standards and conditions satisfactory to the federal government.

In the case of post-secondary education, these fears proved to be unfounded. A proposed federal discussion paper on post-secondary education did not materialize, and the threatened freeze was not implemented. In the case of health care, however, the provinces did find themselves threatened with significant cuts in federal support. Ottawa and the provinces failed to agree on new standards for the health care programs by the April 1983 cut-off date, and the federal government acted unilaterally to address what it perceived to be a crisis in the health care fields. Faced by rapidly growing health care costs, provincial health departments and commissions had resorted to a variety of special charges to ration the use of facilities, impose discipline on users, and raise additional revenue. A federal discussion paper issued in July 1983[8] set out Ottawa's position that necessary hospital and medical services must be available to all Canadians regardless of their financial circumstances. In the federal view—supported by many observers outside government—user fees for hospital care and extra billing by doctors were undermining this basic principle of the joint programs.

The discussion paper was followed by the introduction in December 1983 of the Canada Health Act (passed in 1984),[9] which replaced the Hospital Insurance and Diagnostic Services Act and the Medical Care Act. The new legislation permitted the federal government to reduce the cash EPF payments to a province by the total amount of extra billing or user fees allowed in the province. Ottawa would hold the amounts of these penalties in trust; if a province eliminated extra billing and user fees within three years of the enactment of the legislation, the money would be released (without interest).

---

[8] Canada, Department of National Health and Welfare, *Preserving Universal Medicare: A Government of Canada Position Paper* (Ottawa: Supply and Services, 1983).

[9] SC 1984, c. 6.

The Act also increased the minimum percentage of the population to be covered by a qualifying provincial health insurance plan from 95 percent to 100 percent. It provided as well for the separate calculation of the health care and post-secondary education elements of EPF from 1983-84 on.

In July 1984, the minister of national health and welfare, Monique Bégin, announced that seven provinces—New Brunswick, Quebec, Ontario, Manitoba, Saskatchewan, Alberta, and British Columbia—would collectively lose $9.5 million per month because of extra billing and user fees. In the same month, Nova Scotia, which had not allowed the practice, became the first province to pass legislation banning extra billing. By the deadline of March 31, 1987, the rest of the provinces too had banned the practice. In Quebec, user fees for certain chronic-care patients were in dispute, but the province eventually rescinded them. The federal government withheld a total of $192 million before the last of the provinces capitulated. By March 31, 1988, it had released the full amount to the provinces.

EPF in Decline

The Canada Health Act proved to be only temporarily successful as a means of enforcing national health-care standards. Health-care costs continued to rise, and the provinces continued to contemplate measures for controlling these costs that threatened the basic principle of a national minimum standard. Meanwhile, as the value of the tax points that had been transferred to the provinces under the EPF arrangements grew, the cash payments under EPF declined; by 1991, it was clear that any federal threat to withhold the payments would probably have little deterrent value.

Quite apart from the decline in the cash payments occasioned by the growth in the value of the tax points, these payments had already been reduced by a series of unilateral moves by a federal government that was under great pressure to reduce its deficit. The "6 and 5" anti-inflation program, introduced in 1983, sought to hold a number of federal programs to rates of growth substantially lower than those that had prevailed for several years. Ottawa did not apply the program to many of its transfers to the provinces, but it did impose it on per capita entitlements for the post-secondary education portion of EPF. The GNP escalator used to determine the per capita amounts was arbitrarily held to 6 percent in 1983-84 and 5 percent in 1984-85. Population growth, however, resulted in increases in the total entitlements that were somewhat larger than the increases in the per capita amounts—about 7 percent in 1983-84 and about 6 percent in 1984-85.

In 1986, further pressure to reduce the deficit led the federal government to reduce the rate of growth in the GNP-based escalator for all EPF entitlements. For 1986-87 and subsequent years, the escalator would be 2 percentage points less than the calculated growth in GNP. In 1989, Ottawa reduced the rate of growth in per capita entitlements by a further percentage point. In 1990, it froze the per capita entitlements at their 1989-90 levels for two years, and the 1991 federal budget extended the freeze until the end of

1995-96. The effect of federal restraint on its cash payments to the provinces was exacerbated by the fact that the value of the tax room continued to grow. The successive declines in EPF payments increased the likelihood that the provinces would challenge the federal government's opposition to user fees and extra billing for health-care services.

In order to forestall this eventuality, Finance Minister Michael Wilson announced in 1991 that he intended to change the legislation: henceforth penalties under the Canada Health Act would be applicable to other payments (such as equalization and CAP payments) if an offending province had no cash entitlement under EPF.[10]

The Canadian Health and Social Transfer

Ottawa's efforts to maintain minimum national standards for major social programs were repeatedly undercut by its own efforts—stimulated by rising deficits—to reduce spending, a motive that became especially compelling as the country struggled out of the recession of the early 1990s. In 1996, the federal government took the major step of absorbing the last of the major shared-cost programs, the Canada assistance plan (CAP), into EPF.

The new arrangement had a new name: the Canadian health and social transfer (CHST). In its essence, however, it was an extended version of the EPF program, and it retained EPF's combination of cash payments and tax-point transfers. The initial entitlement for 1996-97 was set at $26.9 billion in tax points and cash and distributed in accordance with the provincial shares of EPF and CAP in 1995-96. The total entitlement was reduced to $25.1 billion for 1997-98, 1998-99, and 1999-2000, and the provinces' shares were adjusted to reflect changes in their shares of total population. The adjustments to provincial shares will continue until the end of the current arrangement in 2002-03. Total entitlements will begin to grow again in 2000-01: the growth rate will be GDP growth less 2 percentage points in 2000-01, GDP growth less 1.5 percentage points in 2001-02, and GDP growth less 1 percentage point in 2002-03. The value of the tax point is expected to grow more rapidly than the total entitlement, so the cash transfers will decline over time. The federal government has guaranteed that the annual total cash transfer will not drop below $11 billion.

The shift from EPF to the CHST reduced federal cash transfers to the provinces and increased provincial flexibility in what had been the last major area of cost-sharing on the original basis, social welfare. Its net effect, therefore, was a further reduction in Ottawa's ability to impose national standards on the provinces. Yet the gain in flexibility did not entirely reconcile the provinces to the loss of federal funding, especially since it was possible to argue that the CHST formula magnified a pattern of inequity that had already been present under the EPF regime.

---

[10] Budget Implementation Act, 1991, SC 1991, c. 51, section 4.

The apparent inequity emerged from the calculation of the cash payments under the CHST. In Ottawa's view, its support for the CHST programs consisted of both tax-point transfers and cash payments. Once transferred, however, the tax points were no longer under the control of the federal government, and the provinces quickly ceased to regard them as a form of federal support. Nevertheless, in calculating the cash payments under the CHST, Ottawa subtracted the value of the tax points from the total entitlement, with the result that the per capita value of the cash transfers varied substantially from province to province. The per capita value of the tax points was much greater in the wealthier provinces than it was in the poorer ones, and so the per capita value of the cash payments was substantially smaller in the former than in the latter. Thus the CHST formula involved an element of equalization; this element had been present under EPF as well, but the larger scope of the new program magnified its prominence.

The wealthier provinces, pressed by high deficits and diminished revenues, were in no mood to support any increase in regional redistribution. Their dissatisfaction with the apparent bias of the CHST put the federal government under pressure to abandon this attempt to maintain a rough parity across the provinces in the resources available for major social programs and to adopt instead a program of equal per capita cash transfers.

19

Conclusions

The fathers of Confederation set out to establish a strong federal state, one in which there would be no doubt about the subordination of the provinces to the central government. Yet now, though there has been no fundamental change in the country's constitutional basis since 1867, Canada is routinely characterized as a relatively weak federation. The provinces enjoy substantially more autonomy than do, for example, the states of the United States, though the perceived weakness of the federalism of the United States was precisely what Canada's founders had set out to avoid. Moreover, as this is being written, the provinces, or at any rate the larger and richer ones, appear to be eager to enlarge their already considerable autonomy.

This book has attempted to show how the fiscal dimension of Canadian federalism has evolved over the past 130 years, to produce—for the time being, at least—a state of affairs that is at once a wide departure from the constitutional formula devised in 1867 and a return to it. The departure consists in the fact that the federal government does not, as it was intended to do, unequivocally dominate Canada's fiscal landscape. The return consists in the fact that the federal government and the provinces, after a long period of sharing certain responsibilities, have for some years now been moving toward a separation of functions quite similar to the one established in the beginning. Depending on one's point of view, then, the present state of affairs is either an overturning of the founders' intentions or a rediscovery of those intentions. The causes of this ambiguous outcome are complex, but their general outlines are not difficult to trace.

Ottawa Ascendant (1)

The designers of the constitution saw several good reasons for preferring a strong federalism to a weak one. Canada was a vast, thinly populated domain: only a strong national government could muster the resources necessary to develop it and defend it. Defence was necessary not only against foreign pressure—in particular, pressure from a United States with a sometimes hyperbolic sense of its manifest destiny—but also against the wayward tendencies of some of the provinces and territories themselves; and indeed much of Ottawa's effort in the early years went into either suppressing by arms or co-opting by the provision of railways a variety of separatist movements and inclinations in the West. Finally, there was the fresh example of the American civil war, which could be attributed in part to a constitution that failed to give Washington an unambiguous primacy over the states.

The desire to establish a strong federalism determined the division of fiscal powers and responsibilities under the British North America (BNA) Act of 1867. The powers and responsibilities given to the provinces were relatively specific and inflexible. Those given to the federal government were general and highly flexible. Any responsibility not explicitly assigned to the provinces was implicitly reserved to the federal government. In addition, the federal government enjoyed a general power to legislate for "the peace, order and good government of Canada." The result—so it was hoped—was an arrangement that would keep provincial activity within determinate bounds but give the federal government enough scope and flexibility to maintain its dominance, and thus hold the federation together, as time moved on and circumstances changed.

Many of the responsibilities that were assigned to the provinces, and for the most part passed on by them to local governments, had to do with social welfare, broadly defined. The provinces were responsible for education, poor relief, hospitals, and asylums. In 1867, the high noon of laissez-faire, these matters were not regarded as major functions of government, and much of the responsibility for them was left to charitable institutions. The most important task of government was to develop and protect a context in which private economic activity could thrive. Thus Ottawa assumed responsibility for defence and for "national" undertakings in the areas of communications and transportation. In raising the revenue they needed in order to meet their responsibilities, the provinces were limited to levying direct taxes, whereas the federal government could levy either direct taxes or indirect taxes. In practice, the provinces passed on most of their taxing authority to local governments, which drew most of their revenue from property taxes. The federal government relied largely on customs and excise duties and other indirect levies.

In the context of the times, this division of fiscal powers and responsibilities did ensure the primacy of the federal government. Indeed, the provinces were left with such slender resources that they required federal subsidies in order to carry out even the limited functions that were left to them. Provincial complaints about the size of these subsidies were frequent and heartfelt during the first half-century of Confederation. Nevertheless, the provinces had to make only a very limited use of their own tax powers in order to supply the deficiency. Experiments with personal and corporate income taxes, wealth taxes, and sales taxes did not account for more than 10 percent of provincial revenues (excluding local revenues) during the years before the First World War. The habit of provincial dependency on federal transfers became entrenched, and neither level of government could readily imagine an alternative.

Ottawa Descendent (1)

From the beginning, however, there were factors latent in the constitution, and in the composition of the country itself, that would eventually work to undermine the federal government's primacy. One factor was the uniqueness of the province of Quebec. Its difference in language and culture from the other nine provinces proved to be a fact that resisted the solvent power of the federalist formula. Exertions of federal authority affronted the province's sense of its essential distinctness. Opposition to federal initiatives became habitual and increasingly rigorous. Ottawa repeatedly faced a disagreeable choice: it could attempt to force Quebec's compliance and thereby increase the province's resentment of federal authority; or it could allow Quebec to exempt itself from federally initiated policies and thereby stir resentment among the other provinces—which would then have to be placated in their turn.

Another factor that worked against federal primacy was the provinces' gradual accumulation of population and wealth. As the provincial economies grew, provincial government revenues—and provincial governments—grew as well. At the end of the 1920s, the combined budgets of the provinces were already half again as large as the federal budget. As provincial governments grew more considerable in their own right, they became increasingly impatient of federal tutelage and of the constraints on provincial initiative that came with dependency on federal grants. Eventually, after fairly rude beginnings, the provinces built up modern and effective bureaucracies that were able to hold their own against the mandarins of Ottawa, and federal-provincial fiscal relations became increasingly a matter of negotiation rather than of unilateral federal initiative.

Still another factor that, over time, forced the federal government to yield ground to the provinces was the composition of the Canadian federation. There were not many provinces, and two of them—Ontario and Quebec—were large enough from the beginning to stand up to Ottawa on their own. These two were later joined by British Columbia. The others, the prairie provinces and the Atlantic provinces, generally constituted two distinct blocs.

This arrangement sometimes worked to the federal government's advantage. Ottawa could, for example, muster support for a given policy by enlisting the smaller or poorer provinces against the larger or richer ones. In general, however, the fact that the federal government had to deal with a few large provinces and provincial blocs worked against its efforts to retain the upper hand in federal-provincial relations. In most contentious situations, enough provinces were able to find enough common ground to force the federal government to modify its position.

Finally, Ottawa's gradual loss of primacy in its fiscal relations with the provinces is attributable in part—perhaps in large part—to the very division of responsibilities under the British North America (BNA) Act that was intended to secure its dominance. In allocating sole responsibility for matters such as education and social welfare to the provinces, the fathers of Confederation were giving what they saw as lesser functions of government to the lower level of government. Indeed, as was noted above, they assumed that the provinces would pass these functions downward to local governments, which would, in their turn, leave them largely to private enterprise and private charity. There was no reason to suppose, in 1867, that these local responsibilities would eventually became one of the largest areas of government expenditure. Yet this is what happened. After the First World War, the provinces undertook large new expenditures in areas such as education, mother's allowances, child welfare, pensions, and unemployment relief.

Many factors brought about this unexpected elevation of the social welfare function of government and the resulting need—equally unexpected—for large provincial revenues. Demand for education increased as society and the economy became more complex. Increasing urbanization and mobility eroded the tradition of family or community responsibility for the ill, the elderly, and the unlucky. Growing industrialization led to cyclical unemployment and a consequent need for organized unemployment relief. Advances in medical knowledge and medical technology created a new emphasis on public health measures. In general, society was becoming a vastly more complicated and bureaucratic affair than it had been in 1867.

The social welfare functions of government became not only more important in their own right but also relatively more important than many of the established responsibilities of the federal government. The tasks associated with the initial project of nation-building—the development of infrastructure, the opening of the West—were largely complete by the end of the First World War. In the 1920s, even the newer provinces were large enough and mature enough to assume most of the responsibility for economic development within their own boundaries. The war led, somewhat paradoxically, to a decline in the importance of Ottawa's responsibility for national defence, since in the course of it the United States abandoned its already diminished role as the primary threat to Canada's security and became an ally. In general, then, the federal government experienced over time a relative decline in demand for the services that it had a mandate to provide.

These two tendencies—the expansion of provincial activity and the relative and absolute contraction of federal activity—imply an obvious result: the end of strong central leadership of the federation. Each of the two world wars, of course, temporarily reversed the trend: Ottawa drew enormous power into its hands and the provinces, for the most part, receded demurely. During the First World War, for example, the federal government entered for the first time into tax fields—personal and corporate income taxes and sales taxes—that the provinces had come to regard as belonging to themselves alone. After the war, however, this federal surge receded almost as rapidly as it had advanced. Ottawa maintained a position in the income tax and sales fields, but in a relatively small way. The provinces, meanwhile, having entered ambitiously into spending on social welfare and infrastructure, entered new tax fields and enlarged their presence in established fields. Ottawa, preoccupied with paying down its enormous war debts, contributed to the provinces' rising revenue needs in only a very limited way. The net result of growing provincial tax activity and federal aloofness was an unprecedented degree of provincial independence in fiscal matters.

By the end of the 1920s, the provinces had largely escaped from federal leadership. The strongly centralized federation established in 1867 had taken just 60 years to become a relatively decentralized entity in which the federal government presided in an informal and somewhat lackadaisical way over a loose collection of strong and jealously independent provinces.

At the time, this outcome did not seem to be an unfortunate one. It was possible to argue that the constitution had more than fulfilled the hopes of its designers. When the country was new and many of the provinces were small, raw, and inexperienced, the constitution had allowed the federal government to guide them firmly and surely to maturity. Once that maturity had been accomplished, the constitution had worked silently and automatically to withdraw the guiding hand and leave the provinces to their own capable devices.

The evolution of federal-provincial fiscal relations might have ended at this point, but it did not. At the end of the 1920s came the Great Depression, which swiftly overwhelmed provincial resources and forced the federal government, almost in spite of itself, to reintroduce the guiding hand.

The provinces had, as a rule, left responsibility for unemployment relief to local governments, which met the costs out of their own resources. The unemployment levels of the depression years reduced this arrangement to tatters. Local governments, overwhelmed, looked to the provinces, and the provinces were unable to take up the burden. The federal government came belatedly and reluctantly to the rescue with large ad hoc grants and loans. Some provinces became virtual wards of Ottawa.

Meanwhile, all three levels of government were casting about for ways in which to extract more revenue out of a shrunken economy. The variety of taxes was enormous, and the incidence of taxation varied enormously from place to place. The tax system as a whole became remarkable for its complexity and inefficiency—and for its inequity as well, since taxes tended to be highest in the parts of the country least able to pay them. Moreover, much of the variation in taxes, and in levels of relief as well, was a consequence of deliberate competition among the provinces, which were at pains both to keep capital from flowing out of their jurisdictions and to keep the unemployed from flowing in.

Thus the decentralized Canada that had emerged inadvertently from the provisions of the BNA Act failed its first substantial test. The harmonious concert of provinces, loosely overseen by a federal government with little business of its own, had dissolved in confusion and competition. In 1940, the report of the Rowell-Sirois commission looked back on the experience of the 1930s and recommended that the federal government assume stewardship not only over unemployment relief but over "national needs" generally. The provinces, chastened by their recent misadventures, did not strenuously object.

In 1941, as a first step in this new direction, the federal government introduced compulsory unemployment insurance. Meanwhile, the country was again at war, and again the federal government drew to itself the lion's share of tax power. In 1941, the provinces agreed to turn over their room in the income tax fields in return for federal payments. Ottawa was to enjoy sole occupancy of these fields until 1947.

With the end of the war and the Wartime Tax Rental Agreements, there was no reason—in theory at least—why the constitution should not operate to restore the provinces to their pre-depression autonomy. Yet nothing of the kind happened. The federal government went boldly and directly from leadership in war to leadership in peace, and it maintained its primacy, without serious challenge, for 30 years. The history of federal-provincial fiscal relations over the past half century is largely the story of how the federal government kept the upper hand for a time and then gradually—and not altogether unwillingly—lost it again.

Ottawa Ascendant (2)

There are several reasons why the federal government succeeded in holding the centre of the stage for the first few decades after the Second World War, in spite of the fact that the focus of government expenditure had shifted even more decisively than it had after the First World War to areas of provincial responsibility.

The most obvious reason for Ottawa's success was the example of recent experience. The depression and the war had brought about an important shift in the climate of opinion, among public and politicians alike, about the appropriate role of government in society and the economy. Canadians were less willing than they had been in the past to believe that unfettered private enterprise was the best guarantee of a stable and broadly distributed prosperity. In addition, they had noted both the failure of all levels of government to deal adequately with the depression and the federal government's success in coordinating national effort during the war.

During the depression, the problems of relief and economic recovery had been left largely to the provinces; the federal government had intervened reluctantly and in an unplanned, ad hoc fashion, making it clear meanwhile that it was waiting for the economy to correct itself. By contrast, the highly centralized and strongly interventionist federalism of the war years had not merely "won the war": it had also ended the depression and restored prosperity. Strong federal leadership was, apparently, more effective and efficient than uncoordinated provincial striving. Therefore the federal government, rather than the provinces, was the appropriate agency to oversee the postwar tasks of reconstruction and development, and to take the steps necessary to prevent future depressions.

The war had also encouraged Canadians to think in national terms. It had broken down (or at any rate mitigated) the parochialism of regional loyalty and interregional competition. In any case, the depression had already shown that "province-building" was poor economic strategy. Every region had a stake in the well-being of all of the other regions. This new interest in interregional equity had its parallel in a growing belief in the responsibility of government to provide some approximation of equity among individuals as well—at least to the extent of ensuring that all Canadians enjoyed basic access to the requirements of a decent life.

In general, then, Canadians were willing to see some portion of their tax dollars go to the less well-off members of the community and the less well-off regions of the country. It was an obvious role for the federal government, a role in keeping with its overarching responsibility to "the nation," to collect and distribute the revenues needed to redress disparities in levels of public services among the provinces and disparities in well-being among individual Canadians.

Another reason why Ottawa retained its dominance after the war is the fact that the end of the war found the federal government firmly in control of the major sources of public revenue. Memories of the tax mess of the 1930s made everyone reluctant to see a simple reversion of personal and corporate income room to the provinces. A nationally uniform income tax system would be more equitable and less distorting, and certainly much simpler, than a federal system plus 10 different provincial systems.

Continued federal control of the major revenue sources had advantages even from the provinces' point of view. It saved the provinces the trouble and expense of maintaining separate tax administrations, and it meant that Ottawa would receive the blame for high taxes or the complexities of the tax system. For the time being, then, the federal government continued to collect all income taxes in most of the provinces, making payments to the provinces according to formulas that varied over time.

Ottawa Descendent (2)

The strong federalism of the decades after the Second World was in large part artificial. Ottawa was leading the way in areas of responsibility that, under the constitution, belonged to the provinces alone. Moreover, the financial basis of its leadership was its domination of tax fields to which the provinces had an equally valid claim.

Given this state of affairs, the federal government was generally obliged to proceed by negotiation rather than unilateral action. Canada's federalism was unusual in this respect. Few other national governments took such pains to consult the state or provincial governments in advance of major initiatives, or to accommodate the junior governments' preferences in the final arrangements.

Negotiations for one purpose or another and of a greater or lesser degree of formality were in progress almost constantly. As a rule, however, the most important negotiations were those that occurred in advance of the renewal of the five-year tax collection agreements. These discussions encompassed not only the tax agreements themselves, but also matters such as equalization payments and cost-sharing. In the intervals between the tax-agreement negotiations, formal federal-provincial conferences and meetings of first ministers or finance ministers provided venues for the introduction of new federal proposals and the airing of complaints about existing programs.

The federal government usually took the initiative. Ottawa proposed a given course of action, the provinces contemplated the proposal for a time, and then the negotiations—sometimes rough, sometimes smooth—proceeded until a compromise emerged that was acceptable, thought rarely altogether agreeable, to all parties.

The provinces became so accustomed to the pattern of prior consultation, negotiation, and compromise that when the federal government did act unilaterally their indignation was extreme. Federal leadership, in their view, was a matter of the initiation and coordination of policy; it did not properly extend to the imposition of policy. Taken to its extreme, as it sometimes was, this view implied that the federal government was at bottom an instrument of the provinces, a means by which they adjusted differences among themselves, rather than a policy maker in its own right.

The occasional passages of noisy contention between Ottawa and the provinces revealed the essential uncertainty of the federal government's constitutional position, particularly in the matters of taxation and social policy—an uncertainty that the generally temperate process of negotiation and compromise tended to disguise. Ottawa's readiness to negotiate may have been in some part a matter of good will, but it was also a consequence of the federal government's essential powerless to proceed in any other way.

The coyote in the cartoons can run in midair for quite some time before gravity claims him. In Ottawa's case, gravity was the constitution. Over time, the provinces' constitutional right to responsibility for social welfare spending, and to the revenue sources necessary to support that spending, gradually shifted the balance between the federal government and the provinces. The established pattern of negotiation and compromise was both a consequence of the constitutional reality and a means by which provincial primacy slowly asserted itself. With each successive compromise, the federal government retreated slightly from the position it had held before.

But if erosion of the federal government's position was inevitable, the extent and the timing of this process depended on circumstance. The first serious stirrings of provincial restlessness came in the late 1950s and early 1960s. Post-war reconstruction was complete; the provincial and municipal sectors had become, once again, collectively quite as large as the federal sector. The provinces felt that some degree of decentralization was in order, and Ottawa was accommodating—to a point.

One adjustment in this period was the replacement, in 1962, of the tax rental agreements by tax collection agreements. The federal government continued to determine the terms of income taxation and collect the tax, and it retained title to its existing share of the tax room. A portion of the nominal tax room was, however, "abated" to the provinces, which were allowed to apply tax rates of their own choosing to the abated portion, provided that the rate was expressed as a percentage of the tax calculated according to the federal formula. This change gave the provinces more freedom of action but left the taxes under federal control. Moreover, by providing an allowance for taxpayers who also paid income taxes in Quebec, the federal government recognized the fundamental right of the provinces to impose income taxes.

In 1972, the federal government made a further concession. It dropped the abatement of federal tax in favour of an actual withdrawal from an equivalent amount of tax room. This room passed into the hands of the provinces. The provincial rate was expressed as a percentage of the federal tax, as before, but the resulting tax now showed up on the form as an additional amount. Thus there were now two distinct taxing authorities in each province, though still, in most provinces, only one collection agency—the federal government.

By the early 1960s, the provinces were also growing resentful of the terms attached to the federal government's conditional transfers and shared-cost programs, which they felt distorted provincial priorities. They also felt that their increasing needs entitled them to a larger share—in the form of either more tax room or larger transfers—of the revenues collected by the federal government.

Again, Ottawa was accommodating. In 1964, it offered to allow any province to "contract out" of the joint arrangements—that is, to forgo the federal grants in exchange for an abatement of federal tax room to the province; the arrangement was supposed to be a temporary one, until some permanent financing arrangement agreeable to everyone was worked out. In the event, no new arrangement emerged and only Quebec took advantage of the contracting-out option. Prevailing opinion still preferred a strong federal structure to a weak one; it was felt that contracting-out would weaken federalism and, with it, the principle of national minimum standards. The provinces, apart from Quebec, were not prepared to go cut loose altogether from the conditional programs. In the absence of any immediate federal offer of a middle ground, they accepted the status quo.

One circumstance that strengthened Ottawa's position during the early post-war decades was prosperity. The long run of economic growth through the 1950s and 1960s and into the 1970s kept revenues high for both levels of government; they had little reason to compete for tax room. Federal transfers to the provinces for social programs were generous enough to temper provincial resentment of the federal conditions that came with the money. The provinces grumbled about federal high-handedness, but fiscal relations between the two levels of government continued, as a rule, to be characterized by negotiation rather than confrontation.

It remained to be seen what would happen if prosperity faltered. The test came with the oil-price crises of the 1970s.

The enormous rise in oil and gas prices in the 1970s, which enriched some provinces—particularly Alberta—and threw others into economic disarray, revealed the inherent brittleness of federal-provincial fiscal harmony. It also showed that Ottawa's ability to impose its will in fiscal matters had its limits even within its own exclusive sphere of indirect taxation. The federal government's unilateral introduction in 1980 of the national energy program, which gave Ottawa effective control over the pricing, production, distribution, and taxation of oil and natural gas, was the boldest display of federal authority in fiscal matters since the Second World War. Yet a series of equally unilateral provincial moves—cuts in oil production, court challenges, threats to sabotage the federal government's cherished scheme of repatriating the constitution—eventually obliged the federal government to compromise. The new constitution, introduced in 1982, changed the terms of the original document to allow the provinces to levy indirect taxes on natural resources.

This was not the first retreat on Ottawa's part occasioned by the oil-price issue. Alberta's revenues from oil and gas production were so enormous that they made nonsense out of the existing equalization formula: a calculation of entitlements that took Alberta's resource revenue into account would have given equalization transfers to every province except Alberta, including well-to-do provinces such as Ontario. In order to avoid this absurd outcome, which was beyond its means in any case, Ottawa introduced legislation in 1978 that denied equalization payments to any province whose average per capita income was above the national average. In 1982, after lengthy and ultimately fruitless wrangling with the provinces, the federal government unilaterally replaced the old all-province standard for the calculation of payments with a "five-province" standard that eliminated both the richest and the four poorest provinces from the formula.

The new scheme was seen as federal retreat in two senses. In the first place, Ottawa's total outlay for equalization would be smaller under the new formula than it would have been under the old one. A more fundamental objection was that the new formula was a step backward from the broad inclusiveness and evenhandedness of the original principle of equalization. Alberta's windfall may have made the principle untenable, but it was difficult not to notice that the federal government was no longer exerting its leadership in order to expand its commitments to the provinces and to the ideal of minimum national standards. Instead, it was unilaterally reducing its commitments.

Alberta's good fortune was an episode in the larger event of the worldwide oil price rise, which created inflationary pressures on government budgets everywhere. For Ottawa and the provinces, one common source of budgetary woe was the shared-cost programs for post-secondary education, medical care, hospitals, and welfare. Since the federal government matched provincial expenditures in the latter two areas dollar for dollar, the provinces found it difficult to resist pressures to channel their own spending into the joint programs. Thus provincial spending drove the shared-cost programs; Ottawa could only look on helplessly and pay. The provinces, however, had an additional grievance: in order to receive the money, they had to spend it in accordance with conditions laid down by Ottawa, though constitutionally the spending areas in question were provincial domains.

The solution was the replacement in 1977 of the shared-cost programs by the established programs financing (EPF) formula. The new formula consolidated existing federal payments for post-secondary education, medical care, and hospitalization and provided that one half of the compensation was to be in the form of tax points, which would grow as collections in each province grew, and cash payments, which would be linked to the growth of GNP (later, GDP). The provinces would be able to distribute the federal compensation among the three program areas more or less as they wished. Thus Ottawa achieved more control over the level of spending on social programs at the price of a significant loss of control over how the money was spent.

This outcome represented a significant shift in the balance between the federal government and the provinces. Moreover, it prepared the way for further erosion of federal control over social programs. In 1982, a still cash-strapped federal government changed the EPF formula: the value of the tax points would now be deducted from the total federal compensation, as now determined by GNP growth, and the cash payment would be equal to what remained. Since the value of the tax points grew more rapidly than did GNP, the cash payment would inevitably become smaller and smaller.

The federal government did not feel that its contribution to social spending was diminished by these arrangements, since in its view the tax points conceded to the province under the EPF formula were still federal property. Ottawa was, in effect, loaning the tax points to the provinces year by year. Thus it continued to take these tax points into account in calculating its total transfers to the provinces.

The provinces saw the various transfers of tax points in another light. In their view, the federal government was simply returning what had never really belonged to it, since the provinces had as much right to a share of the income tax fields as Ottawa had. In practical terms, the provinces had the better of the argument: the tax points were now in their hands, and they were not likely to give them back. Moreover, as the cash payments under EPF diminished, so did Ottawa's ability to enforce the conditions it attached to the payments.

The late 1970s were the watershed years for the federal government. The economic recovery program it introduced in 1978 established a pattern of retrenchment in the face of rising deficits and declining revenues that would continue into the 1990s. Instead of initiating new "national" social programs, Ottawa would hereafter seek ways in which to reduce its disbursements for existing programs. Federal-provincial cooperation under federal leadership yielded increasingly to federal-provincial competition for diminished resources.

Federal leadership, from the provinces' point of view, had two principal aspects: federal willingness to shower the provinces with money, and federal insistence that much of the money be spent in ways that did not necessary agree with provincial priorities. The provinces complained equally about the decline of federal leadership in the first sense and its persistence in the second sense. Ottawa, for its part, was as eager to enforce national standards as it was to reduce its expenditure. In 1984, for example, the federal government reduced EPF payments to the provinces in order to compel them to outlaw extra billing and user fees for medical services. Within a few years of this episode, however, the dwindling of the payments—a process accelerated by Ottawa's imposition of a sequence of caps on their rate of growth—had largely eliminated the deterrent value of federal threats to withhold them.

The career of the goods and services tax (GST) provided another example of Ottawa's declining ability to secure provincial cooperation. When Ottawa introduced the tax in 1991, it confidently supposed that the provinces would hasten to harmonize their retail sales tax bases with the more inclusive federal base and accept federal administration of the whole, on the pattern of the collection agreements for income taxes. Initially, only Quebec responded to the federal offer—on its own terms. Years later, in 1996, three of the Atlantic provinces agreed to harmonize their taxes with the GST. The larger and richer provinces stayed aloof.

Also in 1996, the federal government extended block funding under the EPF formula to include the last of the major shared-cost programs, the Canada assistance plan. The new program—the Canadian health and social transfer (CHST)—was another retreat from the principle of national minimum standards in the provision of social services, all the more so because the cash portion of the CHST transfers, like those of the EPF transfers, would diminish over time.

This is being written in 1997, a symmetrical 50 years since the first of the peacetime tax rental agreements. These agreements and their successors, the tax collection agreements, gave the federal government a command over the country's fiscal resources that allowed it to undertake a generation-long campaign to realize a wide variety of ambitious "national" goals: a reduction in regional economic disparities, universal access to public services of a high minimum standard, and an extension of the definition of "public services" to include many matters that had previously been left to the private sector, non-profit and otherwise.

Fifty years later, the major strategic devices that Ottawa deployed in order to realize these goals are still in working order. Equalization, conditional grants, and the tax collection agreements themselves, though diminished in scope and therefore diminished as well in their power to realize the goals for which they were designed, continue to help bind the provinces together under the aegis of the federal government. Nevertheless, it is clear that the "heroic" period of fiscal federalism is over, at least for the foreseeable future.

This result, it has been suggested here, was probably inevitable. The framers of the constitution failed to see how the twentieth century would unwind; therefore they placed what would prove to be the most important areas of government activity entirely outside of the federal government's direct control. This constitutional irony was bound in the long run to work against Ottawa and in favour of the provinces. But the federal government's diminished leadership has also been a product of circumstance. The 1970s were for governments everywhere what the 1930s had been for private enterprise. Inflation, economic stagnation, rising deficits, and rising taxes consumed the prestige of government in the 1970s even as depression and massive unemployment had consumed the prestige of the private sector 40 years earlier. If the solution then had been more government, the solution now seemed to be less government. The ideal of cooperation mediated by a strong central authority yielded to an ideal of competition mildly regulated by more or less localized authorities. Centralization gave way to decentralization, intervention to non-intervention.

The politicians who presided in Ottawa during the 1980s and 1990s were not aloof from this shift in opinion, and the federal government's loss of leadership was not entirely involuntary. Nor did the devolution of responsibilities to the provinces stop there. By the mid-1990s, several provinces had started shifting both revenues and responsibilities downward to local governments. Since the responsibilities tended to be larger than the revenues, municipalities in their turn were obliged to turn over some of the established functions of government to private enterprise and private charity.

Thus the end was like the beginning.

But only to a point. We are, as yet, a long way from a return to 1867. Nor would it be wise to assume that the future will be like the present. It can be said, however, that the future of federal-provincial fiscal relations depends on the outcome of the larger constitutional debate. Given the present state of affairs, any revision of the constitution drawn up in the near future is not likely to strengthen the federal government's role in the federation. On the other hand, the constitutional debate has been in progress for a long time; by the time it is resolved, if it is ever resolved, circumstances may have changed again and the climate of opinion with them.

Appendix

Federal Transfers to the Provinces, 1942-43 to 1995-96

Table A.1 Federal Transfers to the Provinces, 1942-43

	PEI	NS	NB	Que.	Ont.	Man.	Sask.	Alta.	BC	Yukon & NWT	Total
				thousands of dollars							
Specific-purpose transfers											
Health	0.2	1.1	0.9	6.1	6.1	1.3	1.5	1.2	1.5	—	19.9
Old age pensions	208.6	1,948.1	1,606.4	7,048.9	9,633.7	2,093.4	2,043.4	1,833.6	2,443.2	2.0	28,861.2
Blind persons' pensions	15.2	107.4	129.6	379.1	266.4	59.8	58.0	41.0	58.4	—	1,114.8
Other welfare	—	—	—	125.8	2.8	16.3	—	35.2	—	—	180.1
Education	9.5	16.2	24.5	98.5	4.2	32.1	24.1	36.8	49.0	—	295.0
Other	—	—	—	55.3	—	—	—	—	—	—	55.3
	233.4	2,072.8	1,761.5	7,713.8	9,913.1	2,202.9	2,127.1	1,947.8	2,552.0	2.0	30,526.3
Joint war programs	—	208.3	274.3	1,187.5	2,863.7	373.1	524.1	578.8	1,107.4	—	7,122.1
Total specific-purpose transfers[a]	233.4	2,281.1	2,035.8	8,901.3	12,776.8	2,576.0	2,651.2	2,526.6	3,659.4	2.0	37,648.4
General-purpose transfers											
Statutory subsidies	381.9	709.0	735.6	2,873.9	3,173.6	1,722.5	2,052.2	1,801.0	1,040.4	—	14,490.1
Current tax agreements	694.3	3,347.7	3,650.1	21,508.7	27,597.5	6,105.4	5,699.2	3,479.8	13,858.7	—	85,941.6
Gasoline tax guarantee	—	84.1	470.4	577.3	1,529.0	5,612.2	—	—	—	—	8,273.0
Total general-purpose transfers	1,160.3	4,527.1	4,963.0	25,911.6	36,383.3	7,827.9	7,751.4	5,280.8	14,899.1	—	108,704.7
Total transfers	1,393.7	6,808.2	6,998.8	34,812.9	49,160.1	10,403.9	10,402.6	7,807.4	18,558.5	2.0	146,353.1
Total provincial revenue ($ million)	2.0	16.3	11.7	96.9	108.0	18.6	24.2	25.5	40.8	—	344.0

—Nil or less than $500.

[a] Total includes $4,700 not allocated by province.

Sources: Public Accounts and Canadian Tax Foundation, *Canadian Fiscal Facts, Principal Statistics of Canadian Public Finance* (Toronto: the foundation, 1957).

Table A.2 Federal Transfers to the Provinces, 1943-44

	PEI	NS	NB	Que.	Ont.	Man.	Sask.	Alta.	BC	Yukon & NWT	Total
				thousands of dollars							
Specific-purpose transfers											
Health	1.3	9.6	7.5	64.9	46.4	9.4	12.2	10.2	9.1	—	170.7
Old age pensions	268.5	2,137.2	1,732.7	8,535.4	10,310.6	2,002.6	2,352.4	2,062.8	2,791.0	2.4	32,195.6
Blind persons' pensions	19.5	114.0	136.4	452.1	284.0	60.2	64.0	47.9	65.8	—	1,244.0
Other welfare	—	—	—	68.4	—	1.4	15.6	0.3	—	—	85.6
Education	6.8	14.5	22.1	90.4	7.0	28.5	25.4	21.8	42.7	—	259.2
	296.1	2,275.3	1,898.7	9,211.1	10,648.0	2,102.1	2,469.7	2,143.0	2,908.8	2.4	33,955.1
Joint war programs	18.6	242.0	284.7	1,582.6	2,211.1	302.5	432.9	411.2	675.9	—	6,163.6
Total specific-purpose transfers[a]	314.7	2,517.3	2,183.4	10,793.7	12,859.1	2,404.6	2,902.6	2,554.2	3,584.5	2.4	40,118.7
General-purpose transfers											
Statutory subsidies	381.9	705.1	732.4	2,866.6	3,155.0	1,717.9	2,092.2	1,794.8	1,003.4	—	14,449.4
Current tax agreements	680.6	2,911.1	3,650.1	20,316.8	29,182.3	5,331.4	5,800.7	3,759.0	12,046.2	—	83,678.3
Gasoline tax guarantee	46.9	696.5	399.2	1,863.4	7,440.3	334.2	496.0	—	480.1	—	11,756.6
Total general-purpose transfers	1,109.4	4,312.7	4,781.7	25,046.8	39,777.6	7,383.5	8,388.9	5,553.8	13,529.7	—	109,884.3
Total transfers	1,424.1	6,830.0	6,965.1	35,840.5	52,636.7	9,788.1	11,291.5	8,108.0	17,114.2	2.4	150,003.0
Total provincial revenue ($ million)	2.0	16.8	12.3	97.5	117.6	19.3	29.6	27.0	39.0	—	361.0

—Nil or less than $500.

[a]Total contains $2,400 unallocated by province.

Sources: Same as table A.1.

Table A.3 Federal Transfers to the Provinces, 1944-45

	PEI	NS	NB	Que.	Ont.	Man.	Sask.	Alta.	BC	Yukon & NWT	Total
				thousands of dollars							
Specific-purpose transfers											
Health	1.4	8.8	9.1	64.7	52.2	10.6	12.9	9.7	10.5	—	179.9
Old age pensions	311.6	2,807.9	2,391.0	10,386.1	12,291.1	2,879.9	2,794.9	2,401.4	3,236.0	3.1	39,503.0
Blind persons' pensions	22.0	140.0	161.6	530.2	331.2	85.1	74.2	54.3	73.3	—	1,472.0
Education	8.2	15.7	22.3	168.2	6.0	26.8	22.1	16.3	41.4	—	327.0
Other	0.2	0.3	0.4	45.1	—	0.4	—	—	—	—	46.3
	343.4	2,972.7	2,584.4	11,194.3	12,680.6	3,002.8	2,904.1	2,481.7	3,361.2	3.1	41,528.3
Joint war programs	17.4	235.5	188.1	927.2	1,078.8	142.4	329.4	342.4	276.8	—	3,537.9
Total specific-purpose transfers	360.8	3,208.2	2,772.5	12,121.5	13,759.4	3,145.2	3,233.5	2,824.1	3,638.0	3.1	45,066.2
General-purpose transfers											
Statutory subsidies	381.9	705.1	732.4	2,866.6	3,155.0	1,717.0	2,028.6	1,855.2	1,003.4	—	14,445.3
Current tax agreements	701.9	2,911.1	3,650.1	20,319.5	28,327.8	5,410.2	5,817.7	3,794.6	12,044.1	—	82,977.1
Gasoline tax guarantee	19.0	480.0	359.0	778.6	7,694.9	275.0	125.8	—	624.6	—	10,356.9
Total general-purpose transfers	1,102.8	4,096.2	4,741.5	23,964.7	39,177.7	7,402.2	7,972.1	5,649.8	13,672.1	—	107,779.3
Total transfers	1,463.6	7,304.4	7,514.0	36,086.2	52,937.1	10,547.4	11,205.6	8,473.9	17,310.1	3.1	152,845.5
Total provincial revenue ($ million)	2.2	17.6	12.8	100.7	115.7	20.3	30.3	28.6	41.0	—	369.2

—Nil or less than $500.

Sources: Same as table A.1.

Table A.4 Federal Transfers to the Provinces, 1945-46

thousands of dollars

	PEI	NS	NB	Que.	Ont.	Man.	Sask.	Alta.	BC	Yukon & NWT	Total
Specific-purpose transfers											
Health	1.6	8.0	7.8	58.6	55.3	10.7	12.5	12.6	13.0	—	180.0
Old age pensions	322.4	2,914.0	2,498.9	10,823.3	13,129.8	2,684.1	2,903.0	2,526.2	3,485.9	3.6	41,291.2
Blind persons' pensions	22.8	142.7	162.0	568.4	341.6	79.5	76.8	57.6	75.4	—	1,526.7
Education	6.3	16.6	28.1	79.7	75.7	26.7	37.3	14.5	41.6	—	326.6
Other	0.2	0.5	0.4	187.0	—	0.1	—	—	—	—	187.9
	353.2	3,081.7	2,697.2	11,717.2	13,602.4	2,801.0	3,029.6	2,610.9	3,615.9	3.6	43,512.8
Joint war programs	67.1	349.7	451.8	1,066.1	2,865.2	350.6	470.7	543.2	337.5	—	6,501.7
Total specific-purpose transfers	420.3	3,431.4	3,149.0	12,783.3	16,467.6	3,151.6	3,500.3	3,154.1	3,953.4	3.6	50,014.5
General-purpose transfers											
Statutory subsidies	381.9	705.1	732.4	2,866.6	3,155.0	1,717.3	2,049.8	1,835.1	1,003.4	—	14,446.6
Current tax agreements[a]	701.9	2,911.1	3,650.1	20,199.3	28,269.7	5,547.8	5,826.8	15,189.3	12,046.6	—	94,342.7
Gasoline tax guarantee	—	391.0	83.6	—	2,440.8	276.3	11.0	—	506.5	—	3,709.1
Total general-purpose transfers	1,083.8	4,007.2	4,466.1	23,065.9	33,865.5	7,541.4	7,887.6	17,024.4	13,556.5	—	112,498.4
Total transfers	1,504.1	7,438.6	7,615.1	35,849.2	50,333.1	10,693.0	11,387.9	20,178.5	17,509.9	3.6	162,512.9
Total provincial revenue ($ million)	3.0	19.0	16.0	119.0	134.0	22.0	35.0	34.0	47.0	—	429.0

—Nil or less than $500.

[a] Includes an adjustment to Alberta.

Sources: Public Accounts and M.C. Urquhart and K.A.H. Buckley, eds., *Historical Statistics of Canada* (Toronto: Macmillan, 1965).

Table A.5 Federal Transfers to the Provinces, 1946-47

	PEI	NS	NB	Que.	Ont.	Man.	Sask.	Alta.	BC	Yukon & NWT	Total
					thousands of dollars						
Specific-purpose transfers											
Health	5.4	15.9	12.6	62.2	72.3	15.7	18.7	17.1	20.0	—	240.0
Old age pensions	350.8	3,093.2	2,649.0	11,466.9	13,886.4	2,826.7	3,085.2	2,699.4	3,767.6	4.2	43,829.6
Blind persons' pensions	24.2	147.5	166.4	605.8	359.9	86.6	81.9	62.2	80.4	0.3	1,615.1
Education	162.0	1,000.0	767.8	2,435.3	5,555.6	638.8	787.8	1,274.9	830.9	—	13,453.0
Agriculture	26.0	81.9	88.0	355.2	137.1	18.1	34.8	53.0	43.6	—	837.6
Other	—	17.6	7.5	1,100.7	—	112.5	24.9	449.9	9.3	—	1,722.5
Total specific-purpose transfers	568.4	4,356.1	3,691.3	16,026.1	20,011.2	3,698.4	4,033.3	4,556.5	4,751.8	4.5	61,697.9
General-purpose transfers											
Statutory subsidies	381.9	705.1	732.4	2,866.6	3,155.0	1,709.0	2,034.7	1,794.6	1,003.4	—	14,382.8
Tax agreements—1942	743.3	4,085.5	5,187.6	20,586.1	28,546.5	5,571.4	5,818.2	5,809.2	12,038.5	—	88,386.3
Tax agreements—1947	350.8	2,805.0	2,838.4	—	—	—	—	—	—	—	5,994.2
Total general-purpose transfers	1,475.9	7,595.6	8,758.4	23,452.7	31,701.5	7,280.4	7,852.9	7,603.8	13,041.9	—	108,763.3
Total transfers	2,044.3	11,951.7	12,449.7	39,478.8	51,712.7	10,978.8	11,886.2	12,160.3	17,793.7	4.5	170,461.2
Total provincial revenue ($ million)	4.0	22.0	20.0	151.0	151.0	23.0	37.0	36.0	58.0	—	502.0

—Nil or less than $500.

Sources: Same as table A.4.

Table A.6 Federal Transfers to the Provinces, 1947-48

	PEI	NS	NB	Que.	Ont.	Man.	Sask.	Alta.	BC	Yukon & NWT	Total
	thousands of dollars										
Specific-purpose transfers											
Health	4.8	14.0	11.5	65.4	68.2	14.1	16.4	17.2	20.0	—	231.7
Old age pensions	478.9	3,943.6	3,634.3	14,714.3	17,999.9	3,727.4	3,837.0	3,466.1	5,171.0	5.8	56,978.4
Blind persons' pensions ...	29.4	181.8	217.4	801.7	464.9	115.0	107.6	81.3	108.6	0.4	2,108.0
Education	51.2	625.4	469.5	3,564.3	2,175.0	502.2	512.2	613.6	491.3	—	6,004.6
Agriculture	25.1	86.0	94.2	371.3	111.3	38.6	35.3	48.7	29.1	—	839.5
Other	—	8.7	2.2	615.1	14.5	172.7	65.1	918.0	28.6	—	1,824.9
Total specific-purpose transfers	589.4	4,859.5	4,429.1	20,132.2	20,833.8	4,570.0	4,573.6	5,144.9	5,848.6	6.2	70,987.1
General-purpose transfers											
Statutory subsidies[a]	656.9	2,005.1	1,632.4	2,866.6	3,155.0	1,722.2	10,079.7	10,272.8	1,003.4	—	33,394.1
Prior tax agreements	—	—	—	20,586.1	28,964.0	3,655.7	3,132.8	3,278.8	3,383.9	—	63,001.3
Current tax agreement	1,226.4	7,525.0	5,866.4	—	—	9,496.0	10,261.0	9,903.9	15,217.0	—	59,495.6
Total general-purpose transfers	1,883.3	9,530.2	7,498.7	23,452.7	32,119.0	14,873.9	23,473.4	23,455.5	19,604.3	—	155,891.0
Total transfers	2,472.7	14,389.7	11,927.8	43,584.9	52,952.8	19,443.9	28,047.0	28,600.4	25,452.9	6.2	226,878.1
Total provincial revenue ($ million)	5.0	32.0	29.0	194.0	223.0	34.0	53.0	48.0	72.0	—	690.0

—Nil or less than $500.

[a] Figures for Saskatchewan and Alberta include special payments of $8.0 million.

Sources: Same as table A.4.

Table A.7 Federal Transfers to the Provinces, 1948-49

	PEI	NS	NB	Que.	Ont.	Man.	Sask.	Alta.	BC	Yukon & NWT	Total
				thousands of dollars							
Specific-purpose transfers											
General health grants	155.8	414.7	453.6	2,557.1	1,408.8	436.3	645.6	297.5	1,159.0	—	7,528.4
Old age pensions	593.1	4,658.6	3,960.4	16,273.9	20,292.5	4,127.1	4,115.3	3,840.2	6,363.5	7.7	64,232.2
Blind persons' pensions	30.9	224.5	263.0	939.0	564.3	134.3	124.1	104.7	146.9	0.4	2,532.1
Other health and social services[a]	5.5	14.1	11.9	64.3	69.2	18.2	17.0	34.2	5,130.1	—	5,435.2
Vocational training	63.6	291.4	331.7	2,144.4	1,352.3	294.7	663.4	536.0	490.5	—	6,168.1
Other	5.2	89.4	99.0	536.2	128.7	214.3	83.0	218.5	4,584.6	—	5,958.7
Total specific-purpose transfers	854.1	5,692.7	5,119.6	22,514.9	23,815.8	5,224.9	5,648.9	5,031.1	17,874.6	8.1	91,853.7
General-purpose transfers											
Statutory subsidies	656.9	2,005.1	1,632.4	2,866.6	3,155.0	1,715.6	2,041.5	2,018.0	1,003.4	—	17,094.7
Current tax agreements	1,769.7	10,673.0	8,477.6	—	—	13,409.2	14,069.5	14,021.4	21,966.6	—	84,386.9
Total general-purpose transfers	2,426.6	12,678.1	10,110.0	2,866.6	3,155.0	15,124.8	16,111.0	16,039.4	22,970.0	—	101,481.6
Total transfers	3,280.7	18,370.8	15,229.6	25,381.5	26,970.8	20,349.7	21,759.4	21,070.5	40,844.6	8.1	193,335.3
Total provincial revenue ($ million)	5.0	33.0	28.0	203.0	220.0	36.0	56.0	63.0	101.0	—	745.0

—Nil or less than $500.

[a] Total includes $70,829 not allocated by province.

Sources: Same as table A.4.

Table A.8 Federal Transfers to the Provinces, 1949-50

	Nfld.	PEI	NS	NB	Que.	Ont.	Man.	Sask.	Alta.	BC	Yukon & NWT	Total
					millions of dollars							
Specific-purpose transfers												
General health grants	0.7	0.2	0.7	0.5	5.0	4.1	0.8	1.3	1.4	1.3	—	15.7
Old age pensions	2.2	0.9	6.1	5.1	22.3	27.9	5.6	5.4	5.2	9.1	—	89.7
Blind persons' pensions	—	—	0.3	0.4	1.3	0.8	0.2	0.2	0.1	0.2	—	3.5
Other health and social services	—	—	—	—	—	—	—	—	—	0.1	—	0.3
Vocational training	—	—	0.5	0.6	0.9	1.2	0.3	0.4	0.5	0.6	—	5.1
Agriculture	—	—	0.1	0.1	0.7	0.1	—	—	—	—	—	1.1
Other	—	—	—	0.1	0.1	—	0.4	0.1	0.2	0.1	—	1.0
Total specific-purpose transfers	2.9	1.2	7.6	6.7	30.3	34.1	7.3	7.3	7.5	11.4	—	116.4
General-purpose transfers												
Statutory subsidies	1.9	0.7	2.0	1.6	2.9	3.2	1.8	2.1	2.1	1.0	—	19.2
Current tax agreements	4.9	1.7	9.6	7.6	—	—	10.7	12.6	11.9	17.8	—	76.9
Special grant	6.5	—	—	—	—	—	—	—	—	—	—	6.5
Share of utilities tax	—	—	0.2	0.1	0.8	0.4	0.3	—	0.6	0.7	—	3.1
Total general-purpose transfers	13.3	2.4	11.8	9.4	3.7	3.5	12.8	14.7	14.5	19.5	—	105.6
Total transfers	16.2	3.6	19.4	16.1	34.0	37.6	20.1	22.0	22.0	30.9	—	221.9
Total provincial revenue	18.0	5.0	34.0	30.0	207.0	236.0	38.0	61.0	88.0	124.0	—	841.0

—Nil or less than $500.

Sources: Same as table A.4.

Table A.9 Federal Transfers to the Provinces, 1950-51

	Nfld.	PEI	NS	NB	Que.	Ont.	Man.	Sask.	Alta.	BC	Yukon & NWT	Total
					millions of dollars							
Specific-purpose transfers												
General health grants	0.7	0.2	1.0	0.6	6.1	4.5	1.1	1.4	1.5	1.7	—	18.9
Old age pensions	3.8	0.9	6.6	5.4	24.5	30.1	6.0	5.8	5.9	10.3	—	99.3
Blind persons' pensions	0.1	0.3	—	0.4	1.4	0.8	0.2	0.2	0.2	0.2	—	3.9
Other health and social services[a]	—	—	—	—	1.2	—	12.5	—	—	—	—	13.9
Vocational training	0.1	0.1	0.4	0.2	0.9	1.2	0.4	0.5	0.5	0.2	—	4.4
Trans-Canada Highway	1.0	0.1	—	—	—	2.7	0.3	0.4	0.2	2.5	—	7.2
Other	—	0.1	0.1	0.1	0.7	0.3	0.3	0.1	0.2	0.2	—	2.1
Total specific-purpose transfers	5.7	1.8	8.2	6.7	34.8	39.6	20.7	8.4	8.4	15.1	—	149.7
General-purpose transfers												
Statutory subsidies	1.5	0.7	2.0	1.6	2.9	3.2	1.8	2.1	2.1	1.0	—	18.7
Current tax agreements	7.2	2.1	11.4	10.1	—	—	14.0	15.4	14.8	19.2	—	94.1
Special grant	6.5	—	—	—	—	—	—	—	—	—	—	6.5
Share of utilities tax	—	—	0.2	0.1	0.4	0.5	0.2	—	0.6	0.9	—	2.9
Total general-purpose transfers	15.3	2.7	13.5	11.9	3.3	3.6	15.9	17.5	17.5	21.0	—	122.2
Special payments to territories											0.2	0.2
Total transfers	20.9	4.5	21.7	18.7	38.1	43.3	36.6	25.9	25.8	36.2	0.3	272.1
Total provincial revenue	21.0	5.0	36.0	32.0	239.0	266.0	41.0	67.0	105.0	139.0	—	951.0

—Nil or less than $50,000.

[a] Total includes $124,100 not allocated by province.

Sources: Same as table A.4.

Table A.10　Federal Transfers to the Provinces, 1951-52

	Nfld.	PEI	NS	NB	Que.	Ont.	Man.	Sask.	Alta.	BC	Yukon & NWT	Total
					millions of dollars							
Specific-purpose transfers												
General health grants	0.7	0.2	1.1	1.1	7.3	7.1	1.1	1.5	1.6	2.5	—	24.3
Old age pensions	3.1	0.7	5.0	4.2	19.1	23.3	4.6	4.5	4.6	8.1	—	77.2
Blind persons' pensions	0.1	—	0.3	0.3	1.1	0.7	0.2	0.1	0.1	0.2	—	3.0
Old age assistance	—	—	0.1	0.2	0.7	0.7	0.1	0.1	0.1	0.3	—	2.3
Blind persons' allowances	—	—	0.1	0.1	0.3	0.1	—	—	—	—	—	0.7
Vocational training	0.1	—	0.4	0.3	1.0	1.3	0.3	0.5	0.4	0.3	—	4.4
Trans-Canada Highway	1.0	0.4	—	1.1	—	5.0	0.8	0.9	0.9	2.6	—	12.8
Other	—	0.1	0.4	0.2	1.9	1.1	0.3	0.2	0.3	1.5	—	5.9
Total specific-purpose transfers	5.0	1.5	7.3	7.3	31.3	39.3	7.4	7.9	8.2	15.4	—	130.7
General-purpose transfers												
Statutory subsidies	1.6	0.7	2.1	1.7	3.3	3.6	1.8	2.0	2.1	1.3	—	20.1
Current tax agreements	7.7	2.2	12.5	9.4	—	—	14.6	16.5	14.8	19.1	—	96.9
Special grant	6.5	—	—	—	—	—	—	—	—	—	—	6.5
Share of utilities tax	0.1	—	0.1	0.2	0.6	0.6	0.3	—	0.8	1.0	—	3.7
Total general-purpose transfers	15.9	2.8	14.7	11.3	35.1	4.3	16.7	18.6	17.7	21.4	—	127.2
Special payments to territories											0.2	0.2
Total transfers	20.9	4.4	22.0	18.6	35.1	43.6	24.1	26.5	25.9	36.8	0.2	258.1
Total provincial revenue	25.0	6.0	39.0	41.0	277.0	304.0	46.0	75.0	106.0	157.0	—	1,076.0

—Nil or less than $50,000.

Sources: Same as table A.4.

Table A.11 Federal Transfers to the Provinces, 1952-53

	Nfld.	PEI	NS	NB	Que.	Ont.	Man.	Sask.	Alta.	BC	Yukon & NWT	Total
					millions of dollars							
Specific-purpose transfers												
General health grants	0.8	0.2	1.3	1.2	8.0	8.3	1.5	2.0	2.1	2.0	—	27.3
Old age assistance	0.8	0.1	0.9	1.1	6.9	4.6	1.0	1.0	1.0	1.7	—	19.1
Blind persons' allowances	0.1	—	0.3	0.3	1.1	0.6	0.2	0.1	0.1	0.2	—	3.0
Vocational training	0.1	0.4	0.2	0.2	1.0	2.1	0.2	0.3	0.6	0.2	—	5.0
Trans-Canada Highway	0.6	0.4	—	0.6	—	4.1	1.0	1.7	2.8	2.7	—	14.0
Other	—	0.1	0.2	0.1	0.8	1.7	0.3	0.2	0.3	1.7	—	5.5
Total specific-purpose transfers	2.5	0.8	2.9	3.5	17.8	21.4	4.2	5.3	6.9	8.5	—	73.8
General-purpose transfers												
Statutory subsidies	1.6	0.7	2.1	1.7	3.3	3.6	1.8	2.0	2.1	1.3	—	20.1
Previous tax arrangements	2.1	0.7	2.2	2.5	—	—	2.9	2.5	5.0	5.8	—	23.8
Current tax agreements	10.7	3.3	18.1	15.0	—	123.3	23.1	23.6	27.3	40.4	—	284.8
Share of utilities tax	0.1	—	0.2	0.2	0.9	0.5	0.4	—	1.0	1.1	—	4.4
Special grant	5.7	—	—	—	—	—	—	—	—	—	—	5.7
Total general-purpose transfers	20.1	4.6	22.5	19.4	4.2	127.4	28.2	28.2	35.4	48.6	—	338.7
Special payments to territories											0.6	0.6
Total transfers	22.6	5.5	25.4	22.9	22.0	148.8	32.4	33.5	42.4	57.1	0.6	413.1
Total provincial revenue	32.0	7.0	47.0	47.0	285.0	365.0	55.0	91.0	144.0	185.0	—	1,258.0

—Nil or less than $50,000.
Sources: Same as table A.4.

Table A.12 Federal Transfers to the Provinces and Local Governments, 1953-54

	Nfld.	PEI	NS	NB	Que.	Ont.	Man.	Sask.	Alta.	BC	Yukon & NWT	Total
					millions of dollars							
Provinces												
Specific-purpose transfers												
General health grants	0.9	0.2	1.5	1.5	9.6	7.3	1.7	1.9	1.8	2.6	—	29.2
Old age assistance	0.9	0.1	1.0	1.2	7.2	4.7	1.1	1.0	1.1	1.9	—	20.3
Blind persons' allowances	0.1	—	0.3	0.3	1.1	0.6	0.1	0.1	0.1	0.2	—	2.9
Vocational training	0.1	0.1	0.2	0.2	0.9	1.3	0.2	0.2	0.5	0.3	—	4.1
Trans-Canada Highway	0.9	0.1	—	0.3	—	2.5	1.5	2.1	2.7	3.3	—	13.4
Agriculture and other natural resources	—	0.1	0.2	1.1	0.4	0.8	0.2	0.1	0.1	1.0	—	3.9
Other	—	—	—	—	0.2	0.4	0.1	0.1	0.1	0.2	—	1.2
Total specific-purpose transfers[a]	2.8	0.7	3.2	4.7	19.3	17.6	5.0	5.5	6.5	9.5	0.5	75.6
General-purpose transfers												
Statutory subsidies	1.6	0.7	2.1	1.7	3.3	3.6	1.8	2.0	2.1	1.3	—	20.1
Current tax agreements	11.8	3.7	19.5	16.2	—	134.4	25.0	25.3	29.8	43.5	—	309.2
Share of utilities tax	0.2	—	0.3	0.3	2.1	1.1	0.6	—	1.4	0.9	—	6.8
Special grant	4.8	—	—	—	—	—	—	—	—	—	—	4.8
Total general-purpose transfers	18.4	4.3	21.8	18.1	5.4	139.2	27.4	27.3	33.3	45.7	—	341.0
Special payments to territories											0.6	0.6
Total transfers to provinces	21.2	5.0	25.1	22.8	24.7	156.7	32.3	32.9	39.8	55.1	1.1	417.1
Local governments												
Grants in lieu of taxes	—	—	0.5	0.2	0.1	2.2	—	—	0.1	0.1	—	3.4
Other	—	—	—	—	0.1	0.5	0.1	—	0.1	0.1	—	0.9
Total transfers to local governments	—	—	0.5	0.2	0.2	2.7	0.2	—	0.2	0.2	—	4.3
Total transfers	21.2	5.0	25.5	23.0	25.2	159.5	32.6	32.9	40.1	55.4	1.1	421.4
Total provincial revenue	32.0	8.0	49.0	49.0	299.0	371.0	56.0	98.0	186.0	186.0	—	1,334.0

—Nil or less than $50,000.

[a] Total includes payments of $118,300 for education not allocated by province.

Sources: Same as table A.4.

Table A.13 Federal Transfers to the Provinces and Local Government, 1954-55

	Nfld.	PEI	NS	NB	Que.	Ont.	Man.	Sask.	Alta.	BC	Yukon & NWT	Total
					millions of dollars							
Provinces												
Specific-purpose transfers												
General health grants	0.8	0.3	1.5	1.5	9.6	8.0	2.0	2.6	2.3	2.9	—	31.6
Old age assistance	0.9	0.1	1.1	1.3	7.4	4.9	1.1	1.1	1.2	1.9	—	20.9
Blind persons' allowances	0.1	—	0.2	0.3	1.0	0.6	0.1	0.1	0.1	0.2	—	2.9
Disabled persons' allowances	—	—	—	—	—	0.4	—	—	—	—	—	0.4
Vocational training	0.1	—	0.4	0.2	0.6	1.1	0.2	0.3	0.5	0.3	—	3.7
Trans-Canada Highway	2.0	—	0.1	0.5	—	6.3	2.1	2.0	1.8	3.4	—	18.1
Other	0.1	0.1	0.2	0.5	0.3	1.2	0.2	0.2	0.3	1.3	—	4.6
Total specific-purpose transfers[a]	4.1	0.5	3.5	4.3	19.0	22.5	5.8	6.3	6.1	9.9	0.1	82.2
General-purpose transfers												
Statutory subsidies	1.6	0.7	2.1	1.7	3.3	3.6	1.9	2.1	2.2	1.3	—	20.4
Current tax arrangements	12.5	3.9	20.5	17.0	—	142.7	26.2	26.6	31.8	46.1	—	327.4
Share of utilities tax	0.2	—	0.3	0.2	1.7	1.3	—	—	1.7	1.8	—	7.3
Special grant	4.0	—	—	—	—	—	—	—	—	—	—	4.0
Total general-purpose transfers	18.3	4.6	22.8	18.9	5.0	147.7	28.1	28.8	35.7	49.1	—	359.0
Special payments to territories	—	—	—	—	—	—	—	—	—	—	0.6	0.6
Total transfers to provinces	22.4	5.1	26.4	23.2	23.9	170.2	33.8	35.1	41.8	59.1	1.0	443.0
Local governments												
Grants in lieu of taxes	—	—	0.6	0.2	0.3	2.0	—	—	0.1	0.1	—	3.4
Other	—	—	—	—	0.1	0.9	—	—	0.1	0.3	—	1.3
Total transfers to local governments	—	—	0.6	0.2	0.4	2.9	—	—	0.2	0.3	—	4.7
Total transfers	22.4	5.1	27.0	23.4	24.3	173.1	33.8	35.1	42.0	59.4	1.0	447.7
Total provincial revenue	33.0	8.0	51.0	51.0	339.0	399.0	57.0	99.0	175.0	200.0	—	1,412.0

—Nil or less than $50,000.

[a] Total includes $164,800 for language instruction not allocated by province.

Sources: Same as table A.4.

Table A.14 Federal Transfers to the Provinces and Local Governments, 1955-56

	Nfld.	PEI	NS	NB	Que.	Ont.	Man.	Sask.	Alta.	BC	Yukon & NWT	Total
					millions of dollars							
Provinces												
Specific-purpose transfers												
General health grants	1.0	0.4	1.6	1.3	10.1	9.2	2.2	2.8	2.6	2.4	—	33.5
Old age assistance	0.9	0.1	1.0	1.3	7.4	4.9	1.1	1.2	1.2	1.8	—	20.9
Blind persons' allowances	0.1	—	0.3	0.3	1.0	0.6	0.1	0.1	0.1	0.2	—	2.9
Disabled persons' allowances	0.1	0.1	0.3	0.2	2.6	1.7	0.2	0.2	0.3	0.1	—	5.7
Vocational training	0.1	—	0.4	0.2	0.6	1.1	0.4	0.3	0.5	0.3	—	4.0
Trans-Canada Highway	2.2	0.5	0.2	1.3	—	3.4	1.4	2.0	1.6	3.4	—	16.1
Other	0.8	0.1	0.7	0.4	0.3	2.0	0.3	0.2	0.3	1.0	0.3	6.4
Total specific-purpose transfers	5.3	1.2	4.4	5.0	22.0	22.9	5.6	6.8	6.6	9.3	0.3	89.5
General-purpose transfers												
Statutory subsidies	1.6	0.7	2.1	1.7	3.3	3.6	1.8	2.1	2.2	1.3	—	20.3
Current tax arrangements	12.5	3.7	19.9	16.6	—	138.3	25.7	26.0	31.6	45.4	—	319.6
Share of utilities tax	0.2	0.1	0.4	0.2	1.0	1.6	0.1	—	2.0	2.4	—	7.9
Special grant	3.1	—	—	—	—	—	—	—	—	—	—	3.1
Total general-purpose transfers	17.4	4.4	22.3	18.5	4.3	143.6	27.6	28.1	35.7	49.1	—	350.9
Special payments to territories											0.6	0.6
Total transfers to provinces	22.6	5.6	26.7	23.5	26.4	166.4	33.2	34.9	42.4	58.4	0.9	441.0
Local governments												
Grants in lieu of taxes	—	—	1.1	0.6	0.9	4.0	0.1	0.1	0.3	0.3	—	7.2
Other	0.1	—	.	0.8	0.1	1.0	0.4	—	0.3	0.1	—	2.9
Total transfers to local governments	0.1	—	1.1	1.4	1.0	5.0	0.5	0.1	0.6	0.4	—	10.1
Total transfers	22.7	5.6	27.7	24.9	27.3	171.5	33.7	35.0	43.0	58.8	0.9	451.1
Total provincial revenue	33.0	8.0	54.0	53.0	413.0	432.0	59.0	103.0	225.0	231.0	—	1,611.0

—Nil or less than $50,000.

Sources: Public Accounts; Dominion Bureau of Statistics, *Financial Statistics of the Government of Canada*, no. 8502-521-35; and M.C. Urquhart and K.A.H. Buckley, eds., *Historical Statistics of Canada* (Toronto: Macmillan, 1965).

Table A.15 Federal Transfers to the Provinces and Local Governments, 1956-57

	Nfld.	PEI	NS	NB	Que.	Ont.	Man.	Sask.	Alta.	BC	Yukon & NWT	Total
					millions of dollars							
Provinces												
Specific-purpose transfers												
General health grants	1.0	0.3	1.7	1.9	10.3	10.5	2.7	2.1	2.6	3.2	0.1	36.3
Old age assistance	1.0	0.1	1.0	1.3	7.1	4.7	1.1	1.2	1.2	1.7	—	20.3
Blind persons' allowances	0.1	—	0.3	0.3	1.0	0.6	0.1	0.1	0.2	0.2	—	3.0
Disabled persons' allowances	0.2	0.1	0.3	0.3	3.6	1.9	0.2	0.2	0.3	0.2	—	7.2
Vocational training	0.1	—	0.4	0.2	0.6	1.1	0.3	0.3	0.5	0.4	—	4.0
Trans-Canada Highway	1.1	0.4	1.0	3.3	—	4.9	3.1	2.7	1.9	6.5	—	24.8
Natural resources incl. agriculture	0.2	0.1	0.1	0.7	0.4	0.9	0.2	0.1	0.1	0.9	—	3.7
Other	2.8	0.1	—	0.8	0.5	1.0	0.9	1.1	0.2	4.5	0.8	12.7
Total specific-purpose transfers	6.6	1.1	4.8	8.7	23.5	25.4	8.5	7.7	7.0	17.5	0.9	111.9
General-purpose transfers												
Statutory subsidies	1.6	0.7	2.1	1.7	3.3	3.6	2.0	2.1	2.3	1.3	—	20.6
Current tax arrangements	13.8	3.1	22.3	17.8	—	160.6	27.9	27.4	37.3	55.7	—	365.9
Share of utilities tax	0.2	—	0.2	0.2	1.2	1.4	0.1	0.1	1.8	1.4	—	6.6
Special grant	2.3	—	—	—	—	—	—	—	—	—	—	2.3
Total general-purpose transfers	17.8	3.8	24.6	19.7	4.5	165.6	30.0	29.6	41.4	58.4	—	395.4
Special payments to territories											0.8	0.8
Total transfers to provinces	24.4	4.9	29.4	28.5	28.0	191.1	38.5	37.3	48.4	75.9	1.8	508.1
Local governments												
Grants in lieu of taxes	—	0.1	1.2	0.5	1.2	4.8	0.8	0.3	0.3	0.6	—	9.7
Other	—	—	—	1.0	0.2	1.2	0.3	0.1	0.9	0.1	—	3.8
Total transfers to local governments	—	0.1	1.2	1.5	1.4	5.9	1.1	0.4	1.2	0.7	—	13.5
Total transfers	24.4	4.9	30.6	29.9	29.4	197.0	39.6	37.7	49.6	76.6	1.8	521.6
Total provincial revenue	37.0	8.0	58.0	57.0	446.0	482.0	66.0	122.0	241.0	273.0	—	1,790.0

—Nil or less than $50,000.

Sources: Same as table A.14.

Table A.16 Federal Transfers to the Provinces and Local Governments, 1957-58

	Nfld.	PEI	NS	NB	Que.	Ont.	Man.	Sask.	Alta.	BC	Yukon & NWT	Total
					millions of dollars							
Provinces												
Specific-purpose transfers												
General health grants	1.1	0.3	1.9	1.8	8.3	9.9	2.2	2.3	2.9	3.8	0.1	34.6
Old age assistance, blind and disabled persons' allowances	1.7	0.3	2.1	2.3	16.1	8.9	1.7	1.9	2.1	2.5	0.1	39.7
Vocational training	0.2	0.1	0.4	0.3	—	0.5	0.3	0.3	1.4	0.7	—	4.2
Trans-Canada Highway	0.9	1.2	3.5	3.6	—	12.4	2.7	3.3	5.3	16.4	—	49.4
Natural resources incl. agriculture	0.2	0.1	0.1	1.1	0.3	1.1	0.4	0.3	0.2	1.0	—	4.9
Other	2.1	0.1	0.1	0.5	0.1	3.7	0.9	0.8	0.3	3.7	0.3	12.5
Total specific-purpose transfers	6.0	2.1	8.2	9.6	24.8	36.6	8.4	8.9	12.2	28.2	0.5	145.3
General-purpose transfers												
Statutory subsidies	1.6	0.7	2.1	1.7	3.3	3.6	2.0	2.1	2.3	1.3	—	20.6
Current tax arrangements	4.4	0.8	9.0	12.6	—	74.4	18.4	13.9	28.9	51.4	—	213.9
Recovery of overpayments	-0.1	-0.2	—	-0.2	—	—	-0.2	-0.3	—	—	—	-1.0
Equalization	11.6	3.0	17.4	8.6	43.1	—	13.9	19.2	14.7	4.5	—	136.0
Stabilization	—	0.4	—	—	—	—	—	—	—	3.0	—	3.5
Share of utilities tax	0.2	0.1	0.4	0.2	1.7	1.3	0.1	0.1	2.0	1.3	—	7.4
Special grant	1.4	—	—	—	—	—	—	—	—	—	—	1.4
Total general-purpose transfers	19.1	4.6	28.9	23.0	48.0	79.4	34.2	34.9	47.9	61.6	—	381.6
Special payments to territories											1.0	1.0
Total transfers to provinces	25.1	6.7	37.0	32.5	72.8	115.9	42.6	43.9	60.1	89.8	1.5	528.0
Local governments												
Grants in lieu of taxes	—	0.1	1.9	0.8	2.4	8.2	1.0	0.6	1.0	1.5	0.1	17.6
Other	—	—	0.2	0.4	0.3	2.1	0.1	—	0.5	0.7	—	4.2
Total transfers to local governments	—	0.1	2.1	1.1	2.7	10.3	1.1	0.7	1.5	2.2	0.1	21.8

(Table A.16 is concluded on the next page.)

Table A.16 Concluded

	Nfld.	PEI	NS	NB	Que.	Ont.	Man.	Sask.	Alta.	BC	Yukon & NWT	Total
					millions of dollars							
Total transfers	25.2	6.7	39.1	33.7	75.5	126.2	43.7	44.5	61.6	91.9	1.6	549.8
Total provincial revenue	39.0	9.0	64.0	62.0	515.0	595.0	74.0	136.0	246.0	282.0	—	2,022.0

—Nil or less than $50,000.
Source: Same as table A.14.

Table A.17 Federal Transfers to the Provinces and Local Governments, 1958-59

	Nfld.	PEI	NS	NB	Que.	Ont.	Man.	Sask.	Alta.	BC	Yukon & NWT	Total
					millions of dollars							
Provinces												
Specific-purpose transfers												
Hospital insurance	2.9	—	1.6	—	—	13.1	7.1	8.4	8.8	12.8	—	54.7
Other health	0.9	0.4	1.9	1.7	15.9	11.8	2.4	3.0	3.5	4.3	0.1	46.0
Old age assistance	1.7	0.2	1.6	1.8	10.6	6.7	1.6	1.8	1.9	2.3	0.1	30.2
Blind and disabled persons' allowances	0.5	0.2	1.0	0.9	9.9	4.4	0.6	0.6	0.7	0.7	—	19.6
Unemployment assistance	3.0	0.1	0.3	0.2	—	9.3	1.6	1.4	1.9	6.1	—	23.9
Vocational training	0.2	0.1	0.5	0.4	—	3.1	0.3	0.4	1.6	1.0	—	7.6
Trans-Canada Highway	4.8	0.5	2.5	11.4	—	15.9	1.8	0.2	2.2	11.9	—	51.1
Natural resources incl. agriculture	0.3	0.1	0.2	0.6	0.9	2.1	0.5	0.5	0.4	1.5	—	7.1
Other	0.3	—	0.6	0.5	0.4	2.5	0.3	1.2	0.3	2.2	0.3	8.5
Total specific-purpose transfers	14.5	1.6	10.2	17.5	37.7	68.8	16.3	17.6	21.4	42.8	0.4	248.8
General-purpose transfers												
Statutory subsidies	1.6	0.7	2.1	1.7	3.3	3.6	2.0	2.1	2.3	1.3	—	20.6
Current tax arrangements	4.7	0.8	11.8	13.6	—	93.3	20.7	14.4	38.4	51.3	—	249.0
Recovery of overpayments	-0.1	-0.2	—	-0.2	—	—	-0.2	-0.3	—	—	—	-1.0
Equalization	12.2	3.1	15.6	8.7	55.0	—	12.9	19.9	8.0	8.2	—	143.4
Stabilization	—	0.4	—	—	—	—	—	—	—	5.3	—	5.7
Share of utilities tax	0.3	—	0.5	0.2	2.3	1.6	—	0.1	2.2	1.5	—	8.7
Special grants	22.1	2.5	7.5	7.5	—	—	—	—	—	—	—	39.6
Total general-purpose transfers	40.7	7.3	37.4	31.5	60.6	98.6	35.4	36.1	50.8	67.6	—	466.0
Special payments to territories											1.0	1.0
Total transfers to provinces	55.2	8.9	47.6	49.0	98.3	167.4	51.7	53.7	72.2	110.4	1.5	715.8

(Table A.17 is concluded on the next page.)

Table A.17 Concluded

	Nfld.	PEI	NS	NB	Que.	Ont.	Man.	Sask.	Alta.	BC	Yukon & NWT	Total
					millions of dollars							
Local governments												
Grants in lieu of taxes	0.1	0.1	1.9	0.9	2.8	9.8	1.5	0.7	1.7	2.2	0.2	22.0
Other	—	—	0.1	1.0	2.7	3.3	—	0.2	0.5	0.5	—	8.3
Total transfers to local governments .	0.1	0.1	2.1	1.9	5.5	13.1	1.5	0.9	2.1	2.8	0.2	30.3
Total transfers	55.4	9.0	49.7	50.9	103.8	180.5	53.3	54.6	74.3	113.1	1.6	746.1
Total provincial revenue	62.0	13.0	76.0	71.0	557.0	647.0	77.0	141.0	236.0	296.0	—	2,176.0

—Nil or less than $50,000.

Sources: Public Accounts; Dominion Bureau of Statistics, *Financial Statistics of the Government of Canada*, no. 8502-521-35; M.C. Urquhart and K.A.H. Buckley, eds., *Historical Statistics of Canada* (Toronto: Macmillan, 1965); and Department of Finance, unpublished data.

Table A.18   Federal Transfers to the Provinces and Local Governments, 1959-60

	Nfld.	PEI	NS	NB	Que.	Ont.	Man.	Sask.	Alta.	BC	Yukon & NWT	Total
					millions of dollars							
Provinces												
Specific-purpose transfers												
Hospital insurance	4.7	0.4	8.2	4.6	—	71.9	11.3	13.4	15.7	20.4	—	150.6
Other health	1.1	0.4	1.5	1.4	15.2	15.1	2.3	2.3	2.9	4.0	0.1	46.2
Old age assistance	1.7	0.2	1.6	1.8	10.7	6.6	1.6	1.8	2.0	2.4	0.1	30.3
Blind and disabled persons' allowances	0.6	0.2	1.1	0.9	9.8	4.7	0.6	0.6	0.8	0.8	—	20.2
Unemployment assistance	3.7	0.1	0.7	0.4	7.8	14.0	2.4	1.8	2.1	7.2	—	40.2
Trans-Canada Highway	5.4	1.2	3.1	8.1	—	18.4	1.7	—	1.1	14.2	—	53.3
Natural resources incl. agriculture	0.2	0.1	0.2	0.2	1.1	1.7	0.6	3.4	2.0	1.5	—	11.1
Other	0.6	1.3	3.7	1.9	1.9	8.0	2.1	3.0	4.4	4.4	—	31.3
Total specific-purpose transfers	17.9	4.0	20.1	19.2	46.4	140.4	22.6	26.3	30.9	55.0	0.3	383.1
General-purpose transfers												
Statutory subsidies	1.6	0.7	2.1	1.7	3.3	3.6	2.1	2.1	2.4	1.3	—	20.7
Current tax arrangements	5.7	1.5	11.3	9.4	—	106.2	26.5	20.1	40.3	58.8	—	279.7
Recovery of overpayments	-0.1	-0.2	—	-0.2	—	—	-0.2	-0.3	—	—	—	-1.0
Equalization	14.3	3.0	20.7	16.9	68.6	—	13.0	20.2	15.1	11.3	—	183.0
Stabilization	—	-0.2	—	—	—	—	—	—	—	-2.2	—	-2.3
Share of utilities tax	0.2	—	0.2	0.1	1.5	1.0	—	—	1.2	0.4	—	4.8
Special grants	15.5	2.5	7.5	7.5	—	—	—	—	—	—	—	33.0
Total general-purpose transfers	37.2	7.4	41.7	35.4	73.4	110.9	41.3	42.1	59.0	69.5	—	517.9
Special payments to territories											1.0	1.0
Total transfers to provinces	55.1	11.3	61.9	54.6	119.8	251.3	63.9	68.4	89.9	124.5	1.3	902.0

(Table A.18 is concluded on the next page.)

Table A.18 Concluded

	Nfld.	PEI	NS	NB	Que.	Ont.	Man.	Sask.	Alta.	BC	Yukon & NWT	Total
					millions of dollars							
Local governments												
Grants in lieu of taxes	0.1	0.1	2.1	0.9	4.0	9.9	1.3	0.7	1.6	1.9	0.1	22.6
Other	—	—	0.2	1.7	0.6	2.3	0.1	0.8	0.3	0.4	—	6.3
Total transfers to local governments .	0.1	0.1	2.4	2.6	4.6	12.1	1.3	1.6	1.9	2.3	0.1	28.9
Total transfers	55.2	11.4	64.3	57.2	124.4	263.4	65.2	69.9	91.8	126.8	1.3	931.0
Total provincial revenue	60.0	14.0	90.0	77.0	605.0	778.0	100.0	146.0	279.0	314.0	—	1,463.0

—Nil or less than $50,000.
Sources: Same as table A.17.

Table A.19 Federal Transfers to the Provinces and Local Governments, 1960-61

	Nfld.	PEI	NS	NB	Que.	Ont.	Man.	Sask.	Alta.	BC	Yukon & NWT	Total
					millions of dollars							
Provinces												
Specific-purpose transfers												
Hospital insurance	5.1	1.0	9.6	7.9	13.9	84.5	13.0	14.5	16.9	22.5	—	188.9
Other health	0.8	0.5	2.9	1.6	14.1	15.8	3.0	2.4	2.8	4.1	0.5	48.5
Old age assistance	1.7	0.2	1.6	1.7	11.0	6.6	1.6	1.8	2.0	2.3	0.1	30.6
Blind and disabled persons' allowances	0.6	0.2	1.2	0.9	9.5	5.0	0.7	0.7	0.8	0.9	—	20.5
Unemployment assistance	2.8	0.1	1.6	1.4	14.2	12.9	3.3	2.3	2.6	10.3	0.1	51.5
Trans-Canada Highway	6.6	0.6	3.3	3.5	—	17.9	0.5	—	0.3	16.1	—	48.7
Other[a]	1.4	1.7	3.0	3.2	3.4	11.8	3.8	4.9	6.3	7.1	—	46.6
Total specific-purpose transfers	19.1	4.3	23.3	20.3	66.0	154.6	26.0	26.5	31.4	63.5	0.8	435.8
General-purpose transfers												
Statutory subsidies	1.6	0.7	2.1	1.7	3.3	3.6	2.1	2.1	2.4	1.3	—	20.7
Current tax arrangements	5.1	1.1	11.2	9.3	—	113.8	26.0	16.9	39.6	65.6	—	288.9
Recovery of overpayments	-0.1	-0.2	—	-0.2	—	—	-0.2	-0.3	—	—	—	-1.0
Equalization	15.4	3.5	21.0	17.4	71.1	—	14.1	23.7	17.5	5.9	—	189.7
Stabilization	—	0.2	—	—	—	—	—	—	—	2.1	—	2.3
Share of utilities tax	0.1	—	0.3	0.1	1.2	0.6	—	0.1	1.4	0.3	—	4.2
Special grants	15.5	2.5	7.5	7.5	—	—	—	—	—	—	—	33.0
Total general-purpose transfers	37.6	7.8	42.1	35.8	75.6	118.0	42.0	42.5	61.0	75.2	—	537.5
Special payments to territories	—	—	—	—	—	—	—	—	—	—	1.1	1.1
Total transfers to provinces	56.7	12.1	65.5	56.1	141.5	272.6	67.9	69.0	92.4	138.7	1.9	974.4

(Table A.19 is concluded on the next page.)

Table A.19 Concluded

	Nfld.	PEI	NS	NB	Que.	Ont.	Man.	Sask.	Alta.	BC	Yukon & NWT	Total
					millions of dollars							
Local governments												
Grants in lieu of taxes	0.1	0.1	2.1	1.1	4.9	9.9	1.5	0.8	1.6	2.4	0.1	24.7
Other	—	—	0.4	1.7	0.6	5.4	0.3	0.4	0.7	0.9	—	10.5
Total transfers to local governments .	0.2	0.1	2.5	2.8	5.5	15.3	1.8	1.2	2.3	3.3	0.1	35.2
Total transfers	56.9	12.2	68.0	58.9	147.0	287.9	69.7	70.2	94.7	142.0	2.0	1,009.6
Total provincial revenue	64.0	16.0	92.0	87.0	641.0	833.0	104.0	149.0	246.0	320.0	—	2,552.0

—Nil or less than $50,000.

[a] Other specific-purpose transfers to Quebec net of overpayment in previous years of university grants, $746,000.

Sources: Public Accounts; Dominion Bureau of Statistics, *Financial Statistics of the Government of Canada*, no. 8502-521-35; M.C. Urquhart and K.A.H. Buckley, eds., *Historical Statistics of Canada* (Toronto: Macmillan, 1965); Statistics Canada, *Financial Statistics of Provincial Governments*, catalogue no. 68-207; and Department of Finance, unpublished data.

Table A.20 Federal Transfers to the Provinces and Local Governments, 1961-62

	Nfld.	PEI	NS	NB	Que.	Ont.	Man.	Sask.	Alta.	BC	Yukon & NWT	Total
					millions of dollars							
Provinces												
Specific-purpose transfers												
Hospital insurance	6.3	1.4	11.9	9.5	73.0	104.5	15.2	16.0	19.7	25.7	0.7	283.9
Other health	1.5	0.3	2.7	1.6	13.1	16.5	3.0	2.5	3.9	3.9	0.1	49.0
Old age assistance	1.7	0.2	1.6	1.8	10.9	6.9	1.7	1.8	2.0	2.3	0.1	30.8
Blind and disabled persons' allowances	0.6	0.3	1.3	1.0	8.9	5.3	0.7	0.7	0.8	1.0	—	20.5
Unemployment assistance	4.4	0.2	1.7	1.4	38.2	17.0	4.2	4.2	4.2	16.4	0.1	92.0
Education	3.0	0.2	1.2	1.6	8.8	12.1	1.2	1.5	3.6	2.8	0.3	36.2
Trans-Canada Highway	2.2	0.3	1.8	2.4	2.7	13.0	0.9	0.1	0.7	12.5	—	36.5
Other[a]	2.0	1.4	3.2	3.3	13.2	12.0	4.2	3.7	5.9	7.8	0.1	56.5
Total specific-purpose transfers	21.6	4.3	25.4	22.6	168.7	187.1	31.0	30.4	40.8	72.4	1.3	605.6
General-purpose transfers												
Statutory subsidies	1.7	0.7	2.1	1.7	4.0	4.6	2.1	2.1	2.8	1.7	—	23.5
Current tax arrangements	8.9	1.8	14.1	10.2	—	120.7	28.5	19.3	43.5	65.5	—	312.6
Recovery of overpayments	-0.1	-0.2	—	-0.2	—	—	-0.2	-0.3	—	—	—	-1.0
Equalization	11.2	2.8	18.2	16.0	62.6	—	11.9	21.2	14.9	5.9	—	164.7
Stabilization	—	0.2	—	—	—	—	—	—	—	3.0	—	3.1
Share of utilities tax	0.1	0.1	0.5	0.1	2.1	0.7	0.1	0.1	1.9	0.9	—	6.4
Special grants	15.5	2.5	7.5	7.5	—	—	—	—	—	—	—	33.0
Total general-purpose transfers	37.3	7.9	42.4	35.4	68.7	125.9	42.4	42.4	63.1	77.0	—	542.3
Special payments to territories											1.1	1.1
Total transfers to provinces	58.9	12.2	67.8	58.0	237.4	313.0	73.4	72.8	103.8	149.4	2.4	1,149.0

(Table A.20 is concluded on the next page.)

Table A.20 Concluded

	Nfld.	PEI	NS	NB	Que.	Ont.	Man.	Sask.	Alta.	BC	Yukon & NWT	Total
						millions of dollars						
Local governments												
Grants in lieu of taxes	0.1	0.1	2.1	1.0	3.5	11.8	1.6	0.9	1.7	2.1	0.1	25.0
Other	0.1	—	0.2	1.7	1.4	5.4	0.3	0.3	1.0	0.7	—	11.1
Total transfers to local governments	0.2	0.1	2.3	2.7	4.9	17.2	1.9	1.2	2.7	2.8	0.1	36.1
Total transfers	59.1	12.3	70.1	60.7	242.3	330.2	75.3	74.0	106.5	152.2	2.5	1,185.1
Total provincial revenue	68.9	17.9	102.3	84.3	758.1	927.1	118.0	156.7	273.0	346.4	4.2	2,856.8

—Nil or less than $50,000.

[a] Other specific-purpose transfers to Quebec net of overpayment in previous years of university grants, $2.2 million.

Sources: Same as table A.19.

Table A.21 Federal Transfers to the Provinces and Local Governments, 1962-63

	Nfld.	PEI	NS	NB	Que.	Ont.	Man.	Sask.	Alta.	BC	Yukon & NWT	Total
					millions of dollars							
Provinces												
Specific-purpose transfers												
Hospital insurance	7.5	1.7	13.5	10.9	88.7	122.1	17.3	18.3	25.8	30.0	0.8	336.7
Other health	1.5	0.5	2.8	1.9	14.1	15.8	2.6	2.5	4.3	4.3	0.7	50.9
Old age assistance	2.0	0.4	2.0	2.1	13.8	8.5	2.0	2.2	2.5	2.7	0.1	38.2
Blind and disabled persons' allowances	0.8	0.4	1.6	1.2	10.2	6.5	0.8	0.9	1.0	1.2	—	24.5
Unemployment assistance	4.3	0.2	1.6	1.6	33.6	23.8	4.6	4.6	6.2	15.9	0.1	96.5
Education	13.2	1.0	3.6	2.6	20.4	126.8	3.8	5.4	24.5	6.3	1.0	208.5
Transportation	1.8	1.2	2.3	2.9	13.0	7.7	1.2	0.7	1.4	12.0	—	44.1
Other	0.5	0.2	1.1	1.3	16.5	10.5	4.1	3.7	4.9	6.2	0.1	49.2
Total specific-purpose transfers	31.7	5.5	28.4	24.5	210.3	321.8	36.5	38.2	70.5	78.6	2.8	848.8
General-purpose transfers												
Statutory subsidies	1.7	0.7	2.1	1.7	4.0	4.6	2.1	2.1	2.8	1.7	—	23.5
Current tax arrangements Share of federal estate tax	0.3	0.1	2.3	0.9	—	—	2.4	0.9	2.4	7.3	—	16.6
Equalization (includes stabilization)	13.3	3.0	18.2	15.3	66.3	—	12.3	23.3	7.0	—	—	158.5
Adjustments for previous years	0.3	0.2	2.8	0.7	11.5	-0.2	4.0	4.2	4.9	-4.8	—	23.5
Share of utilities tax	0.2	0.1	0.5	—	4.5	1.0	—	—	2.6	1.1	—	10.0
Special grants	18.5	3.5	10.5	10.5	—	—	—	—	—	—	—	43.0
Total general-purpose transfers	34.2	7.4	36.4	29.1	86.3	5.4	20.8	30.5	19.7	5.3	—	275.2
Special payments to territories											3.5	3.5
Total transfers to provinces	65.9	13.0	64.8	53.6	296.6	327.2	57.4	68.7	90.1	83.9	6.3	1,127.5

(Table A.21 is concluded on the next page.)

Table A.21 Concluded

	Nfld.	PEI	NS	NB	Que.	Ont.	Man.	Sask.	Alta.	BC	Yukon & NWT	Total
					millions of dollars							
Local governments												
Grants in lieu of taxes	0.2	0.1	2.1	0.9	5.0	15.2	1.4	0.9	1.7	2.2	0.1	29.9
Other	—	—	0.3	2.2	0.6	11.1	0.4	0.4	1.4	1.4	—	17.7
Total transfers to local governments .	0.2	0.1	2.4	3.1	5.6	26.3	1.8	1.3	3.1	3.6	0.1	47.6
Total transfers	66.1	13.1	67.2	56.7	302.2	353.5	59.2	70.0	93.2	87.5	6.4	1,175.1
Total provincial revenue	76.1	19.2	113.8	90.1	864.6	1,095.3	130.6	201.3	293.9	363.9	6.9	3,255.8

—Nil or less than $50,000.

Sources: Public Accounts; Statistics Canada, *Federal Government Finance*, catalogue no. 68-211; and *Provincial Government Finance*, catalogue no. 68-207.

Table A.22 Federal Transfers to the Provinces and Local Governments, 1963-64

	Nfld.	PEI	NS	NB	Que.	Ont.	Man.	Sask.	Alta.	BC	Yukon & NWT	Total
					millions of dollars							
Provinces												
Specific-purpose transfers												
Hospital insurance	8.7	1.9	15.2	12.6	113.8	136.0	19.7	21.3	28.3	33.7	1.0	392.2
Other health	2.2	0.4	2.8	2.3	14.4	16.7	2.9	3.1	4.6	3.9	0.1	53.4
Old age assistance	1.9	0.4	2.1	2.1	13.9	9.1	2.1	2.2	2.6	2.8	0.1	39.2
Blind and disabled persons' allowances	0.8	0.4	1.7	1.3	9.7	7.2	0.8	0.9	1.0	1.3	—	25.2
Unemployment assistance	4.5	0.4	1.8	1.9	39.4	24.5	5.8	4.6	8.0	16.3	0.2	107.4
Vocational education	5.8	1.7	4.7	2.3	22.9	69.2	1.8	3.7	15.1	9.0	—	136.2
Transportation	12.1	2.0	2.1	6.0	10.1	6.6	0.9	0.6	1.3	10.7	—	52.2
Natural resources, incl. agriculture	0.4	0.2	0.7	0.8	4.5	3.4	7.7	1.6	1.3	2.1	—	22.6
Other	0.7	0.5	0.4	0.5	13.8	7.8	1.6	2.0	3.7	4.1	1.4	36.5
Total specific-purpose transfers	36.7	7.6	31.4	29.6	242.6	280.7	43.2	40.0	65.8	83.8	2.7	864.1
General-purpose transfers												
Statutory subsidies	1.7	0.7	2.1	1.7	4.0	4.6	2.1	2.1	2.9	1.7	—	23.6
Current tax arrangements												
Share of federal estate tax	0.3	0.1	2.3	0.9	—	—	2.3	1.1	3.1	—	—	10.1
Equalization (includes stabilization)	14.6	3.2	19.5	16.3	65.6	—	12.0	23.0	2.0	—	—	156.2
Adjustments for previous years	0.3	0.7	-0.5	0.2	3.2	—	1.6	-0.5	5.5	-0.2	—	10.2
Share of utilities tax	0.2	0.1	0.6	—	4.6	1.0	—	—	2.7	0.5	—	9.9
Special grants	18.5	3.5	10.5	10.5	—	—	—	—	—	—	—	43.0
Total general-purpose transfers	35.6	8.1	34.6	29.7	77.4	5.6	18.0	25.7	16.0	2.0	—	252.8
Special payments to territories											4.5	4.5
Total transfers to provinces	72.5	15.7	66.0	59.3	320.0	286.4	61.3	65.8	81.8	85.2	7.2	1,121.4

(Table A.22 is concluded on the next page.)

Table A.22 Concluded

	Nfld.	PEI	NS	NB	Que.	Ont.	Man.	Sask.	Alta.	BC	Yukon & NWT	Total
						millions of dollars						
Local governments												
Grants in lieu of taxes	0.2	0.1	3.7	0.8	4.7	14.8	1.9	1.0	2.1	2.7	0.1	31.9
Other	—	—	0.3	2.2	3.5	8.4	0.8	0.9	1.1	2.7	—	20.3
Total transfers to local governments .	0.2	0.1	4.0	3.0	8.2	23.2	2.7	1.9	3.2	5.4	0.1	52.2
Total transfers	72.5	15.8	70.0	62.3	328.2	309.6	64.0	67.7	85.0	90.6	7.3	1,173.6
Total provincial revenue	81.0	19.3	113.7	94.6	948.4	1,181.9	136.2	216.9	319.7	398.5	8.4	3,518.5

—Nil or less than $50,000.

Sources: Same as table A.21.

Table A.23 Federal Transfers to the Provinces and Local Governments, 1964-65

	Nfld.	PEI	NS	NB	Que.	Ont.	Man.	Sask.	Alta.	BC	Yukon & NWT	Total
	millions of dollars											
Provinces												
Specific-purpose transfers												
Hospital insurance	9.6	2.1	15.9	13.8	128.2	151.5	20.9	23.5	31.4	36.1	0.9	433.9
Other health	1.5	0.4	2.6	2.2	16.4	17.7	3.0	2.5	5.2	5.0	0.1	56.6
Old age assistance	2.2	0.5	2.3	2.3	16.6	10.5	2.3	2.3	2.9	3.0	0.1	45.0
Blind and disabled persons' allowances	1.1	0.4	2.0	1.4	11.0	8.6	0.9	1.0	1.1	1.4	0.1	29.0
Unemployment assistance	4.7	0.3	1.9	1.4	41.0	21.0	5.4	4.6	9.2	17.9	0.1	107.6
Education	0.8	0.4	2.4	4.0	40.8	28.0	1.9	2.6	8.4	8.0	0.3	97.6
Transportation	23.7	1.6	5.2	10.8	33.2	6.3	1.0	0.4	0.6	3.7	—	86.7
Natural resources	0.8	0.2	0.9	1.1	6.6	3.9	9.9	2.9	1.6	2.1	—	29.9
Labour, employment, and immigration	0.2	0.2	0.1	0.3	25.2	6.7	1.8	1.7	2.5	4.4	—	42.9
Other	0.1	0.1	0.4	1.3	12.3	1.7	0.5	0.4	0.7	0.7	0.6	18.7
Total specific-purpose transfers	44.7	6.2	33.5	38.6	331.3	256.0	47.6	41.9	63.8	82.2	2.3	948.0
General-purpose transfers												
Statutory subsidies	1.6	0.7	2.1	1.7	4.0	4.6	2.1	2.1	2.9	1.7		23.6
Current tax arrangements												
Share of federal estate tax	0.5	0.1	3.5	2.0	8.8	15.1	3.7	1.6	4.7	—		40.1
Equalization (includes stabilization)	19.1	4.7	25.5	22.5	98.3	—	19.2	25.0	0.4	—		214.9
Adjustments for previous years	-0.7	0.7	0.7	0.8	4.8		2.5	-1.0	4.6	—		12.4
Share of utilities tax	0.2	0.1	0.7	0.1	4.3	1.1			2.9	0.3		9.7
Special grants	18.5	3.5	10.5	10.5	—	—				—		43.0
Provincial taxes and fees	0.4	—	0.2	—	1.7	1.2				0.4		3.8
Total general-purpose transfers	39.8	9.8	43.3	37.7	121.9	22.0	27.7	27.8	15.4	2.3		347.5
Special payments to territories											5.0	5.0
Total transfers to provinces	84.3	16.1	76.8	76.3	453.1	277.9	75.2	69.7	79.2	84.5	7.3	1,300.5

(Table A.23 is concluded on the next page.)

Table A.23 Concluded

	Nfld.	PEI	NS	NB	Que.	Ont.	Man.	Sask.	Alta.	BC	Yukon & NWT	Total
					millions of dollars							
Local governments												
Grants in lieu of taxes	0.1	0.1	2.6	1.6	7.6	16.1	2.3	1.0	2.2	2.7	0.2	36.4
Other	0.5	—	0.9	2.2	1.9	14.8	1.6	0.8	1.1	1.9	—	25.9
Total transfers to local governments .	0.6	0.1	3.5	3.8	9.5	30.9	3.9	1.8	3.3	4.6	0.2	62.3
Total transfers	84.9	16.2	80.3	80.1	462.6	308.8	79.1	71.5	82.5	89.1	7.5	1,362.8
Total provincial revenue	94.3	21.3	129.3	109.5	1,239.8	1,358.2	162.5	236.4	383.1	463.8	9.3	4,207.5

—Nil or less than $50,000.

Sources: Same as table A.21.

Table A.24   Federal Transfers to the Provinces and Local Governments, 1965-66

	Nfld.	PEI	NS	NB	Que.	Ont.	Man.	Sask.	Alta.	BC	Yukon & NWT	Total
					millions of dollars							
Provinces												
Specific-purpose transfers[a]												
Hospital insurance	11.7	2.4	18.1	14.9	28.3	171.9	23.1	25.9	36.9	40.5	1.1	374.7
Other health	2.0	0.6	3.1	1.5	4.3	18.9	3.3	2.8	4.2	5.0	0.8	46.5
Old age and blind and disabled persons' allowances	3.2	0.9	4.2	3.7	—	19.0	3.1	3.2	4.0	4.2	0.1	45.5
Unemployment assistance	4.5	0.4	1.9	1.7	24.6	27.6	5.6	4.4	11.0	19.9	0.1	101.7
Vocational education	3.7	0.3	2.5	1.8	54.2	54.9	3.5	2.9	16.7	19.6	0.4	160.4
Trans-Canada Highway	23.1	1.1	6.8	13.7	33.5	3.1	0.2	0.2	—	1.8	—	83.4
Natural resources	0.9	0.2	1.9	1.6	12.9	6.8	10.2	2.6	1.5	3.5	—	42.0
Labour, employment, and immigration	0.2	0.3	0.1	0.6	24.8	6.6	1.1	1.3	2.2	4.0	—	41.3
Other	3.6	1.4	1.6	5.1	21.4	4.9	2.6	1.7	1.5	1.7	0.4	45.8
Total specific-purpose transfers	52.9	7.6	40.1	44.5	204.0	313.2	52.6	45.0	78.0	100.3	3.1	941.4
General-purpose transfers												
Statutory subsidies	1.7	0.7	2.1	1.7	4.0	4.6	2.1	2.1	2.9	1.7	—	23.6
Current tax arrangements												
Share of federal estate tax	0.8	0.2	1.9	2.3	10.6	16.0	3.0	1.9	4.7	—	—	41.4
Equalization	23.6	5.9	33.7	29.1	127.9	—	24.3	28.9	—	—	—	273.4
Adjustments for previous years	-1.1	0.1	1.6	1.2	-0.9	0.9	1.0	-1.8	1.3	0.9	—	3.3
Share of utilities tax	0.3	0.1	0.7	—	1.0	1.3	—	—	2.6	0.4	—	6.4
Youth allowance recovery	—	—	—	—	-4.9	—	—	—	—	—	—	-4.9
Special grants	18.5	3.5	10.5	10.5	—	—	—	—	—	—	—	43.0
Total general-purpose transfers	43.8	10.4	50.5	44.9	137.7	22.8	30.5	31.2	11.5	3.0	—	386.1
Special payments to territories	—	—	—	—	—	—	—	—	—	—	5.5	5.5
Total transfers to provinces	96.6	18.0	90.6	89.4	341.7	336.0	83.1	76.2	89.4	103.3	8.6	1,333.0

(Table A.24 is concluded on the next page.)

Table A.24 Concluded

	Nfld.	PEI	NS	NB	Que.	Ont.	Man.	Sask.	Alta.	BC	Yukon & NWT	Total
					millions of dollars							
Local governments												
Grants in lieu of taxes	0.4	0.2	3.0	1.3	7.2	17.7	2.0	1.2	1.9	2.8	0.2	37.8
Other	0.1	—	1.5	2.7	17.5	22.3	4.3	2.6	2.7	6.8	—	60.6
Total transfers to local governments .	0.5	0.2	4.5	4.0	24.7	40.0	6.3	3.8	4.6	9.6	0.2	98.4
Total transfers[b]	97.1	18.2	95.1	93.4	366.4	376.0	89.4	80.0	94.0	112.9	8.8	1,431.4
Total provincial revenue	168.9	34.7	210.9	186.0	1,808.9	2,089.5	273.7	356.0	651.2	699.8	13.0	6,492.6

—Nil or less than $50,000.

[a] Specific-purpose transfers to Quebec include payments under opting-out, Established Programs (Interim Arrangements) Act, $81.5 million. [b] Total transfer figure for Quebec is net of overpayment in previous years of $1.6 million in university grants.

Sources: Public Accounts; Statistics Canada, *Federal Government Finance*, catalogue no. 68-211; Statistics Canada, *Provincial Government Finance*, catalogue no. 68-207; and Statistics Canada, *Public Finance Historical Data 1965/66 to 1991/92, Financial Management System*, catalogue no. 68-512.

Table A.25   Federal Transfers to the Provinces and Local Governments, 1966-67

	Nfld.	PEI	NS	NB	Que.	Ont.	Man.	Sask.	Alta.	BC	Yukon & NWT	Total
					millions of dollars							
Provinces												
Specific-purpose transfers												
Hospital insurance	13.1	2.7	20.5	16.7	33.1	194.7	26.4	28.4	41.9	47.8	1.1	426.4
Other health	2.0	0.7	5.3	2.0	7.0	19.4	3.1	2.9	4.8	7.0	0.3	54.3
Old age and blind and disabled persons' allowances	2.8	0.8	3.8	3.1	-0.1	16.7	2.5	1.5	3.2	3.6	0.1	38.1
Unemployment assistance	9.9	0.6	3.4	2.0	33.3	42.9	7.4	7.5	13.9	22.2	0.2	143.3
Vocational education	4.1	0.2	7.3	3.9	74.0	85.5	11.3	8.3	24.4	16.6	0.4	235.9
Trans-Canada Highway	5.8	0.4	18.3	10.6	41.8	2.9	—	0.4	0.3	0.4	—	81.0
Natural resources	1.8	0.5	2.9	1.9	14.4	5.9	2.1	3.1	2.4	4.8	—	39.9
Labour, employment, and immigration	0.4	0.4	0.5	0.5	19.6	7.9	1.3	2.2	2.9	3.5	—	39.0
Other	9.5	1.8	4.4	3.1	36.2	18.5	18.7	5.5	4.4	3.3	0.5	105.7
Total specific-purpose transfers[a]	49.4	8.2	66.2	43.7	259.2	394.3	72.7	59.7	98.3	109.3	2.7	1,163.8
General-purpose transfers												
Statutory subsidies	1.7	0.7	2.1	1.7	4.0	4.6	2.1	2.1	2.9	1.7	—	23.6
Current tax arrangements												
Share of federal estate tax	1.0	0.2	2.0	2.3	11.5	17.9	3.2	2.2	4.4	—	—	44.7
Equalization	27.2	7.1	39.7	34.2	147.6	—	27.7	33.0	—	—	—	316.4
Adjustments for previous years	2.0	0.2	2.1	1.1	8.7	1.9	5.9	1.4	0.2	4.6	—	28.2
Share of utilities tax	0.3	0.1	0.6	—	0.6	1.1	0.1	—	2.9	0.2	—	6.0
Youth allowance recovery	—	—	—	—	-4.1	—	—	—	—	—	—	-4.1
Special grants	18.5	3.5	10.5	10.5	—	—	—	—	—	—	—	43.0
Total general-purpose transfers	50.7	11.7	57.1	49.9	168.3	25.4	39.0	38.8	10.5	6.6	—	457.9
Special payments to territories											6.4	6.4
Total transfers to provinces	100.1	19.9	123.3	93.6	427.5	419.7	111.7	98.6	108.8	115.8	9.1	1,628.1

(Table A.25 is concluded on the next page.)

Table A.25 Concluded

	Nfld.	PEI	NS	NB	Que.	Ont.	Man.	Sask.	Alta.	BC	Yukon & NWT	Total
					millions of dollars							
Local governments												
Grants in lieu of taxes	0.2	0.2	2.9	1.0	7.6	18.4	2.1	1.2	2.3	3.0	0.2	39.0
Other	2.6	0.3	3.3	4.8	14.9	22.2	6.3	3.9	5.2	6.7	—	70.4
Total transfers to local governments .	2.8	0.5	6.2	5.8	22.5	40.6	8.4	5.1	7.5	9.7	0.2	109.4
Total transfers	102.9	20.4	129.5	99.4	450.0	460.3	120.1	103.7	116.3	125.5	9.3	1,737.5
Total provincial revenue	184.5	39.6	256.0	212.0	2,064.6	2,571.8	327.5	397.1	692.3	794.1	15.3	7,554.9

—Nil or less than $50,000.

[a] Specific-purpose transfers to Quebec include net payments under opting-out, Established Programs (Interim Arrangements) Act, $57.6 million.

Sources: Public Accounts; Statistics Canada, *Federal Government Finance*, catalogue no. 68-211.

Table A.26 Federal Transfers to the Provinces and Local Governments, 1967-68

	Nfld.	PEI	NS	NB	Que.	Ont.	Man.	Sask.	Alta.	BC	Yukon & NWT	Total
	millions of dollars											
Provinces												
Specific-purpose transfers												
Hospital insurance	15.5	3.4	24.0	19.5	44.5	234.8	30.6	32.3	49.8	57.4	1.4	513.1
Other health	1.7	0.6	10.9	2.7	12.2	28.4	3.5	3.0	5.8	8.2	0.2	77.3
Canada assistance plan	17.9	1.7	10.3	7.2	109.8	100.3	15.6	13.4	26.5	32.7	—	335.4
Other welfare	2.3	1.1	3.3	2.7	-0.4	6.2	2.8	0.9	4.0	4.9	0.2	28.3
Vocational education	6.5	1.2	14.0	2.3	82.5	59.8	8.2	12.3	9.1	8.9	0.3	205.1
Post-secondary education	1.9	1.2	5.2	2.4	40.6	19.5	7.1	8.2	17.5	4.4	—	108.0
Trans-Canada Highway	9.5	0.9	12.9	11.2	22.1	5.2	1.1	1.0	0.5	0.5	—	64.7
Natural resources	5.4	0.6	9.7	5.9	5.5	7.1	7.2	2.6	2.6	1.7	—	48.3
Labour, employment, and immigration	0.2	0.6	0.4	0.2	15.1	7.0	0.8	1.3	2.6	2.5	—	30.8
Other	5.1	3.0	5.9	11.6	7.0	6.4	1.3	1.2	1.5	3.4	2.3	48.9
Total specific-purpose transfers	65.9	14.3	96.6	65.7	339.1	475.0	78.1	76.2	119.8	124.7	4.4	1,459.8
General-purpose transfers												
Statutory subsidies	1.7	0.7	2.1	1.7	4.0	4.6	2.1	2.2	3.0	1.7	—	23.7
Special grant	8.0	—	—	—	—	—	—	—	—	—	—	8.0
Current tax arrangements												
Share of federal estate tax	1.0	0.2	5.1	1.9	13.1	19.8	3.7	2.9	5.9	—	—	53.7
Equalization	67.8	14.1	77.1	66.3	249.6	—	43.5	26.4	—	—	—	544.8
Adjustments for previous years	-2.6	-0.5	-4.4	-4.6	-18.6	0.8	-2.1	-4.1	2.5	—	—	-33.5
Share of utilities tax	0.4	0.1	0.6	—	0.7	1.6	0.3	—	2.9	0.2	—	6.7
Youth allowance recovery	—	—	—	—	-18.8	—	—	—	—	—	—	-18.8
Grants in lieu of taxes	—	—	—	0.8	—	—	—	—	—	0.4	—	1.2
Total general-purpose transfers	76.3	14.6	80.6	66.2	230.0	26.8	47.5	27.4	14.2	2.2	—	585.7
Special payments to territories	—	—	—	—	—	—	—	—	—	—	9.4	9.4
Total transfers to provinces	142.4	28.8	177.1	131.9	569.1	501.8	125.7	103.6	134.0	126.9	13.8	2,054.8

(Table A.26 is concluded on the next page.)

Table A.26 Concluded

	Nfld.	PEI	NS	NB	Que.	Ont.	Man.	Sask.	Alta.	BC	Yukon & NWT	Total
	millions of dollars											
Local governments												
Grants in lieu of taxes	0.2	0.2	2.9	0.1	8.4	20.6	2.6	1.2	2.3	3.3	0.3	42.1
Other	0.4	—	2.6	2.2	7.3	21.9	2.6	2.6	3.9	4.3	0.1	48.0
Total transfers to local governments .	0.6	0.2	5.5	2.3	15.7	42.5	5.2	3.8	6.2	7.6	0.4	90.1
Total transfers	142.8	29.0	182.6	134.2	584.8	544.3	130.9	107.4	140.2	134.5	14.2	2,144.9
Total provincial revenue	238.5	49.7	322.0	291.8	2,564.2	3,046.3	403.6	440.6	758.9	892.7	22.6	9,030.8

—Nil or less than $50,000.

[a] Specific-purpose transfers to Quebec include net payments under opting-out, Established Programs (Interim Arrangements) Act, $153.0 million.

Sources: Public Accounts; Statistics Canada, *Federal Government Finance*, catalogue no. 68-211; and Statistics Canada, *Provincial Government Finance*, catalogue no. 68-207.

Table A.27 Federal Transfers to the Provinces and Local Governments, 1968-69

	Nfld.	PEI	NS	NB	Que.	Ont.	Man.	Sask.	Alta.	BC	Yukon & NWT	Total
					millions of dollars							
Provinces												
Specific-purpose transfers[a]												
Hospital insurance	19.0	3.7	28.2	22.7	63.7	284.7	35.5	33.0	61.7	71.9	1.6	625.6
Medical care	—	—	—	—	—	—	—	11.3	—	21.7	—	33.0
Canada assistance plan[b]	21.1	2.6	11.1	9.9	127.3	119.0	14.0	14.1	28.8	37.2	0.2	385.2
Vocational education	0.2	0.4	10.2	10.1	57.5	9.6	7.2	6.9	1.9	5.1	—	109.0
Post-secondary education	3.3	1.1	12.3	4.0	62.9	117.3	10.1	15.7	33.0	17.1	—	276.6
Trans-Canada Highway	9.1	0.2	10.0	3.2	8.8	3.1	1.2	0.6	0.6	0.5	—	37.3
Natural resources	3.8	0.8	8.6	3.3	7.5	7.5	3.8	3.7	3.9	2.5	0.4	45.9
Labour, employment, and immigration	0.1	0.2	—	0.1	10.5	5.9	0.6	0.7	1.9	1.9	—	22.0
Other	7.8	4.5	16.9	8.4	12.0	43.3	5.2	4.1	9.0	11.3	1.2	123.6
Total specific-purpose transfers	64.6	13.1	97.2	61.8	350.2	590.4	77.7	90.1	140.7	169.2	3.4	1,658.2
General-purpose transfers												
Statutory subsidies	1.7	0.7	2.1	1.7	4.0	4.6	2.1	2.1	3.0	1.7	—	23.7
Special grant	8.0	—	—	—	—	—	—	—	—	—	—	8.0
Current tax arrangements												
Share of federal estate tax	0.2	0.5	5.6	1.5	14.7	21.7	4.2	3.2	7.4	—	—	59.1
Equalization	72.7	14.2	82.2	74.9	283.4	—	40.4	18.8	—	—	—	586.7
Adjustments for previous years	0.1	—	0.2	0.2	-1.7	—	0.4	0.4	-0.5	-0.7	—	-1.5
Share of utilities tax	1.2	0.2	1.9	0.1	2.9	5.5	0.9	—	7.4	0.6	0.2	21.0
Youth allowance recovery	—	—	—	—	-16.8	—	—	—	—	—	—	-16.8
Grants in lieu of taxes	—	—	—	0.9	—	—	—	—	—	0.4	—	1.3
Total general-purpose transfers	84.0	15.7	92.1	79.4	286.5	31.8	48.1	24.6	17.3	2.0	0.2	681.5
Special payments to territories											11.8	11.8
Total transfers to provinces	148.4	28.8	189.3	141.2	636.7	622.2	125.7	114.7	158.0	171.2	15.4	2,351.5

(Table A.27 is concluded on the next page.)

Table A.27 Concluded

	Nfld.	PEI	NS	NB	Que.	Ont.	Man.	Sask.	Alta.	BC	Yukon & NWT	Total
					millions of dollars							
Local governments												
Grants in lieu of taxes	0.3	0.2	3.0	—	9.6	21.8	2.7	1.3	2.9	3.8	0.3	46.0
Other	0.2	0.1	3.4	1.9	4.6	19.9	2.7	1.0	2.7	3.6	0.1	40.0
Total transfers to local governments	0.5	0.3	6.4	1.9	14.2	41.7	5.4	2.3	5.6	7.4	0.4	86.0
Total transfers	148.9	29.1	195.7	143.1	650.9	663.9	131.1	117.0	163.6	178.6	15.8	2,437.5
Total provincial revenue	270.2	56.4	349.0	325.0	2,921.9	3,634.6	449.7	484.1	966.1	1,091.6	25.9	10,574.5

—Nil or less than $50,000.

[a] Specific-purpose transfers to Quebec include net payments under opting-out, Established Programs (Interim Arrangements) Act, $186.9 million. [b] Canada assistance plan payment to Quebec includes amounts under the categorical welfare programs.

Sources: Same as table A.26

Table A.28 Federal Transfers to the Provinces and Local Governments, 1969-70

	Nfld.	PEI	NS	NB	Que.	Ont.	Man.	Sask.	Alta.	BC	Yukon & NWT	Total
					millions of dollars							
Provinces												
Specific-purpose transfers[a]												
Hospital insurance	21.0	4.0	32.3	25.1	55.4	320.9	40.4	42.5	67.3	80.5	1.9	691.3
Medical care	9.5	—	13.7	—	—	65.0	17.8	17.7	21.2	36.1	—	181.0
Canada assistance plan[b]	20.3	3.3	15.2	11.8	119.7	132.3	19.3	17.2	31.4	43.1	0.4	414.0
Vocational education	—	1.1	8.6	9.7	36.9	16.2	1.9	7.1	2.3	3.2	—	87.0
Post-secondary education	4.4	1.0	12.5	5.7	91.3	105.0	12.9	15.7	40.0	16.9	—	305.3
Natural resources	4.2	7.8	5.5	10.3	13.0	9.7	6.3	3.3	3.8	2.6	4.4	70.9
Other	18.3	3.1	21.5	17.8	33.3	46.3	8.1	7.8	8.4	13.3	3.3	181.3
Total specific-purpose transfers	77.7	20.2	109.5	80.4	349.5	695.4	106.6	111.3	174.5	195.8	10.0	1,930.8
General-purpose transfers												
Statutory subsidies	1.7	0.7	2.1	1.7	4.0	4.6	2.1	2.1	3.0	1.7	—	23.8
Special grant	8.0	—	—	—	—	—	—	—	—	—	—	8.0
Current tax arrangements												
Share of federal estate tax	0.6	0.5	1.5	1.1	12.3	26.8	6.0	3.9	7.3	—	—	59.9
Equalization	83.5	16.7	86.7	79.8	362.3	—	35.8	10.5	0.2	—	—	675.3
Share of utilities tax	0.9	0.2	1.8	0.1	3.2	8.8	1.0	—	7.0	0.5	0.2	23.8
Youth allowance recovery	—	—	—	—	−23.0	—	—	—	—	—	—	−23.0
Grants in lieu of taxes	—	—	—	2.4	—	—	—	—	—	0.4	—	2.8
Total general-purpose transfers	94.6	18.0	92.1	85.2	358.8	40.2	44.9	16.5	17.6	2.5	0.2	770.7
Special payments to territories											16.9	16.9
Total transfers to provinces	172.3	38.2	201.6	165.5	708.3	735.6	151.5	127.9	192.1	198.3	27.1	2,718.4

(Table A.28 is concluded on the next page.)

Table A.28 Concluded

	Nfld.	PEI	NS	NB	Que.	Ont.	Man.	Sask.	Alta.	BC	Yukon & NWT	Total
					millions of dollars							
Local governments												
Grants in lieu of taxes	0.2	0.2	3.4	—	9.6	23.0	3.4	1.3	2.8	3.9	0.3	48.2
Other	2.1	—	3.2	5.2	6.1	23.1	2.1	2.1	4.0	2.0	0.1	49.1
Total transfers to local governments .	2.3	0.2	6.6	5.2	15.7	46.2	5.5	3.4	6.0	5.9	0.4	97.3
Total transfers	174.6	38.4	208.2	170.7	724.0	781.8	157.0	131.3	198.1	204.2	27.5	2,815.7
Total provincial revenue	314.4	69.3	439.4	383.5	3,246.6	4,578.5	561.8	514.2	1,124.6	1,323.2	54.4	12,609.9

—Nil or less than $50,000.

[a] Specific-purpose transfers to Quebec include net payments under opting-out, Established Programs (Interim Arrangements) Act. [b] Canada assistance plan payment to Quebec includes amounts under the categorical welfare programs.

Sources: Same as table A.26.

Table A.29 Federal Transfers to the Provinces and Local Governments, 1970-71

	Nfld.	PEI	NS	NB	Que.	Ont.	Man.	Sask.	Alta.	BC	Yukon & NWT	Total
					millions of dollars							
Provinces												
Specific-purpose transfers[a]												
Hospital insurance	24.0	4.8	37.5	28.1	69.9	368.8	46.9	44.0	82.5	95.5	2.2	804.1
Medical care	12.3	0.8	17.8	3.4	56.1	174.5	23.2	22.5	38.1	51.9	—	400.5
Canada assistance plan[b]	22.0	3.8	16.7	15.2	155.6	176.4	28.2	20.6	39.3	68.2	1.2	547.2
Vocational education	8.6	2.2	9.4	11.0	76.5	7.8	19.1	13.8	1.4	19.9	—	169.5
Post-secondary education	5.9	13.9	1.3	7.6	114.1	143.4	17.5	15.1	54.1	15.5	0.8	389.1
Agriculture and primary industries	1.9	11.7	1.7	14.7	14.9	5.9	6.9	2.5	4.9	3.3	13.7	82.2
Trade and industry	33.5	—	10.2	26.6	24.5	—	1.6	0.6	0.7	—	—	97.8
Other	12.7	0.6	4.6	12.7	51.1	54.9	11.2	6.3	10.9	11.9	1.0	177.5
Total specific-purpose transfers	120.8	37.7	99.4	119.4	562.8	931.6	154.5	125.2	232.0	266.1	18.9	2,668.5
General-purpose transfers												
Statutory subsidies	1.7	0.7	2.1	1.7	4.0	4.6	2.1	2.1	3.0	1.7	—	23.8
Special grant	8.0	—	—	—	—	—	—	—	—	—	.	8.0
Current tax arrangements												
Share of federal estate tax	0.5	0.2	3.4	1.7	13.0	26.3	4.4	3.6	7.3	—	—	60.4
Equalization	93.7	21.9	90.3	79.9	545.0	2.1	52.3	42.1	-0.3	—	—	927.0
Share of utilities tax	1.0	0.2	1.6	0.1	3.0	10.6	0.7	—	6.0	0.5	0.2	24.1
Youth allowance recovery	—	—	—	—	-27.5	—	—	—	—	—	—	-27.5
Grants in lieu of taxes	—	—	—	2.9	—	—	—	—	—	0.1	—	2.9
Total general-purpose transfers	104.8	23.0	97.5	86.3	537.5	43.6	59.6	47.9	16.1	2.2	0.2	1,018.7
Special payments to territories											32.4	32.4
Total transfers to provinces	225.6	60.7	196.8	205.7	1,100.4	975.2	214.1	173.1	248.1	268.4	51.5	3,719.6

(Table A.29 is concluded on the next page.)

Table A.29 Concluded

	Nfld.	PEI	NS	NB	Que.	Ont.	Man.	Sask.	Alta.	BC	Yukon & NWT	Total
					millions of dollars							
Local governments												
Grants in lieu of taxes	0.3	0.2	4.1	—	10.5	26.2	3.1	1.4	2.8	3.9	0.5	53.0
Other	1.6	—	1.0	3.1	13.3	22.3	2.9	1.8	2.9	2.7	—	51.7
Total transfers to local governments	1.9	0.2	5.1	3.1	23.8	48.5	6.0	3.2	5.7	6.6	0.5	104.7
Total transfers	227.5	60.9	201.9	208.8	1,124.2	1,023.7	220.1	176.3	253.8	275.0	52.0	3,824.3
Total provincial revenue	356.1	85.1	467.4	433.7	4,092.1	5,257.0	661.3	563.1	1,215.1	1,464.0	79.9	14,674.7

—Nil or less than $50,000.

[a] Specific-purpose transfers to Quebec include net payments under opting-out, Established Programs (Interim Arrangements) Act. [b] Canada assistance plan payment to Quebec includes amounts under the categorical welfare programs.

Sources: Public Accounts; and Statistics Canada, *Federal Government Finance*, catalogue no. 68-211.

Table A.30 Federal Transfers to the Provinces and Local Governments, 1971-72

	Nfld.	PEI	NS	NB	Que.	Ont.	Man.	Sask.	Alta.	BC	Yukon & NWT	Total
					millions of dollars							
Provinces												
Specific-purpose transfers[a]												
Hospital insurance	27.1	5.2	42.8	34.7	99.2	427.5	53.5	49.5	94.8	107.1	2.3	943.8
Medical care	14.4	2.9	20.7	16.2	159.8	203.7	27.5	25.4	45.0	60.0	0.9	576.4
Canada assistance plan[b]	25.6	4.0	21.9	20.2	197.0	211.1	36.3	25.3	42.9	68.6	1.3	654.1
Post-secondary education	6.3	1.4	16.0	8.2	149.7	157.2	19.4	16.1	61.4	14.7	—	450.5
Other education	4.3	1.0	5.0	11.7	78.3	21.5	13.8	8.1	1.0	14.3	0.5	159.7
Transportation	11.2	—	10.2	5.2	1.9	4.5	—	0.2	—	0.7	—	34.0
Natural resources	2.7	13.6	1.4	11.5	33.5	7.4	7.5	2.9	1.5	3.8	—	86.0
Other	15.5	0.5	8.5	12.2	32.8	30.8	7.0	5.4	9.1	15.9	0.8	138.4
Total specific-purpose transfers	107.1	28.6	126.4	120.1	752.3	1,063.8	165.0	132.7	255.7	285.0	5.8	3,042.6
General-purpose transfers												
Statutory subsidies	1.7	0.7	2.2	1.8	4.5	5.5	2.1	2.1	3.1	2.1	—	25.8
Special grant	8.0	—	—	—	—	—	—	—	—	—	—	8.0
Current tax arrangements												
Share of federal estate tax	—	0.1	5.0	1.2	17.5	25.7	4.9	2.9	8.6	—	—	65.9
Equalization	120.6	23.2	93.8	97.2	543.6	—	58.6	115.6	—	—	—	1,052.5
Share of utilities tax	2.0	0.4	2.0	—	2.8	10.5	0.5	—	5.3	0.9	0.3	24.6
Youth allowance recovery	—	—	—	—	-32.0	—	—	—	—	—	—	-32.0
Grants in lieu of taxes	—	—	—	2.7	—	—	—	—	—	0.5	—	3.2
Total general-purpose transfers	132.2	24.2	102.9	103.0	536.4	41.7	66.3	120.7	16.9	3.5	0.3	1,148.0
Special payments to territories											61.6	61.6
Total transfers to provinces	239.4	52.8	229.3	223.0	1,288.7	1,105.5	231.5	253.4	272.6	288.5	67.7	4,252.2

(Table A.30 is concluded on the next page.)

Table A.30 Concluded

	Nfld.	PEI	NS	NB	Que.	Ont.	Man.	Sask.	Alta.	BC	Yukon & NWT	Total
					millions of dollars							
Local governments												
Grants in lieu of taxes	0.4	0.2	3.8	—	12.0	26.7	3.3	1.5	3.0	4.8	0.3	55.9
Other	3.3	0.4	2.5	3.0	22.1	31.9	5.0	3.1	5.7	5.0	0.3	82.6
Total transfers to local governments .	3.7	0.6	6.3	3.0	34.1	58.6	8.3	4.6	8.7	9.8	0.6	138.5
Total transfers	243.1	53.4	235.6	226.0	1,322.8	1,164.1	239.8	258.0	281.3	298.3	68.3	4,390.7
Total provincial revenue	435.3	98.0	555.1	503.7	4,662.6	5,628.4	709.5	636.9	1,366.2	1,664.6	101.5	16,361.7

—Nil or less than $50,000.

[a] Specific-purpose transfers to Quebec include net payments under opting-out, Established Programs (Interim Arrangements) Act. [b] Canada assistance plan payment to Quebec includes amounts under the categorical welfare programs.

Sources: Same as table A.29.

Table A.31 Federal Transfers to the Provinces and Local Governments, 1972-73

	Nfld.	PEI	NS	NB	Que.	Ont.	Man.	Sask.	Alta.	BC	Yukon & NWT	Total
					millions of dollars							
Provinces												
Specific-purpose transfers[a]												
Hospital insurance	30.6	6.2	47.2	39.3	39.6	485.0	64.4	55.2	105.8	123.3	3.4	1,000.0
Medical care	15.3	3.2	22.6	18.5	175.2	225.0	30.2	26.6	48.0	64.7	1.6	630.9
Canada assistance plan[b]	26.0	4.4	22.2	22.9	197.8	210.6	36.2	29.1	53.1	70.0	1.6	674.0
Post-secondary education	6.2	1.4	17.1	8.0	179.4	161.7	20.0	14.2	53.7	19.3	—	481.1
Transportation	5.2	0.1	9.2	10.0	10.1	4.9	0.2	0.1	0.1	0.1	—	40.1
Natural resources	3.8	15.5	3.2	10.7	37.8	8.9	7.4	2.1	8.5	6.5	—	104.4
Regional development	17.6	0.1	11.0	6.2	29.3	—	1.4	0.8	1.0	—	—	67.4
Other	7.9	2.2	4.3	9.1	50.3	46.1	10.0	7.6	10.1	7.3	4.5	159.2
Total specific-purpose transfers	112.5	33.1	136.7	124.9	719.5	1,142.1	169.8	135.7	280.3	291.1	11.1	3,156.7
General-purpose transfers												
Statutory subsidies	1.7	0.7	2.2	1.8	4.5	5.5	2.1	2.1	3.1	2.1	—	25.8
Special grant	8.0	—	—	—	—	—	—	—	—	—	—	8.0
Current tax arrangements												
Share of federal estate tax	-0.4	0.4	0.2	—	0.8	7.9	1.5	1.1	0.9	—	—	12.4
Equalization	114.4	25.1	146.8	125.2	501.9	—	89.8	173.6	—	—	—	1,176.8
Share of utilities tax	3.3	1.5	3.7	—	12.1	36.0	1.1	0.1	18.9	3.3	0.9	80.9
Youth allowance recovery	—	—	—	—	-39.4	—	—	—	—	—	—	-39.4
Grants in lieu of taxes	—	—	—	2.9	—	—	—	—	—	0.7	—	3.6
Total general-purpose transfers	127.1	27.6	152.8	129.8	479.8	49.4	94.6	176.9	22.9	6.2	0.9	1,268.1
Special payments to territories											74.6	74.6
Total transfers to provinces	127.1	27.6	152.8	129.8	479.8	49.4	94.6	176.9	22.9	6.2	86.6	1,353.7

(Table A.31 is concluded on the next page.)

Table A.31 Concluded

	Nfld.	PEI	NS	NB	Que.	Ont.	Man.	Sask.	Alta.	BC	Yukon & NWT	Total
					millions of dollars							
Local governments												
Grants in lieu of taxes	0.3	0.1	4.1	—	10.9	31.6	3.5	1.7	3.0	5.0	0.4	60.5
Other	4.5	0.6	1.9	2.9	27.5	29.0	5.0	2.2	7.2	7.4	0.3	88.6
Total transfers to local governments	4.8	0.7	6.0	2.9	38.4	60.6	8.5	3.9	10.2	12.4	0.7	149.1
Total transfers	244.3	61.4	295.4	257.7	1,237.7	1,252.1	272.9	316.6	313.3	309.7	87.3	4,648.5
Total provincial revenue	467.0	114.0	628.7	559.7	5,216.2	6,327.0	837.8	725.7	1,535.2	1,878.8	129.4	18,419.7

—Nil or less than $50,000.

[a] Specific-purpose transfers to Quebec include net payments under opting-out, Established Programs (Interim Arrangements) Act. [b] Canada assistance plan payment to Quebec includes amounts under the categorical welfare programs.

Sources: Same as table A.29.

Table A.32 Federal Transfers to the Provinces and Local Governments, 1973-74

	Nfld.	PEI	NS	NB	Que.	Ont.	Man.	Sask.	Alta.	BC	Yukon & NWT	Total
					millions of dollars							
Provinces												
Specific-purpose transfers[a]												
Hospital insurance	34.6	6.9	53.2	43.4	11.0	530.0	73.9	60.2	119.8	140.3	3.5	1,076.7
Medical care	16.7	3.5	24.8	20.1	185.4	243.3	31.2	27.7	52.7	70.7	1.8	678.0
Canada assistance plan[b]	24.7	5.1	27.7	30.1	195.5	207.3	37.9	35.4	52.7	83.3	2.6	702.3
Post-secondary education	5.4	0.9	22.5	7.3	196.1	153.6	17.7	13.8	54.7	13.1	—	485.1
Transportation and communications	11.0	0.5	10.5	13.5	9.7	0.1	—	—	0.5	1.2	—	47.1
Natural resources	7.2	17.2	6.2	16.9	41.4	8.7	6.4	8.7	10.5	5.9	—	129.0
Regional development	12.5	—	3.6	13.3	55.2	—	1.4	0.8	2.4	—	—	89.2
Other	13.4	0.5	1.8	9.1	89.9	50.8	6.6	3.2	9.4	5.2	2.9	192.5
Total specific-purpose transfers	125.2	34.7	150.3	153.4	784.1	1,193.8	175.3	149.9	302.7	319.7	10.8	3,399.9
General-purpose transfers												
Statutory subsidies	1.7	0.7	2.2	1.8	4.5	5.5	2.1	2.1	3.1	2.1	—	25.8
Special grant	8.0	—	—	—	—	—	—	—	—	—	—	8.0
Current tax arrangements												
Share of federal estate tax	-0.1	—	-1.0	0.1	-0.1	1.5	-0.1	0.2	-0.3	—	—	0.1
Equalization	156.9	35.0	189.9	145.2	664.8	23.3	127.5	166.5	6.0	2.0	—	1,517.1
Revenue guarantee	0.8	0.2	—	1.2	5.0	22.3	3.9	2.3	5.2	1.7	—	42.6
Share of utilities tax	1.9	0.4	0.2	—	2.4	12.5	0.5	—	6.1	1.9	0.5	26.4
Youth allowance recovery	—	—	—	—	-53.1	—	—	—	—	—	—	-53.1
Grants in lieu of taxes	—	0.2	—	2.3	—	—	—	—	—	0.5	—	3.0
Oil export tax payments	—	—	—	—	—	—	1.2	15.7	122.1	4.3	—	143.3
Total general-purpose transfers	169.3	36.4	191.3	150.6	623.4	65.1	135.1	186.6	142.2	12.6	0.5	1,713.1
Special payments to territories											84.8	84.8
Total transfers to provinces	294.5	71.2	341.5	304.0	1,407.5	1,258.9	310.1	336.7	444.9	332.3	96.1	5,197.8

(Table A.32 is concluded on the next page.)

Table A.32 Concluded

	Nfld.	PEI	NS	NB	Que.	Ont.	Man.	Sask.	Alta.	BC	Yukon & NWT	Total
					millions of dollars							
Local governments												
Grants in lieu of taxes	0.4	0.2	5.1	—	14.8	28.4	4.3	1.7	3.5	5.0	0.5	64.0
Other	4.3	0.9	4.7	2.9	27.4	29.7	4.5	1.6	6.0	18.3	0.5	100.9
Total transfers to local governments	4.7	1.1	9.8	2.9	42.2	58.1	8.8	3.3	9.5	23.3	1.0	164.9
Total transfers	299.2	72.3	351.3	306.9	1,449.7	1,317.0	319.1	340.0	454.4	355.6	97.1	5,362.7
Total provincial revenue	555.1	139.5	779.0	675.7	5,954.2	7,362.6	953.7	892.5	2,020.8	2,353.2	142.7	21,828.8

—Nil or less than $50,000.

[a] Specific-purpose transfers to Quebec include net payments under opting-out, Established Programs (Interim Arrangements) Act. [b] Canada assistance plan payment to Quebec includes amounts under the categorical welfare programs.

Sources: Public Accounts; Statistics Canada, *Federal Government Finance*, catalogue no. 68-211; and Department of Finance, unpublished data.

Table A.33 Federal Transfers to the Provinces and Local Governments, 1974-75

	Nfld.	PEI	NS	NB	Que.	Ont.	Man.	Sask.	Alta.	BC	Yukon & NWT	Total
					millions of dollars							
Provinces												
Specific-purpose transfers[a]												
Hospital insurance	42.1	8.0	62.7	51.9	35.0	651.9	84.8	72.5	142.3	187.4	4.3	1,342.7
Medical care	18.3	3.9	27.2	22.4	207.2	275.2	34.9	30.6	59.4	81.5	1.9	762.7
Canada assistance plan[b]	33.2	7.0	31.2	35.2	240.8	300.6	49.9	34.8	67.1	139.8	6.8	946.6
Post-secondary education	4.8	1.1	19.2	6.3	233.0	142.7	15.9	13.2	52.5	14.9	—	503.6
Natural resources	8.4	19.1	6.6	9.1	30.7	12.6	7.6	20.1	10.4	7.9	—	132.4
Trade and industry	35.6	—	4.6	26.5	18.8	4.6	8.0	0.5	2.9	2.5	—	104.0
Regional development	11.3	—	10.1	7.4	21.2	0.1	1.3	0.5	1.6	0.4	—	53.8
Other	13.3	1.2	5.4	12.0	99.2	69.4	15.7	8.7	17.7	11.5	3.6	257.6
Total specific-purpose transfers	167.0	40.5	166.8	170.7	885.8	1,456.9	218.0	180.9	354.1	446.0	16.6	4,103.3
General-purpose transfers												
Statutory subsidies	1.7	0.7	2.2	1.8	4.5	5.5	2.2	2.1	3.1	2.1	—	25.8
Special grant	8.0	—	—	—	—	—	—	—	—	—	—	8.0
Current tax arrangements												
Share of federal estate tax	—	—	-0.3	-0.3	2.1	0.7	0.4	-0.2	0.8	—	—	3.7
Equalization	197.5	43.0	231.4	189.5	1,085.5	214.1	151.9	103.7	44.9	25.5	—	2,287.0
Revenue guarantee	10.7	2.4	15.0	16.3	107.4	206.8	29.3	20.9	43.9	22.5	—	475.2
Share of utilities tax	1.7	0.5	0.2	—	0.9	7.6	1.4	—	12.5	1.8	0.4	27.0
Youth allowance recovery	—	—	—	—	-98.7	—	—	—	—	—	—	-98.7
Grants in lieu of taxes	—	0.1	—	1.9	—	—	0.5	—	—	1.2	0.6	3.8
Oil export tax payments	—	—	—	—	—	—	—	12.2	95.4	3.1	—	111.1
Total general-purpose transfers	219.6	46.6	248.9	209.2	1,101.8	434.7	185.7	138.7	200.5	56.1	1.0	2,842.9
Special payments to territories											94.5	94.5
Total transfers to provinces	386.7	87.1	415.6	379.9	1,987.6	1,891.7	403.7	319.7	554.6	502.1	112.1	7,040.7

(Table A.33 is concluded on the next page.)

Table A.33 Concluded

	Nfld.	PEI	NS	NB	Que.	Ont.	Man.	Sask.	Alta.	BC	Yukon & NWT	Total
					millions of dollars							
Local governments												
Grants in lieu of taxes	0.7	0.1	4.3	0.1	14.6	33.1	5.1	1.9	3.5	5.5	0.5	69.5
Other	3.8	0.4	2.6	3.0	20.9	28.5	2.0	0.7	4.8	8.7	0.1	75.4
Total transfers to local governments .	4.5	0.5	6.9	3.1	35.5	61.6	7.1	2.6	8.3	14.2	0.6	144.9
Total transfers	391.2	87.6	422.5	383.0	2,023.1	1,953.3	410.8	322.3	562.9	516.3	112.7	7,185.6
Total provincial revenue	688.9	159.8	903.5	793.7	7,638.2	8,866.7	1,118.4	1,265.6	3,249.0	2,930.3	158.4	27,772.5

—Nil or less than $50,000.

[a] Specific-purpose transfers to Quebec include payments under opting-out, Established Programs (Interim Arrangements) Act. [b] Canada assistance plan payment to Quebec includes amounts under the categorical welfare programs.

Sources: Same as table A.32.

Table A.34   Federal Transfers to the Provinces and Local Governments, 1975-76

	Nfld.	PEI	NS	NB	Que.	Ont.	Man.	Sask.	Alta.	BC	Yukon & NWT	Total
					millions of dollars							
Provinces												
Specific-purpose transfers[a]												
Hospital insurance	53.9	10.3	78.8	65.2	31.3	855.7	104.2	88.6	195.0	252.3	5.2	1,740.5
Medical care	19.0	4.1	28.3	23.5	215.7	287.7	35.7	32.1	61.4	86.4	2.0	795.8
Canada assistance plan[b]	36.8	9.0	41.1	50.3	287.6	414.9	60.3	42.0	97.6	185.4	5.7	1,230.7
Post-secondary education	5.3	1.1	26.5	5.9	240.9	167.5	18.2	12.4	42.8	14.4	—	535.0
Natural resources	2.8	33.3	3.3	8.9	21.0	17.3	10.7	45.8	16.6	7.9	—	167.6
Trade and industry	46.3	—	18.4	33.5	38.1	15.1	12.1	10.4	4.7	2.8	—	181.4
Other	9.4	1.2	14.6	19.3	130.6	105.8	34.2	27.3	31.0	22.4	12.0	408.0
Total specific-purpose transfers	173.4	58.9	210.9	206.5	965.2	1,864.0	275.5	258.7	449.1	571.7	24.9	5,058.9
General-purpose transfers												
Statutory subsidies	1.7	0.7	2.2	1.8	4.5	5.5	2.2	2.1	3.1	2.1	—	25.8
Special grant	8.0	—	—	—	—	—	—	—	—	—	—	8.0
Current tax arrangements												
Share of federal estate tax	—	0.1	-0.6	—	-0.4	-1.1	0.2	0.1	0.7	—	—	-1.1
Equalization	191.3	49.0	281.3	202.5	999.2	—	150.5	47.8	—	—	—	1,921.6
Revenue guarantee	10.1	2.2	14.7	14.1	100.4	192.1	26.5	18.3	42.0	40.1	—	460.5
Share of tax on undistributed income	0.3	—	0.2	0.3	3.8	5.6	0.7	0.2	1.2	1.8	—	14.0
Share of utilities tax	1.8	0.5	—	—	2.5	7.0	1.2	0.1	16.5	2.3	0.5	32.3
Youth allowance recovery	—	—	—	—	-114.7	—	—	—	—	—	—	-114.7
Grants in lieu of taxes	—	0.5	—	1.4	—	—	—	—	—	0.8	0.5	3.3
Oil export tax payments	—	—	—	—	—	—	—	—	0.2	—	—	0.2
Total general-purpose transfers	213.2	53.1	298.4	219.4	995.2	209.0	181.2	68.6	63.8	47.0	1.0	2,350.0
Special payments to territories											145.1	145.1
Total transfers to provinces	386.7	112.0	509.3	426.0	1,960.4	2,073.0	456.7	327.3	512.9	618.7	171.0	7,554.0

(Table A.34 is concluded on the next page.)

Table A.34 Concluded

	Nfld.	PEI	NS	NB	Que.	Ont.	Man.	Sask.	Alta.	BC	Yukon & NWT	Total
					millions of dollars							
Local governments												
Grants in lieu of taxes	0.7	—	5.2	—	15.2	35.5	5.7	2.1	4.7	8.2	0.7	78.0
Other	6.6	1.2	2.6	4.1	35.8	50.2	5.8	3.8	6.7	10.9	0.4	128.1
Total transfers to local governments .	7.3	1.2	7.8	4.1	51.0	85.7	11.5	5.9	11.4	19.1	1.1	206.1
Total transfers	394.0	113.2	517.1	430.1	2,011.4	2,158.7	468.2	333.2	524.3	637.8	172.1	7,760.1
Total provincial revenue	797.6	193.3	1,060.4	943.3	8,702.4	9,940.6	1,332.8	1,441.0	3,706.0	3,325.0	226.7	31,669.1

—Nil or less than $50,000.

[a] Specific-purpose transfers to Quebec include payments under opting-out, Established Programs (Interim Arrangements) Act. [b] Canada assistance plan payment to Quebec includes amounts under the categorical welfare programs.

Sources: Public Accounts; and Statistics Canada, *Federal Government Finance*, catalogue no. 68-211.

Table A.35   Federal Transfers to the Provinces and Local Governments, 1976-77

	Nfld.	PEI	NS	NB	Que.	Ont.	Man.	Sask.	Alta.	BC	Yukon & NWT	Total
					millions of dollars							
Provinces												
Specific-purpose transfers[a]												
Hospital insurance	67.3	12.5	98.2	81.7	−16.1	1,019.9	124.4	109.4	219.6	290.2	7.2	2,014.4
Medical care	24.1	5.2	35.6	29.7	270.4	360.0	45.0	41.9	82.3	106.7	2.6	1,003.6
Canada assistance plan[b]	40.3	10.7	46.8	67.3	391.4	408.7	53.1	63.5	107.2	184.7	5.0	1,378.8
Post-secondary education	6.7	1.5	21.3	8.7	335.6	189.9	19.5	15.0	39.0	11.5	—	648.7
Transportation	0.4	0.1	0.1	—	10.0	6.9	15.7	10.1	32.1	57.7	—	133.0
Agriculture	3.4	34.6	1.2	5.1	10.6	13.1	12.5	30.6	20.3	4.9	—	136.2
Trade and industry	44.8	—	31.8	34.3	42.7	10.0	13.0	12.1	4.4	3.5	2.7	199.3
Other	7.4	5.6	42.3	24.9	123.1	157.7	31.4	7.8	28.2	20.4	4.8	453.6
Total specific-purpose transfers	194.6	70.2	277.2	251.6	1,168.0	2,166.1	314.6	290.5	533.1	679.5	22.3	5,967.6
General-purpose transfers												
Statutory subsidies	1.7	0.7	2.2	1.8	4.5	5.5	2.2	2.1	3.1	2.1	—	25.8
Special grant	8.0	—	—	—	—	—	—	—	—	—	—	8.0
Current tax arrangements												
Equalization	223.2	59.9	283.4	211.4	1,189.5	—	171.4	−52.3	—	—	—	2,086.6
Revenue guarantee	18.6	4.0	25.3	21.3	219.5	379.4	41.2	39.0	73.3	121.6	—	943.1
Share of undistributed income tax	0.1	—	0.4	0.3	3.4	6.2	0.9	0.5	1.8	2.1	—	15.6
Adjustments for previous years	0.3	—	−0.5	−0.3	−2.9	−3.4	0.3	−0.3	2.0	—	—	−4.9
Share of utilities tax	2.3	0.3	—	—	2.0	4.7	1.4	—	25.5	2.2	0.2	38.7
Youth allowance recovery	—	—	—	—	−130.3	—	—	—	—	—	—	−130.3
Grants in lieu of taxes	—	0.3	—	3.4	—	—	—	—	—	0.8	0.4	4.9
Total general-purpose transfers	254.2	65.2	310.7	237.8	1,285.7	392.4	217.3	−11.0	105.7	128.8	0.6	2,987.5
Special payments to territories											197.1	197.1
Total transfers to provinces	448.8	135.4	587.9	489.4	2,453.7	2,558.4	532.0	279.5	638.8	808.3	220.0	9,152.1

(Table A.35 is concluded on the next page.)

Table A.35 Concluded

	Nfld.	PEI	NS	NB	Que.	Ont.	Man.	Sask.	Alta.	BC	Yukon & NWT	Total
					millions of dollars							
Local governments												
Grants in lieu of taxes	0.7	—	5.0	—	17.4	44.5	5.6	2.5	5.7	8.0	1.1	90.6
Other	18.2	3.2	12.5	18.6	56.5	72.1	6.3	4.5	9.7	39.5	1.1	241.1
Total transfers to local governments .	18.9	3.2	17.5	18.6	73.9	116.6	11.9	7.0	15.4	47.5	2.2	332.7
Total transfers	467.7	138.6	605.4	508.0	2,527.6	2,675.0	543.9	286.5	654.2	855.8	222.2	9,484.8
Total revenue	920.2	209.9	1,208.8	1,030.6	10,285.5	11,615.7	1,557.8	1,619.2	4,655.2	4,100.8	282.8	37,486.5

—Nil or less than $50,000.

[a] Specific-purpose transfers to Quebec include payments under opting-out, Established Programs (Interim Arrangements) Act. [b] Canada assistance plan payment to Quebec includes amounts under the categorical welfare programs.

Sources: Same as table A.34.

Table A.36 Federal Transfers to the Provinces and Local Governments, 1977-78

	Nfld.	PEI	NS	NB	Que.	Ont.	Man.	Sask.	Alta.	BC	Yukon & NWT	Total
					millions of dollars							
Provinces												
Specific-purpose transfers[a]												
Hospital insurance	43.2	8.2	66.8	49.7	471.5	654.1	84.1	70.5	144.2	161.7	5.1	1,759.1
Medical care	26.5	5.4	40.4	31.8	265.7	396.7	50.3	44.3	90.4	109.4	3.2	1,064.2
Canada assistance plan[b]	40.0	7.4	47.6	51.1	365.3	409.8	54.5	55.8	115.8	198.9	5.9	1,352.1
Post-secondary education	26.7	5.4	41.7	34.0	311.5	386.0	56.2	45.7	60.8	127.6	3.0	1,098.5
Transportation	—	0.4	5.2	0.9	11.9	0.9	14.6	10.8	25.7	40.1	—	110.4
Agriculture	3.0	30.2	0.1	0.7	7.5	13.6	11.6	40.2	19.5	5.1	—	131.6
Trade and industry	55.5	—	34.3	43.4	117.6	11.0	14.6	9.4	5.5	7.4	0.9	299.6
Other	8.5	1.1	8.3	18.1	184.0	107.7	32.3	11.7	27.1	23.1	6.4	428.6
Total specific-purpose transfers	203.5	58.1	244.6	229.4	1,734.8	1,979.9	318.2	288.5	489.1	673.3	24.5	6,243.9
General-purpose transfers												
Statutory subsidies	1.7	0.7	2.2	1.8	4.5	5.5	2.2	2.1	3.4	2.1	—	26.1
Special grant	8.0	—	—	—	—	—	—	—	—	—	—	8.0
Current tax arrangements												
Equalization	262.9	62.8	365.5	265.2	1,226.7	—	213.5	-13.0	—	—	—	2,383.5
Revenue guarantee	13.3	2.7	18.4	16.4	143.9	210.4	31.4	38.2	66.3	59.5	—	600.4
Share of undistributed income tax	0.3	0.2	0.3	0.3	3.5	6.2	0.5	0.5	1.9	1.8	—	15.3
Share of utilities tax	2.1	0.4	—	—	1.7	8.1	1.2	—	31.9	0.5	0.2	46.1
Reciprocal taxation agreements	2.1	1.2	7.4	2.8	11.1	22.1	—	—	—	—	—	46.6
Youth allowance recovery	—	—	—	—	-122.5	—	—	—	—	—	—	-122.5
Grants in lieu of taxes	—	0.7	—	4.8	—	—	—	—	—	1.5	0.4	7.4
Total general-purpose transfers	290.2	68.3	393.7	291.2	1,269.0	252.2	248.8	27.8	103.5	65.4	0.6	3,010.8
Special payments to territories											224.4	224.4
Total transfers to provinces	493.7	126.7	638.3	520.6	3,003.8	2,232.1	566.9	316.3	592.5	738.7	249.5	9,479.1

(Table A.36 is concluded on the next page.)

Table A.36 Concluded

	Nfld.	PEI	NS	NB	Que.	Ont.	Man.	Sask.	Alta.	BC	Yukon & NWT	Total
					millions of dollars							
Local governments												
Grants in lieu of taxes	1.0	—	7.2	—	25.3	54.2	7.9	3.1	7.0	11.6	1.0	118.3
Other	5.6	3.3	12.5	8.5	55.7	57.7	4.5	9.5	8.7	20.9	1.2	188.3
Total transfers to local governments	6.6	3.3	19.7	8.5	81.0	111.9	12.4	12.6	15.7	32.5	2.2	306.6
Total transfers	500.3	130.0	658.0	529.1	3,084.8	2,344.0	579.3	328.9	608.2	771.2	251.7	9,785.7
Total provincial revenue	1,038.9	237.0	1,343.7	1,129.3	11,825.5	12,422.6	1,653.5	1,819.3	6,092.1	4,698.7	319.8	42,580.4

—Nil or less than $50,000.

[a] Specific-purpose transfers to Quebec include payments under opting-out, Established Programs (Interim Arrangements) Act. [b] Canada assistance plan payment to Quebec includes amounts under the categorical welfare programs.

Sources: Same as table A.34.

Table A.37   Federal Transfers to the Provinces and Local Governments, 1978-79

	Nfld.	PEI	NS	NB	Que.	Ont.	Man.	Sask.	Alta.	BC	Yukon & NWT	Total
					millions of dollars							
Provinces												
Specific-purpose transfers[a]												
Hospital insurance	56.5	11.6	85.1	68.5	494.5	821.9	104.4	94.5	168.1	218.5	6.4	2,130.0
Medical care[b]	19.1	3.9	28.7	23.1	166.6	276.9	35.1	31.9	56.5	73.6	2.1	717.5
Extended health services	12.7	2.7	18.7	15.5	139.7	187.5	22.9	21.1	43.4	56.2	1.4	521.8
Post-secondary education	35.8	7.6	52.4	44.4	336.6	506.2	73.4	65.1	93.3	150.6	4.0	1,369.4
Canada assistance plan	39.6	10.0	46.7	61.5	576.5	419.2	58.1	57.5	115.6	204.5	8.9	1,598.1
Transportation	10.0	3.7	10.9	10.4	22.7	5.8	11.4	23.4	31.3	13.4	18.4	161.2
Agriculture	0.5	29.0	0.1	0.1	2.7	16.0	11.0	36.1	21.5	4.3	—	121.3
Trade and industry	52.2	—	46.2	46.5	130.7	6.0	10.6	10.7	7.8	7.7	—	318.5
Other	21.9	2.3	16.8	25.7	189.1	174.1	40.5	22.1	55.7	43.4	10.6	602.2
Total specific-purpose transfers	248.3	70.8	305.6	295.7	2,059.1	2,413.6	367.4	362.4	593.2	772.2	51.8	7,540.0
General-purpose transfers												
Statutory subsidies	1.7	0.7	2.2	1.8	4.5	5.5	2.2	2.1	3.3	2.1	—	26.0
Special grant	8.0	—	—	—	—	—	—	—	—	—	—	8.0
Current tax arrangements												
Equalization	324.9	63.9	360.9	314.4	1,382.3	—	227.2	73.5	—	—	—	2,747.2
Revenue guarantee	3.2	0.6	3.8	3.2	31.5	43.6	5.4	2.5	14.8	13.2	—	121.6
Share of undistributed income tax	0.1	—	0.4	0.2	5.5	6.7	0.6	0.4	1.1	1.9	—	16.8
Reciprocal taxation agreements	4.9	2.9	13.9	7.4	30.3	41.1	—	—	—	—	—	100.4
Youth allowance recovery	—	—	—	—	-131.3	—	—	—	—	—	—	-131.3
Provincial sales tax reduction	8.6	1.4	1.9	2.7	40.0	-56.9	4.7	5.0	—	15.8	—	23.2
Share of utilities tax	6.9	1.4	—	—	2.1	15.1	0.2	0.1	55.7	0.2	0.7	82.4
Grants in lieu of taxes	—	0.2	—	1.7	—	—	—	—	—	—	5.0	7.0
Total general-purpose transfers	358.3	71.2	383.0	331.5	1,364.9	55.0	240.3	83.6	74.9	33.2	5.7	3,001.3

(Table A.37 is concluded on the next page.)

Table A.37 Concluded

millions of dollars

	Nfld.	PEI	NS	NB	Que.	Ont.	Man.	Sask.	Alta.	BC	Yukon & NWT	Total
Special payments to territories ...											225.7	225.7
Total transfers to provinces	606.6	141.9	688.5	627.2	3,424.0	2,468.6	607.6	446.0	668.1	805.4	283.2	10,767.2
Local governments												
Grants in lieu of taxes	1.8	—	6.5	—	36.8	59.5	7.3	3.4	8.8	9.9	1.2	135.0
Specific-purpose grants	5.1	4.7	8.8	9.9	74.5	88.1	9.5	13.2	11.9	34.7	1.4	261.9
Total transfers to local governments	6.9	4.7	15.2	9.9	111.3	147.6	16.8	16.5	20.7	44.6	2.6	396.9
Total transfers	613.5	146.7	703.8	637.1	3,535.3	2,616.2	624.4	462.5	688.8	850.0	285.7	11,164.1
Total provincial revenue	1,225.7	260.6	1,494.7	1,314.9	13,099.0	13,896.5	1,782.6	2,074.1	7,543.7	5,165.4	370.1	48,227.3

—Nil or less than $50,000.

[a] Specific-purpose transfers to Quebec include transfers under opting-out, Established Programs (Interim Arrangements) Act. [b] Transfers under Medical care include extended health care.

Sources: Same as table A.34.

Table A.38 Federal Transfers to the Provinces and Local Governments, 1979-80

	Nfld.	PEI	NS	NB	Que.	Ont.	Man.	Sask.	Alta.	BC	Yukon & NWT	Total
					millions of dollars							
Provinces												
Specific-purpose transfers[a]												
Hospital insurance	66.0	14.4	97.8	82.0	512.9	924.4	121.1	112.4	184.6	269.9	6.7	2,392.1
Medical care	22.6	4.9	33.4	28.0	175.1	315.8	41.4	38.4	63.0	92.2	2.3	817.0
Extended health services	14.0	3.0	20.7	17.1	154.0	207.7	25.2	23.4	49.0	62.7	1.6	578.4
Post-secondary education	41.6	9.0	61.1	51.2	356.8	577.3	84.6	70.2	115.2	170.1	4.2	1,541.2
Canada assistance plan	43.2	10.3	53.7	66.4	496.9	472.6	60.2	60.1	127.4	255.6	7.0	1,653.2
Transportation	18.5	3.0	15.4	11.8	21.7	4.2	8.2	7.5	2.0	10.1	23.7	125.9
Agriculture	—	27.7	0.2	0.1	3.2	9.9	10.7	38.4	21.1	4.8		116.1
Trade and industry	68.2	—	38.9	51.6	118.6	16.9	16.9	19.0	7.6	21.9	0.6	360.0
Other	9.9	3.4	13.1	18.5	139.4	133.9	16.6	12.5	56.5	32.6	10.3	447.7
Total specific-purpose transfers	284.0	75.7	334.3	326.7	1,978.6	2,662.7	384.9	381.9	626.4	919.9	56.4	8,031.6
General-purpose transfers												
Statutory subsidies	9.7	0.7	2.2	1.8	4.5	5.5	2.2	2.1	3.4	2.1	—	34.1
Current tax arrangements												
Equalization	340.0	80.2	418.4	378.5	1,707.1	—	366.1	31.1	—	—	—	3,321.4
Revenue guarantee	2.2	0.3	2.5	2.7	22.2	9.5	5.7	3.8	7.6	15.7	—	72.1
Share of undistributed income tax	0.1	0.1	0.2	0.2	5.3	5.7	0.6	0.4	1.6	1.7	—	15.9
Share of utilities tax	5.7	0.9	—	—	1.1	22.9	2.2	0.1	32.5	0.9	0.6	66.9
Youth allowance recovery	—	—	—	—	-157.8	—	—	—	—	—	—	-157.8
Reciprocal taxation agreements	5.8	2.8	14.8	8.8	33.0	40.2	—	—	—	—	—	105.3
Provincial sales tax reduction	2.7	0.7	3.6	4.9	—	31.3	4.1	3.6	—	14.0	—	64.8
Grants in lieu of taxes	—	—	0.3	—	1.6	1.5	—	—	—	—	5.3	8.6
Total general-purpose transfers	366.2	85.6	442.0	396.8	1,616.8	116.6	380.8	41.0	45.0	34.4	5.9	3,531.2
Special payments to territories											253.9	253.9
Total transfers to provinces	650.2	161.3	776.2	723.6	3,595.4	2,779.4	765.7	423.0	671.4	954.3	316.2	11,816.7

(Table A.38 is concluded on the next page.)

Table A.38 Concluded

	Nfld.	PEI	NS	NB	Que.	Ont.	Man.	Sask.	Alta.	BC	Yukon & NWT	Total
					millions of dollars							
Local governments												
Grants in lieu of taxes	1.4	—	6.7	—	26.7	63.1	7.4	3.1	8.4	11.6	1.5	129.9
Other	4.2	2.8	6.2	6.0	46.5	71.5	5.7	12.5	22.7	23.0	—	201.1
Total transfers to local governments	5.6	2.8	12.9	6.0	73.2	134.6	13.1	15.6	31.1	34.6	1.5	331.0
Total transfers	655.8	164.1	789.1	729.6	3,668.6	2,914.0	778.8	438.6	702.5	988.9	317.7	12,147.7
Total provincial revenue	1,358.1	285.1	1,684.3	1,515.2	14,582.4	15,801.7	2,084.3	2,356.8	8,535.7	6,232.4	411.7	54,847.7

—Nil or less than $50,000.

a Specific-purpose transfers to Quebec include transfers under opting-out, Established Programs (Interim Arrangements) Act.

Sources: Same as table A.34.

Table A.39   Federal Transfers to the Provinces and Local Governments, 1980-81

	Nfld.	PEI	NS	NB	Que.	Ont.	Man.	Sask.	Alta.	BC	Yukon & NWT	Total
					millions of dollars							
Provinces												
Specific-purpose transfers												
Hospital insurance[a]	70.4	15.0	104.8	85.8	492.5	973.1	128.9	118.2	200.7	283.6	7.2	2,480.3
Medical care[a]	24.2	5.2	36.3	29.7	170.8	337.2	44.7	41.0	69.6	98.2	2.5	859.6
Extended health services[a]	15.5	3.3	22.9	18.9	168.1	229.7	27.6	26.0	55.9	70.7	1.7	640.4
Post-secondary education[a]	45.1	9.5	70.1	55.0	325.0	627.0	84.3	77.5	112.9	193.7	4.7	1,605.0
Canada assistance plan[a]	53.2	12.6	62.3	80.0	586.7	547.5	72.5	75.6	160.3	314.7	7.9	1,973.3
Transportation	6.0	1.3	4.7	13.4	15.9	1.8	2.4	10.2	3.8	11.8	11.5	82.9
Agriculture	1.5	31.2	0.2	0.2	4.3	13.5	13.1	50.5	28.4	6.4	—	149.2
Trade and industry	39.1	—	43.7	50.9	94.4	27.0	20.9	12.2	7.6	30.1	2.6	328.4
Other	11.4	2.5	12.8	15.8	198.9	67.9	41.7	32.0	38.8	16.6	10.6	448.5
Total specific-purpose transfers	266.4	80.6	357.8	349.7	2,056.6	2,824.7	436.1	443.2	678.0	1,025.8	48.7	8,567.6
General-purpose transfers												
Statutory subsidies	9.7	0.7	2.2	1.8	4.5	5.5	2.2	2.1	3.4	2.1	—	34.1
Current tax arrangements												
Equalization	387.3	89.8	454.2	332.8	1,848.9	—	404.0	73.4	—	—	—	3,590.4
Share of undistributed income tax	0.4	—	0.7	1.4	13.4	18.5	1.8	1.0	3.6	4.9	—	45.6
Share of utilities tax	12.0	2.1	—	—	4.2	52.4	7.6	0.3	51.0	5.2	1.4	136.2
Reciprocal taxation agreements	9.8	1.9	38.2	9.8	33.2	52.3	—	—	—	—	—	145.3
Youth allowance recovery	—	—	—	—	-163.4	—	—	—	—	—	—	-163.4
Grants in lieu of taxes	—	0.2	—	5.3	—	—	—	—	—	1.0	0.5	7.0
Total general-purpose transfers	419.2	94.7	495.2	351.0	1,740.9	128.7	415.5	76.7	57.9	13.3	1.9	3,794.8
Special payments to territories											266.5	266.5
Total transfers to provinces	685.5	175.4	853.0	700.7	3,797.5	2,953.5	851.6	519.9	735.9	1,039.1	317.1	12,629.1

(Table A.39 is concluded on the next page.)

Table A.39 Concluded

	Nfld.	PEI	NS	NB	Que.	Ont.	Man.	Sask.	Alta.	BC	Yukon & NWT	Total
					millions of dollars							
Local governments												
Grants in lieu of taxes	1.7	0.2	10.3	1.6	35.4	75.4	7.7	4.0	8.2	11.7	1.4	157.7
Other	7.5	0.2	7.1	7.1	31.1	57.0	9.7	4.9	16.2	8.6	2.7	151.8
Total transfers to local governments	9.2	0.4	17.4	8.7	66.5	132.4	17.4	8.9	24.4	20.3	4.1	309.5
Total transfers	694.7	175.8	870.4	709.4	3,864.0	3,085.9	869.0	528.8	760.3	1,059.4	321.2	12,938.6
Total provincial revenue	1,482.7	320.4	1,898.5	1,604.6	16,347.0	17,202.3	2,283.7	2,822.9	9,808.6	6,817.4	557.5	61,145.6

—Nil or less than $50,000.

[a] Cash transfers under Federal-Provincial Fiscal Arrangements and Established Programs Financing Act, 1977.

Sources: Same as table A.34.

Table A.40 Federal Transfers to the Provinces and Local Governments, 1981-82

	Nfld.	PEI	NS	NB	Que.	Ont.	Man.	Sask.	Alta.	BC	Yukon & NWT	Total
					millions of dollars							
Provinces												
Specific-purpose transfers												
Hospital insurance[a]	74.4	15.8	108.9	90.3	519.0	1,043.8	130.9	124.6	236.8	284.4	7.4	2,636.4
Medical care[a]	25.6	5.4	37.5	31.1	178.7	359.4	45.1	42.9	81.5	97.9	2.6	907.7
Extended health services[a]	17.4	3.7	25.5	21.1	188.6	256.6	30.7	29.2	64.3	80.6	1.9	719.7
Post-secondary education	46.5	9.8	69.4	55.7	347.8	640.7	81.5	78.2	127.7	183.9	4.7	1,646.1
Canada assistance plan	60.3	16.5	73.2	93.0	678.7	634.9	88.5	90.2	245.5	344.7	12.0	2,337.5
Agriculture	0.3	21.0	0.2	0.5	8.8	16.1	14.8	58.3	32.2	5.5	—	157.7
Trade and industry	35.4	—	55.5	44.8	97.7	34.2	18.0	25.4	6.0	84.0	2.0	402.9
Other	21.6	1.4	13.4	27.1	165.9	90.3	13.5	12.9	44.0	41.6	21.6	452.9
Total specific-purpose transfers	281.5	73.6	383.6	363.6	2,185.2	3,076.0	423.0	461.7	838.0	1,122.6	52.2	9,260.9
General-purpose transfers												
Statutory subsidies	9.8	0.7	2.3	1.8	4.7	6.1	2.2	2.2	3.5	2.5	—	35.6
Equalization	466.6	111.5	554.6	437.7	2,399.6	—	404.6	103.7	—	—	—	4,478.2
Youth allowance recovery	—	—	—	—	-203.9	—	—	—	—	—	—	-203.9
Share of utilities tax	8.9	1.4	—	—	3.3	8.3	5.6	0.2	54.9	5.1	0.7	88.5
Reciprocal taxation agreements	7.9	2.9	32.4	9.8	37.5	50.8	—	—	—	—	—	141.4
Provincial sales tax reduction	-0.7	-0.2	-1.3	-0.6	—	-4.4	—	-0.1	—	-1.8	—	-9.1
Other	—	0.6	—	3.1	3.0	0.7	—	—	0.3	1.1	0.3	9.1
Total general-purpose transfers	492.5	116.9	588.0	451.8	2,244.3	61.5	412.4	106.0	58.7	6.9	1.0	4,539.8
Special payments to territories											336.1	336.1
Total transfers to provinces	774.0	190.5	971.6	815.4	4,429.5	3,137.5	835.4	567.7	896.7	1,129.5	389.3	14,340.6

(Table A.40 is concluded on the next page.)

Table A.40 Concluded

	Nfld.	PEI	NS	NB	Que.	Ont.	Man.	Sask.	Alta.	BC	Yukon & NWT	Total
					millions of dollars							
Local governments												
Grants in lieu of taxes	2.5	0.3	16.0	2.4	50.2	104.1	10.4	5.1	10.6	16.1	2.1	219.8
Other	6.6	0.4	5.0	9.0	38.8	40.4	7.9	2.1	3.6	10.7	—	124.6
Total transfers to local												
governments	9.1	0.7	21.0	11.4	89.0	144.5	18.3	7.2	14.2	26.8	2.1	344.4
Total transfers	783.1	191.2	992.6	826.8	4,518.5	3,282.0	853.7	574.9	910.9	1,156.3	391.4	14,481.2
Total provincial revenue	1,632.3	366.8	2,178.5	1,817.9	19,419.1	19,584.4	2,690.4	3,133.7	11,269.0	8,055.0	552.2	70,699.3

—Nil or less than $50,000.

[a] Cash transfers under Federal-Provincial Fiscal Arrangements and Established Programs Financing Act, 1977.

Sources: Same as table A.34.

Table A.41   Federal Transfers to the Provinces and Local Governments, 1982-83

	Nfld.	PEI	NS	NB	Que.	Ont.	Man.	Sask.	Alta.	BC	Yukon & NWT	Total
					millions of dollars							
Provinces												
Specific-purpose transfers												
Hospital insurance[a]	62.0	13.9	97.8	78.5	452.8	956.1	120.6	121.0	224.7	281.7	8.9	2,418.1
Medical care[a]	21.3	4.8	33.7	27.0	151.9	329.2	41.5	41.7	77.4	97.0	3.1	828.5
Extended health care[a]	17.7	3.9	27.6	22.3	221.0	288.1	34.0	31.8	81.8	94.4	2.6	825.2
Post-secondary education	39.4	8.9	62.2	50.0	306.5	608.3	77.5	77.6	143.0	179.2	5.7	1,558.2
Canada assistance plan	67.1	18.6	89.3	110.9	807.8	767.3	97.2	123.3	314.2	477.2	14.9	2,887.9
Agriculture	3.2	14.6	0.3	6.4	2.6	32.0	14.9	57.0	37.6	6.8	1.0	176.4
Resource conservation	10.6	1.0	3.4	8.8	33.8	26.3	18.9	437.7	318.7	33.5	4.9	897.6
Trade and industry	22.8	—	23.7	0.3	17.1	19.6	10.1	11.0	6.0	9.4	2.0	122.0
Other	25.5	3.7	11.9	29.3	175.7	141.6	14.8	7.5	18.9	37.1	22.8	488.7
Total specific-purpose transfers	269.6	69.5	350.0	333.6	2,169.1	3,168.2	429.4	908.5	1,222.3	1,216.3	65.9	10,202.5
General-purpose transfers												
Statutory subsidies	9.7	0.7	2.2	1.8	4.8	6.1	2.2	2.1	3.6	2.5	—	35.8
Equalization	535.3	123.6	616.6	546.4	3,082.6	—	479.8	-117.1	—	—	—	5,267.1
Youth allowance recovery	—	—	—	—	-225.3	—	—	—	—	—	—	-225.3
Share of utilities tax	13.6	0.9	—	—	3.8	-14.2	0.2	—	130.9	6.7	-0.3	141.6
Reciprocal taxation agreements	10.1	4.1	25.7	14.0	43.6	60.0	—	—	—	—	—	157.4
Other	—	0.5	—	5.2	0.2	1.1	—	—	—	2.3	0.6	10.0
Total general-purpose transfers	568.8	129.7	644.5	567.4	2,909.7	52.9	482.1	-115.0	134.6	11.5	0.3	5,386.6
Special payments to territories											362.2	362.2
Total transfers to provinces	838.4	199.2	994.5	901.0	5,078.8	3,221.1	911.5	793.5	1,356.9	1,227.8	428.4	15,951.4

(Table A.41 is concluded on the next page.)

Table A.41 Concluded

	Nfld.	PEI	NS	NB	Que.	Ont.	Man.	Sask.	Alta.	BC	Yukon & NWT	Total
					millions of dollars							
Local governments												
Grants in lieu of taxes	3.7	0.3	12.4	2.4	41.3	98.8	12.0	4.8	13.4	23.0	1.9	214.0
Other	2.9	0.2	3.9	9.7	23.3	24.4	10.4	3.1	4.5	6.5	1.3	90.2
Total transfers to local governments	6.6	0.5	16.3	12.1	64.6	123.2	22.4	7.9	17.9	29.5	3.2	304.2
Total transfers	845.0	199.7	1,010.8	913.1	5,143.4	3,344.3	933.9	801.4	1,374.8	1,257.3	431.6	16,255.6
Total provincial revenue	1,758.2	390.1	2,333.2	2,010.6	21,412.5	21,376.7	3,038.5	3,294.6	12,457.7	8,783.8	632.7	77,488.6

—Nil or less than $50,000.

[a] Cash transfers under established programs financing arrangements.

Sources: Same as table A.34.

Table A.42   Federal Transfers to the Provinces and Local Governments, 1983-84

	Nfld.	PEI	NS	NB	Que.	Ont.	Man.	Sask.	Alta.	BC	Yukon & NWT	Total
					millions of dollars							
Provinces												
Specific-purpose transfers												
Hospital insurance[a]	92.5	19.9	137.8	113.1	751.8	1,307.9	159.5	172.0	254.7	421.7	8.9	3,439.9
Medical care[a]	31.9	6.8	47.4	38.9	258.9	450.3	54.9	59.2	87.8	145.2	3.1	1,184.3
Extended health care[a]	21.8	4.7	32.4	26.6	246.5	333.3	38.7	37.4	88.7	106.8	2.7	939.5
Post-secondary education[a]	56.1	12.1	83.6	68.6	480.3	790.2	95.7	104.1	150.9	254.9	5.5	2,101.8
Canada assistance plan	72.8	17.1	95.9	116.6	1,043.8	868.5	110.5	146.2	336.4	538.7	12.5	3,359.0
Transportation	27.6	7.7	9.4	8.7	51.4	0.1	2.8	1.5	1.9	17.3	9.2	137.6
Agriculture	1.2	9.9	0.4	3.2	2.8	21.0	13.1	55.8	43.1	5.5	1.0	156.9
Trade and industry	17.9	—	0.4	20.6	18.8	10.5	16.4	6.0	1.7	4.7	1.0	98.0
Natural resources	14.7	2.2	3.7	12.7	45.5	15.1	20.4	214.0	83.6	50.2	6.6	468.9
Other	6.9	3.5	6.9	16.9	50.9	102.5	15.3	4.7	13.0	14.7	17.3	253.0
Total specific-purpose transfers	343.4	83.9	417.9	425.9	2,950.7	3,899.4	527.3	800.9	1,061.8	1,559.7	67.8	12,138.9
General-purpose transfers												
Statutory subsidies	9.7	0.7	2.3	1.8	4.7	6.1	2.2	2.2	3.6	2.5	—	35.7
Equalization	494.6	127.4	606.5	517.3	3,135.0	—	477.6	—	—	—	—	5,358.4
Stabilization	—	—	—	—	—	—	—	—	—	80.0	—	80.0
Share of public utilities tax	12.2	2.7	—	—	9.4	-13.0	-0.9	-0.1	165.8	4.7	-0.1	180.7
Reciprocal taxation agreements	11.1	4.1	25.5	15.8	50.9	65.0	8.7	—	—	16.7	—	197.9
Youth allowance recovery	—	—	—	—	-206.1	—	—	—	—	—	—	-206.1
Other	—	4.4	0.4	8.0	0.1	—	—	—	—	2.4	0.5	15.9
Total general-purpose transfers	527.6	139.2	634.7	543.0	2,994.0	58.2	487.6	2.1	169.4	106.3	0.5	5,662.6
Special payments to territories	—	—	—	—	—	—	—	—	—	—	462.0	462.0
Total transfers to provinces	871.0	223.2	1,052.6	968.8	5,944.6	3,957.7	1,014.9	803.0	1,231.2	1,666.6	530.2	18,263.5

(Table A.42 is concluded on the next page.)

Table A.42 Concluded

	Nfld.	PEI	NS	NB	Que.	Ont.	Man.	Sask.	Alta.	BC	Yukon & NWT	Total
					millions of dollars							
Local governments												
Grants in lieu of taxes	3.7	0.6	22.7	4.5	38.0	103.7	12.6	4.3	16.0	20.2	2.3	228.7
Other	12.3	0.3	7.4	9.3	31.1	70.5	8.3	4.7	2.3	12.7	0.7	159.3
Total transfers to local governments	16.0	0.9	30.1	13.8	69.1	174.2	20.9	9.0	18.3	32.9	3.0	388.0
Total transfers	887.0	224.1	1,082.7	981.8	6,013.7	4,131.9	1,035.8	812.0	1,249.5	1,699.5	533.2	18,651.5
Total provincial revenue	1,948.2	432.1	2,598.5	2,291.7	23,353.1	23,551.7	3,507.7	3,601.8	12,862.3	9,628.8	760.9	84,536.8

—Nil or less than $50,000.

ᵃ Cash transfers to provinces under established programs financing arrangements.

Sources: Same as table A.34.

Table A.43   Federal Transfers to the Provinces and Local Governments, 1984-85

	Nfld.	PEI	NS	NB	Que.	Ont.	Man.	Sask.	Alta.	BC	Yukon & NWT	Total
					millions of dollars							
Provinces												
Specific-purpose transfers												
Established programs financing arrangements												
Insured health services	139.4	30.2	209.9	169.0	1,166.9	1,934.5	265.6	264.8	470.5	654.7	16.1	5,321.5
Extended health services	23.2	5.0	34.9	28.6	262.4	358.6	43.2	40.3	94.4	115.3	2.8	1,008.9
Post-secondary education	59.7	12.9	89.9	73.7	463.6	837.4	114.6	115.1	201.8	289.5	6.7	2,264.8
Subtotal	222.3	48.1	334.7	271.3	1,892.9	3,130.5	423.4	420.2	766.7	1,059.5	25.6	8,595.1
Canada assistance plan	75.9	18.2	107.7	130.5	1,147.9	978.8	141.3	147.2	355.4	620.0	13.9	3,736.6
Resource conservation and industrial development	40.3	24.4	35.7	8.5	26.9	30.0	41.6	289.3	1,637.6	66.2	8.2	2,208.7
Agriculture	0.7	6.3	0.9	1.2	31.3	21.3	18.2	65.7	52.1	7.3	0.3	205.1
Transportation	30.1	3.1	7.3	34.4	19.4	0.2	0.4	—	0.2	14.5	4.9	114.6
Other	14.2	2.2	15.9	35.4	196.8	139.1	28.9	10.1	22.2	66.5	35.3	567.0
Total specific-purpose transfers	383.5	102.3	502.2	481.3	3,315.2	4,299.9	653.8	932.5	2,834.2	1,834.0	88.2	15,427.1
General-purpose transfers												
Statutory subsidies	9.7	0.7	2.3	1.8	4.7	6.1	2.2	2.2	3.6	2.5	—	35.8
Equalization	533.0	128.9	622.7	531.1	3,101.6	—	477.9	—	—	—	—	5,395.2
Stabilization	—	—	—	—	—	—	—	—	—	94.0	—	94.0
Youth allowance recovery	—	—	—	—	-213.1	—	—	—	—	—	—	-213.1
Share of public utilities tax	10.7	4.0	—	—	22.2	51.0	6.1	—	193.8	3.4	1.3	292.5
Reciprocal taxation agreements	13.1	4.0	13.0	19.8	55.5	71.6	12.4	—	—	19.7	—	209.0
Other[a]	—	8.0	21.0	1.4	—	0.1	—	—	—	2.9	0.4	35.9
Total general-purpose transfers	566.5	145.6	659.0	554.1	2,971.0	128.8	498.6	2.2	197.4	122.5	1.7	5,847.3
Special payments to territories											494.8	494.8
Total transfers to provinces	950.0	247.9	1,161.2	1,035.4	6,499.2	4,428.7	1,152.4	934.7	3,031.6	1,956.5	584.7	21,769.4

(Table A.43 is concluded on the next page.)

Table A.43 Concluded

	Nfld.	PEI	NS	NB	Que.	Ont.	Man.	Sask.	Alta.	BC	Yukon & NWT	Total
						millions of dollars						
Local governments												
Grants in lieu of taxes	3.1	0.5	18.7	3.4	57.8	129.2	11.0	6.0	15.1	27.4	2.7	274.9
Other	12.0	0.4	3.9	11.4	13.2	49.0	7.8	1.7	2.5	14.0	1.2	117.1
Total transfers to local governments	15.1	0.9	22.6	14.8	71.0	178.2	18.8	7.7	17.6	41.4	3.9	392.0
Total transfers	965.1	248.8	1,183.8	1,050.2	6,570.2	4,606.9	1,171.2	942.4	3,049.2	1,997.9	588.6	22,374.5
Total provincial revenue	2,075.2	446.7	2809.4	2,490.7	24,446.7	26,460.2	3,747.0	3,725.3	13,949.7	10,122.0	813.7	91,086.7

—Nil or less than $50,000.

[a] Grant in lieu of taxes to Nova Scotia made under the terms of the Canada-Nova Scotia oil and gas agreement, $21.0 million.

Sources: Same as table A.34.

Table A.44   Federal Transfers to the Provinces and Local Governments, 1985-86

	Nfld.	PEI	NS	NB	Que.	Ont.	Man.	Sask.	Alta.	BC	Yukon & NWT	Total
					millions of dollars							
Provinces												
Specific-purpose transfers												
Established programs financing arrangements												
Insured health services	141.9	31.1	214.7	172.5	1,124.9	1,920.0	262.3	280.9	478.0	669.8	15.4	5,311.5
Extended health services	24.6	5.4	37.4	30.5	279.1	384.7	45.3	43.4	99.0	122.2	3.1	1,074.7
Post-secondary education	60.6	13.3	91.7	75.1	461.2	832.1	111.7	120.8	205.7	299.2	6.5	2,277.8
Subtotal	227.1	49.8	343.8	278.1	1,865.2	3,136.8	419.3	445.1	782.7	1,091.2	25.0	8,663.9
Canada assistance plan	75.7	20.7	104.5	136.9	1,198.3	1,052.3	141.3	148.6	389.8	593.5	14.4	3,876.1
Natural resources (including agriculture and industrial development)	27.1	26.0	101.8	15.9	40.6	42.9	44.2	201.6	171.6	25.1	17.6	714.4
Protection	4.9	0.5	6.0	5.6	11.1	61.1	3.8	9.3	20.9	18.8	2.7	144.8
Transportation	20.5	9.7	10.1	43.7	16.2	1.2	0.8	—	0.2	14.9	5.5	122.8
Other	13.3	2.2	17.4	43.1	204.4	113.1	30.5	13.5	29.2	67.8	27.0	561.5
Total specific-purpose transfers	368.6	108.9	583.6	523.3	3,335.8	4,407.4	639.9	818.1	1,394.4	1,811.3	92.2	14,083.5
General-purpose transfers												
Statutory subsidies	9.7	0.7	2.3	1.8	4.7	6.1	2.2	2.2	3.6	2.5	—	35.8
Equalization	663.4	131.8	571.3	624.9	2,744.1	—	420.3	—	—	—	—	5,155.8
Supplementary fiscal equalization	15.0	5.0	20.0	20.0	110.0	—	50.0	—	—	—	—	220.0
Youth allowance recovery	—	—	—	—	-251.5	—	—	—	—	—	—	-251.5
Share of public utilities tax	11.2	4.1	—	—	4.6	55.7	4.6	—	216.0	2.7	0.1	299.1
Reciprocal taxation agreements	14.7	4.5	22.1	22.7	57.9	82.1	16.7	—	216.0	22.2	—	242.8
Other[a]	—	—	4.9	—	—	—	—	—	—	—	—	4.9
Total general-purpose transfers	714.0	146.1	620.5	669.4	2,669.8	143.9	493.7	2.2	219.6	27.4	0.1	5,706.9

(Table A.44 is concluded on the next page.)

Table A.44 Concluded

	Nfld.	PEI	NS	NB	Que.	Ont.	Man.	Sask.	Alta.	BC	Yukon & NWT	Total
					millions of dollars							
Special payments to territories											586.2	586.2
Total transfers to provinces	1,082.6	254.9	1,204.2	1,192.8	6,005.8	4,551.3	1,133.7	820.3	1,614.0	1,838.7	678.5	20,376.6
Local governments												
Grants in lieu of taxes	3.2	0.4	17.3	3.1	49.7	117.0	14.5	6.2	15.0	24.9	2.6	253.8
Other	16.1	0.1	2.1	4.9	14.2	24.5	5.3	0.7	5.6	13.2	1.1	88.0
Total transfers to local governments	19.3	0.5	19.4	8.0	63.9	141.5	19.8	6.9	20.6	38.1	3.7	341.8
Total transfers	1,101.9	255.4	1,223.6	1,200.8	6,069.7	4,692.8	1,153.5	827.2	1,634.6	1,876.8	682.2	20,718.4
Total provincial revenue	2,274.7	490.9	2,974.7	2,795.4	26,300.1	29,143.5	4,079.8	3,983.8	13,838.1	10,752.0	941.0	97,574.0

—Nil or less than $50,000.

a Grant in lieu of taxes to Nova Scotia made under the terms of the Canada-Nova Scotia oil and gas agreement, $4.9 million.

Sources: Same as table A.34.

Table A.45 Federal Transfers to the Provinces and Local Governments, 1986-87

	Nfld.	PEI	NS	NB	Que.	Ont.	Man.	Sask.	Alta.	BC	Yukon & NWT	Total
					millions of dollars							
Provinces												
Specific-purpose transfers												
Established programs financing arrangements												
Insured health services	140.6	31.1	214.9	181.4	1,085.6	2,002.8	262.6	254.6	515.5	779.3	14.4	5,483.0
Extended health care services	25.8	5.7	39.4	32.2	294.5	407.3	48.1	45.5	106.4	129.4	3.3	1,137.7
Post-secondary education	60.2	13.3	92.2	75.1	434.8	809.9	112.5	109.3	207.4	311.6	6.1	2,232.3
Subtotal	226.6	50.1	346.5	288.7	1,814.9	3,220.0	423.2	409.4	829.3	1,220.3	23.8	8,853.0
Canada assistance plan	85.5	19.8	124.4	145.1	1,107.8	1,132.2	154.6	160.7	427.3	632.1	12.0	4,001.4
Resource conservation and industrial development	20.1	16.3	45.9	14.6	27.2	33.8	36.1	90.6	78.7	28.7	12.6	404.4
Protection	12.1	0.8	7.6	4.5	26.5	73.5	16.4	11.6	29.7	22.2	2.6	207.5
Other	35.4	3.6	31.0	50.9	229.8	99.2	46.6	15.0	40.6	87.9	41.5	681.5
Total specific-purpose transfers	379.7	90.6	555.4	503.8	3,206.2	4,558.7	676.9	687.3	1,405.6	1,991.2	92.5	14,147.8
General-purpose transfers												
Statutory subsidies	9.7	0.7	2.3	1.8	4.7	6.1	2.2	2.2	3.6	2.5	—	35.8
Equalization	736.2	148.0	681.8	632.8	2,891.4	—	443.4	168.6	—	—	—	5,702.2
Supplementary fiscal equalization	—	—	—	—	—	—	65.0	—	—	—	—	65.0
Youth allowance recovery	—	—	—	—	-264.2	—	—	—	—	—	—	-264.2
Fiscal stabilization and revenue guarantee	—	—	—	—	—	—	—	4.3	—	0.4	—	4.7
Share of public utilities tax	11.6	4.0	—	—	4.0	13.5	4.1	0.1	220.0	—	0.7	257.9
Reciprocal taxation	13.9	5.2	26.5	22.0	58.4	94.8	13.6	—	—	21.5	—	255.8
Other	—	—	—	—	—	0.1	—	—	—	—	—	0.1
Total general-purpose transfers	771.4	157.9	710.6	656.6	2,694.4	114.4	528.3	175.1	223.7	24.4	0.7	6,057.3

(Table A.45 is concluded on the next page.)

Table A.45 Concluded

	Nfld.	PEI	NS	NB	Que.	Ont.	Man.	Sask.	Alta.	BC	Yukon & NWT	Total
					millions of dollars							
Special payments to territories											624.8	624.8
Total transfers to provinces	1,151.1	248.4	1,265.9	1,160.4	5,900.6	4,673.0	1,205.2	862.4	1,629.2	2,015.6	718.0	20,829.9
Local governments												
Grants in lieu of taxes	4.5	1.5	34.7	19.5	52.0	111.4	13.5	0.3	18.3	29.2	2.9	287.7
Other	11.7	0.3	2.7	3.5	8.0	26.4	8.8	0.9	3.3	13.5	0.6	79.9
Total transfers to local governments	16.2	1.8	37.4	23.0	60.0	137.8	22.3	1.2	21.6	42.7	3.5	367.6
Total transfers	1,167.3	250.2	1,303.3	1,183.4	5,960.6	4,810.8	1,227.5	863.6	1,650.8	2,058.3	721.5	21,197.5
Total provincial revenue	2,445.4	526.2	3,182.6	2,854.6	27,781.4	32,796.6	4,476.9	3,837.7	10,571.4	11,243.0	1,028.9	100,744.7

—Nil or less than $50,000.

Sources: Same as table A.34.

Table A.46 Federal Transfers to the Provinces, 1987-88

	Nfld.	PEI	NS	NB	Que.	Ont.	Man.	Sask.	Alta.	BC	Yukon & NWT	Total
					millions of dollars							
Specific-purpose transfers												
Established programs financing arrangements[a]												
Insured health services	138.7	31.5	216.2	173.9	985.4	1,957.7	265.1	251.7	572.3	745.4	22.4	5,360.3
Extended health care services	26.4	6.0	41.0	33.2	305.5	435.6	50.5	47.0	112.7	136.3	3.9	1,198.1
Post-secondary education	59.5	13.5	92.7	74.4	391.1	815.7	113.7	107.5	243.0	321.2	9.6	2,241.9
Subtotal	224.6	51.0	349.9	281.5	1,682.0	3,209.0	429.3	406.2	928.0	1,202.9	35.9	8,800.3
Canada assistance plan[b]	88.4	21.7	128.2	152.4	1,100.7	1,319.8	164.2	157.5	442.9	652.8	17.1	4,245.7
Agriculture	10.2	13.2	7.4	12.6	49.1	40.1	24.1	71.0	59.2	37.6	—	324.6
Employment	73.8	12.8	59.5	57.5	383.7	394.2	66.3	55.2	121.6	184.7	—	1,409.3
Protection	3.9	2.0	6.6	5.0	108.6	79.9	9.1	9.1	18.5	24.4	9.1	276.2
Other	125.7	17.9	70.2	105.2	279.6	395.3	73.2	83.2	90.3	67.7	59.9	1,368.2
Total specific-purpose transfers	526.6	118.6	621.8	614.2	3,603.7	5,438.3	766.2	782.2	1,660.5	2,170.1	122.0	16,424.3
General-purpose transfers												
Statutory subsidies	9.7	0.7	2.3	1.8	4.7	6.1	2.2	2.2	3.7	2.5	—	35.9
Equalization	781.8	147.9	686.1	710.3	3,065.6	—	620.5	374.0	—	—	—	6,386.2
Youth allowance recovery	—	—	—	—	-289.5	—	—	—	—	—	—	-289.5
Share of public utilities tax	9.8	3.3	—	—	-2.0	89.9	5.2	0.3	223.1	10.0	1.0	340.6
Reciprocal taxation	10.4	4.9	36.4	20.6	55.5	90.8	18.0	—	—	24.5	—	261.1
Total general-purpose transfers[c]	811.7	156.8	724.8	732.7	2,834.3	186.8	645.9	376.5	226.8	37.0	1.0	6,734.3
Special payments to territories											738.4	738.4
Total transfers	1,338.3	275.4	1,346.6	1,346.9	6,438.0	5,625.1	1,412.1	1,158.7	1,887.3	2,207.1	861.4	23,897.0
Total provincial revenue	2,667.9	568.6	3,462.8	3,153.2	30,668.9	36,075.7	5,274.1	4,445.9	12,740.1	12,416.1	1,118.9	112,592.2

—Nil or less than $50,000. [a] Cash portion of transfers. [b] Quebec takes a tax abatement in addition to cash transfer for Canada assistance plan. [c] Excludes grants in lieu of property taxes. Data not avilable. Sources: Same as table A.34.

Table A.47 Federal Transfers to the Provinces, 1988-89

millions of dollars

	Nfld.	PEI	NS	NB	Que.	Ont.	Man.	Sask.	Alta.	BC	Yukon & NWT	Total
Specific-purpose transfers												
Established programs financing arrangements[a]												
Insured health services	138.2	31.6	218.3	176.2	959.2	1,897.0	269.4	244.5	666.3	786.9	19.9	5,407.5
Extended health care services	27.4	6.3	43.2	34.8	324.8	462.9	53.4	49.5	117.5	147.2	3.8	1,270.6
Post-secondary education	58.0	13.2	91.7	74.1	371.1	776.5	113.2	103.1	285.4	332.8	8.5	2,227.5
Subtotal	223.6	51.1	353.2	285.1	1,655.1	3,136.4	436.0	397.1	1,069.2	1,266.9	32.2	8,905.6
Canada assistance plan[b]	91.3	22.6	152.9	149.8	1,129.0	1,511.0	197.8	155.2	487.9	663.1	23.1	4,583.6
Agriculture	10.5	6.5	2.4	10.8	47.7	47.9	35.8	97.6	87.3	60.6	—	407.2
Employment	84.2	12.3	59.6	62.1	378.6	361.2	58.9	50.8	123.6	171.1	—	1,362.3
Protection	7.2	0.8	8.1	6.0	49.6	101.4	9.6	9.8	22.1	25.4	9.3	249.4
Housing	31.3	5.3	41.3	24.1	91.4	265.1	33.4	66.3	59.3	42.8	62.6	723.0
Official languages in education	4.6	1.4	4.6	28.0	76.8	76.8	8.4	13.1	9.3	10.5	1.5	235.3
Other	93.7	13.3	101.9	60.7	151.8	143.3	43.9	16.7	52.7	65.5	12.1	755.1
Total specific-purpose transfers	546.4	113.3	724.0	626.6	3,580.0	5,643.1	823.8	806.6	1,911.4	2,305.9	140.8	17,221.5
General-purpose transfers												
Statutory subsidies	9.7	0.7	2.3	1.8	4.7	6.1	2.2	2.2	3.7	2.5	—	35.9
Equalization	870.3	184.9	816.2	781.4	3,472.4	—	863.3	383.2	—	—	—	7,371.7
Adjustments related to census	0.8	—	—	-3.0	-79.9	—	—	—	—	—	—	-82.2
Youth allowance recovery	—	—	—	—	-328.2	—	—	—	—	—	—	-328.2
Share of public utilities tax	10.6	2.0	—	—	15.8	54.0	4.8	0.3	196.8	16.0	0.9	301.3
Reciprocal taxation	13.9	4.9	33.3	26.9	60.3	109.1	15.6	—	—	21.0	—	285.1
Total general-purpose transfers[c]	905.3	192.5	851.8	807.1	3,145.1	169.2	885.9	385.7	200.5	39.5	0.9	7,583.6

(Table A.47 is concluded on the next page.)

Table A.47 Concluded

	Nfld.	PEI	NS	NB	Que.	Ont.	Man.	Sask.	Alta.	BC	Yukon & NWT	Total
Special payments to territories ...											850.9	850.9
					millions of dollars							
Total transfers	1,451.7	305.8	1,575.8	1,433.7	6,725.1	5,812.3	1,709.7	1,192.3	2,111.9	2,345.4	992.6	25,656.0
Total provincial revenue	2,910.7	637.3	3,766.6	3,437.5	33,024.3	41,511.1	5,592.5	4,763.7	12,602.6	13,619.9	1,225.8	123,092.0

—Nil or less than $50,000.
[a] Cash portion of transfers. [b] Quebec takes a tax abatement in addition to cash transfer for Canada assistance plan. [c] Excludes grants in lieu of property taxes. Data not avilable.
Sources: Same as table A.34.

Table A.48 Federal Transfers to the Provinces, 1989-90

	Nfld.	PEI	NS	NB	Que.	Ont.	Man.	Sask.	Alta.	BC	Yukon & NWT	Total
					millions of dollars							
Specific-purpose transfers												
Established programs financing arrangements[a]												
Insured health services	137.3	31.5	213.7	173.1	958.5	1,860.5	261.6	256.4	626.9	779.5	18.2	5,317.3
Extended health care services	29.2	6.7	45.5	36.8	343.2	491.3	55.6	51.8	125.0	156.7	4.0	1,345.8
Post-secondary education	57.1	13.2	88.9	72.0	366.0	755.2	109.6	107.5	263.0	326.0	7.7	2,166.1
Subtotal	223.6	51.4	348.1	281.9	1,667.7	3,107.0	426.8	415.7	1,014.9	1,262.2	29.9	8,829.2
Canada assistance plan[b]	101.0	23.9	157.2	158.9	1,106.4	1,761.5	194.5	152.9	513.2	693.8	22.1	4,885.3
Agriculture	1.8	7.2	5.4	4.4	25.1	57.1	4.9	13.3	7.7	16.1	—	143.0
Employment	91.3	12.8	61.7	82.1	397.5	345.6	59.5	53.5	125.7	182.1	—	1,411.7
Protection	7.9	0.3	10.1	6.1	44.1	105.5	10.5	10.2	25.4	29.6	7.3	257.0
Housing	26.7	3.0	29.1	12.8	57.9	220.1	29.9	59.9	46.3	21.7	47.4	554.9
Official languages in education	4.0	1.6	5.6	29.9	76.1	86.4	8.9	9.4	10.3	11.0	2.1	245.1
Other	103.0	18.3	75.2	56.2	134.7	151.6	26.7	20.0	73.1	81.3	10.6	750.9
Total specific-purpose transfers	559.3	118.5	692.4	632.3	3,509.5	5,834.8	761.7	734.9	1,816.6	2,297.8	119.4	17,077.1
General-purpose transfers												
Statutory subsidies	9.7	0.7	2.3	1.8	4.7	6.1	2.2	2.2	3.7	2.5	—	35.9
Equalization	891.3	195.1	896.4	871.4	3,707.5	—	909.7	608.7	75.1	—	—	8,155.1
Youth allowance recovery	—	—	—	—	-342.3	—	—	—	—	—	—	-342.3
Share of public utilities tax	8.4	2.5	—	—	12.8	102.4	1.4	0.1	140.9	9.8	1.1	279.5
Reciprocal taxation	17.0	6.5	29.8	27.9	67.6	132.8	15.6	—	—	22.0	—	319.1
Total general-purpose transfers[c]	926.4	204.8	928.5	901.1	3,450.3	241.3	928.9	611.0	219.7	34.3	1.1	8,447.3

(Table A.48 is concluded on the next page.)

Table A.48 Concluded

	Nfld.	PEI	NS	NB	Que.	Ont.	Man.	Sask.	Alta.	BC	Yukon & NWT	Total
					millions of dollars							
Special payments to territories											921.1	921.2
Total transfers	1,485.7	323.3	1,620.9	1,533.4	6,959.8	6,076.1	1,690.6	1,345.9	2,036.3	2,332.1	1,041.6	26,445.5
Total provincial revenue[d]	3,240.4	682.1	4,024.6	3,715.5	34,794.4	45,844.1	5,950.0	5,039.7	13,073.6	15,277.7	1,343.5	132,985.6

—Nil or less than $50,000. [a]Cash portion of transfers. [b]Quebec takes a tax abatement in addition to cash transfer for Canada assistance plan. [c]Excludes grants in lieu of property taxes. Data not avilable. [d]Estimates.

Sources: Same as table A.34.

Table A.49 Federal Transfers to the Provinces, 1990-91

	Nfld.	PEI	NS	NB	Que.	Ont.	Man.	Sask.	Alta.	BC	Yukon & NWT	Total
					millions of dollars							
Specific-purpose transfers												
Established programs financing arrangements[a]												
Insured health services	129.9	29.6	201.7	164.1	850.4	1,556.7	248.4	227.4	582.6	700.3	17.8	4,708.8
Extended health care services	28.6	6.5	44.2	36.0	338.0	485.0	54.3	50.0	122.0	155.6	4.0	1,324.2
Post-secondary education	53.7	12.1	83.4	67.8	309.0	600.5	102.0	93.9	242.2	289.6	7.3	1,861.5
Subtotal	212.2	48.2	329.3	267.9	1,497.4	2,642.2	404.7	371.3	946.8	1,145.5	29.1	7,894.5
Canada assistance plan[b]	119.0	28.7	189.1	173.7	1,264.6	2,474.8	227.1	158.8	554.0	748.9	28.3	5,966.9
Agriculture	2.2	5.1	6.8	9.6	10.2	16.0	2.5	165.1	93.3	5.0	—	315.5
Employment	39.2	4.1	25.4	48.2	239.0	226.3	26.0	29.1	68.2	75.1	—	780.5
Protection	6.3	5.5	10.5	7.0	46.8	113.1	9.8	10.6	21.6	27.7	9.8	268.6
Housing	43.3	6.0	43.5	26.5	154.5	370.1	49.8	74.0	66.2	64.6	62.4	961.0
Official languages in education	4.0	4.7	8.7	25.8	76.9	88.1	10.0	11.6	10.1	10.9	2.0	252.7
Other	125.6	15.6	62.2	57.3	137.5	153.8	34.4	17.4	39.5	46.7	6.2	696.9
Total specific-purpose transfers	551.8	117.9	675.5	616.0	3,426.9	6,084.4	764.3	837.9	1,799.7	2,124.4	137.8	17,136.6
General-purpose transfers												
Statutory subsidies	9.7	0.7	2.3	1.8	4.7	6.1	2.2	2.2	3.7	2.5	—	35.9
Equalization	942.1	206.2	980.3	908.8	3,591.4	—	970.0	661.8	—	—	—	8,260.6
Youth allowance recovery	—	—	—	—	-383.0	—	—	—	—	—	—	-383.0
Share of public utilities tax	8.7	1.4	—	—	26.5	49.4	0.2	0.4	147.7	1.4	0.6	236.3
Reciprocal taxation	13.1	4.4	19.3	22.5	51.6	111.4	10.4	—	—	14.4	—	247.2
Total general-purpose transfers[c]	973.6	212.7	1,001.9	933.1	3,291.2	166.9	982.8	664.4	151.4	18.3	0.6	8,397.0

(Table A.49 is concluded on the next page.)

Table A.49 Concluded

	Nfld.	PEI	NS	NB	Que.	Ont.	Man.	Sask.	Alta.	BC	Yukon & NWT	Total
					millions of dollars							
Special payments to territories . . .											1,058.8	1,058.8
Total transfers	1,525.4	330.6	1,677.4	1,549.1	6,718.1	6,251.3	1,747.1	1,502.3	1,951.1	2,142.7	1,197.2	26,592.4
Total provincial revenue[d]	3,204.0	720.5	4,231.6	3,902.1	36,721.8	48,061.8	6,046.6	5,701.2	14,958.8	16,934.9	1,439.5	141,922.8

—Nil or less than $50,000.
[a] Cash portion of transfers. [b] Quebec takes a tax abatement in addition to cash transfer for Canada assistance plan. [c] Excludes grants in lieu of property taxes. Data not available. [d] Estimates.

Sources: Same as table A.34.

Table A.50 Federal Transfers to the Provinces, 1991-92

	Nfld.	PEI	NS	NB	Que.	Ont.	Man.	Sask.	Alta.	BC	Yukon & NWT	Total
					millions of dollars							
Specific-purpose transfers												
Established programs financing arrangements[a]												
Insured health services ...	137.1	30.8	214.6	172.0	850.2	2,126.3	261.7	225.3	584.4	655.9	17.8	5,276.2
Extended health care services	29.8	6.7	46.9	37.5	357.0	522.5	57.1	51.6	131.5	167.4	4.2	1,412.3
Post-secondary education	57.4	12.9	89.8	72.0	312.4	875.0	109.5	93.6	243.7	268.4	7.4	2,142.1
Subtotal	224.3	50.4	351.3	281.5	1,519.6	3,523.8	428.3	370.5	959.6	1,091.7	29.4	8,830.6
Canada assistance plan[b]	132.9	34.8	217.7	206.9	1,546.5	2,158.8	253.1	177.0	623.3	747.3	31.9	6,130.3
Agriculture	1.8	5.4	8.6	8.0	4.5	13.6	0.3	—	1.8	5.2	—	49.2
Employment	30.1	2.8	21.2	37.7	167.4	172.1	23.3	25.9	55.7	73.5	—	609.6
Protection	8.3	2.5	10.4	6.1	59.3	132.1	9.7	10.0	24.0	31.4	10.4	304.1
Housing	47.2	6.7	67.0	32.8	167.7	419.0	56.4	79.8	88.9	72.9	85.8	1,124.2
Official languages in education	3.9	3.5	7.2	27.5	81.8	91.3	10.4	13.2	10.6	11.5	2.0	263.1
Other	156.6	24.5	46.5	65.7	143.3	193.8	37.2	23.9	44.1	50.9	8.3	794.7
Total specific-purpose transfers	605.1	130.6	729.9	666.2	3,690.1	6,704.5	818.7	700.3	1,808.0	2,084.4	167.8	18,105.8
General-purpose transfers												
Statutory subsidies	9.7	0.7	2.3	1.8	4.7	6.1	2.2	2.2	3.7	2.5	—	35.9
Equalization	910.4	179.0	960.2	810.0	3,547.0	—	1,046.6	622.0	—	—	—	8,075.1
Youth allowance recovery	—	—	—	—	-402.2	—	—	—	—	—	—	-402.2
Share of public utilities tax	7.5	3.9	—	—	19.6	—	—	0.5	156.7	—	0.6	188.9
Share of income tax on preferred share dividends	—	—	0.7	0.1	1.8	7.7	1.1	0.1	0.4	2.9	—	14.9
Revenue guarantees and stabilization adjustments	—	—	—	—	—	—	—	2.5	195.6	—	—	198.1
Reciprocal taxation	8.5	0.4	3.4	0.2	14.4	6.1	-0.2	—	—	6.5	—	39.4
Total general-purpose transfers[c]	936.1	184.0	966.6	812.1	3,185.3	19.9	1,049.7	627.3	356.4	11.9	0.6	8,150.1

(Table A.50 is concluded on the next page.)

Table A.50 Concluded

	Nfld.	PEI	NS	NB	Que.	Ont.	Man.	Sask.	Alta.	BC	Yukon & NWT	Total
					millions of dollars							
Special payments to territories											1,042.3	1,042.3
Total transfers	1,541.2	314.6	1,696.5	1,478.3	6,875.4	6,724.4	1,868.4	1,327.6	2,164.4	2,096.3	1,210.7	27,298.2
Total provincial revenue[d]	3,425.9	765.7	4,411.2	4,094.4	38,596.8	47,758.3	6,172.5	5,672.8	15,952.4	18,029.6	1,520.9	146,400.5

—Nil or less than $50,000. [a]Cash portion of transfers. [b]Quebec takes a tax abatement in addition to cash transfer for Canada assistance plan. [c]Excludes grants in lieu of property taxes. Data not available. [d]Estimates.

Sources: Same as table A.34.

Table A.51 Federal Transfers to the Provinces, 1992-93

	Nfld.	PEI	NS	NB	Que.	Ont.	Man.	Sask.	Alta.	BC	Yukon & NWT	Total
	millions of dollars											
Specific-purpose transfers												
Established programs financing arrangements[a]												
Insured health services	158.9	36.3	260.0	211.9	1,315.6	2,633.6	309.6	291.4	652.2	921.3	22.4	6,813.2
Extended health care services	29.3	6.6	47.7	38.9	372.3	563.1	56.6	51.1	137.7	184.7	5.2	1,493.4
Post-secondary education	68.6	15.7	112.3	91.5	538.6	1,119.1	133.8	126.4	277.5	394.2	9.4	2,887.1
Subtotal	256.9	58.6	420.0	342.3	2,226.5	4,315.8	500.0	468.9	1,067.4	1,500.2	37.0	11,193.7
Canada assistance plan[b]	151.4	35.5	248.6	227.3	1,825.7	2,282.9	294.2	197.0	619.0	803.2	37.3	6,722.1
Agriculture	1.4	5.2	9.2	7.8	2.5	11.2	8.8	8.4	4.8	4.3	—	63.5
Employment	39.0	4.1	22.5	40.3	149.0	125.1	17.6	22.3	43.0	63.3	—	526.4
Protection	6.8	2.2	9.4	6.2	50.0	106.4	9.8	10.0	22.7	28.5	9.6	261.6
Housing	49.6	7.7	55.0	31.7	156.5	447.7	48.0	87.5	84.7	86.2	91.5	1,146.2
Official languages in education	3.8	1.7	7.1	26.2	81.5	98.0	10.0	14.2	10.9	12.1	2.0	267.4
Other	211.9	25.7	49.0	51.6	258.6	323.4	134.7	323.4	300.9	63.0	14.4	1,756.7
Total specific-purpose transfers	720.8	140.8	820.8	733.5	4,750.4	7,710.7	1,023.1	1,131.7	2,153.3	2,560.9	191.8	21,937.7
General-purpose transfers												
Statutory subsidies	9.7	0.7	2.3	1.8	5.0	6.9	2.2	2.2	3.8	2.8	—	37.6
Equalization	817.6	173.3	811.8	1,055.5	3,333.6	—	774.0	411.0	—	—	—	7,376.9
Youth allowance recovery	—	—	—	—	-376.1	—	—	—	—	—	—	-376.1
Share of public utilities tax	8.8	3.5	10.3	—	6.4	-0.3	-4.1	0.3	176.2	1.3	0.6	202.9
Share of income tax on preferred share dividends	3.8	0.3	2.2	1.3	25.6	101.9	3.9	2.9	13.0	16.8	0.4	172.2
Revenue guarantees and stabilization adjustments	—	4.0	—	—	—	300.0	—	30.0	—	—	—	334.0
Total general-purpose transfers[c]	840.0	181.9	826.6	1,058.6	2,994.6	408.5	775.9	446.4	193.0	21.0	1.0	7,747.4

(Table A.51 is concluded on the next page.)

Table A.51 Concluded

millions of dollars

	Nfld.	PEI	NS	NB	Que.	Ont.	Man.	Sask.	Alta.	BC	Yukon & NWT	Total
Special payments to territories ...											1,073.3	1,073.3
Total transfers	1,560.8	322.6	1,647.4	1,792.1	7,744.9	8,119.2	1,799.0	1,578.1	2,346.3	2,581.9	1,266.0	30,758.3
Total provincial revenue[d]	3,343.9	741.2	4,533.8	4,263.1	39,459.4	46,302.7	6,375.9	6,079.4	13,583.1	18,884.1	1,612.9	145,179.4

—Nil or less than $50,000.
[a]Cash portion of transfers. [b]Quebec takes a tax abatement in addition to cash transfer for Canada assistance plan. [c]Excludes grants in lieu of property taxes. Data not available. [d]Actual.

Sources: Public Accounts; and Statistics Canada, *Unpublished data, January 1997.*

Table A.52 Federal Transfers to the Provinces, 1993-94

	Nfld.	PEI	NS	NB	Que.	Ont.	Man.	Sask.	Alta.	BC	Yukon & NWT	Total
	millions of dollars											
Specific-purpose transfers												
Established programs financing arrangements[a]												
Insured health services	140.7	31.4	220.5	179.7	984.5	2,317.4	268.0	240.0	614.2	760.2	19.6	5,776.2
Extended health care services	29.5	6.7	46.7	38.1	366.1	542.6	56.7	50.9	135.0	178.7	4.8	1,455.9
Post-secondary education	59.3	13.2	93.0	75.7	376.3	964.3	113.0	101.2	257.7	316.3	8.1	2,378.2
Subtotal	229.6	51.3	360.2	293.4	1,726.9	3,824.4	437.7	392.1	1,006.9	1,255.2	32.5	9,610.3
Canada assistance plan[b]	173.6	37.5	264.5	208.5	2,013.9	2,520.7	307.0	227.4	587.9	839.5	38.7	7,219.2
Agriculture	0.8	7.7	5.2	7.0	21.0	34.0	21.8	71.6	41.9	5.7	—	216.6
Employment	61.8	3.9	20.5	39.9	164.1	133.4	15.8	20.6	44.3	70.0	—	574.3
Protection	6.9	2.1	9.1	5.9	45.9	103.1	9.5	9.7	21.7	27.5	7.6	249.0
Housing	54.0	7.8	57.6	31.4	168.8	427.3	57.2	90.4	81.4	92.6	104.0	1,172.6
Official languages in education	3.4	1.6	7.9	23.6	72.1	91.0	8.8	8.9	10.5	11.0	2.0	240.8
Other	138.8	25.4	56.5	98.6	218.4	289.5	129.1	186.8	159.3	65.4	15.5	1,383.3
Total specific-purpose transfers	668.9	137.2	781.6	708.4	4,431.1	7,423.5	986.9	1,007.6	1,953.9	2,366.9	200.3	20,666.1
General-purpose transfers												
Statutory subsidies	9.8	0.7	2.3	1.9	5.1	7.2	2.2	2.2	3.8	2.9	—	38.0
Equalization	903.1	158.0	813.6	809.7	3,802.5	—	801.5	467.5	—	—	—	7,755.9
Youth allowance recovery	—	—	—	—	-381.5	—	—	—	—	—	—	-381.5
Share of public utilities tax	10.1	2.3	29.0	—	12.6	0.9	6.5	0.1	173.1	2.3	1.3	238.1
Revenue guarantees and stabilization adjustments	15.0	—	25.0	—	—	227.3	30.0	—	—	—	—	297.3
Total general-purpose transfers[c]	938.0	160.9	869.9	811.6	3,438.6	235.3	840.2	469.8	176.9	5.2	1.3	7,947.7

(Table A.52 is concluded on the next page.)

Table A.52 Concluded

	Nfld.	PEI	NS	NB	Que.	Ont.	Man.	Sask.	Alta.	BC	Yukon & NWT	Total
					millions of dollars							
Special payments to territories ...											1,055.6	1,055.6
Total transfers	1,606.8	298.2	1,651.5	1,520.0	7,869.7	7,658.8	1,827.1	1,477.4	2,130.8	2,372.1	1,257.1	29,669.4
Total provincial revenue[d]	3,378.4	769.6	4,403.3	4,357.3	40,394.7	48,355.7	6,508.0	5,981.4	15,192.7	21,140.8	1,727.2	152,209.1

—Nil or less than $50,000.
[a] Cash portion of transfers. [b] Quebec takes a tax abatement in addition to cash transfer for Canada assistance plan. [c] Excludes grants in lieu of property taxes. Data not available. [d] Revised estimates.
Sources: Same as table A.51.

Table A.53   Federal Transfers to the Provinces, 1994-95

	Nfld.	PEI	NS	NB	Que.	Ont.	Man.	Sask.	Alta.	BC	Yukon & NWT	Total
					millions of dollars							
Specific-purpose transfers												
Established programs financing arrangements[a]												
Insured health services ...	145.9	34.0	234.1	190.4	1,042.1	2,401.5	283.4	254.1	609.1	848.2	21.1	6,064.0
Extended health care services ...	29.9	7.0	48.2	39.2	372.2	561.0	58.4	52.3	140.1	189.0	4.8	1,502.1
Post-secondary education .	61.8	14.4	99.1	80.7	375.0	1,001.2	120.0	107.6	260.3	356.6	8.9	2,485.7
Subtotal	237.7	55.5	381.4	310.2	1,789.3	3,963.7	461.8	414.1	1,009.6	1,393.8	34.8	10,051.8
Canada assistance plan[b] ...	199.2	36.2	263.9	203.3	2,030.5	2,576.2	331.5	236.5	479.4	882.2	40.6	7,279.4
Agriculture	1.9	1.8	5.5	1.0	15.6	10.9	3.5	3.9	14.5	2.0	0.1	60.8
Employment	22.1	2.5	16.7	37.7	137.6	125.6	12.7	16.1	34.5	58.2	0.7	464.3
Protection	7.3	2.4	10.2	6.7	48.1	109.4	10.5	10.7	23.3	28.9	10.2	267.8
Housing	52.7	8.0	52.9	32.2	164.9	455.3	64.1	94.9	81.4	93.6	100.4	1,200.3
Official languages in education .	5.0	1.7	8.0	25.4	67.6	92.2	11.1	11.2	13.0	10.9	2.3	248.2
Other	146.5	20.9	81.6	98.0	454.5	507.6	139.0	545.0	140.3	162.3	118.9	2,414.7
Total specific-purpose transfers ..	672.4	128.9	820.1	714.5	4,708.1	7,841.0	1,034.2	1,332.4	1,796.0	2,631.9	307.9	21,987.4
General-purpose transfers												
Statutory subsidies	9.8	0.7	2.3	1.9	5.1	7.2	2.3	2.2	3.9	2.9	—	38.1
Equalization	958.3	200.7	1,146.3	887.5	3,716.0	—	1,080.1	554.5	—	—	—	8,543.4
Youth allowance recovery ...	—	—	—	—	-393.0	—	—	—	—	—	—	-393.0
Share of public utilities tax ..	8.1	2.3	4.5	—	-9.1	56.0	4.0	0.3	159.1	27.7	1.2	254.1
Revenue guarantees and stabilization adjustments	16.1	5.0	30.0	25.0	125.0	184.4	12.9	-20.0	—	—	—	378.4
Total general-purpose transfers[c]	992.3	208.6	1,183.1	914.3	3,444.1	247.6	1,099.3	536.9	163.0	30.6	1.2	8,821.1

(Table A.53 is concluded on the next page.)

Table A.53 Concluded

	Nfld.	PEI	NS	NB	Que.	Ont.	Man.	Sask.	Alta.	BC	Yukon & NWT	Total
						millions of dollars						
Special payments to territories ...											1,195.8	1,195.8
Total transfers	1,664.7	337.5	2,003.3	1,628.8	8,152.1	8,088.5	2,133.5	1,869.3	1,959.0	2,662.5	1,504.9	32,004.2
Total provincial revenue[d]	3,610.9	833.8	4,795.6	4,597.0	40,650.3	50,604.7	6,980.6	6,441.5	17,101.7	23,261.8	1,771.5	160,649.4

—Nil or less than $50,000.
[a] Cash portion of transfers. [b] Quebec takes a tax abatement in addition to cash transfer for Canada assistance plan. [c] Excludes grants in lieu of property taxes. Data not available. [d] Revised estimates.

Sources: Same as table A.51.

Table A.54 Federal Transfers to the Provinces, 1995-96

millions of dollars

	Nfld.	PEI	NS	NB	Que.	Ont.	Man.	Sask.	Alta.	BC	Yukon & NWT	Total
Specific-purpose transfers												
Established programs financing arrangements[a]												
Insured health services	135.3	32.0	219.9	176.2	916.5	2,299.9	266.9	235.9	581.7	836.3	20.7	5,721.3
Extended health care services	29.5	7.0	48.0	38.9	377.2	569.4	58.3	52.0	140.9	193.0	4.9	1,519.3
Post-secondary education	57.0	13.5	92.6	74.0	370.2	951.7	112.4	99.2	236.7	349.5	8.6	2,365.3
Subtotal	221.8	52.5	360.5	289.2	1,663.9	3,821.0	437.6	387.0	959.4	1,378.8	34.2	9,605.8
Canada assistance plan[b]	207.5	36.4	285.1	206.5	1,997.3	2,507.6	328.4	242.9	493.3	837.2	42.4	7,184.5
Agriculture	0.3	0.7	3.1	1.2	11.5	7.7	11.1	64.8	5.4	1.8	—	107.4
Employment	18.0	5.5	14.9	26.7	157.2	63.1	9.3	17.8	12.5	52.7	2.5	380.2
Protection	6.9	2.2	9.7	6.3	46.4	105.4	9.8	10.4	22.4	27.8	7.8	255.2
Housing	51.1	8.4	49.8	34.4	182.4	416.5	52.9	102.0	78.8	97.8	107.7	1,181.8
Official languages in education	3.0	1.6	8.5	20.6	53.9	73.3	10.3	14.4	13.8	9.5	5.1	214.0
Other	123.6	21.1	80.0	151.0	544.8	656.7	132.8	148.0	125.0	97.5	25.5	2,106.1
Total specific-purpose transfers	632.3	128.4	811.6	736.0	4,657.5	7,651.1	992.3	987.4	1,710.4	2,502.9	225.2	21,035.0
General-purpose transfers												
Statutory subsidies	9.8	0.7	2.3	1.9	5.1	7.2	2.3	2.2	3.9	2.9	—	38.1
Equalization	912.0	187.9	1,118.5	921.0	4,376.5	—	1,067.5	217.3	—	—	—	8,800.6
Youth allowance recovery	—	—	—	—	-417.1	—	—	—	—	—	—	-417.1
Share of public utilities tax	13.8	-0.5	-3.1	—	5.6	45.5	3.6	0.1	16.0	—	0.7	81.6
Revenue guarantees and stabilization adjustments	—	3.9	—	5.0	-53.3	366.9	—	-10.0	—	—	—	312.5
Total general-purpose transfers[c]	935.5	191.9	1,117.7	927.8	3,916.8	419.5	1,073.3	209.6	19.9	2.9	0.7	8,815.8

(Table A.54 is concluded on the next page.)

Table A.54 Concluded

	Nfld.	PEI	NS	NB	Que.	Ont.	Man.	Sask.	Alta.	BC	Yukon & NWT	Total
					millions of dollars							
Special payments to territories											1,195.7	1,195.7
Total transfers	1,567.8	320.3	1,929.2	1,663.8	8,574.3	8,070.7	2,065.6	1,196.9	1,730.3	2,505.8	1,421.6	31,046.4
Total provincial revenue[d]	3,656.9	828.3	5,046.5	4,854.3	44,038.7	54,185.4	7,158.2	6,195.5	16,578.2	24,206.1	1,839.1	168,587.2

—Nil or less than $50,000.
[a]Cash portion of transfers. [b]Quebec takes a tax abatement in addition to cash transfer for Canada assistance plan. [c]Excludes grants in lieu of property taxes. [d]Data not available. [d]Revised estimates.
    Sources: Same as table A.51.

Index